Hampshire County Death Records (1866 - 1922)

Compiled by
Vicki Bidinger Horton

Clearfield Company
Baltimore, Maryland

Originally published
Romney, West Virginia
1993

Reprinted for Clearfield Company by
Genealogical Publishing Company
Baltimore, Maryland
2005, 2013

ISBN 978-0-8063-5161-2

Made in the United States of America

INTRODUCTION

This book contains data extracted from the Hampshire County, West Virginia death records as they appear in the Hampshire County Death Record Books I and II. These books cover the years of 1866 through 1922. The information contained in the death record books varied considerably. Some are very informative while others contained only the name of the deceased and the date of death.

When the information is available this book includes, name of deceased, sex/race, died (date/age/place), father, mother, born (date/place), burial place, informant, designation of informant, consort, county death record book/page number and notes. The order in which the data appears is alphabetical by the last name of the deceased.

The spelling throughout this book is given as found in the original records. It should be noted that there were frequently variations in the spelling of the same name. These variations often occurred within the same record.

Some deaths are listed twice in two different records because they were reported by two different individuals, such as a family member as well as a doctor.

The index contains an alphabetical listing of all fathers, mothers, and informants contained in each death record. If a particular name is found in more than one death record, there is a separate index listing for each.

The following abbreviations have been used:

D:	-	Died
F:	-	Father
M:	-	Mother
B:	-	Born
BUR:	-	Burial
I:	-	Informant
DOI:	-	Designation of Informant
C:	-	Consort
B/P:	-	Book/Page
N:	-	Notes

Dedicated to Sylvia Stella Talbot

Who won't let me give up.

1 Abe, Emma - white female D: Oct 6, 1881; Maryland F: Abe, Jno A M: Abe, Martha B: Maryland DOI: father B/P: 1/31

2 Abe, Leona - white female D: Jan 24, 1917 B/P: 2/3

3 Abell, Alvie - white female D: June 21, 1903; 10y; Hampshire F: Abell, Geo. M: Abell, Sallie B: 1893 DOI: father B/P: 1/80

4 Abell, Chas. - married white male D: Aug 20, 1899; 32y; Slanesville B: Hampshire BUR: Hampshire B/P: 1/105 N: blacksmith

5 Abell, Robt. E. - white male D: Feb 25, 1908; 1d; B: Hampshire B/P: 2/3

6 Abell, Sallie - married white female D: July 9, 1907; 35y B: Hampshire B/P: 2/3

7 Abell, Sallie A. - married white female D: July 9, 1907; 41y 7m 6d B: Hampshire B/P: 2/3

8 Abie, Nellie - white female D: Feb 13, 1911; B/P: 2/3

9 Abrel, Geo. - white male D: May 18, 1885; 68y; Hampshire B: Hampshire I: Leith, M.J. DOI: friend B/P: 1/42

10 Abrel, Israel - white male D: Dec 8, 1885; 39y; Hampshire B: Hampshire I: Alderton, J.S. DOI: friend B/P: 1/42

11 Abrel, John D: Jan 4, 1871; 2d; Hampshire F: Abrel, Lemuel M: Abrel, Sarah B/P: 1/6

12 Abrel, Joseph - white male D: July 13, 1883; 70y; Hampshire F: Abrel, Joseph M: Abrel, Margaret B: Hampshire I: Abrel, John C: Abrel, Lucinda C. B/P: 1/37

13 Abrel, Lucinda C. - white female D: Dec 18, 1883; 71y; Hampshire F: Oats, Dan'l M: Oats, Mary B: Hampshire I: Abrel, John DOI: son C: Abrel, Joseph B/P: 1/37

14 Abrell, Bertie - single white female D: Dec 27, 1896; 13y; near Bloomery B: Hampshire B/P: 1/95

15 Adams, Elizabeth - single white female D: Aug 21, 1884; 95y 6m 11d; Hampshire B: Hampshire I: Bowen, Dr. DOI: physician B/P: 1/39

16 Adams, Jacob - married white male D: June 9, 1906; 72y B: Hampshire B/P: 2/3 N: farmer

17 Adams, Margaret Ann - white female D: Feb 20, 1867; 45y 9m 14d; Springfield F: Taylor, Simon M: Taylor, Rachel B: near Springfield DOI: husband C: Adams, William B/P: 1/2

18 Adams, S.P. - married white male D: Nov 20, 1904; 60y B/P: 2/3 N: farmer

19 Adams, S.V. - white female D: Feb 5, 1888; 32y; Hampshire B: Hampshire DOI: husband C: Adams, S. B/P: 1/45

20 Adams, Sallie - white female D: Dec 8, 1901; 30y; Hampshire F: Sirbaugh, L. I: Largent, Jas. B/P: 1/77

21 Adams, Sarah - widow white female D: Jan 2, 1908; 58y; B: Hampshire B/P: 2/3

22 Aker, Edgar - single white male D: Dec 31, 1904; 15y; B/P: 2/3 N: pupil

23 Alabang, Rahama - married white female D: Oct 28, 1922; 87y 1m; Hampshire M: Alabang, Elizabeth B: Hampshire I: Lupton, Geo. A. B/P: 1/136 N: housewife

24 Albaugh, Lorena - white female D: July 22, 1867; 7m 3d; Green Spring Depot F: Albaugh, Daniel M: Albaugh, Elizabeth Ellen B: Green Spring Depot DOI: father B/P: 1/2

25 Albin, Dorothy - white female D: Dec 25, 1874; 65 y; Hampshire B: Hampshire I: Albin, Mary J. DOI: daughter C: Albin, James B/P: 1/12

26 Albin, James W. - white male D: Aug 21, 1874; 59y 8m 9d; Hampshire B: Frederick Co VA I: Albin, Mary J. DOI: daughter C: Albin, D. B/P: 1/12

27 Albough, Anna - white female D: Sept 14, 1879; 11m 21d; Hampshire F: Albough, John W. M: Albough, Ada B: Hampshire DOI: mother B/P: 1/26

28 Albright, Elizabeth - white female D: Dec 7, 1885; 58y; Hampshire I: Malcom, Sarah B/P: 1/42

29 Albright, Henry - white female D: Dec 19, 1900; 39y 29d; Mill Creek F: Hiett, Henry M: Hiett, Herriott B: Nov 20, 1861 DOI: husband C: Albright, Ed B/P: 1/72

30 Albright, Ivy - widow white female D: July 13, 1912; 76y 12d B/P: 2/3

31 Albright, William - married white male D: Sept 8, 1910; 81y 8m; B: Hampshire B/P: 2/3

32 Alderton, Elizabeth - white female D: Oct 11, 1896; 45y; Hampshire B: Oct 11, 1851 DOI: daughter B/P: 1/63

33 Alderton, James W. - widower white male D: Feb 22, 1897; 45y 5m 7d; Bloomery F: Alderton, William B: Sept 15, 1851 I: Alderton, Amanda DOI: daughter B/P: 1/66

34 Alderton, Lucinda - married white female D: Apr 23, 1912; 68y B: Gore District B/P: 2/3

35 Alderton, M.A. - white female D: Sept 5, 1888; 12d; Hampshire F: Alderton, H. M: Alderton, A. B: Hampshire DOI: father B/P: 1/45

36 Alderton, Margaret - white female D: Apr 23, 1876; 64y; Hampshire F: Miller, Coonrod B: Morgan Co. DOI: husband C: Alderton, William B/P: 1/20

37 Alderton, Margaret - white D: May 29, 1872; 23y; Hampshire F: Alderton, William B: Hampshire I: Hiett, Evan & Jane DOI: friend B/P: 1/8

38 Alderton, Margaret A. - white female D: July 30, 1883; 22y 9m 3d; Hampshire F: Alderton, Jacob M: Alderton, Ann M. B: Hampshire DOI: mother B/P: 1/37

39 Alderton, Peter - single white male D: Mar 26, 1876; 20y 9m 28d; Hampshire F: Alderton, Jacob M: Alderton, Ann B: Hampshire I: Alderton, Mrs. DOI: mother B/P: 1/20

40 Alderton, Richard - single white male D: Dec 1, 1909; 60y B: Hampshire B/P: 2/3

41 Alderton, Sarah A - white female D: Jan 19, 1873; 21y 8m 14d; Hampshire F: Alderton, Jacob M: Alderton, Mariah B: Hampshire DOI: father B/P: 1/11

42 Alderton, W.W. - white male D: Oct 29, 1892; 20y; Hampshire F: Alderton, S.P. M: Alderton, H.E. B: Hampshire DOI: father B/P: 1/57

43 Alderton, William - white male D: June 15, 1883; 75y; Hampshire F: Alderton, William B: Morgan Co., VA I: Alderton, Richard DOI: son C: Alderton, Margaret B/P: 1/37

44 Alderton, Wm. C. - white male D: Oct 5, 1885; 32y; Hampshire F: Alderton, A. M: Alderton, Ann B: Hampshire

DOI: wife C: Alderton, Ann B/P: 1/42 N: railroader

45 Alexander, Ettie - colored female D: Sept 10, 1874; 1y 1d; Hampshire M: Alexander, Nancy B: Hampshire DOI: mother B/P: 1/12

46 Alexander, Millie - colored female D: Nov 7, 1881; 57y; Hampshire B: Hampshire DOI: husband C: Alexander, Joseph B/P: 1/30

47 Alkire, Anna E. - white female D: Sept 22, 1880; 1m 12d; Hampshire F: Alkire, Wigfiel S. M: Alkire, Belzora J. B: Hampshire DOI: father B/P: 1/28

48 Alkire, B.J. - white female D: Dec 1, 1896; 44y; Hampshire B: Dec 21, 1852 DOI: husband C: Alkire, Scott B/P: 1/63

49 Alkire, Belle - married white female D: Sept 21, 1896; 42y; near Slanesville B: WV BUR: Salem Church B/P: 1/91

50 Alkire, Raymond Peter - white male D: Jan 19, 1917; 19d B/P: 2/3

51 Alkire, Rebecca A. - white female D: Feb 18, 1883; 56y; Hampshire F: Smoot, Silas B: Hampshire DOI: husband C: Alkire, Peter B/P: 1/37

52 Allamong, Christopher C. - white male D: 26 May 1882; 56y; Sherman District F: Allamong, Casper B: Frederick Co VA I: Allamong, Jery DOI: son C: Allamong, Mary E. B/P: 1/33

53 Allamong, Jeremiah A. - white male D: 1904 B/P: 2/3

54 Allamong, Mary E. - widow white female D: Dec 8, 1914; 86y 7m 13d B: Hampshire B/P: 2/3

55 Allen, Annie E. - white female D: Nov 4, 1892; 48y; Hampshire B: Hampshire DOI: husband C: Allen, E. B/P: 1/57

56 Allen, Elizabeth - white female D: Oct 17, 1876; 78y 4m 2d; Hampshire B: Frederick Co VA DOI: husband C: Allen, Thomas B/P: 1/20 N: mother's name was Hazzard

57 Allen, Jacob - widower colored male D: Nov 20, 1914; 88y B: Hampshire B/P: 2/3

58 Allen, Laura M.A. - white female D: Oct 15, 1881; 2y 15d; Hampshire F: Allen, Thomas E. M: Allen, Mary E. B: Hampshire DOI: mother B/P: 1/31

59 Allen, Lucy V. - white female D: Feb 16, 1892; 26y 1d; Hampshire F: Taylor, Alfred M: Taylor, Virginia B: Hardy County DOI: husband C: Allen, F.P. B/P: 1/53

60 Allen, Mary E. - white female D: Apr 28, 1886; 34y 2m 13d; Hampshire F: Catlet, Jos. M: Catlet, Annie B: Hampshire DOI: husband C: Allen, Thos E. B/P: 1/44

61 Allen, Oscar - single white male D: Mar 9, 1889; 4m; near Springfield B: WV BUR: Frankfort B/P: 1/125

62 Allen, Susan D. - white female D: April 26, 1874; 64y; Hampshire B: Frederick Co VA DOI: husband C: Allen, Neal B/P: 1/12

63 Allen, Susan D.K. - white female D: Apl 26, 1875; 64y; Romney B: Pennsylvania DOI: husband C: Allen, Neal B/P: 1/14

64 Allender, Ann M. - white female D: Oct 25, 1885; 27y 1m 1d; Hampshire F: Allender, Thomas M: Allender, Ellen B: Hampshire DOI: father B/P: 1/42

65 Allender, Eleanor - white female D: May 17, 1885; 52y 1m 19d; Hampshire B: Hampshire DOI: husband C: Allender, Thos B/P: 1/42

66 Allender, Sarah - white female D: Nov 25, 1873; 8y 5m 17d; Hampshire F: Alderton, William M: Alderton, Eleanor B: Hampshire I: Allender, Thomas DOI: son C: Allender, James B/P: 1/11

67 Alverson, Arthur - white male D: Oct 9, 1882; 21y; Sherman District F: Alverson, A.M. M: Alverson, Margaret B: WV I: Poland, A.C. DOI: friend B/P: 1/33

68 Amica, R.C. - white female D: Sept 1898; 56y; Bloomery District F: Anderson, I: Riley, R.F. DOI: friend C: Amica, W.H. B/P: 1/69

69 Amica, Washington - white male D: Mar 3, 1881; 8d; Hampshire F: Amica, Wm. A. M: Amica, Rebecca B: Hampshire DOI: father B/P: 1/31

70 Amick, Gracy - white female D: Apr 15, 1894; 2m; Capon F: Amick, W.H. M: Amick, Gracy B: Sherman District DOI: father B/P: 1/59

71 Amick, Wm. O. - single white male D: Oct 16, 1898; 21y; Capon District F: Amick, Frank DOI: father B/P: 1/68

72 Anderson, Andrew - married white male D: Jan 23, 1915; 44y B: Hampshire B/P: 2/3 N: carpenter

73 Anderson, Christena - white female D: Oct 11, 1881; 85y; Hampshire B: Hampshire I: Anderson, Geo N. DOI: grandson C: Anderson, Jas B/P: 1/30

74 Anderson, Daniel - white male D: Oct 9, 1884; 87y 1m 22d; Hampshire F: Anderson, Daniel M: Anderson, Elizabeth B: Hampshire I: Anderson, Eliza DOI: daughter C: Anderson, Mary (dec'd) B/P: 1/38

75 Anderson, Edgar - colored male D: July 30, 1872; 2y 2m 28d F: Anderson, Willis M: Anderson, Margaret B: Hampshire I: Wills, Rebecca DOI: friend B/P: 1/8

76 Anderson, Eliza - white female D: Sept 6, 1894; 74y; Capon DOI: son B/P: 1/59

77 Anderson, Elizabeth - white female D: Nov 1881; 60y; Hampshire B: Virginia I: Anderson, Dan DOI: son C: Anderson, Dan'l B/P: 1/30

78 Anderson, Hannah - white female D: May 13, 1899; 7d; Purgitsville F: Anderson, Jas M: Anderson, Eliza B: May 6 DOI: father B/P: 1/71

79 Anderson, Hunter - single white male D: Dec 3, 1910; 38y 7m 15d; B/P: 2/3 N: clerk

80 Anderson, J. Wm. - widowed white male D: 1922; 78y 6m 21d; Hampshire M: Anderson, Mariah B: Virginia I: Brill, H.P. B/P: 1/133 N: farmer

81 Anderson, Jas. E. - married white male D: Jan 22, 1922; 72y 2m 9d; Hampshire F: Anderson, Israel M: Anderson, Margaret B: Frederick Co., VA I: Anderson, Dewey L. B/P: 1/133 N: agriculture

82 Anderson, John M. - white male D: July 28, 1875; 52y; Hampshire B: Hampshire DOI: wife C: Anderson, Rebecca B/P: 1/14 N: farmer

83 Anderson, Joseph P. - single white male D: Dec 6, 1867; 25 y; Timber Ridge F: Anderson, Paul P. B: Timber Ridge DOI: father B/P: 1/2

84 Anderson, Julius M. - white male D: June 10, 1913; 63y 8d; I: Anderson, Martha J. Mrs. B/P: 23

85 Anderson, Marcellus - white male D: Oct 3, 1888; 19y 6m 3d; Capoon District F: Anderson, B.F. M: Anderson, R. B: Hampshire DOI: father B/P: 1/47

86 Anderson, Margaret - married colored female D: Mar 12, 1872; 25y; Hampshire F: Brook, Henry M: Anderson, Ann B: Hampshire I: Wills, Rebecca DOI: friend C: Anderson, Willis B/P: 1/8

87 Anderson, Margaret E. D: Aug 10, 1870; 15y 4m; Hampshire M: Anderson, Elizabeth B/P: 1/5

88 Anderson, Margaret - white female D: Mar 28, 1900; 79y 11m; Capon I: Anderson, William DOI: son B/P: 1/71

89 Anderson, Mary - single white female D: January 15, 1867; 84y; Timber Ridge B: Timber Ridge I: Anderson, Paul P. DOI: nephew B/P: 1/2

90 Anderson, Matilda - widow white female D: Feb 28, 1897; 84y; Bloomery BUR: Bloomery B/P: 1/95

91 Anderson, Rebecca - single white female D: Nov 20, 1873; 22y 5m 2d; Hampshire B: Frederick Co., VA I: Wright, David DOI: brother in law B/P: 1/10

92 Anderson, S.E. - white male D: Sept 28, 1891; 25y; Hampshire F: Anderson, G.N. M: Anderson, Eliza B: Hampshire DOI: father B/P: 1/53

93 Arkel, William - married white male D: May 14, 1913; 32y B: Hampshire B/P: 2/3

94 Armstrong, Anne - widow white female D: Dec 26, 1908; 80y B: Hampshire B/P: 2/3

95 Armstrong, J.D. - white male D: 1893 C: Armstrong, Ann B/P: 1/58 N: ex-judge

96 Arnold, Albert S. - married white male D: Apr 30, 1914; 49y 4m 17d B: Hampshire DOI: wife B/P: 2/3

97 Arnold, Amanda - white female D: Dec 22, 1882; 5m 3d; Hampshire F: Arnold, M.W. M: Arnold, Cath. B: Hampshire DOI: mother B/P: 1/34

98 Arnold, Anna M. - white female D: June 19, 1897; 40y 19d; Gore F: Snyder, Peter M: Snyder, S.R. B: May 30, 1857 DOI: husband C: Arnold, D.A. B/P: 1/66

99 Arnold, Annie - married white female D: Sept 10, 1895; 21y; Hampshire B/P: 1/90

100 Arnold, Annie - married white female D: Sept 10, 1896; 21y 1m 1d; Mill Creek B: Sept 10, 1875 DOI: mother B/P: 1/62

101 Arnold, David W. - single white male D: May 1888; 60y; Mill Creek District F: Arnold, Daniel B: Hampshire I: Arnold, Jas. DOI: brother B/P: 1/47 N: farmer

102 Arnold, Elijah - white male D: Oct 5, 1885; 83y; Hampshire B: Hampshire I: Arnold, Jesse DOI: son B/P: 1/42

103 Arnold, Elizabeth - white female D: May 28, 1879; 5y 2m 15d; Hampshire F: Arnold, Millard W. M: Arnold, Catherine B: Hampshire DOI: father B/P: 1/26

104 Arnold, Elizabeth - white female D: Dec 28, 1893; 81y 4m; Hampshire I: Arnold, J.W. B/P: 1/58

105 Arnold, Evaline - white female D: Jan 8, 1892; 64y; Hampshire F: Arnold, William M: Arnold, Mahala B: Hampshire I: Arnold, T.M. DOI: brother B/P: 1/53

106 Arnold, Evan - single white male D: Apr 9, 1878; 26y; Hampshire F: Arnold, Lewis M: Arnold, Emily B: Hampshire DOI: father B/P: 1/23 N: farmer

107 Arnold, Hattie - married white female D: Dec 6, 1914; 60y 4m 15d B: Hampshire B/P: 2/3

108 Arnold, Hiram - white male D: May 21, 1909; 12y B: Bloomery District B/P: 2/3

109 Arnold, Jacob R. - widower white male D: Feb 15, 1915; 66y 4m 3d B: Hampshire B/P: 2/3

110 Arnold, James - white male D: May 11, 1895; 76y 4m; Mill Creek District F: Arnold, Daniel B: Sept 11, 1819 I: Arnold, David DOI: son B/P: 1/61

111 Arnold, Jas W. - white male D: Aug 8, 1901; 2y; Hampshire F: Arnold, J.L. M: Arnold, Sallie I: Largent, J.L. B/P: 1/77

112 Arnold, John W. - white male D: July 5, 1903; 19y; Sherman District B/P: 1/81

113 Arnold, Laverna - white female D: June 19, 1884; 5y 8m 11d; Hampshire F: Arnold, G.B. M: Arnold, Maggie B: Hampshire DOI: father B/P: 1/39

114 Arnold, Maggie A - white female D: Sept 26, 1875; 6y 2m 10d; Hampshire F: Arnold, Tilberry M: Arnold, Margaret B: Hampshire DOI: father B/P: 1/14

115 Arnold, Maggie B. - white female D: Aug 4, 1884; 34y 7m 9d; Hampshire F: Shelley, David B: Hampshire DOI: husband C: Arnold, G.B. B/P: 1/39

116 Arnold, Mahala - white female D: July 1881; 73y; Hampshire B: Hampshire I: Arnold, T.M. DOI: son C: Arnold, Wm. B/P: 1/30

117 Arnold, Mamie - married white female D: Oct 31, 1918; 22y; Hampshire B/P: 1/126 N: housewife

118 Arnold, Mary - white female D: Sept 25, 1875; 74y; Hampshire M: Sloan, Charlotte B: Hampshire I: Arnold, Geo DOI: son C: Arnold, David B/P: 1/16

119 Arnold, Mary - white female D: July 4, 1885; 77y; Hampshire B: Hampshire I: Arnold, Jesse DOI: son B/P: 1/42

120 Arnold, Mary Margaret E. D: Aug 25, 1869; 3y 9m 27d; Hampshire F: Arnold, Jesse M: Arnold, Jane B: Hampshire B/P: 1/4

121 Arnold, Oliver - white male D: Oct 2, 1917; 9y 5m B/P: 2/3

122 Arnold, Paul - married white male D: Nov 25, 1918; 33y 6m; Hampshire B/P: 1/126 N: farmer

123 Arnold, Robt C. - white male D: Sept 26, 1875; 3y 4m; Hampshire F: Arnold, Tilbery M: Arnold, Margaret B: Hampshire DOI: father B/P: 1/14

124 Arnold, Virginia - white female D: Dec 25, 1879; 1y 2m; Hampshire F: Arnold, David M: Arnold, Anna A B: Sherman District DOI: father B/P: 1/25

125 Arnold, Virginia B. - white female D: Dec 30, 1901; 52y; Hampshire I: Arnold, G.S. B/P: 1/77

126 Arnold, W.B. - white female D: Mar 15, 1899; 2m 1d; Gore District F: Arnold, J.R. M: Arnold, N. B: Jan 4, 1899 DOI: father B/P: 1/70

127 Arnold, Wilde B. - single white female D: Mar 15, 1899; 2m; Gore District B: Hampshire BUR: Arnold Graveyard B/P: 1/107

128 Arnold, William B. - single white male D: Nov 1, 1873; 20y 1m 31d; Hampshire F: Arnold, George W. M: Arnold, Sarah B: Hampshire DOI: mother B/P: 1/11 N: farmer

129 Athey, Maria C. - white female D: Nov 1884; 70y; Hampshire B: Hampshire I: Ludwick, J.G. DOI: son in law C: Athey, Thos C. B/P: 1/38

130 Athey, Sarah W. - white female D: Sept 25, 1878; 40y; Hampshire F: Brent, G.A. M: Brent, Sophina B: Frederick Co DOI: husband C: Athey, Jno W. B/P: 1/24

131 Athey, Thomas - white male D: Feb 7, 1887; 70y; Mill Creek District F: Athey, Thos. M: Athey, Magaret B: Hardy County, VA I: Purgit, William DOI: friend C: Athey, Margaret B/P: 1/43

132 Atkins, Mary E. - widow white female D: Dec 31, 1909; 75y 9m B/P: 2/3

133 Austin, Jno. N. - widower colored male D: Nov 26, 1906; 43y 5m 11d B: Hampshire B/P: 2/3 N: barber

134 Austin, Pearl - single colored female D: Jan 23, 1906; 8y 10m 20d; B: Hampshire Co B/P: 2/3

135 Bailey, Albert - white male D: Sept 12, 1906; 19y 4m B/P: 2/4

136 Bailey, Mahala - white female D: July 20, 1897; 61y; Sherman District B: Mineral County DOI: husband C: Bailey, Thornton B/P: 1/64

137 Bailey, Thornton - widower white male D: Jan 20, 1914; 79y 2m 4d B/P: 2/6

138 Baird, Sarah C. - white female D: Oct 1, 1899; 42y; Romney F: Dailey, R.W. B: 1858 B/P: 1/71

139 Baird, Wm. N. - married white male D: Oct 16, 1915; 61y 11m 17d B/P: 2/7 N: clerk

140 Baker, A.C. - white male D: Jan 18, 1901; 50y; Hampshire I: Baker, Sarah B/P: 1/77

141 Baker, Ann - white female D: July 9, 1912; 72y 2m 9d; B: Sherman District B/P: 2/6

142 Baker, Buzie H. - white male D: Aug 18, 1913; 62y 4m 13d B/P: 2/6 N: farmer

143 Baker, Catherine - white female D: Feb 1, 1907; 62y 5m 16d B/P: 2/4

144 Baker, Elizabeth - white female D: May 10, 1896; 32y 10m; Sherman District F: Stallman, John B: July 1863 DOI: father B/P: 1/62

145 Baker, Geo - white male D: Nov 2, 1913; 63y B/P: 2/6 N: farmer

146 Baker, Hannah - white female D: May 10, 1883; 30y 12d; Hampshire B: Hampshire DOI: husband C: Baker, Jacob V. B/P: 1/36

147 Baker, Lena May - white female D: Oct 8, 1908; 2y 7m 8d B/P: 2/4

148 Baker, Mary E. - white female D: Nov 19, 1910; 1m B/P: 2/5

149 Baker, Woodrow Wilson - white male D: Apr 11, 1919; 2y 8m 10d B/P: 2/7

150 Baldwin, Ida - white female D: Aug 29, 1907; 27y B/P: 2/4

151 Balis, H. - white female D: June 28, 1892; 45y; Hampshire B: Hampshire DOI: husband C: Balis, Sanford B/P: 1/53

152 Bank, Daniel - married black male D: Feb 24, 1899; 67y; Romney B: Romney BUR: Romney B/P: 1/106

153 Banks, Alexander - colored male D: Mar 11, 1875; 1m 17d; Romney F: Banks, William M: Banks, Agnes B: Romney, Hampshire DOI: mother B/P: 1/14

154 Banks, Earl - colored male D: 1897; 1y 6m; Romney F: Banks, Erving M: Banks, Nettie B: Romney DOI: father B/P: 1/64

155 Banks, Frances - single colored female D: Nov 22, 1894; 38y; Romney B: Romney BUR: Romney B/P: 1/82

156 Banks, Nettie - married colored female D: Aug 10, 1897;

22y; Romney F: Jackson, Jacob B: Romney DOI: father B/P: 1/64

157 Banks, Sallie - single colored female D: Nov 21, 1880; 73y; Hampshire B: Virginia I: Banks, Abram DOI: son B/P: 1/27

158 Banks, Sallie - colored female D: Oct 21, 1881; 78y; Hampshire B: Virginia I: Banks, Abram DOI: son B/P: 1/30

159 Barber, G.T. - widower white male D: Sept 24, 1908; 94y B/P: 2/4

160 Barnes, Adison - white male D: Dec 18, 1889; 15y; Hampshire F: Barnes, Peter M: Barnes, M. B: Hampshire DOI: father B/P: 1/51

161 Barnes, Ambrose - white male D: Dec 17, 1872; 1m; Hampshire F: Barnes, Abraham M: Barnes, Margaret B: Hampshire DOI: father B/P: 1/8

162 Barnes, Charles T. - white male D: Aug 1889; 1y; Romney District F: Barnes, F.P. M: Barnes, Alverda B: Romney District DOI: father B/P: 1/49

163 Barnes, Christina - married white female D: Aug 23, 1909; 30y 16m 2d B/P: 2/5

164 Barnes, Dessie - white female D: Feb 13, 1910; 1y 7m B/P: 2/5

165 Barnes, Elizabeth - white female D: Nov 4, 1910; 4m B/P: 2/5

166 Barnes, Isaac P. - white male D: Dec 10, 1889; 18y; Hampshire F: Barnes, Peter M: Barnes, M. B: Hampshire DOI: father B/P: 1/51

167 Barnes, Isaac P. - single white male D: Jan 4, 1910; 86y 9m 3d B/P: 2/5

168 Barnes, J.C. - white male D: Dec 10, 1889; 5y; Hampshire F: Barnes, Peter M: Barnes, M. B: Hampshire DOI: father B/P: 1/51

169 Barnes, Jane - married white female D: Dec 30, 1887; 43y 3m 6d; Jersey Mountain B: Hampshire BUR: Three Churches B/P: 1/122

170 Barnes, Lester Roy - white male D: May 20, 1909; 10m 25d

B/P: 2/5

171 Barnes, Mary - white female D: Nov 17, 1883; 52y; Hampshire F: Figgins, B: Warren County, VA DOI: husband C: Barnes, Isau P. B/P: 1/37

172 Barnes, Minnie G. - married white female D: Oct 31, 1912; 34y 11m B/P: 2/6

173 Barnes, Miss - single white female D: July 28, 1912; 4m B/P: 2/6

174 Barnes, P.J.O. - white male D: Nov 3, 1889; 8y; Hampshire F: Barnes, Peter M: Barnes, M. B: Hampshire DOI: father B/P: 1/51

175 Barnes, Rena - married white female D: Feb 17, 1904; 24y B: Hampshire B/P: 2/4

176 Barnesworth, Mr. - white male D: Feb 1, 1913; B/P: 2/6

177 Barr, Cora See - white female D: Feb 8, 1868; 4 y; N.R. Meeting H. F: Barr, Oscar B: N R Meeting House DOI: father B/P: 1/3

178 Barr, Joseph E. - white male D: July 13, 1881; 14y 11m 17d; Hampshire F: Barr, Jas. H. M: Barr, Margaret B: Frederick Co., VA DOI: mother B/P: 1/31

179 Barr, Leisa J - single white female D: Jan 25, 1873; 7y 10d; Hampshire F: Barr, Oscar M: Barr, Lucy B: Hampshire DOI: father B/P: 1/10

180 Barr, Thomas M - white male D: Dec 9, 1873; 6m 12d; Hampshire F: Barr, James H. M: Barr, Margaret A. B: Hampshire DOI: father B/P: 1/11

181 Barret, Harold E. - white male D: May 20, 1913; 5y 1m 2d; B/P: 2/6

182 Barrett, Marion - white male D: Dec 13, 1896; 2y 2m; B: Hampshire BUR: Christian Church B/P: 1/96

183 Barrett, Marvin - white male D: Aug 7, 1896; 14d; B: Timber Ridge BUR: High View B/P: 1/97

184 Barrow, Dorman W. - white male D: Nov 28, 1896; 13y 8m 27d; Bloomery District B: Virginia BUR: Capon Chapel B/P: 1/97

185 Barrow, G. - white male D: Aug 13, 1913; 1y 8m B/P: 2/6

186 Barrow, Milton - white male D: Aug 27, 1913; 62y 5m 21d; B/P: 2/6

187 Bartlet, Vincent - colored male D: 1873 B/P: 1/11

188 Bartlett, Clarence - colored female D: June 30, 1885; 5y; Hampshire F: Bartlett, Vincent M: Bartlett, Cath B: Hampshire DOI: father B/P: 1/42

189 Bartlett, Nora - single colored female D: June 5, 1909; 11y 8m 23d; B/P: 2/5

190 Bartlett, Sidney - married colored female D: Aug 28, 1906; 33y B/P: 2/4

191 Bates, James E. - white male D: July 7, 1883; 1y 6m; Hampshire F: Bates, Benj. M: Bates, Mary B: Pennsylvania I: Gibson, Ellen DOI: friend B/P: 1/37

192 Bates, Mary - white female D: July 30, 1883; 25y; Hampshire F: Russell, William M: Russell, Catharine B: Hampshire I: Gibson, Ellen DOI: sister C: Bates, Benj. B/P: 1/37

193 Bauer, Kate - white female D: June 8, 1899; 67y; B: 1833 DOI: husband B/P: 1/71

194 Bauer, Kate - married white female D: June 8, 1899; 67y 8m 28d; Hampshire B: Germany BUR: Mineral County B/P: 1/107

195 Baylis, Sanford - widower white male D: Mar 2, 1909; 77y B/P: 2/5 N: farmer

196 Beall, Eli D: Nov 14, 1870; 81y; Hampshire F: Beall, Elish M: Beall, Ann C: Beall, Margaret B/P: 1/5

197 Beall, Margaret - white female D: Jun 1, 1873; 73y 6m 20d; Hampshire F: Caudy, James M: Caudy, Elizabeth B: Hampshire I: Frye, Benj H DOI: grandson C: Beall, Eli B/P: 1/11

198 Bean, Anna Claude - married white female D: Aug 28, 1915; 22y DOI: husband B/P: 2/6

199 Bean, Annie - white female D: Oct 23, 1908; 21y 4m B/P: 2/5

200 Bean, Bill - married white male D: 1910 B/P: 2/5

201 Bean, Elizabeth - widow white female D: Oct 12, 1889; 82y 7m; Inkerman, Hardy Co. B: Hardy County BUR: Hardy County B/P: 1/124

202 Bean, Emily - white female D: Oct 30, 1883; 56y 7m; Hampshire B: Hampshire DOI: husband C: Bean, Erasmus B/P: 1/36

203 Bean, Fred - white male D: Mar 3, 1907; 61y B/P: 2/4

204 Bean, John W.W. - married white male D: Nov 29, 1889; 60y 9m 19d; Hampshire B: Hampshire B/P: 1/124

205 Bean, John Warren - married white male D: Nov 17, 1889; 60y 9m 19d; near Doman, Hardy Co. B: Hardy County BUR: Asberry Church B/P: 1/124

206 Bean, Pearl R. - white female D: Oct 23, 1907; 2m 2d B/P: 2/4

207 Bean, Rosa - white female D: Mar 26, 1915; 25y 6m 27d B/P: 2/6

208 Bean, Rosa May - married white female D: Mar 24, 1915; 26y 6m 1d DOI: husband B/P: 2/6

209 Bean, William Wesley - white male D: June 3, 1913; 71y B/P: 2/6

210 Beasted, Ella - white female D: May 2, 1913; 20d B/P: 2/6

211 Beatty, Isabella M. - white female D: May 4, 1889; 1d; Romney District F: Beatty, Hugh M: Beatty, Nancy A. B: Romney District DOI: father B/P: 1/49

212 Beatty, John H. - married white male D: Jan 20, 1908; 59y 2m 8d B/P: 2/4

213 Beatty, Nancy - widow white female D: May 20, 1922; 65y 4m 2d; Hampshire F: Starnes, Jno. M: Starnes, Sarah B: Hampshire Co. I: Beatty, J.W. B/P: 1/133 N: housewife

214 Beatty, Sarah E. - widow white female D: Apr 17, 1910; 62y B/P: 2/5

215 Beatty, V.C. - white male D: Aug 5, 1902; 2y 6m; Romney District F: Beatty, Jno. A. B: May 4, 1899 DOI: father B/P: 1/78

216 Beatty, Virginia - married white female D: Dec 4, 1918; 29y 1d; Hampshire B/P: 1/126 N: housewife

217 Bedinger, Charles - white male D: Dec 16, 1866; North River F: Bedinger, Joseph M: Bedinger, C B: North River DOI: father B/P: 1/1

218 Beery, Cora - single white female D: Aug 29, 1909; 21y 6m 27d B/P: 2/5

219 Beery, David - white male D: Mar 7, 1884; 75y 4m 25d; Hampshire F: Beery, David M: Beery, Ann B: Hampshire I: Beery, Jacob D. DOI: son C: Beery, Elizabeth B/P: 1/38

220 Beery, Myrtle - single white female D: Sept 11, 1899; 9y 7m 10d; Augusta B: Hampshire BUR: Augusta B/P: 1/107

221 Beery, Zulemma - white female D: Nov 28, 1907; 55y 10m 7d B/P: 2/4

222 Belford, Myrtle - single white female D: Apr 22, 1897; 9m; Cold Stream B: Cold Stream BUR: Cold Stream B/P: 1/95

223 Bell, Edward A - single white male D: Sept 7, 1873; 5 m; Hampshire F: Bell, Edward M: Bell, Mary A. B: Hampshire DOI: mother B/P: 1/10

224 Belt, Earl - white male D: Apr 12, 1910; 14m B/P: 2/5

225 Bennett, Bessie - white female D: Jan 6, 1903; 42y; Romney DOI: husband C: Bennett, M.I. B/P: 1/81

226 Bennett, Catharine - white female D: Apr 12, 1907; 11m B/P: 2/4

227 Bennett, E.J. - white female D: Feb 16, 1901; 63y; Hampshire I: Bennett, B.E. B/P: 1/77

228 Bennett, Edgar - single white male D: Feb 15, 1895; 2y; Hampshire B: Hampshire B/P: 1/89

229 Bennett, Florence R. - single white female D: Aug 13, 1876; 12y 11m 15d; Hampshire F: Bennett, Martin L. M: Bennett, Margaret B: Hampshire DOI: father B/P: 1/20

230 Bennett, James A. - married white male D: May 12, 1915; 50y B/P: 2/6

231 Bennett, Joseph Edger - white male D: Feb 10, 1895; 1y

8m; Mill Creek District F: Bennett, W.D. B: Oct 11, 1891 DOI: mother B/P: 1/60

232 Bennett, M.L. - white female D: Sept 21, 1901; 63y; Hampshire I: Bennett, J.A. B/P: 1/77

233 Bennett, Maggie - married white female D: Nov 17, 1902; 30y; Sherman District F: Bean, D.M. B: 1873 DOI: father B/P: 1/78

234 Bennett, Margaret - white female D: Apr 30, 1893; 52y; Hampshire DOI: husband B/P: 1/58 N: cause of death: violence

235 Bennett, Minnie - married white female D: Mar 29, 1914; 45y 6m 11d B/P: 2/6

236 Bennett, Mrs. - married white female D: Mar 2, 1904; 32y B: Hampshire B/P: 2/4

237 Bennett, R.P. - white male D: Mar 21, 1888; 3m 3d; Hampshire F: Bennett, J.A. M: Bennett, M.L. B: Hampshire DOI: father B/P: 1/45

238 Bennett, Wilbur E. - white male D: May 29, 1902; 1y 9m; Capon District F: Bennett, D.C.A. M: Bennett, Neomie B: Aug 23, 1901 B/P: 1/78

239 Bennington, S.D. - married white male D: May 9, 1892; 61y; Hampshire I: Thomas, Doctor DOI: physician B/P: 1/57 N: minister

240 Berkhimer, A.F. - white male D: Aug 12, 1889; 1y 11m 22d; Hampshire F: Berkhimer, H. M: Berkhimer, V. B: Hampshire DOI: father B/P: 1/51

241 Berry, William A. - white male D: July 4, 1896; 13y 8m 23d; Mill Creek F: Berry, John B: Mar 4, 1882 DOI: father B/P: 1/62

242 Betson, Catherine - white female D: Oct 10, 1880; 59y; Hampshire F: Henderson, Wm M: Henderson, Catherine B: Ohio DOI: husband C: Betson, Patrick B/P: 1/28

243 Bias, Emily - colored female D: May 1886; Hampshire F: Bias, Joseph M: Bias, Hannah B: Hampshire DOI: father B/P: 1/44

244 Bias, Geo - colored male D: Jan 1, 1872; 6m; Hampshire F: Bias, Joseph M: Bias, Ellen B: Hampshire I: Washington,

George DOI: friend B/P: 1/8

245 Bidinger, George - white male D: Sept 19, 1889; 10m; Hampshire F: Bidinger, George M: Bidinger, Rebecca B: Hampshire DOI: father B/P: 1/51 N: twin see 1262

246 Bidinger, Rebecca - white female D: Feb 27, 1889; 4m; Hampshire F: Bidinger, George M: Bidinger, Rebecca B: Hampshire DOI: father B/P: 1/51 N: twin

247 Bidinger, Rebecca - white female D: Nov 1888; 35y; Hampshire B: Hampshire I: Short, Ed C: Bidinger, Geo B/P: 1/45

248 Billmyer, Jenette - white female D: Nov 16, 1895; 61y; Sherman District B: Nov 16, 1834 I: Billmyer, Richard DOI: sib B/P: 1.61

249 Billmyre, Chlorice - whtie female D: Apr 17, 1891; 1m; Hampshire F: Billmyre, R.D. M: Billmyre, Eliza B: Hampshire DOI: father B/P: 1/53

250 Billmyre, Ethel - single white female D: June 23, 1914; 22y 2m 12d B/P: 2/6

251 Bird, Mary Myrtle - white female D: June 28, 1892; 5m 25d; Augusta F: Bird, Marcellus M: Bird, Manda B: Augusta DOI: father B/P: 1/56

252 Biser, Damisas - white female D: Apr 16, 1876; 46y 2m 10d; Hampshire F: Canrell, John B: Hampshire DOI: husband C: Biser, Solomon B/P: 1/18

253 Biser, Frederick - married white male D: July 20, 1901; 78y; Mill Creek District I: Biser, Isaac DOI: son B/P: 1/76 N: farmer

254 Biser, Hannah - white female D: Nov 17, 1883; 81y; Hampshire B: Hampshire I: Biser, Frederick DOI: husband C: Biser, Jacob B/P: 1/36

255 Biser, Jacob M. - single white male D: June 12, 1897; 20y 7m 14d; Mill Creek F: Biser, Silas B: Mill Creek DOI: father B/P: 1/64

256 Biser, John E. - wingle white male D: July 27, 1921; 6m 2d; Hampshire F: Biser, Geo. M: Biser, Madora B: Mineral County DOI: father B/P: 1/131

257 Biser, Margaret - single white female D: Sept 17, 1883;

51y; Hampshire F: Biser, Jacob M: Biser, Hannah B: Hampshire I: Biser, Frederick DOI: son B/P: 1/36

258 Biser, Mrs. - widow white female D: Dec 25, 1912; 62y B: Romney B/P: 2/6

259 Biser, Sarah - white female D: Apr 10, 1905; 90y 6m B: Hampshire B/P: 2/4

260 Blackburn, Eva C - single white female D: Sept 8, 1902; 7m; Mill Creek District F: Blackburn, Richard M: Blackburn, Lulu B: Mar 8, 1899 B/P: 1/78

261 Blair, Jno W. - white male D: Feb 10, 1905; 88y 2m B/P: 2/4

262 Blaker, Fenton D. - white male D: Sept 10, 1886; 66y; Capon District B: Hampshire I: Blaker, Charles DOI: son C: Blaker, Elizabeth B/P: 1/43

263 Blaker, Nannie - white female D: Sept 16, 1882; 8y 5d; Hampshire F: Blaker, J.F. M: Blaker, I. B: Hampshire DOI: father B/P: 1/34

264 Blaker, Samuel M. - white male D: Feb 29, 1884; 24y; Hampshire F: Blaker, F.D. M: Blaker, Evaline B: Hampshire DOI: father C: Blaker, Elizabeth B/P: 1/38

265 Bloom, Mrs. - married white female D: Apr 25, 1894; 40y; Hampshire B: Hampshire BUR: Salem Church B/P: 1/84

266 Bloom, Thomas Dent - married white male D: Jan 4, 1919; 45y 3m 3d B/P: 2/7 N: farmer

267 Bloxham, Elam - single white male D: Mar 14, 1908; 96y 6m 13d B/P: 2/5 N: farmer

268 Bloxham, Thomas - white male D: Sept 9, 1868; 80y; Pleasant Dale B: Louden Co, VA DOI: son B/P: 1/3

269 Blue, Ann Eliza - married white female D: Jan 12, 1898; 61y 3m 22d; Romney District DOI: father B/P: 1/68 N: parents: Vance & Rebecca

270 Blue, Annie Eliza - married white female D: Jane 12, 1898; 61y 3m 23d; Romney BUR: Romney B/P: 1/95

271 Blue, Eleanor - white female D: Jan 29, 1908; 59y B/P: 2/5

272 Blue, Fanny - white female D: Sept 18, 1872; 9m; Hampshire F: Blue, Isaac P M: Blue, Susan M. B: Hampshire DOI: father B/P: 1/8

273 Blue, Garret I. - white male D: June 21, 1872; 73y 2m 26d; Hampshire F: Blue, John B: Hampshire I: Blue, Marcellus DOI: son C: Blue, Sarah B/P: 1/8 N: farmer

274 Blue, Geo W. - white male D: July 1889; 4y 6m; Hampshire F: Blue, Jas. M: Blue, Sarah B: Hampshire DOI: father B/P: 1/51

275 Blue, George - white male D: Apr 18, 1889; 3y; near S. Branch Depot B: WV BUR: Levels Roads B/P: 1/125

276 Blue, Helen - white female D: July 27, 1907; 6y 3m 27d B/P: 2/4

277 Blue, Isaac B - married white male D: Nov 15, 1873; 33y 10m 7d; Hampshire F: Blue, Thomas M: Blue, Sarah A B: Hampshire DOI: mother C: Blue, Susanah B/P: 1/11

278 Blue, Jas. P. - white male D: Sept 19, 1904; 6y 4m 4d B: Hampshire B/P: 2/4

279 Blue, John - single white male D: June 30, 1903; 69y; Hampshire F: Blue, Garrett M: Blue, Sallie B: 1834 B/P: 1/81 N: assessor

280 Blue, John L. - white male D: May 7, 1880; 69y 2m 15d; Hampshire F: Blue, J. Michael M: Blue, Fannie B: Hampshire I: Blue, James R. DOI: son B/P: 1/28

281 Blue, Mary - white female D: Feb 16, 1892; 19y; Hampshire F: Blue, J.P. M: Blue, Mary B: Hampshire DOI: father B/P: 1/57

282 Blue, Sarah A. - white female D: Nov 11, 1878; 67y; Hampshire F: Parsons, J. M: Parsons, Catherine B: Hampshire I: Blue, Jas DOI: son C: Blue, Thos. L. B/P: 1/24

283 Blue, William - married colored male D: Aug 26, 1913; 22y B/P: 2/6 N: killed by train

284 Bobo, Harriett Ann - white female D: June 6, 1898; 55y; F: Mitcalf, Wade DOI: husband B/P: 1/68

285 Boher, Elizabeth - white female D: Apr 20, 1892; 23y; Hampshire B: Hampshire DOI: husband C: Boher, F. B/P: 1/57

286 Bohrer, Asa C. - white male D: Jan 9, 1915; 26y 4m B/P: 2/6

287 Bohrer, Eather - white female D: Sept 1, 1879; 6m 3d; Hampshire F: Bohrer, Washington M: Bohrer, Elizabeth B: Hampshire DOI: father B/P: 1/26

288 Bohrer, Mrs. - married white female D: Apr 19, 1908 B/P: 2/5

289 Bohrer, Wash - married white male D: May 9, 1898; 60y; Forks of Capon BUR: Forks of Capon B/P: 1/98 N: farmer & blacksmith

290 Bohrer, Washington - white male D: May 8, 1898; 64y; Bloomery District F: Bohrer, Arch M: Bohrer, Sarah DOI: wife C: Bohrer, Elizabeth B/P: 1/69

291 Boley, Edith - white female D: Oct 4, 1905; 23y B: Hampshire B/P: 2/4

292 Bond, William - white male D: Nov 25, 1881; 90y; Hampshire B: New York I: Vance, J. DOI: friend B/P: 1/30 N: carpenter

293 Bonett, Rachel A - white female D: Mar 26, 1880; 64y; Hampshire DOI: husband C: Bonnett, William B/P: 1/27

294 Bonney, Marthy J. - white female D: Oct 29, 1892; 73y; Romney B: Romney I: Herndon, G.H. B/P: 1/56

295 Bonney, Mary J. - white female D: Dec 21, 1888; 54y; Romney District B: Hampshire DOI: husband C: Bonney, John B/P: 1/47

296 Boon, Rosa Ellen - white female D: Mar 22, 1895; 10m; Sherman District F: Boon, D.A. M: Boon, Sarah C. B: Jan 10, 1894 DOI: mother B/P: 1/61

297 Boone, David - white male D: Apr 4, 1892; 2m; Hampshire F: Boone, J.J. M: Boone, Sarah C. B: Hampshire DOI: father B/P: 1/53

298 Boone, Loring - white male D: Aug 14, 1908; 10m 7d B/P: 2/5

299 Boone, Minnie G. - white female D: Aug 1890; 2y; Capon District F: Boone, Jas J. M: Boone, Sarah E. B: Hampshire DOI: father B/P: 1/52

300 Boone, Ola Elsie - white female D: Dec 24, 1915; 6y 5m B/P: 2/6

301 Bowen, Ann - single white female D: June 1, 1904; 40y B: Hampshire B/P: 2/4

302 Bowen, Benja. S. - white male D: Feb 2, 1909; 45y 3m 16d B/P: 2/5

303 Bowen, Etta - white female D: 1906; B/P: 2/4

304 Bowen, Luree - white male D: Sept 4, 1915; 6d B/P: 2/6

305 Bowen, Mrs. - widow white female D: Mar 2, 1899; 70y; Slanesville B: Hampshire BUR: Salem B/P: 1/103

306 Bowen, Robb T. - single white male D: July 28, 1911; 26y B: Gore district B/P: 2/6

307 Bowen, Sarah J. - widow white female D: Mar 3, 1898; 85y; Gore District I: Bowers, Anna DOI: daughter B/P: 1/69

308 Bower, Harriet - single white female D: Nov 6, 1909; 46y 5m 3d B/P: 2/5

309 Bowers, Ellen - single white female D: Dec 19, 1889; 6y; BUR: Romney B/P: 1/124

310 Bowers, Hannah L. - white female D: May 19, 1873; 12y 5m 9d; Hampshire F: Bowers, John W M: Bowers, Elizabeth B: Page Co., VA DOI: mother B/P: 1/11

311 Bowers, Laura B. - white female D: Aug 10, 1881; 2y 4m; Hampshire F: Bowers, Joseph M: Bowers, Rebecca B: Frederick Co., VA DOI: mother B/P: 1/31

312 Bowers, Mary - widow white female D: May 19, 1900; 73y; Springfield B: WV BUR: Springfield B/P: 1/108

313 Bowman, Benj W. - white male D: May 20, 1886; 2y 7d; Hampshire F: Bowman, Jos. M: Bowman, Rhoda B: Hampshire DOI: father B/P: 1/44

314 Bowman, Cary A D: July 15, 1871; 10d; Hampshire F: Bowman, John A M: Bowman, Barbara B/P: 1/6

315 Bowman, Eleanor - white female D: Aug 17, 1879; 73y; Hampshire F: Arnold, John M: Arnold, Rose B: Hampshire I: Barnes, Margaret DOI: daughter C: Bowman, Andrew B/P: 1/26

316 Bowman, Geo O. - white male D: Oct 1903; 76y; Kirby I: Timbrook, I.F. B/P: 1/81

317 Bowman, Henry - widow white male D: Nov 5, 1910; 78y B/P: 2/5

318 Bowman, James H. - white male D: Dec 24, 1907; 2y 6m 7d B/P: 2/4

319 Bowman, Jas. H. - white male D: Dec 31, 1908; 2y 6m 7d B/P: 2/4

320 Bowman, Lee - married white female D: Feb 15, 1908; 42y 3m B/P: 2/4

321 Bowman, Mary - white female D: Feb 10, 1874; 79y 23d; Hampshire B: Germany I: Bowman, Jacob DOI: son C: Bowman, George B/P: 1/12

322 Bowman, Mrs. - white female D: Dec 28, 1915; 70y B/P: 2/6

323 Bowman, Ray Ernest - white male D: June 6, 1917; stillborn B/P: 2/7

324 Bowman, Rettie - single white female D: Dec 3, 1894; 22y; near Springfield BUR: Ebenezer B/P: 1/82

325 Bowman, Rhoda - married white female D: Mar 3, 1908; 70y B/P: 2/5

326 Bowman, Susan - married white female D: Jan 20, 1897; 67y 20d; Hampshire B: Hampshire B/P: 1/96

327 Bowman, Wm D: June 10, 1869; 2m; Hampshire F: Bowman, George O. B: Hampshire B/P: 1/4

328 Bradfield, J.P. - white male D: Nov 15, 1899; 67y 4m 2d; Bloomery District F: Bradfield, James M: Bradfield, Margaret B: July 13, 1832 DOI: wife C: Bradfield, Margaret B/P: 1/70

329 Bradfield, Jas - white male D: Sept 4, 1901; 74y; Hampshire I: Bradfield, Charlotte B/P: 1/77

330 Bradfield, Thomas A - white male D: May 1883; 24y 3m 11d; Hampshire F: Bradfield, Jno P. M: Bradfield, Margaret B: Hampshire DOI: father B/P: 1/37

331 Bradfield, William K. - white male D: Mar 28, 1905; B/P: 2/4

332 Bradford, William B - married white male D: June 7, 1876; 40y 1m 17d; Hampshire F: Bradford, Nathan M: Bradford, Margarite B: Hampshire DOI: father B/P: 1/20

333 Brady, Hannah - white female D: Dec 12, 1881; 86y; Hampshire F: Parker, Robt. B: Hampshire I: Brady, James DOI: son B/P: 1/31

334 Brady, Isaac T. - white male D: Dec 3, 1893; 56y; Weston F: Brady, Samuel D. M: Brady, Susan C: Brady, Sally B/P: 1/58

335 Brady, Jas. Burr - single white male D: Apr 9, 1922; 55y 6m 29d; Hampshire F: Brady, Isaac M: Brady, Sallie B: Romney B/P: 1/133 N: engineer

336 Brady, Mrs. - married white female D: Feb 12, 1897; 70y; Romney BUR: Romney B/P: 1/94

337 Brahier, Joseph C. - white male D: Sept 11, 1872; 6m 20d; Winchester F: Brahier, Eugene M: Brahier, Mary B: Hampshire DOI: mother B/P: 1/8

338 Brannon, Eliza J. - white female D: Feb 1, 1902; 64y; Hampshire F: Brelsford, Thos. M: Brelsford, Bettie B: Feb 1838 I: Brannon, W. DOI: son B/P: 1/79

339 Brathwaite, Mary C. - white female D: Mar 7, 1903; 76y; Hampshire F: Mason B: 1828 I: Brathwaite, W.A. DOI: son B/P: 1/80

340 Brelsford, Alverda - white female D: Dec 6, 1882; 3y 8m 2d; Hampshire F: Brelsford, Jas. W. M: Brelsford, M. B: Hampshire DOI: father B/P: 1/34

341 Brelsford, Elizabeth - married white female D: Oct 1875; 67y; Hampshire F: Walker, Spencer M: Walker, Nancy B: Loudoun Co VA DOI: husband C: Brelsford, Thomas B/P: 1/16

342 Brelsford, Florence - white female D: Apr 22, 1897; 8m 7d; Bloomery F: Brelsford, William B: July 15, 1896 DOI: father B/P: 1/66

343 Brelsford, James - white male D: July 29, 1889; 48y; Hampshire I: Malcolm, C. DOI: friend C: Brelsford, Marth B/P: 1/51

344 Brelsford, Jesse - single white male D: Oct 9, 1882; 74y; Hampshire F: Brelsford, D. M: Brelsford, M. B: Hampshire I:

Brennan, Eliza J. DOI: neice B/P: 1/34

345 Brelsford, Maggie A. - white female D: Oct 30, 1899; 11y; Bloomery District F: Brelsford, G.W. M: Brelsford, Sallie B: Oct 30, 1888 DOI: father B/P: 1/70

346 Brelsford, Maggie - single white female D: Oct 1, 1899; 11y; Bloomery District B: Hampshire BUR: Sandy Ridge B/P: 1/109

347 Brelsford, Martha - white female D: Apr 9, 1889; Hampshire I: Malcolm, C. DOI: friend C: Brelsford, James B/P: 1/51

348 Brelsford, Rebecca - widower white female D: Jan 18, 1913; 80y B/P: 2/6

349 Brill, Alfred A. - married white male D: July 19, 1914; 83y 7m 14d DOI: son B/P: 2/6

350 Brill, Amos W. - white male D: Dec 22, 1905; 72y B/P: 2/4 N: farmer

351 Brill, Blanche - white female D: July 31, 1890; 19d; Capon District F: Brill, Jas H. M: Brill, Catherine B: Hampshire DOI: father B/P: 1/52

352 Brill, Caroline - white female D: Mar 1, 1896; 61y 1m 1d; Capon District F: Brill, S. B: Feb 1858 I: Anderson, Elias B/P: 1/62

353 Brill, Charles W. - white male D: Sept 1, 1880; 1y 5m; Hampshire F: Brill, Levi M: Brill, Mary B: Hampshire DOI: father B/P: 1/27

354 Brill, Edger - white male D: Aug 5, 1866; Capon Springs F: Brill, J.A. M: Brill, Eliza B: Capon Springs DOI: mother B/P: 1/1

355 Brill, Elias - white male D: Dec 25, 1896; 38y 2m; Capon District B/P: 1/62

356 Brill, Eliza A. - white female D: Dec 20, 1902; 65y; Capon District F: Lafollette, Amos M: Lafollette, R. B: 1838 B/P: 1/78

357 Brill, Elizabeth - white female D: Mar 9, 1900; 84y; Sherman F: Brill, William M: Brill, Maria B/P: 1/72

358 Brill, Elizabeth H. - widow white female D: Mar 10, 1900;

84y 10m 11d; Kirby B: Hampshire BUR: Grassy Lick Church B/P: 1/108

359 Brill, Etta V. - white female D: Apr 8, 1889; 5y; Sherman District F: Brill, I.B. M: Brill, Annie M. B: Sherman District DOI: father B/P: 1/49

360 Brill, Ettie Victoria D: Apr 18, 1889; 5y 5m 29d; B: WV BUR: Grassy Lick Church B/P: 1/125

361 Brill, Eva Ellen - married white female D: 1922; 71y 5m 5d; Hampshire F: Cooper, Nathan M: Cooper, Rebecca B: WV I: Lupton, Geo A B/P: 1/133 N: housewife

362 Brill, Flavius D: Sept 15, 1870; 24y 6m; F: Brill, Samuel B/P: 1/5

363 Brill, H.J. - married white male D: Dec 7, 1914; 70y 5m 3d B/P: 2/6

364 Brill, Hampton J. - married white male D: Dec 7, 1914; 70y 5m 13d DOI: wife B/P: 2/6

365 Brill, Harrison - widower white male D: Jan 14, 1910; 69y 1m 1d B/P: 2/5 N: farmer

366 Brill, Jno A. - white male D: Nov 1890; 64y; Capon District B: Hampshire I: Brill, Walter DOI: son C: Brill, Mary B/P: 1/52

367 Brill, John - white male D: June 17, 1922; 74y 3m 7d; Hampshire F: Brill, Sam'l M: Brill, Martha B: WV I: Lupton, Geo. A. B/P: 1/133 N: farmer

368 Brill, John - white male D: Nov 10, 1880; 9m; Hampshire F: Brill, John A M: Brill, Eliza A B: Hampshire I: Brill, James W. DOI: uncle B/P: 1/27

369 Brill, Lernon E. - married white male D: Oct 25, 1918; 41y 10m 17d; Hampshire B/P: 1/126 N: farmer

370 Brill, Loreu S. - white male D: Oct 25, 1881; 10d; Hampshire F: Brill, L. E. M: Brill, Mary B: Hampshire DOI: father B/P: 1/30

371 Brill, Lula - white female D: Sept 7, 1867; 2m; Timber Ridge F: Brill, Lemuel B: Timber Ridge DOI: father B/P: 1/2

372 Brill, Mariah Christena - single white female D: Aug 5,

1876; 26y; Hampshire M: Brill, Sidnry B: Hampshire DOI: mother B/P: 1/18

373 Brill, Mariah E. - white female D: May 6, 1899; 43y; F: Saville, Peter M: Saville, Mary B: 1857 B/P: 1/71

374 Brill, Mary - married white female D: Oct 20, 1866; 70Y B: Hampshire DOI: husband C: Brill, Henry B/P: 1/1

375 Brill, Minnie - white female D: 29 Sept 1882; 5y; Capon District F: Brill, Harrison M: Brill, Annie E. B: Hampshire DOI: father B/P: 1/33

376 Brill, Mitchel Glen - white male D: July 11, 1897; 5m 1d; Romney F: Brill, Julius M: Brill, Carrie B: Romney DOI: father B/P: 1/64

377 Brill, Robb C. - white male D: July 28, 1908; 28y 6m 28d B/P: 2/5 N: farmer

378 Brill, Royal Ruthe - white female D: Sept 10, 1896; 8m 14d; Capon District F: Brill, J.H. M: Brill, Emma V. B: Oct 1895 DOI: father B/P: 1/62

379 Brill, Sam'l Edwd. - single white male D: Oct 12, 1876; 13y 2m; Hampshire F: Brill, Sam'l M: Brill, Martha B: Hampshire DOI: father B/P: 1/18

380 Brill, Samuel - white male D: July 10, 1882; 72y; Capon B: Virginia DOI: widow C: Brill, Martha B/P: 1/33

381 Brill, Thos. B. - married white male D: 1909; 59y 8m 26d B/P: 2/5 N: farmer

382 Brill, William M - white male D: Dec 13, 1876; 38y 10m 21d; Hampshire F: Brill, Michael M: Brill, Elanor B: Hampshire DOI: wife C: Brill, Ellen B/P: 1/20

383 Brock, Thos. Henry - married white male D: Aug 22, 1917; 42y 24d; B/P: 2/7 N: farmer

384 Brook, Lucy - single white female D: June 25, 1912; 27y B: Romney District B/P: 2/6

385 Brooks, Anna - single colored female D: Sept 12, 1875; 1y 1m 15d; Hampshire M: Brooks, Alice B: Hampshire I: Brooks, Henry DOI: grandfather B/P: 1/16

386 Brooks, Ellen - married white female D: July 9, 1908; 67y 1m B/P: 2/4

387 Brown, Angus L. - single white male D: Apr 25, 1894; 22y; Mill Creek District F: Brown, George B: Mill Creek District DOI: father B/P: 1/59

388 Brown, Branson - white male D: Aug 1884; 23y; Hampshire F: Brown, Jas. W. M: Brown, Mary B: Hampshire DOI: father B/P: 1/38

389 Brown, Catharine - white female D: Aug 1884; 20y; Hampshire F: Brown, Jas W. M: Brown, Mary B: Hampshire DOI: father B/P: 1/38

390 Brown, Christian - single colore female D: Sept 1, 1877; Glebe I: Poling, Mitchel DOI: overseer of poor B/P: 1/22

391 Brown, Eliza - single white female D: June 10, 1906; 45y B/P: 2/4

392 Brown, Frank - colored male D: Nov 9, 1907; 80y B/P: 2/4

393 Brown, Geo W. - married white male D: June 22, 1910; 73y DOI: wife B/P: 2/5 N: farmer

394 Brown, James - married white male D: Dec 1, 1912; 81y B/P: 2/6

395 Brown, Jessie - colored male D: May 2, 1907; 16d B/P: 2/4

396 Brown, Jno E. - white male D: July 11, 1905; 2y 1m B/P: 2/4

397 Brown, John A - single D: Sept 1, 1870; 2y 6m 1d; Hampshire F: Brown, Sedgwick M: Brown, Ann E. B/P: 1/5

398 Brown, Lottie - single white female D: Oct 12, 1918; Hampshire B/P: 1/126

399 Brown, Perrel - white female D: Apr 20, 1898; 1m 5d; Romney F: Brown, T.J. M: Brown, E.J. DOI: father B/P: 1/68

400 Brown, Sarah A - single white female D: Aug 17, 1866; 3y 3m; Hampshire F: Brown, J. M: Brown, Mary A. B: Hampshire DOI: parent B/P: 1/1

401 Brown, Wesley - widower colored male D: Feb 12, 1908; 75y B/P: 2/4

402 Brown, Wm - single white male D: Oct 7, 1866; Mill Creek F: Brown, George M: Brown, Susan B: Mill Creek DOI: father B/P: 1/1

403 Bucklew, Cora E. - single white female D: Dec 24, 1909; 16y 4m 6d B/P: 2/5

404 Bucklew, Grace - white female D: Jan 2, 1914; 19y B/P: 2/6

405 Bucklew, Margaret - white female D: May 13, 1919; 12y B/P: 2/7

406 Bucklew, Mrs. William - married white female D: June 7, 1911; 50y B: Gore District B/P: 2/6

407 Bucklew, William - white male D: Jan 5, 1912; 45y B: Sherman district B/P: 2/6

408 Buckwalter, Jennie - single white female D: Sept 3, 1910; 71y B/P: 2/5

409 Buckwalter, M.V. - white female D: Sept 1910; 75y B/P: 2/5

410 Buckwalter, Marion - white female D: Sept 5, 1911; 21y 7m B: Gore District B/P: 2/6

411 Buckwalter, Mary - white female D: Sept 1, 1874; 76y 11m 20d; Hampshire F: Buzzard, John M: Buzzard, Mary B: Hampshire I: Buckwalter, John DOI: son C: Buckwalter, Anthony B/P: 1/12

412 Bullet, Louisa - colored female D: Oct 1882; 6y; Hampshire F: Bullet, F. M: Bullet, L. B: Hampshire DOI: father B/P: 1/34

413 Bullet, Millie - colored female D: Aug 7, 1884; 100y; Hampshire B: Hampshire I: Bullet, Frank DOI: son B/P: 1/39

414 Bumbaugh, D. - white female D: June 11, 1890; 6y; Capon District F: Bumbaugh, Jno M: Bumbaugh, Mary B: Hampshire DOI: father B/P: 1/52

415 Bumbaugh, J.A. - white male D: Aug 10, 1898; 6m; Romney District F: Bumbaugh, John G. DOI: father B/P: 1/68

416 Burgstressy, Levi - white male D: Oct 1, 1879; 1m 15d; Hampshire F: Burgstressy, Georg C M: Burgstressy, Ada C. B: Hampshire I: Burgstressy, T.M. DOI: grandfather B/P: 1/26

417 Burket, Ella J. - white female D: Apr 9, 1893; 32y; Hampshire DOI: husband C: Burket, John L. B/P: 1/58

418 Burket, Elmira - white female D: June 4, 1884; 46y; Hampshire B: Hampshire DOI: husband C: Burket, William B/P: 1/39

419 Burket, Florence - married white female D: Jan 14, 1913; 56y B/P: 2/6

420 Burket, H - married white male D: June 14, 1880; 77y 4m 22d; Hampshire F: Burket, Thos M: Burket, Elizabeth B: Hampshire DOI: wife C: Burket, Eleanor B/P: 1/28

421 Burket, James A. - single white male D: Nov 18, 1875; 19y 7m 17d; Hampshire F: Burket, Luther M: Burket, Eliza B: Hampshire DOI: mother B/P: 1/16 N: farmer

422 Burket, Jane - single white female D: Dec 19, 1912; 47y 6m B/P: 2/6

423 Burket, L.A. - white male D: Aug 26, 1892; 67y; Hampshire B: Hampshire I: Burket, J. DOI: son B/P: 1/57

424 Burket, L.E. - white female D: Aug 2, 1892; 25y; Hampshire F: Burket, L.G. M: Burket, E.J. B: Hampshire DOI: father B/P: 1/57

425 Burket, Nancy - white female D: Oct 9, 1879; 63y 11m; Hampshire F: Malcolm, Peter M: Malcolm, Anna B: Hampshire DOI: husband C: Burket, Thos. B/P: 1/26

426 Burket, Sarah - single white female D: Oct 31, 1911; 68y B: Gore District B/P: 2/6

427 Burket, William L. - white male D: Apr 1, 1891; 26y; Hampshire F: Burket, John L. B: Hampshire DOI: wife C: Burket, M.C. B/P: 1/55

428 Burket, Wm H - white male D: Dec 16, 1879; 10y 21d; Hampshire F: Burket, Luther B: Hampshire DOI: father B/P: 1/26

429 Burkett, Catharine - white female D: Sept 1, 1900; 86y; Hampshire B: 1814 I: Burket, J.L. DOI: son B/P: 1/73

430 Burkett, Elizabeth - white female D: July 4, 1906; 73y 3m 18d B/P: 2/4

431 Burkett, J.D. - white male D: Nov 25, 1902; 64y; Hampshire F: Burkett, Jno. M: Burkett, Maria B: June 22, 1838 I: Burkett, Wm. T. DOI: brother C: Burkett, Elmyra B/P: 1/79

432 Burkett, J.D. - single white male D: Nov 25, 1902; 65y; Higginsville B: Hampshire BUR: Three Churches B/P: 1/116

433 Burkett, James - white male D: Jan 2, 1910; 80y B/P: 2/5

434 Burkett, Salemma J. - single white female D: Nov 18, 1911; 58y B: Springfield District B/P: 2/6

435 Burkett, Sam'l - married white male D: Dec 1, 1897; 82y; near Three Churches B: WV BUR: Jersey Mountain B/P: 1/91

436 Burkett, Samuel - married white male D: Dec 1, 1897; 80y 9m; Gore B: Mar 1, 1817 I: Burkett, Lucy DOI: niece B/P: 1/66

437 Burkett, Sarah J. - white female D: June 23, 1900; 29y; Hampshire F: Rouza, S.A. B: 1870 DOI: husband C: Burkett, C.M. B/P: 1/73

438 Burkett, William - white male D: Jan 13, 1907; 80y B/P: 2/4

439 Burwell, Geo. Washington - single white male D: May 4, 1920; stillborn; Hampshire F: Burwell, Allen M: Burwell, Effie B: Hampshire B/P: 1/129

440 Burwell, Minnie - married white female D: Apr 25, 1909; 31y 4m 13d B/P: 2/5

441 Burwell, Wm. Allen - single white male D: May 4, 1920; Stillborn; Hampshire F: Burwell, Allen M: Burwell, Effie B: Hampshire B/P: 1/129

442 Butler, Vance - white male D: Mar 11, 1915; 8d B/P: 2/6

443 Butts, Joseph - white male D: June 2, 1886; 43y; Hampshire B: Hampshire DOI: wife C: Butts, Matilda B/P: 1/44

444 Buzzard, Ethel - white female D: Mar 13, 1906; 24y 5m 3d B/P: 2/4

445 Buzzard, Robt W. - white male D: May 9, 1876; 3y 6m 1d; Hampshire F: Buzzard, Jasper M: Buzzard, Susan B: Hampshire

DOI: father B/P: 1/20

446 Byrd, Elizabeth - white female D: July 18, 1901; 39y; Hampshire I: Byrd, Thos. B/P: 1/77

447 Cain, Catherine - white female D: July 14, 1879; 75y 7m 16d; Hampshire F: Curlett, William M: Curlett, Mary B: Hampshire I: Newman, John C: Cain, Levi B/P: 1/26

448 Caldwel, C.B. - married white male D: Aug 3, 1904; 87y 8m B/P: 2/15

449 Caldwell, G.B. - married white male D: June 1, 1904; 79y B: Pennsylvania B/P: 2/15

450 Caldwell, Miss - white female D: Jan 2, 1905; 28d B: Hampshire B/P: 2/15

451 Caldwell, Mr. - white male D: Jan 20, 1905; 10d B: Hampshire B/P: 2/15

452 Camel, Henry W. - white male D: Sept 27, 1891; 86y; Hampshire F: Camel, Lemuel B: Hampshire DOI: wife C: Camel, Mary B/P: 1/55

453 Campbell, Isabella - white female D: Feb 15, 1887; 73y; Romney District B: Berkeley County DOI: husband C: Campbell, Lemuel B/P: 1/43

454 Carder, Anna - widow white female D: Mar 25, 1909; 81y 6m 1d B/P: 2/16

455 Carder, Elias E. - married white male D: Apr 3, 1909; 45y 3m B/P: 2/16 N: farmer

456 Carder, Frederick D: Dec 11, 1870; 39y 2m M: Carder, Edna B/P: 1/5

457 Carder, Isaac W. - white male D: Oct 20, 1889; 3y; Sherman District F: Carder, F.A. M: Carder, Margaret E. B: Sherman District DOI: father B/P: 1/49

458 Carder, James - white male D: Aug 21, 1910; 83y 10m 2d B/P: 2/16

459 Carder, John - white male D: July 24, 1879; 88y; Hampshire F: Carder, George M: Carder, Elizabeth B: Hampshire I: Carder, Abny DOI: son C: Carder, Lavinia B/P: 1/26

460 Carder, John A. - white male D: Mar 2, 1883; Hampshire F: Carder, Alex M: Carder, Elizabeth B: Rappahannock County VA I: Compton, Z.J. DOI: son in law C: Carder, Sarah L. B/P: 1/37

461 Carder, Joseph - white male D: Sept 20, 1868; 28y 1m; Little Capon M: Carder, Edney B: Hampshire DOI: sister B/P: 1/3

462 Carder, Laura J. - white female D: July 6, 1883; Hampshire F: Carder, Jno A. M: Carder, Sarah L. B: Fayette County, PA I: Compton, Z.J. DOI: brother in law B/P: 1/37

463 Carder, Maria - white female D: Apr 14, 1886; 57y; Sherman District B: Hampshire DOI: husband C: Carder, Jackson B/P: 1/43

464 Carder, Mary E. - married white female D: Jan 18, 1914; 44y 3m B/P: 2/16

465 Carder, Mary J.E.V. - white female D: Jan 1873; 6y; Hampshire F: Carder, Sanford M: Carder, Mary B: Hampshire DOI: father B/P: 1/11

466 Carder, Sanford D: Dec 1, 1869; 30y; Hampshire F: Carder, E B: Hampshire B/P: 1/4

467 Carder, Wayne - single white male D: Dec 5, 1921; 23y 9m 26d; Hampshire F: Carder, L.A. M: Carder, Mary B: WV DOI: father B/P: 1/131 N: sawmill operator

468 Carlile, Miss - white female D: Nov 7, 1908; 1m 14d B/P: 2/15

469 Carlile, Miss - single white female D: Aug 8, 1908; 9d B/P: 2/15

470 Carlise, Isaac - white male D: Feb 9, 1877; Hampshire F: Carlise, Isaac M: Carlise, L. B: Hampshire DOI: father B/P: 1/22

471 Carlyle, Charlie - single white male D: Sept 21, 1920; 40y 4m 19d; Hampshire F: Carlyle, Ben M: Carlyle, B. B: Hampshire B/P: 1/129 N: farmer

472 Carny, Herbert - single white male D: Jan 13, 1922; 13d; Hampshire F: Carny, E.E. M: Carny, Mirel B: WV B/P: 1/133

473 Carrier, Celesta - white female D: June 22, 1908; 10m B/P: 2/15

474 Carrier, Isaac E. - white male D: July 21, 1908; 64y 9m 26d B/P: 2/15 N: farmer

475 Carter, George - single white male D: Mar 7, 1914; 79y 5m 13d B: Gore B/P: 2/16 N: farmer

476 Carter, James - white male D: Nov 22, 1881; 78y 5m 16d; West Va B: Hampshire I: Carter, C.S. DOI: son C: Carter, Mary B/P: 1/29

477 Carter, Mary - white female D: Apr 14, 1886; 70y 7m 17d; Sherman District B: Hampshire I: Carter, Calvin L. DOI: son C: Carter, James B/P: 1/43

478 Catlett, Bertha E. - white female D: Dec 3, 1885; 1m 24d; Hampshire F: Catlett, Harrison M: Catlett, Sarah B: Hampshire I: Doman, Thomas W. DOI: grandfather B/P: 1/42

479 Catlett, Etta V. - single white female D: July 7, 1912; 32y B/P: 2/16

480 Cave, Charles - white male D: Jan 17, 1908; 18y B/P: 2/15

481 Cave, Mrs. - married white female D: May 30, 1894; Hampshire BUR: Bloomery B/P: 1/86

482 Chaney, Henry - white female D: Nov 23, 1872; 1y 8m 18d; Hampshire F: Chaney, Isaac M: Chaney, Marie B: Hampshire DOI: father B/P: 1/8

483 Chaney, Thomas - single white male D: July 23, 1897; Springfield B: Hampshire BUR: Springfield B/P: 1/93

484 Chapman, Jno B. - white male D: July 17, 1908; 62y B/P: 2/15 N: lumberman; murdered

485 Charlton, Mr. - white male D: 1905; 24d B/P: 2/15

486 Cheney, Joseph N. - white male D: May 18, 1883; 6y; Hampshire F: Cheney, Isaac W. M: Cheney, Maria B: Mineral County DOI: father B/P: 1/37

487 Cheshier, Bessie Aldora - white female D: Jan 5, 1887; 2y; Sherman District F: Cheshier, Jas. M: Cheshier, Martha B: Hampshire DOI: father B/P: 1/43

488 Cheshir, Jasper - single white male D: June 23, 1898; 42y; Dillon Run B: West Virginia BUR: St James B/P: 1/96

489 Cheshire, Abe - white male D: Apr 14, 1903; 53y; Sherman District B/P: 1/81

490 Cheshire, Edward P - single white male D: Apr 22, 1877; Hampshire F: Cheshire, James M: Cheshire, Sarah B: Hampshire DOI: father B/P: 1/22 N: farmer

491 Cheshire, Ernest - married white male D: Dec 9, 1918; 27y 2m 27d; Hampshire B/P: 1/126 N: farmer

492 Cheshire, J.L. - white male D: Aug 16, 1894; 4m; Hampshire F: Cheshire, J.W. M: Cheshire, M.A. B: Hampshire DOI: father B/P: 1/60

493 Cheshire, Mandie May - single white female D: Mar 1, 1922; 31y 7m 29d; Hampshire F: Cheshire, Robt. M: Cheshire, Harriet B: Hampshire I: Cheshire, Burr B/P: 1/133

494 Cheshire, Mariah B. - white male D: Jan 23, 1879; 37y 2m 5d; Hampshire B: Hampshire DOI: wife C: Cheshire, Virginia B/P: 1/25

495 Cheshire, Mary Belle - single white female D: Nov 10, 1922; 38y 6m 1d; Hampshire F: Cheshire, Jas. M: Cheshire, Harriet B: Hampshire Co. B/P: 1/133

496 Cheshire, Mrs. Ira - married white female D: Dec 10, 1918; 26y 3m 15d; Hampshire B/P: 1/126 N: housewife

497 Cheshire, Perry - white male D: Sept 17, 1879; 55y; Hampshire F: Cheshire, Uriah M: Cheshire, Ann B: Hampshire DOI: wife C: Cheshire, Eliza B/P: 1/26

498 Cheshire, R. - white female D: Mar 8, 1891; 82y; Sherman District F: Cheshire, Abraham M: Cheshire, Mary B: Hampshire I: Kline, Jos S. DOI: son in law C: Cheshire, Jno B/P: 1/52

499 Cheshire, Sarah - widow white female D: Jan 19, 1909; 76y B/P: 2/16

500 Cheshire, William - white male D: Feb 14, 1900; 80y; Hampshire B: 1820 I: Cheshire, Jas. DOI: son B/P: 1/73

501 Cheshire, William - married white male D: Feb 14, 1900; 70y 6m 7d; Hampshire BUR: Ebenezer B/P: 1/107

502 Chilcott, Eliza - white female D: Jan 1, 1908; 73y B/P: 2/15

503 Christie, Jean - white female D: Feb 1900; 2y; Hampshire F: Christie, Jno. B: 1898 I: Mencer, Jno DOI: uncle B/P: 1/73

504 Clark, Albert - single white male D: Mar 22, 1900; 26y; near Slanesville B: WV BUR: Slanesville B/P: 1/105

505 Clark, James - white male D: July 28, 1908; 41y B/P: 2/15 N: carpenter

506 Clark, James M. - white male D: July 27, 1908; 45y B/P: 2/15 N: carpenter

507 Clark, Joseph - married white male D: Oct 8, 1897; 56y 7m 22d; Capon Bridge B: Virginia BUR: Fairview, VA B/P: 1/95

508 Clark, Joseph D. - white male D: July 5, 1891; 45y; Hampshire F: Clark, Joseph M: Clark, Mary B: Frederick, VA DOI: wife C: Clark, M.J. B/P: 1/55

509 Clark, Joseph T. - white male D: Oct 10, 1897; 56y; Gore F: Clark, Sampson B: 1841 DOI: wife C: Clark, Margaret B/P: 1/66

510 Clark, Sarah E. - white female D: Aug 2, 1905; 70y B/P: 2/15

511 Clayton, Towson - white male D: Mar 11, 1874; 52y; Hampshire F: Clayton, Amos M: Clayton, Elizabeth B: Loudoun Co VA I: Clayton, Emma DOI: daughter C: Clayton, Susan B/P: 1/12 N: physician

512 Clein, C. - white male D: Aug 15, 1875; 5m; Hampshire F: Clein, Joseph M: Clein, Mary B: Hampshire DOI: mother B/P: 1/14

513 Clem, Isaac J. - single white male D: Oct 29, 1919; 10y 1m 22d B/P: 2/16

514 Click, Susan - white female D: July 2, 1898; 88y; Gore District I: Hannas, John DOI: friend B/P: 1/69

515 Cline, Asa R. - white male D: Nov 1, 1893; 3y; Hampshire F: Cline, H.P. DOI: father B/P: 1/58

516 Cline, Henry - married white male D: Aut 10, 1888; 75y; Little Capon Bridge B: Germany BUR: Levels B/P: 1/123

517 Cloud, Anna - white female D: Aug 15, 1901; 35y; Hampshire F: Cloud, Amos I: Cloud, A. B/P: 1/77

518 Cloud, Mr. - white male D: May 18, 1907; B/P: 2/15

519 Cloud, Susie - white female D: Aug 17, 1901; 71y; Hampshire F: Cloud, Amos I: Cloud, A. B/P: 1/77

520 Clower, Breuwes G. - white male D: 1906; 32y 5m 29d B/P: 2/15

521 Coceran, Sam'l - single white male D: 1893; 69y; Hampshire B: WV B/P: 1/58

522 Cockran, Barbra - colored female D: 1872; 83y 5m; Hampshire B: Hampshire I: Washington, Geo. C: Cockran, David B/P: 1/8

523 Coffman, John - widower white male D: Oct 4, 1893; 81y; Hampshire B/P: 1/58

524 Coffman, Mary - white female D: Aug 12, 1888; 60y; Sherman District F: Thompson, Elisha M: Thompson, Elizabeth B: Hampshire I: Coffman, Julius DOI: son C: Coffman, John B/P: 1/47

525 Coffman, Mary - married white female D: Aug 12, 1888; 70y 11m; Hampshire B: Hampshire B/P: 1/123

526 Cogill, F.I. - white female D: Aug 22, 1892; 22y 7d; Hampshire F: Cogill, J. M: Cogill, M. B: Hampshire DOI: father B/P: 1/57

527 Cole, Fannie B V D: Mar 13, 1866; Great Capon F: Cole, Enoch H B: G. Capon DOI: father B/P: 1/1

528 Colehan, Wm. E. - white male D: Feb 24, 1881; 5m; Loudoun Co., VA F: Colehan, Samuel L. M: Colehan, Mary B: Loudoun Co., VA DOI: father B/P: 1/31

529 Coleman, Mary A. - white female D: Aug 19, 1876; 54y 10m 17d; Hampshire F: Kile, John W. M: Kile, Winaford B: Loudoun Co VA I: Coleman,(young) DOI: son C: Coleman, Chas B/P: 1/20

530 Coleman, Winnie - white female D: Feb 1890; 50y; Romney District B: Romney District I: Coleman, John DOI: son B/P: 1/49

531 Collins, Carrie May - white female D: June 5, 1892; 12d; near Romney F: Collins, A.S. M: Collins, Sadie B: Romney DOI: father B/P: 1/56

532 Collins, Catharine D: Aug 4, 1869; 35y 1m 0d; Hampshire F: Williams, Benjamin M: Williams, Martha B: Hampshire C: Collins, Alfred B/P: 1/4

533 Collins, John - white male D: Aug 11, 1894; 2m 11d; near Kirby B: Hampshire BUR: Romney B/P: 1/86

534 Collins, John - white male D: Aug 1, 1894; 2m; Sherman District F: Collins, Geo M: Collins, Sada B: Sherman District DOI: father B/P: 1/59

535 Collins, Perry - married white male D: Mar 27, 1904; 40y B: Hampshire B/P: 2/15

536 Colwell, Edward - white male D: June 23, 1892; 14y; Tucker County F: Colwell, G.B. M: Colwell, C.J. B: Pennsylvania DOI: father B/P: 1/57

537 Combs, Amersy D: June 30, 1871; 17y F: Combs, Andrew B/P: 1/6

538 Combs, Andrew G. - white male D: Oct 1, 1885; 24y 3m; Hampshire F: Combs, Andrew M: Combs, Catharine B: Hampshire DOI: mother B/P: 1/41

539 Combs, Anne - white female D: Apr 4, 1880; 95y; Hampshire I: Combs, Andres DOI: son B/P: 1/27

540 Combs, Catherine - white female D: Jan 20, 1892; 72y; Hampshire B: Hampshire I: Combs, Geo. W. DOI: son C: Combs, Andrew B/P: 1/53

541 Combs, Earl Martin - white male D: Sept 20, 1916; 11d B: Sherman B/P: 2/16

542 Combs, Elizabeth M.S. - married white female D: July 19, 1907; 35y B/P: 2/15

543 Combs, Ethel - white female D: Jane 1891; 3m; Sherman District F: Combs, Wm. A. M: Combs, Elizabeth A. B: Hampshire DOI: father B/P: 1/52

544 Combs, Ida C.L. - white female D: Oct 2, 1885; 17y 11m; Hampshire F: Combs, Andrew M: Combs, Catharine B: Hampshire DOI: mother B/P: 1/41

545 Combs, James H. - widower white male D: May 18, 1907; 63y B/P: 2/15 N: farmer

546 Combs, Janet May - single white female D: May 29, 1922; 11m 17d; Hampshire F: Combs, Alfred M: Combs, Mary B: Purgitsville DOI: father B/P: 1/133

547 Combs, Jesse Winfred - single white male D: Apr 29, 1909; 2y 1m 21d B/P: 2/16

548 Combs, Lelia J. - single white female D: Oct 20, 1902; 11y 6m 23d; Hampshire B: Hampshire BUR: Mt. Zion B/P: 1/114

549 Combs, Mary - widow white female D: Oct 12, 1909; 75y B/P: 2/16

550 Combs, Mary Elizabeth - white female D: Apr 4, 1919; 64y 4m 20d B/P: 2/16

551 Combs, Miss - single white female D: Sept 2, 1909; 9d B/P: 2/16

552 Combs, Neal - single white male D: Jan 18, 1899; 2m 6d; Ruckman B: Ruckman BUR: Grassy Lick Church B/P: 1/101

553 Combs, Payton - Widower white male D: May 4, 1899; 79y 3m 18d; Ruckman B: Hampshire BUR: Mountain Dale B/P: 1/108 N: farmer

554 Combs, Rebecca D: Oct 15, 1871; 25y F: Combs, Andrew B/P: 1/6

555 Combs, Rebecca J. - married white female D: July 24, 1896; 72y 8m 9d; Hampshire B: Hampshire BUR: Mountain Dale B/P: 1/90

556 Combs, Sada - white female D: July 11, 1875; 6m; Hampshire M: Combs, Margaret B: Hampshire I: Combs, Andrew DOI: grandfather B/P: 1/14

557 Combs, Sophoria Ellen - single white female D: Apr 10, 1900; 5m 9d; Kirby B: Hampshire BUR: Grassy Lick Church B/P: 1/107

558 Compton, Edna M - white female D: Aug 4, 1897; 3m 9d; Gore F: Compton, H. M: Compton, E. B: Apr 25, 1897 DOI: father B/P: 1/66

559 Compton, Pauline - white female D: Aug 25, 1900; 5m; Hampshire F: Compton, H.C. M: Compton, Francis B: Apr 29, 1900 DOI: father B/P: 1/73

560 Cookus, Geo T. - white male D: 1905; 47y 8m B/P: 2/15

561 Cool, Bane - white male D: Nov 16, 1891; 31y; Hampshire F: Cool, Jas. M: Cool, Elizabeth B: Hampshire I: Cool, James DOI: brother C: Cool, Mary B/P: 1/53

562 Cool, Malinda - widow white female D: Apr 7, 1915; 76y 5m 9d B/P: 2/16

563 Cool, Wm D: May 15, 1869; 78y; Hampshire F: Cool, Herbert B: Hampshire B/P: 1/4

564 Cooper, Chas. C. - white male D: Nov 19, 1880; Hampshire F: Cooper, Marshal M: Cooper, Fannie B: Hampshire DOI: father B/P: 1/28

565 Cooper, George W - white male D: Feb 12, 1885; 82y; Hampshire B: Hampshire I: Cooper, Hiram DOI: son B/P: 1/42

566 Cooper, Jacob - white male D: Mar 7, 1875; 75y 3m 29d; Hampshire F: Cooper, John M: Cooper, Mary B: Hampshire DOI: wife C: Cooper, Anna B/P: 1/16 N: farmer

567 Cooper, Martha - widow white female D: Nov 23, 1910; 79y B/P: 2.16

568 Cooper, Moridca - white male D: May 8, 1896; 86y; Capon District B: May 1810 DOI: wife B/P: 1/62

569 Cooper, Nannie - single white female D: Feb 28, 1907; 65y B/P: 2/15

570 Corbert, Gurtrude - white female D: Aug 3, 1896; 2y; Romney F: Corbert, John P. M: Corbert, Mary B: Aug 1894 DOI: brother B/P: 1/62

571 Corbet, Gurtrude - white female D: Aug 3, 1895; 1y 6m; Romney District F: Corbet, John M: Corbet, Mary B: 1894 DOI: father B/P: 1/61

572 Corbin, Ann - married white female D: Dec 31, 1902; 67y; Hampshire B: Hampshire BUR: Mt Zion B/P: 1/116

573 Corbin, Ann - single white female D: Dec 13, 1898; 67y; Hampshire B: Hampshire BUR: Hampshire B/P: 1/100

574 Corbin, Bell - white female D: May 10, 1902; 34y 3m; Romney District F: Cheshire, Jas. M: Cheshire, Sarah B: 1869 DOI: husband C: Corbin, Job B/P: 1/78

575 Corbin, Cora Bell - female D: Dec 24, 1901; 4y 2m 5d;

near Romney F: Corbin, Charles M: Corbin, Ella DOI: father B/P: 1/76

576 Corbin, Elizabeth - white female D: June 1, 1881; 67y; Hampshire F: Corbin, Isaih M: Corbin, Nancy B: Hampshire I: Corbin, Francis DOI: brother B/P: 1/31

577 Corbin, Ethel - single white female D: Mar 24, 1919; 20y B/P: 2/16 N: burned to death

578 Corbin, Francis - white male D: Aug 20, 1884; 66y; Hampshire B: Hampshire I: Corbin, Ann DOI: sister B/P: 1/39

579 Corbin, Harry - single white male D: Aug 28, 1894; 4y; Near Hamp. Poor House B: Hampshire B/P: 1/82

580 Corbin, Henry - white male D: Oct 29, 1878; 55y; Hampshire F: Corbin, Isaac M: Corbin, Nancy B: Hampshire DOI: wife C: Corbin, Martha B/P: 1/24

581 Corbin, Jno. - white male D: Feb 5, 1903; 75y; Hampshire F: Corbin, Isaiah M: Corbin, Nancy B: 1829 I: Smith, B.W. DOI: son in law B/P: 1/80

582 Corbin, John - widower white male D: June 30, 1904; 75y 5m 5d; B/P: 2/15

583 Corbin, John - married white male D: Mar 31, 1909; 34y B/P: 2/16 N: farmer

584 Corbin, Manning - white male D: Mar 26, 1894; 34y 2m; Mill Creek District F: Corbin, James B: Mill Creek District DOI: father B/P: 1/59

585 Corbin, Mitchell Ray - single white male D: May 23, 1922; 10d; Hampshire F: Corbin, Harley M: Corbin, Bernadette B: Hampshire I: father B/P: 1/133

586 Corbin, Nancy - white female D: Feb 1875; 79y; Hampshire F: French, Robert M: French, Catherine B: Hampshire I: Corbin, Francis DOI: son C: Corbin, Isaiah B/P: 1/16

587 Corbin, Sarah A. - white female D: Mar 3, 1894; 57y; Mill Creek District B: Mill Creek District DOI: neighbor B/P: 1/59

588 Corbin, Susan - white female D: July 1892; 71y; Hampshire B: Hampshire I: Corbin, George DOI: son C: Corbin, Ashford B/P: 1/53

589 Corder, Bettie - white female D: Sept 22, 1908; 33y B/P: 2/15

590 Corlan, Henry M - single white male D: Oct 15, 1873; 5m 4d; Hampshire F: Corlan, James M: Corlan, Sarah B: Hampshire DOI: father B/P: 1/10

591 Cornwell, Jacob H. - white male D: Dec 23, 1897; 68y; Romney I: Cornwell, W.B. DOI: son B/P: 1/64

592 Cornwell, Marian M - white male D: May 27, 1874; 4m 27d; Hampshire F: Cornwell, Jacob H M: Cornwell, Mary E. B: Hampshire DOI: father B/P: 1/12

593 Cornwell, Mary - white female D: Oct 8, 1892; 11m 10d; Near Romney F: Cornwell, John J. M: Cornwell, Edna B: Romney DOI: father B/P: 1/56

594 Cornwell, Mary Ellen - widow white female D: Apr 25, 1922; 88y; Hampshire F: Taylor, Jno. M: Taylor, Mary B: Hampshire I: Cornwell, Jno. J. B/P: 1/133

595 Cornwell, Nanie V. - white female D: June 9, 1893; 24y 15d; Hampshire DOI: husband C: Cornwell, W.B. B/P: 1/58

596 Coval, W.A.E. - widow white female D: July 26, 1895; 74y; Romney B: 1821 I: Parson, G.W. B/P: 1/61

597 Cowgill, Alice - married white female D: Mar 11, 1907; 76y B/P: 2/15

598 Cowgill, Amanda E. - white female D: Nov 4, 1885; 72y 1m; Hampshire F: Cowgill, Erwin M: Cowgill, Margaret B: Hampshire DOI: father B/P: 1/42

599 Cowgill, Catherine - white female D: Aug 20, 1886; 82y 5m 1d; Hampshire I: Cowgill, John B/P: 1/44

600 Cowgill, Dora - white male D: May 1902; 14y; Hampshire F: Cowgill, Wm. M: Cowgill, E. B: 1888 I: Cowgill, J.E. DOI: uncle B/P: 1/79

601 Cowgill, F. - white male D: Mar 1888; 8m; Hampshire F: Cowgill, J.M. M: Cowgill, M.A. B: Hampshire C: Cowgill, J.M. B/P: 1/45

602 Cowgill, Fred - white male D: Dec 17, 1907; 84y B/P: 2/15 N: farmer

603 Cowgill, Frederick - widower white male D: Dec 14, 1908; 84y 4m B/P: 2/16 N: farmer

604 Cowgill, Harriet - widow white female D: Dec 21, 1909; 80y B/P: 2/16

605 Cowgill, Harriott - white female D: Jan 12, 1908; 74y B/P: 2/15

606 Cowgill, James A. - white male D: Nov 17, 1882; 63y; Hampshire F: Cowgill, H. M: Cowgill, R. B: Hampshire I: Cowgill, A. DOI: son B/P: 1/34

607 Cowgill, James H. - white male D: Feb 6, 1874; 7m 22d; Hampshire F: Cowgill, J.M. M: Cowgill, Margaret B: Hampshire DOI: mother B/P: 1/12

608 Cowgill, Leona - white female D: Mar 16, 1906; 31y B/P: 2/15

609 Cowgill, Mary - white female D: April 1902; 18y; Hampshire F: Cowgill, Wm. M: Cowgill, E. B: 1884 I: Cowgill, J.E. DOI: uncle B/P: 1/79

610 Cowgill, Nancy J. - white female D: July 1874; 52y; Hampshire F: Grant, John M: Grant, Elizabeth B: Hampshire I: Cowgill, E. DOI: brother in law C: Cowgill, Frederic B/P: 1/12

611 Cox, Albert L. - white male D: Sept 9, 1876; 8y 10m 6d; Hampshire F: Cox, John Thomas M: Cox, Rebecca B: Hampshire DOI: father B/P: 1/20

612 Cox, Henry Harrison - widower white male D: Mar 16, 1922; 81y 9m 6d; Hampshire B: Berkeley County I: Cox, B.H. B/P: 1/133 N: farmer

613 Cox, Thomas - married white male D: Mar 17, 1907; 58y B/P: 2/15 N: farmer

614 Crabtree, Alexander K D: Oct 2, 1870; Hampshire F: Crabtree, John M: Crabtree, Amanda B/P: 1/5

615 Crabtree, Anna - white female D: Sept 3, 1872; 3m; Hampshire F: Crabtree, Eli M: Crabtree, Margaret B: Hampshire DOI: father B/P: 1/8

616 Crabtree, Jno D. - white male D: Aug 26, 1906; 3d; B/P: 2/15

617 Crane, Goldie - white female D: Sept 15, 1908; 15y 1m B/P: 2/15

618 Crane, Hunter - white male D: Mar 1891; 2y; Capon District F: Crane, Sam M: Crane, Catherine B: Hampshire DOI: father B/P: 1/52

619 Crane, Hunter - white male D: Apr 1891; 4m; Hampshire F: Crane, S.E. M: Crane, Catherine B: Hampshire DOI: father B/P: 1/53

620 Crane, W. - white male D: July 23, 1888; 1y 3m; Hampshire F: Crane, S. M: Crane C. B: Hampshire DOI: father B/P: 1/45

621 Creamer, A.J. - married white male D: Nov 27, 1908; 84y B/P: 2/16

622 Creamer, A.J. - married white male D: Nov 27, 1909; 84y B/P: 2/16 N: tailor

623 Creswell, Chas. W. - white male D: June 15, 1909; 59y B/P: 2/16 N: farmer

624 Crites, Sallie P. - single white female D: Nov 7, 1912; 9y 9m 4d B: Romney B/P: 2/16

625 Critton, Debbie - single white female D: Jun 3, 1911; 65y B/P: 2/16

626 Critton, Elizabeth - white female D: July 1881; 80y; Hampshire B: Hampshire I: Portmess, Mrs. Washington DOI: niece B/P: 1/31

627 Crock, Benjamin - white male D: Feb 17, 1905; 65y B: Hampshire B/P: 2/15 N: farmer

628 Crock, F.C. - white female D: Oct 7, 1899; 54y 3m; Bloomery District F: Brelsford, N. M: Brelsford, M. B: July 7, 1845 DOI: husband C: Crock, B.L. B/P: 1/70

629 Crock, Mrs. B. - married white female D: Oct 8, 1899; 50y; Spring Gap B: Hampshire BUR: Forks of Capon B/P: 1/105

630 Cross, Annie - single white female D: Dec 26, 1896; 17y; near Slanesville B: WV BUR: Salem Church B/P: 1/91 N: name reads: Cross or Miller

631 Cross, Caroline - white female D: Aug 1873; 5m; Hampshire F: Cross, Robert M: Cross, Harriett B: Hampshire DOI: father

B/P: 1/11

632 Cross, Robt. - married white male D: Apr 29, 1896; abt 50; near Higginsville B: Hampshire BUR: Three Churches B/P: 1/91

633 Cross, Sarah A. - white female D: July 18, 1879; 79 y; Hampshire F: Barker, Barker M: Barker, Elizabeth B: Ohio I: Cross, Robert G DOI: son C: Cross, Wm. B. B/P: 1/26

634 Croston, Catharine D: 1870 B/P: 1/5

635 Croston, Eliza - single white female D: Dec 4, 1899; 80y; Near North River B: WV BUR: North River B/P: 1/106 N: Nationality: Spanish

636 Croston, William - married Spanish male D: June 5, 1894; 100y; North River B: Virginia BUR: Home B/P: 1/85

637 Croston, William - white male D: June 5, 1894; 99y; Hampshire B: Virginia I: Croston, Chas DOI: son B/P: 1/60

638 Crounse, Henry V. - white male D: Jan 14, 1899; 79y; Springfield F: Crounse, J. M: Crounse, M. B: Jan 4, 1820 I: Counse, A. DOI: son B/P: 1/70

639 Crouse, Mr. - single white male D: Nov 16, 1922; 59y 26m 16d; Hampshire F: Crouse, Larice M: Crouse, Nancy B: Morgan Co. I: Crouse, Thomas B/P: 1/133 N: farmer

640 Cummins, Sarah A. - white female D: Jan 3, 1908; B/P: 2/15

641 Cunningham, Ira C. - white male D: Mar 3, 1908; 17d B/P: 2/16

642 Cunningham, Jno. E. - wingle white male D: Dec 31, 1921; 26y 1m 21d; Hampshire F: Cunningham, J.E. M: Cunningham, Mary B: Berkeley Springs DOI: mother B/P: 1/131 N: mechanic

643 Cunningham, Sarah - married white female D: Jan 3, 1909; 77y 11m 26d B/P: 2/16

644 Cupp, Elmer Jesse - single white male D: Aug 24, 1910; 22y 9m 6d B/P: 2/16 N: clerk

645 Cupp, Jacob - married white male D: Feb 13, 1910; 55y B/P: 2/16

646 Curry, Lillian - white female D: Aug 10, 1904; 4m 14d

B/P: 2/15

647 Cutlett, Emma - white female D: Mar 4, 1912; 1d B/P: 2/16

648 Dailey, Elizabeth - white female D: Aug 10, 1912; 80y B/P: 2/23

649 Dailey, Hariet E. - white female D: July 22, 1885; 45y; Hampshire B: Hampshire I: Dailey, Eliza B/P: 1/42

650 Dailey, Jane - white female D: Oct 5, 1885; 78y; Hampshire B: Hampshire I: Dailey, Eliza B/P: 1/42

651 Dailey, John - widower white male D: Jan 15, 1912; 81y B: Springfield B/P: 2/23

652 Dandridge, Wash - married colored male D: Apr 22, 1907; 55y B/P: 2/22 N: farmer

653 Daniel, Eliza J. - white female D: Feb 14, 1880; Hampshire I: Daniels, Alphius DOI: husband B/P: 1/27

654 Daniels, Alpheus - white male D: July 29, 1881; 50y; Hampshire B: Hampshire I: Shull, J.W. DOI: son in law B/P: 1/29

655 Darr, Eliza - married white female D: Dec 14, 1921; 72y; Hampshire F: Nealis, Jas. M: Nealis, Mary B: Penn. I: Darr, Jas. E. B/P: 1/131 N: housewife

656 Darr, Hattie A. - white female D: July 5, 1882; 1y 2d; Hampshire F: Darr, J. M: Darr, Mary C. B: Hampshire DOI: mother B/P: 1/34

657 Darr, John - white male D: Sept 24, 1901; 52y; Hampshire B/P: 1/77

658 Darr, Wm. - white male D: Oct 20, 1886; 65y 9d; Hampshire B: Rappahannock, VA I: Darr, Wm. S. C: Darr, Catherine M. B/P: 1/44

659 Dattor, Pantibone - white male D: Feb 20, 1913; B/P: 2/23

660 Daugherty, Eliza J. - white female D: Aug 31, 1891; 70y 6m 9d; Hampshire F: Haines, Daniel M: Haines, Elizabeth B: Hampshire DOI: husband C: Daugherty, John W. B/P: 1/53

661 Daugherty, Harry - single white male D: Sept 14, 1918; 2y

10m; Hampshire B/P: 1/126

662 Daugherty, James - married white male D: July 30, 1913; 24y 3m 10d B/P: 2/23 N: farmer

663 Davey, M.F. - white male D: Oct 25, 1901; 10y; Mill Creek District F: Davey, William DOI: father B/P: 1/76

664 Davey, Margaret - white female D: Nov 14, 1901; 80y; Mill Creek District I: Davey, Silas DOI: son B/P: 1/76

665 Davey, Sarah J. - white female D: Aug 28, 1905; 20y B/P: 2/22

666 Davey, W.B. - white male D: Nov 12, 1901; 14y; Mill Creek District F: Davey, William DOI: father B/P: 1/76

667 Davey, William L. - single white male D: Dec 31, 1900; 21y; Romney F: Davey, Jack M: Davey, Chrislora DOI: father B/P: 1/72

668 Davis, Arthur B. - married white male D: Nov 15, 1921; 38y; Hampshire F: Davis, John B: WV I: Racey, B.T. B/P: 1/131 N: clerk at Deaf & Blind School

669 Davis, Bashie - single white female D: Dec 9, 1909; 80y B/P: 2/22

670 Davis, Dent Davis - white male D: Jan 19, 1908; 2y 2m 10d B/P: 2/22

671 Davis, Edna L. - white female D: July 22, 1893; 3y 4m; Hampshire F: Davis, Lemuel DOI: father B/P: 1/58

672 Davis, Kate - married white female D: Nov 24, 1920; 56y; Hampshire F: Dennison, Robert M: Dennison, Mary B: WV B/P: 1/129

673 Davis, Margaret D: June 8, 1871; 96y B: Ireland C: Davis, J.R. B/P: 1/6

674 Davis, Martha Ann - white female D: May 24, 1886; 18y; Sherman District F: Davis, R.S. M: Davis, Susan B: Hampshire DOI: father B/P: 1/43

675 Davis, Marvin - single white male D: July 25, 1915; 19y B/P: 2/23

676 Davis, Mary E D: Jan 13, 1871; 27y 6m F: Combs, Payton C: Davis, R.S. B/P: 1/6

677 Davis, Mary E. D: Apr 20, 1871; 3 m 10d F: Davis, R.S. B/P: 1/6

678 Davis, Phebe Lillie - white female D: Nov 19, 1905; 39y 3m B/P: 2/22

679 Davis, Samuel Bayard - white male D: May 27, 1886; 10y; Sherman District F: Davis, R.S. M: Davis, Susan B: Hampshire DOI: father B/P: 1/43

680 Davis, Sarah - married white female D: Sept 17, 1895; 69y; Hampshire B: Hampshire B/P: 1/87

681 Davis, Sarah A D: Nov 27, 1870; 14y 2m 4d; F: Davis, Eli B/P: 1/5

682 Davis, Thos. W. - single white male D: Apr 1, 1896; 12d; Hampshire B: Hampshire B/P: 1/87

683 Davis, Wm. Franklin - single white male D: Oct 12, 1921; 21y 10m 23d; Hampshire F: Davis, Chas. M: Davis, Sarah B: Hampshire DOI: father B/P: 1/131

684 Davy, Annie - white female D: Apr 23, 1891; 17y; Hampshire F: Davy, Geo W. M: Davy, Susan B: Hampshire DOI: father B/P: 1/53

685 Davy, Benj. F. - single white male D: Sept 25, 1909; 60y 3m 28d B/P: 2/22 N: farmer

686 Davy, Catherin - white female D: Oct 29, 1895; 49y 5m; Romney District F: Liller, Henry B: May 23, 1848 DOI: husband C: Davy, John W. B/P: 1/61

687 Davy, Eliza W. - white female D: Oct 12, 1881; 4y; West Va. F: Davy, Silas M: Davy, Lucinda B: Hampshire DOI: father B/P: 1/29

688 Davy, George - widower white male D: Sept 28, 1907; 70y B/P: 2/22

689 Davy, Mrs. Geo. - married white female D: Aug 27, 1907; 75y B/P: 2/22

690 Davy, Nettie C. - white female D: Mar 3, 1892; 11m; Mill Creek F: Davy, Isaac M: Davy, Harriett B: Mill Creek DOI: father B/P: 1/56

691 Davy, Sarah V. - white female D: Jan 16, 1892; 35y;

Hampshire F: Liller, Elijah M: Liller, Christina B: Hampshire DOI: husband C: Davy, William B/P: 1/53

692 Davy, Thompson - single white male D: Aug 9, 1911; 19y 3m 18d B: Sherman District B/P: 2/23

693 Dawson, Harris - single white male D: Aug 30, 1888; 15m; 3 miles from Paw Paw B: WV B/P: 1/123

694 Dawson, McKinley R. - white male D: Dec 5, 1902; 2y 9m; Sherman District F: Dawson, W.T.I. M: Dawson, Lizzie B: 1900 DOI: father B/P: 1/78

695 Day, Alex - white male D: Jan 4, 1901; 76y; Hampshire I: Day, J.W. B/P: 1/77

696 Day, Ann - white female D: Oct 7, 1874; 70y 17d; Hampshire F: Pugh, Jacob M: Pugh, Elizabeth B: Hampshire I: Day, Alexander DOI: son C: Day, William B/P: 1/12

697 Day, Caroline - white female D: Mar 17, 1882; 51y 9m 8d; Hampshire F: Smoot, J. M: Smoot, S. B: Hampshire DOI: husband C: Day, Alex B/P: 1/34

698 Day, Eliza - colored female D: Jan 2, 1891; 26y; Romney District F: Hardy, Thomas M: Hardy, Mary B: Hampshire DOI: husband C: Day, Edward B/P: 1/52

699 Day, George B.C. D: Sept 20, 1870; 2y; Hampshire F: Day, Nimrod M: Day, Susan B/P: 1/5

700 Day, Henrietta - white female D: Oct 8, 1872; 8m 13d; Hampshire F: Day, Alexander M: Day, Caroline B: Hampshire DOI: father B/P: 1/8

701 Day, Jas. Morgan - white male D: Mar 21, 1922; stillborn; Hampshire F: Day, Wm. M: Day, Bessie B: Three Churches DOI: father B/P: 1/133

702 Day, John - married white male D: Apr 3, 1906; 55y B/P: 2/22 N: farmer

703 Day, Margaret A. - white female D: Sept 1875; 26y; Hampshire F: Moreland, Jacob M: Moreland, Sarah A. B: Hampshire DOI: husband C: Day, Thomas L. B/P: 1/16

704 Day, Mary F. - white female D: Oct 8, 1875; 16y 9m 19d; Hampshire F: Day, Alex M: Day, Caroline B: Hampshire DOI: mother B/P: 1/16

705 Day, Nimrod - married white male D: Apr 15, 1913; 80y B/P: 2/23 N: farmer

706 Day, Roy - white male D: July 22, 1908; 5y B/P: 2/22

707 Day, Sallie - white female D: Apr 24, 1913; 22y B/P: 2/23

708 Day, Sarah - single white female D: Oct 6, 1875; 16y 11m; Hampshire M: Durst, Harriet B: Hampshire DOI: mother B/P: 1/16

709 Day, Sarah A. - white female D: Oct 26, 1884; 26y; Hampshire F: Day, Alex M: Day, Caroline B: Hampshire DOI: father B/P: 1/39

710 Day, Thomas - widower white male D: May 14, 1913; 77y B/P: 2/23

711 Day, Thos. - widower white male D: May 15, 1913; 75y B/P: 2/23

712 Day, William - single colored male D: June 15, 1918; 35y; Hampshire B/P: 1/126 N: domestic servant

713 Day, William - white male D: Oct 23, 1873; 72y 9m 11d; Hampshire B: Hampshire DOI: wife C: Day, Ann B/P: 1/11

714 Deacon, John M. - single D: July 12, 1871; 27y; Hampshire F: Deacon, David M: Deacon, Margaret B/P: 1/6

715 Deacon, Norman Grant D: Apr 22, 1870; 2y; Hampshire F: Deacon, Tolbert M: Deacon, Caracy E. B/P: 1/5

716 Dean, Henry W. - white male D: Apr 4, 1908; 2y 5m 18d B/P: 2/22

717 Dean, Isaac D. - white male D: Mar 31, 1908; 4y 13d B/P: 2/22

718 Dean, Jane - married white female D: July 26, 1921; 71y 5m 26d; Hampshire M: Greenwalt, Mary Jane B: Pendleton County I: Buckley, Jas. B/P: 1/131 N: housewife

719 Dean, Maggie Catharine - married white female D: Apr 7, 1908; 30y B/P: 2/22

720 Dean, Mariah - married white female D: Mar 25, 1908; 77y B/P: 2/22

721 Dean, Rachel - married white female D: Jan 10, 1911; 33y B: Sherman District B/P: 2/23

722 Deaver, Althea - single white female D: July 5, 1913; 26y B/P: 2/23

723 Deaver, George - single white male D: Oct 1, 1875; 85y 7m 7d; Hampshire F: Deaver, William M: Deaver, Elizabeth B: Hampshire I: Deaver, Geo Jr. DOI: nephew B/P: 1/16 N: drown

724 Deaver, George - widower white male D: Nov 28, 1908; 83y B/P: 2/22 N: farmer

725 Deaver, Lucinda - married white female D: Mar 10, 1898; 71y; near North River Mills B: Hampshire BUR: Sandy Ridge B/P: 1/91

726 Deaver, Susan - white female D: Aug 1882; 81y; Hampshire B: Hampshire I: Moreland, George DOI: friend C: Deaver, Richard B/P: 1/34

727 Deems, Geo. - married white male D: June 21, 1910; 58y DOI: wife B/P: 2/22

728 Dehaven, Couter - white male D: Aug 7, 1912; 27y 2m 3d B/P: 2/23 N: fruit grower

729 Dehaven, D.H. - married white male D: Sept 1, 1904; 40y B: Frederick Co., VA B/P: 2/22 N: peach grower

730 Dehaven, David - married white male D: Aug 19, 1904; 50y B/P: 2/22

731 Dehaven, Laura - married white female D: Aug 25, 1912; 40y 9m 26d B/P: 2/23

732 Dehaven, Luther - single white male D: Apr 6, 1911; 23y 2m B/P: 2/23 N: sawyer

733 Delaplain, Christopher - white male D: Mar 7, 1902; 82y; Sherman District F: Delaplain, Eli B: 1820 I: Delaplain, J.C. DOI: son B/P: 1/78

734 Delaplain, Emily - white female D: Sept 27, 1905; 81y B/P: 2/22

735 Delaplain, John - white male D: Feb 7, 1908; 1y 6m B/P: 2/22

736 Delaplane, Eli - white male D: Nov 3, 1878; 86y 1m 2d; Hampshire F: Delaplane, Isaac B: Hampshire I: Delaplane, W. DOI: son C: Delaplane, Emily B/P: 1/24

737 Deleplane, Christopher - white male D: July 23, 1899; 84y; Sherman District DOI: daughter B/P: 1/72

738 Delinger, Anna - married white female D: Apr 4, 1899; 56y 2m 10d; Hampshire B: Shenandoah Co., VA BUR: Hanging Rock B/P: 1/103

739 Delinger, Annie - white female D: April 10, 1899; 65y; Capon M: Dilinger, Lucy B: 1835 B/P: 1/71

740 Devilbliss, Edward - married white male D: Jan 29, 1915; 47y 2m 6d B/P: 2/23 N: farmer

741 Devilbliss, Martha I. - white female D: Aug 1, 1915; 1m 17d B/P: 2/23

742 Dicken, D.M. - married white male D: Jan 20, 1913; 66y B/P: 2/23 N: orchardist

743 Dicken, Ellen - white female D: Feb 14, 1905; 53y B/P: 2/22

744 Dicken, L.M. - white male D: May 12, 1878; 1m 21d; Hampshire F: Dicken, D.M. M: Dicken, Mary J. B: Maryland DOI: father B/P: 1/24

745 Digman, Jno H. - white male D: Jan 20, 1884; 6y; Hampshire F: Digman, T.W. M: Digman, Mary B: Hampshire DOI: father B/P: 1/39

746 Doman, Alfred - white male D: Mar 29, 1889; 53y; Hampshire DOI: wife C: Doman, Susan B/P: 1/51

747 Doman, Catherine - white female D: Aug 9, 1897; 70y; Mill Creek B: Maryland DOI: husband C: Doman, John B/P: 1/64

748 Doman, Furley - single white male D: Feb 22, 1895; 28y; Near Higginsville B: Hampshire B/P: 1/85

749 Doman, John W. - white male D: Oct 25, 1891; 22y; Hampshire F: Doman, Wm. H. M: Doman, Mary B: Hampshire DOI: father B/P: 1/55

750 Doman, Mary A. - white female D: July 6, 1891; 43y; Hampshire F: Powelson, Jno. M: Powelson, Catherine B: Hampshire DOI: husband C: Doman, Wm. H. B/P: 1/55

751 Doman, Rebecca - white female D: Sept 25, 1891; 60y; Hampshire F: Pownall, Isaac M: Pownall, Nancy B: Hampshire DOI: husband C: Doman, T.W. B/P: 1/55

752 Doman, Susan - white female D: May 7, 1878; 55y 1m 10d; Hampshire B: Hampshire DOI: husband C: Doman, John W. B/P: 1/23

753 Doman, Susan - widow white female D: Dec 6, 1913; 78y B/P: 2/23

754 Doman, Thos. W. - widower white male D: Mar 19, 1908; 80y B/P: 2/22 N: farmer

755 Doman, William - widower white male D: Aug 18, 1914; 81y 6m 10d B/P: 2/23 N: farmer

756 Donaldson, Mary B. - white female D: Oct 11, 1900; 45y; Hampshire F: Donaldson, William M: Donaldson, Mary B: Nov 2, 1885 DOI: mother B/P: 1/73

757 Donaldson, William - white male D: Dec 11, 1882; 57y; Hampshire F: Donaldson, R. M: Donaldson, R. B: Hampshire DOI: wife C: Donaldson, Mary C. B/P: 1/34

758 Dorn, Wm. B. - white male D: Oct 23, 1876; 59y 14d; Hampshire F: Dorn, Frederick M: Dorn, Elizabeth B: Oldtown, MD DOI: wife C: Dorn, Sarah B/P: 1/20

759 Dorsey, Frank - white male D: July 22, 1884; 72y; Hampshire B: Hampshire DOI: wife C: Dorsey, Annie B/P: 1/39

760 Dorsey, George - married white male D: Feb 13, 1914; 39y B/P: 2/23

761 Dorsey, Harriett S - white female D: Jan 14, 1873; 37 y; Hampshire F: Rersin, Alex M: Rersin, Ann B: Maryland DOI: husband C: Dorsey, Francis B/P: 1/11

762 Dorsey, Howard - white male D: Aug 11, 1896; 1m 20d; Hampshire F: Dorsey, Dallis M: Dorsey, Anna B: June 26, 1896 DOI: father B/P: 1/63

763 Dorsey, John - white male D: June 5, 1914; 71y 2m B/P: 2/23 N: farmer

764 Dorsey, Lula - white female D: July 28, 1905; 18y B/P: 2/22

765 Dorsey, May - single white female D: Apr 18, 1907; 1y B/P: 2/22

766 Dorsey, Mr. - white male D: June 26, 1903; 21y; Green Spring B: Hampshire BUR: Levels B/P: 1/117

767 Dorsey, Sarah - married white female D: Nov 1, 1914; 64y B/P: 2/23

768 Dovey, Newton - white male D: Oct 26, 1902; 20y 6m; Romney F: Dovey, Jno M: Dovey, Anna B: 1882 DOI: father B/P: 1/78

769 Doyl, Mathew - white male D: Apr 4, 1879; 67y 2m 20d; Hampshire DOI: wife C: Doyl, Harriet B/P: 1/25

770 Doyle, Chas. Ashby - married white male D: Nov 6, 1919; 55y 4m B/P: 2/23 N: warehouseman

771 Doyle, Ella M - white female D: July 15, 1888; 2y; Sherman District F: Doyle, Matthew M: Doyle, Harriet J. B: Hampshire DOI: father B/P: 1/47

772 Doyle, Harriet - widow white female D: Feb 28, 1909; 82y 5m B/P: 2/22

773 Doyle, Harriet Jane - married white female D: Apr 7, 1919; 60y 1m 21d B/P: 2/23

774 Doyle, John D: July 18, 1870; 55y B/P: 1/5

775 Doyle, John D: July 10, 1869; 53y F: Doyle, Charles B: Hampshire B/P: 1/4

776 Doyle, Roy Elmar - white male D: Apr 13, 1894; 6y; Sherman District F: Doyle, Chas Ashby B: Sherman District DOI: father B/P: 1/59

777 Drening, Silas H. - white male D: June 10, 1874; 1y 4m 8d; Hampshire F: Drening, James M: Drening, Susan B: Hampshire DOI: mother B/P: 1/12

778 Droher, Rufus Lutz - single white male D: Sept 12, 1888; 7m; B: Hampshire B/P: 1/123

779 Druen, Emmet Beverly - white male D: Oct 8, 1912; 39y B/P: 2/23 N: drowned

780 Duncan, Daisy Gladdys - single white female D: Oct 22,

1918; 6y 4m 4d; Hampshire B/P: 1/126

781 Dunlap, F.C. - white female D: Feb 15, 1890; 30y; Capon District F: Lafollette, Jas. A. B: Capon District DOI: father C: Dunlap, H.W. B/P: 1/49

782 Dunlap, Natalie A. - white female D: Jan 18, 1913; 3m 15d B/P: 2/23

783 Durst, Elizabeth - widow white female D: Nov 20, 1913; 82y B/P: 2/23

784 Durst, Jno. R. - white D: 1902; 75y; Hampshire B: 1827 B/P: 1/79

785 Durst, Lewis - white male D: Nov 21, 1912; 22y B: Springfield B/P: 2/23 N: school teacher

786 Duvall, Walter - white male D: Sept 5, 1905; B/P: 2/22

787 Earsom, Walter - white male D: Mar 29, 1876; 26d; Hampshire F: Earsom, William M: Earsom, Mary J. B: Hampshire DOI: father B/P: 1/20

788 Easter, Mary C. D: Dec 1, 1871; 20y 11m; Hampshire F: Easter, Hiram M: Easter, Catharine B/P: 1/6

789 Eaton, B. - white male D: July 4, 1867; 2y 3m 6d; Timber Ridge F: Eaton, James B: Timber Ridge DOI: father B/P: 1/2

790 Eaton, Balam - married white male D: July 12, 1909; 79y B/P: 2/29

791 Eaton, Eliza E. - married white female D: July 25, 1913; 53y B/P: 2/29

792 Eaton, Margaret E. - white female D: July 16, 1872; 1y 2m 1d; Frederick Co VA F: Eaton, James M: Eaton, Effia B: Frederick Co, VA DOI: mother B/P: 1/8

793 Eaton, Martha - married white female D: Mar 16, 1904; 60y B/P: 2/29

794 Eaton, Mary C. - married white female D: April 4, 1866; 25y 3m 11d; Hampshire F: Eaton, Henry M: Eaton, Catherine B: Hampshire DOI: husband C: Eaton, Balien B/P: 1/1

795 Eaton, Mary Lana - white female D: Feb 13, 1867; 1y 1m 1d; Near Capon Bridge F: Eaton, Baline M: Eaton, Lidia B: near Capon Bridge DOI: father B/P: 1/2

796 Eaton, Walter F. - white male D: Dec 14, 1913; 22y 27d B/P: 2/29 N: farmer

797 Edmonson, Ann - widow black female D: Dec 6, 1898; 85y; North River Mills B: Hampshire BUR: Slanesville B/P: 1/99

798 Edmonson, Annie - colored female D: Sept 23, 1903; 13y; Hampshire F: Edmonson, Robert M: Edmonson, Emily B: 1890 DOI: father B/P: 1/80

799 Edmonson, Selu - colored female D: Sept 17, 1886; 25y; Hampshire B: Hampshire DOI: husband C: Edmonson, Edw. B. B/P: 1/44

800 Edwards, Edward - single white male D: Jan 19, 1908; 40y B/P: 2/29

801 Edwards, Golda Pearl - single white female D: Jan 6, 1918; stillborn; Hampshire B/P: 1/126

802 Edwards, Rebecca - single white female D: Oct 18, 1921; 15d; Hampshire F: Edwards, Ernest M: Edwards, Lilah B: Slanesville I: Edwards, Rebecca B/P: 1/131

803 Edwards, Rebecca - married white female D: May 23, 1922; 60y 4m 4d; Hampshire F: Kidwell, Jas. A. M: Kidwell, Mary B: WV I: Edwards, Robert B/P: 1/133 N: housewife

804 Eiflen, Olive - single white female D: Oct 15, 1920; 7m 2d; Hampshire F: Eiflen, Elmer B: Hampshire B/P: 1/129

805 Elliot, Madison - widower white male D: Feb 3, 1899; Yellow Springs B: Yellow Springs BUR: Timber Ridge B/P: 1/102

806 Emert, Eliza - single white female D: July 20, 1879; 53y; Hampshire F: Emert, Andrew M: Emert, Elizabeth B: Hampshire I: Emert, George W. DOI: brother B/P: 1/26

807 Emmart P. - single white female D: Mar 12, 1890; 71y; Sherman District F: Emmart, Henry M: Emmart, Rebecca B: Hampshire I: Emmart, Lemuel DOI: brother B/P: 1/52

808 Emmart, Andrew - white male D: June 13, 1886; 79y; Sherman District F: Emmart, Henry M: Emmart, Rebecca B: Hampshire I: Emmart, Samuel DOI: brother B/P: 1/43

809 Emmart, Anna - white female D: Oct 11, 1884; 54y; Hampshire F: Emmart, Andrew M: Emmart, Elizabeth B:

Hampshire I: Emmart, Jacob DOI: brother B/P: 1/39

810 Emmart, Anna - white female D: June 8, 1912; 43y 6m 13d B/P: 2/29

811 Emmart, Eliza J. - white female D: Apr 25, 1880; Hampshire I: Emmart, W.J. DOI: daughter B/P: 1/27

812 Emmart, Elizabeth - widow white female D: Jan 28, 1909; 65y B/P: 2/29

813 Emmart, Eve - single white female D: Apr 9, 1874; 58y 2y 21d; Hampshire F: Emmart, John M: Emmart, Nancy B: Hampshire I: Emmart, Nancy DOI: sister B/P: 1/12

814 Emmart, Franklin Lee - single white male D: Feb 8, 1866; 11d F: Emmart, L. M: Emmart, S. B: Hampshire DOI: parent B/P: 1/1

815 Emmart, Geo W. - single white male D: Oct 24, 1883; 63y; Hampshire F: Emmart, Andrew M: Emmart, Elizabeth B: Hampshire I: Emmart, Jacob DOI: brother B/P: 1/37

816 Emmart, George - white male D: June 7, 1878; 55y 9m 14d; Hampshire F: Emmart, Henry M: Emmart, R. B: Hampshire I: Emmart,(young) DOI: son C: Emmart, Barbra B/P: 1/24

817 Emmart, Hannah - white female D: July 15, 1884; 58y; Hampshire F: Emmart, Andrew M: Emmart, Elizabeth B: Hampshire I: Emmart, Jacob DOI: brother B/P: 1/39

818 Emmart, John - white male D: Jan 25, 1872; 55y 2m 5d; Hampshire F: Emmart, John M: Emmart, Nancy B: Hampshire B/P: 1/9

819 Emmart, John - white male D: Apr 15, 1866; Tear Coat B: Tear Coat DOI: son B/P: 1/1

820 Emmart, John R. D: Aug 25, 1870; 10m F: Emmart, Lemuel B/P: 1/5

821 Emmart, L.B. - single white male D: Feb 3, 1899; 28y; Romney BUR: Mt. Zion B/P: 1/102

822 Emmart, Lemuel - white male D: Oct 3, 1900; 75y 11m; Sherman F: Emmart, Henry M: Emmart, Rebecca B: Apr 11, 1824 I: Emmart, John DOI: son B/P: 1/71

823 Emmart, Nancy Jane - single white female D: July 1, 1920; 70y 10m 23d; Hampshire F: Emmart, Jas. B: Mineral County

B/P: 1/129

824 Emmart, Samuel - white male D: Feb 14, 1889; 68y; Sherman District B: Hampshire DOI: wife C: Emmart, Elizabeth B/P: 1/47 N: farmer

825 Emmart, Samuel - married white male D: Feb 14, 1889; 68y 4m 16d; Sherman District B: Virginia BUR: Sherman District B/P: 1/124

826 Emmart, Samuel E. - white male D: Apr 8, 1895; 1y 5m 19d; Sherman District F: Emmart, John W. B: Nov 1893 DOI: father B/P: 1/61

827 Emmert, Ettie - married white female D: Apr 18, 1919; 51y 1m B/P: 2/29

828 Emmertt, Jacob - white male D: Jan 27, 1910; 69y 8m 21d B/P: 2/29 N: farmer

829 Emmett, Lemuel - white male D: May 26, 1898; 3y 25d; Sherman District F: Emmett, W.H. M: Emmett, Emma DOI: father B/P: 1/68

830 Emory, Annie L. - white female D: Aug 2, 1905; 47y 7m B/P: 2/29

831 Endler, Frank R. - white male D: Nove 13, 1881; 17y 9m; Hampshire F: Endler, D.W. M: Endler, Elizabeth B: Hampshire DOI: father B/P: 1/30

832 Endler, Isaac - single white male D: May 1896; 60y; Romney B: Romney BUR: Romney B/P: 1/96 N: Tailor

833 Endler, Isaac E. - single white male D: May 21, 1896; 60y 6m 14d; Hampshire B: Hampshire DOI: Hampshire B/P: 1/87

834 Endler, Mrs. David - white female D: Mar 16, 1912; 78y B: Romney District B/P: 2/29

835 Engler, John - white male D: July 12, 1889; 83y; Hampshire B: Hampshire I: McCauley, Ben DOI: son in law B/P: 1/51 N: minister

836 Engler, Sarah - white female D: May 28, 1889; 79y 3m; Hampshire B: Hampshire I: McCauley, Ben DOI: son in law C: Engler, John B/P: 1/51

837 Epperson, Jno E. - married white male D: July 16, 1921; Hampshire B: WV I: Beatty, Jno. B/P: 1/130 N: farmer;

drowned

838 Ernest, Turley - white male D: Sept 4, 1917; 22y 5m 2d B/P: 2/29

839 Eskridge, Eliza - white female D: Aug 31, 1906; B/P: 2/29

840 Evans, Davis - white male D: Feb 9, 1905; 70y B/P: 2/29

841 Evans, Dora Ann - white female D: Sept 1892; 2y 1m 6d; Hampshire F: Evans, W.O. M: Evans, Sarah C. B: near Glebe DOI: father B/P: 1/56

842 Evans, Ed E - white female D: June 15, 1901; 4m; Romney District F: Evans, W.D. M: Evans, Sarah C. DOI: father B/P: 1/76

843 Evans, Edward - white male D: Aug 10, 1900; 3m; Romney F: Evans, Oscar M: Evans, Sarah B: May 10, 1900 B/P: 1/72

844 Evans, Elizabeth - married white female D: Nov 1, 1876; 91y; Hampshire B: Hampshire I: Evans, E. DOI: son C: Evans, Abrm B/P: 1/18

845 Evans, Jane - white female D: Feb 10, 1910; 85y B/P: 2/29

846 Everet, Catharine - married white female D: Apr 6, 1898; 60y; Hampshire B: West Virginia BUR: Mill Creek B/P: 1/98

847 Everett, Isaac H. - white male D: Oct 16, 1889; 11y 11m 4d; Mill Creek District M: Everett, Mary A. B: Mill Creek I: Everett, Catherine DOI: grandmother B/P: 1/49

848 Everett, Jacob E. - married white male D: Dec 14, 1921; 71y; Hampshire F: Everett, Darius M: Everett, Mary B: Hampshire I: Everett, A.E. B/P: 1/131 N: farmer

849 Everett, John P. - white male D: Sept 26, 1882; 68y; Hampshire F: Everett, A. M: Everett, F. B: New Jersey DOI: wife C: Everett, Mary C. B/P: 1/34

850 Everett, Leona - married white female D: Dec 26, 1922; 16y; Hampshire F: Sulser, Lee M: Sulser, Daisy B: Hardy County I: Arnold, Jno B. B/P: 1/133

851 Everett, Lewis - white male D: 25 May 1882; 66y; Mill Creek Dist B: WV I: Everett, Abijah DOI: son B/P: 1/33

852 Everett, Linda - white female D: Feb 14, 1890; 72y 3m 6d; Mill Creek District B: Mill Creek District DOI: husband C: Everett, John B/P: 1/49

853 Everett, Louis - white male D: Apr 11, 1912; 71y 1m 13d B/P: 2/29

854 Everett, Lula - single white female D: Sept 25, 1910; 18y 3m B/P: 2/29

855 Everett, Mary Ann - white female D: Apr 5, 1898; 55y 8m 2d; Mill Creek District F: Ludwick, Joseph M: Ludwick, Ann DOI: husband B/P: 1/68

856 Everett, Mary F. - white female D: Feb 3, 1892; 80y; Hampshire B: Hampshire I: Everett, G.M. DOI: son B/P: 1/57

857 Everitt, Jacob - married white male D: Mar 14, 1873; 64y 3m 10d; Hampshire F: Everitt, Asa M: Everitt, Margt. B: Hampshire I: Everitt, Derias DOI: brother C: Everitt, Rebecca B/P: 1/10 N: farmer

858 Ewers, A.V. - white female D: Jan 15, 1901; 72y; Hampshire I: Ewers, A.L. B/P: 1/77

859 Ewers, Franklin - white male D: Nov 11, 1889; 65y 6m 6d; Hampshire B: Virginia I: Ewers, L. DOI: son C: Ewers, Anna B/P: 1/51

860 Ewers, Jacob F. - single white male D: Dec 31, 1904; 20y 2m 2d B/P: 2/29 N: clerk

861 Ewers, Nannie - white female D: Nov 17, 1910; 45y B/P: 2/29

862 Ewers, Wilson - colored male D: June 7, 1913; 21y B/P: 2/29 N: struck by train

863 Fahrenbach, Sevilla - widow white female D: Jan 8, 1912; 81y B/P: 2/33

864 Fahs, Joseph - white male D: Nov 26, 1882; 80y; Hampshire B: Hampshire DOI: wife C: Fahs, Maria B/P: 1/34

865 Fairfax, Andrew L. - single black male D: Apr 19, 1889; 8m; Springfield BUR: Springfield B/P: 1/124

866 Fairfax, Daniel - colored male D: Aug 1889; 15y; Hampshire F: Fairfax, Dan M: Fairfax, P. B: Hampshire DOI: father B/P: 1/51

867 Fairfax, Daniel - colored male D: Mar 14, 1892; B: Hampshire I: Thomas, Dr. DOI: physician B/P: 1/57

868 Fairfax, Daniel - single black male D: July 13, 1889; 18y 10m; Springfield B: Springfield BUR: Springfield B/P: 1/124

869 Fairfax, Harriett - single colored female D: June 6, 1876; 55y; Hampshire F: Fairfax, Maskus M: Fairfax, Charlote B: Hampshire I: Long, Jno W. DOI: acquaintance BUR: 1/20

870 Fairfax, Mary - colored female D: Mar 1900; 21y; Hampshire F: Fairfax, David M: Fairfax, Mary B: 1879 DOI: father B/P: 1/74

871 Fairfax, Mary - black female D: Mar 25, 1900; 19y; Springfield BUR: Springfield B/P: 1/109

872 Fairfax, Mary - widow colored female D: Dec 4, 1914; 80y B/P: 2/34

873 Fairfax, Ward - colored male D: July 5, 1905; 24y B/P: 2/33

874 Farley, Geo. W. D: Sept 18, 1869; 5m; Gerrardstown, Berkeley Co F: Farley, George B: Gerrardstown B/P: 1/4

875 Farmer, Anna - white female D: 1896; 79y; Hampshire F: Kidwell B: 1817 I: Farmer, S.J. DOI: sib B/P: 1.63

876 Farmer, Jamima - white female D: Aug 9, 1883; 61y; Hampshire B: Virginia DOI: husband C: Farmer, Davis B/P: 1/36

877 Farmer, Romangus - white male D: Oct 20, 1911; 25y B/P: 2/33 N: drowned

878 Fately, Lula - married white female D: Sept 11, 1912; 23y B: Bloomery District B/P: 2/33

879 Feaster, Catherine V. - widowed white female D: June 1, 1922; 81y 8d; Hampshire F: May, B: Grant County I: Leatherman, Lena B/P: 1/133

880 Feller, Rennie, G. - white female D: Jan 17, 1909; 20y DOI: father B/P: 1/33

881 Fertig, Mima Ray - single white female D: June 4, 1876; 2y 1m; Hampshire F: Fertig, John R M: Fertig, Elizabeth B: Hampshire DOI: father C: 1/18

882 Fidler, Nancy E. - colored female D: Mar 8, 1879; 8m; Hampshire F: Fidler, Joseph M: Fidler, Grace B: Hampshire DOI: mother B/P: 1/25

883 Fields, Forest - white male D: Oct 22, 1904; 8m B/P: 2/33

884 Fields, Franklin Martin - single white male D: Oct 4, 1919; 49y B/P: 2/34 N: farmer

885 Fields, Maude - white female D: July 5, 1912; 23y B: Springfield District B/P: 2/33

886 Fields, Miss - single white female D: 1896; 6 d; Springfield B: Hampshire BUR: Springfield B/P: 1/93

887 Fields, Victoria - married white female D: Nov 12, 1917; 55y B/P: 2/34

888 Fields, W.A. - white male D: Apr 8, 1888; 1m 1d; Hampshire F: Fields, H. M: Fields, V. B: Hampshire DOI: father B/P: 1/45

889 Fields, William - white male D: Nov 8, 1905; 84y B/P: 2/33

890 Finley, Rebecca D. - white female D: Aug 1881; 13m; Hampshire F: Finley, Geo W. M: Finley, Margaret B: Virginia I: Gibson, J.A. DOI: friend B/P: 1/30

891 Firby, Mary - white female D: June 2, 1877; Hampshire B: Rockingham Co VA I: Firby, John DOI: son B/P: 1/22

892 Fishel, Bertie - white female D: Aug 10, 1901; 1y 3m; Capon District F: Fishel, William DOI: father B/P: 1/76

893 Fishel, Chas C. - white male D: Feb 24, 1894; 2y; Hampshire County B: Hampshire County BUR: Spring Gap B/P: 1/84

894 Fishel, Gilbert - white male D: June 17, 1897; 3d; Bloomery F: Fishel, Jacob M: Fishel, M. B: June 14, 1897 DOI: father B/P: 1/66

895 Fishel, Henry - married white male D: July 18, 1896; 65y; Spring Gap BUR: Spring Gap B/P: 1/91

896 Fishel, Jacob - white male D: Aug 4, 1889; 51y; Capon District B: Capon District DOI: wife C: Fishel, Mary A.

B/P: 1/49

897 Fishel, Margaret C - white female D: Sept 19, 1866; Great Capon F: Fishel, Jacob M: Fishel, Mary B: Great Capon DOI: mother B/P: 1/1

898 Fishel, Mr. - married white male D: Oct 20, 1913; 48y B/P: 2/34

899 Fishel, Sam'l - white male D: Oct 19, 1866; Great Capon B/P: 1/1

900 Fishell, Jos. - married white male D: Aug 25, 1897; abt 38y; near Slanesville B: Hampshire BUR: Spring Gap B/P: 1/91

901 Fishell, Marg. M. - single white female D: Jan 8, 1921; 3y 9m; Hampshire F: Fishel, Jacob M: Fishel, Minnie B: Green Spring DOI: father B/P: 1/130

902 Fishell, Miss - single white female D: Apr 28, 1895; 1d; Hampshire B: Hampshire B/P: 1/88

903 Fishell, Mrs. Lee - married white female D: May 29, 1898; 36y; Spring Gap B: Hampshire BUR: Spring Gap B/P: 1/99

904 Fisher, Ann Dean - single colored female D: Dec 12, 1917; 27y 5m 7d B/P: 2/34 N: hairdresser

905 Fisher, Butler B. - white male D: Dec 26, 1878; 68y; Hampshire F: Fisher, Barrick B: Franklin, VA C: Fisher, Rebecca B/P: 1/24

906 Fisher, Cindy J. - colored female D: Oct 15, 1901; 65y; Romney DOI: husband C: Fisher, Robert B/P: 1/76

907 Fisher, David - colored male D: Oct 25, 1877; Hampshire F: Fisher, Robert M: Fisher, Matilda B: Hampshire DOI: father B/P: 1/22

908 Fisher, Florence B - single white female D: Nov 16, 1866; 11y 4m; Hampshire F: Fisher, Jacob M: Fisher, Sarah B: Hampshire DOI: parent B/P: 1/1

909 Fisher, Frances D: Nov 27, 1869; 92y; Hampshire B/P: 1/4

910 Fisher, Harry - colored male D: Nov 15, 1901; 35y; Pittsburg, PA F: Fisher, Richard DOI: father B/P: 1/76

911 Fisher, James C. - white male D: Sept 30, 1872; 15y; Hampshire F: Fisher, Washington M: Fisher, Mary B: Middleton, Maryland DOI: father B/P: 1/8

912 Fisher, John W. - white male D: Sept 30, 1872; 28y; Hampshire F: Fisher, Washington M: Fisher, Isabella B: Hampshire DOI: father B/P: 1/8

913 Fisher, Mary S. - white female D: Apr 26, 1875; 44y 3d; Hampshire F: Cherry, William M: Cherry, Eveline B: Hampshire DOI: husband C: Fisher, Washington B/P: 1/16

914 Fisher, W. - white male D: Dec 24, 1892; 78y; Hampshire B: Hampshire I: Thomas, Dr. DOI: physician B/P: 1/57 N: mechanic

915 Fleming, Martha J. - white female D: May 4, 1898; 15y; Mill Creek District F: Fleming, James DOI: father B/P: 1/68

916 Flemming, Edward A. - white male D: Feb 28, 1905; 54y 1m B/P: 2/33

917 Flemming, James - married white male D: July 26, 1907; 58y B/P: 2/33 N: farmer

918 Flemming, Mary - white female D: July 8, 1904; 21y B/P: 2/33

919 Flemming, Mary C. - white female D: Nov 6, 1897; 43y 1m 2d; Mill Creek District F: Cleavers, B: Mineral County DOI: husband C: Flemming, James W. B/P: 1/64

920 Flemming, Mollie - white female D: Mar 16, 1905; 92y 1m B/P: 2/33

921 Flemming, Sallie L. - white female D: June 12, 1902; 27y 6m; Mill Creek District F: Flemming, Jas. M: Flemming, Sallie B: 1876 DOI: father B/P: 1/78

922 Fletcher, ? - white male D: Jan 10, 1877; Hampshire F: Fletcher, Jas H. M: Fletcher, Sarah J. B: Hampshire DOI: father B/P: 1/22

923 Fletcher, Bessie - single white female D: Aug 23, 1916; 14y B: Green Spring B/P: 2/34

924 Fletcher, Eliza - white female D: Feb 1, 1888; 101y 1m; Hampshire B: Hampshire I: Fletcher, U. DOI: son B/P: 1/45

925 Fletcher, Elizabeth Jane - widow white female D: Apr 9,

1910; 88y B/P: 2/33

926 Fletcher, Flavius Josephu - married white male D: May 26, 1916; 63y 9m 3d B: Capon District B/P: 2/34 N: farmer

927 Fletcher, James - single white male D: Oct 6, 1888; 35y; Hardy County B: Hardy County BUR: Hardy County B/P: 1/123

928 Fletcher, Jas. H. - married white male D: Dec 28, 1922; 86y 7m 15d; Hampshire F: Fletcher, Jas. B: Frederick County, VA I: Lupton, Geo. B/P: 1/136

929 Fletcher, Leo - white D: Sept 16, 1905; 2y B/P: 2/33

930 Fletcher, Letty L - white female D: Sept 22, 1881; 4m; Hampshire F: Fletcher, Jas. H. M: Fletcher, Sarah J. B: Hampshire DOI: father B/P: 1/30

931 Fletcher, Martha D: Nov 12, 1871; 4m 10d F: Fletcher, James H. B/P: 1/6

932 Fletcher, Sarah - widow white female D: June 14, 1898; 71y 7m 14d; Capon Bridge BUR: Fairview, VA B/P: 1/101

933 Fletcher, Stanley - white male D: July 1, 1903; 2y; Kirby F: Fletcher, A.M. M: Fletcher, M. DOI: father B/P: 1/81

934 Flick, Mary Eliza - widow white female D: Feb 6, 1916; 80y B: Springfield B/P: 2/34

935 Florey, Martha - married white female D: Oct 14, 1899; 46y 3m 27d; Sherman District B: Hampshire BUR: Augusta B/P: 1/107

936 Flory, Ellen H. - white female D: Mar 15, 1896; 20y; Hampshire B: Mar 1876 DOI: husband C: Flory, Robt B/P: 1/63

937 Flory, Margaret - widow white female D: June 27, 1906; 86y 10m 12d B/P: 2/33

938 Flory, Martha E. - white female D: Oct 13, 1899; 50y 10m; Tare Coat F: Daugherty, John W. B: Jan 3, 1849 DOI: husband B/P: 1/71

939 Flory, Mary - widowed white female D: June 17, 1922; 78y 9m; Hampshire F: Albin, Jas. M: Albin, Dorothy B: WV I: Stewart, M. B/P: 1/133 N: housewife

940 Fogle, Idalia - white female D: Aug 30, 1896; 4m 27d;

Hampshire F: Fogle, Mark M: Fogle, Mary B: Mar 3, 1896 DOI: father B/P: 1/63

941 Folks, Elmira - colored female D: June 18, 1884; 50y; Hampshire B: Hampshire DOI: husband C: Folks, Aaron B/P: 1/38

942 Folks, Sarah E - single colored female D: Feb 11, 1873; 2 m; Hampshire F: Folks, Aaron M: Folks, Minna B: Hampshire DOI: mother B/P: 1/10

943 Foltz, Ada - single white female D: Feb 17, 1898; abt 8y; near Slanesville B: Hampshire BUR: Salem Church B/P: 1/91

944 Foltz, Benjamin - married white male D: May 25, 1907; 35y B/P: 2/33 N: farmer

945 Foltz, C.W. - single white male D: July 14, 1899; 19y 7m 1d; Springfield District F: Foltz, W.D. M: Foltz, Lizzie B: Dec 13, 1879 DOI: mother B/P: 1/70

946 Foltz, Caro L. - white female D: Nov 10, 1905; 24y B/P: 2/33

947 Foltz, Chas - white male D: Mar 27, 1889; 10y 1m 21d; Hampshire M: Foltz, M.C. B: Hampshire DOI: mother B/P: 1/51

948 Foltz, Floyd W. - white male D: Mar 25, 1907; 12d B/P: 2/33

949 Foltz, J. - white male D: July 18, 1905; 87y B/P: 2/33

950 Foltz, Jacob - white male D: May 26, 1886; 35y; Hampshire F: Foltz, Jacob B: Hampshire DOI: wife C: Foltz, Maggie E. B/P: 1/44

951 Foltz, Jacob - white male D: July 19, 1905; 83y B/P: 2/33 N: farmer

952 Foltz, Levi - widower white male D: Jan 21, 1895; 75y; near Slanesville B: Hampshire BUR: Private Graveyard B/P: 1/83

953 Foltz, M. - white male D: Apr 11, 1907; 1y B/P: 2/33

954 Foltz, Maroin - white male D: Jan 20, 1919; stillborn B/P: 2/34

955 Foltz, Minnie - married white female D: Jan 20, 1919; 26y

5m 17d B/P: 2/34

956 Foltz, Miss - single white female D: June 24, 1897; 15m; near Slanesville B: Hampshire BUR: Benj. Foltz nr Slanesville B/P: 1/91

957 Foltz, N.P. - white male D: June 23, 1897; 1y 9m 4d; Gore F: Foltz, J.W. M: Foltz, Ida B: Sept 19, 1896 DOI: mother B/P: 1/66

958 Foltz, Roy W. - white male D: Apr 11, 1906; 2m B/P: 2/33

959 Foltz, S. - white male D: Sept 2, 1888; 75y; Hampshire B: Hampshire I: Foltz, J.F. DOI: son C: Foltz, Rebecca B/P: 1/45 N: miller

960 Foltz, Taylor - white male D: Nov 5, 1912; 68y B/P: 2/33

961 Foltz, Wm. Sr. - married white male D: June 14, 1897; 73y; near Slanesville B: Hampshire BUR: Benj. Foltz nr Slanesville B/P: 1/91

962 Foote, Mary Belle - white female D: July 29, 1917; 71y 4m 17d B/P: 2/34

963 Ford, Charlotte N. - colored female D: May 20, 1901; 84y; Romney District I: Ford, Oscar DOI: son B/P: 1/76 N: Parents: Richard & Ruth

964 Foreman, Anna - white female D: July 13, 1894; 82y; Hampshire B: Virginia I: Foreman, DOI: nephew B/P: 1/60

965 Foreman, Carl C. - white male D: Sept 2, 1902; 11y; Hampshire F: Foreman, Jas. M: Foreman, Syona B: 1891 DOI: father B/P: 1/79

966 Foreman, Maurice - white male D: Sept 20, 1901; 21y; Mineral County F: Foreman, Joseph M: Foreman, S. DOI: father B/P: 1/76

967 Fout, Harriet - married white female D: Aug 3, 1913; 72y B/P: 2/34

968 Fowler, Robert - single colored male D: Apr 5, 1878; 14y 11m 19d; Hampshire F: Fowler, William M: Fowler, Sarah B: Hampshire DOI: father B/P: 1/23

969 Fox, David - widower white male D: Nov 28, 1921; 83y 3m

26d; Hampshire F: Fox, Vaus M: Fox, Rebecca B: Romney B/P: 1/131 N: farmer

970 Fox, Rebecca - white female D: Feb 14, 1889; 92y; Romney District B: Hampshire I: Fox, David DOI: son B/P: 1/47

971 Fox, Ursula Blue - married white female D: Dec 21, 1931; 74y 3m 12d; Hampshire F: Blue, Garrett M: Blue, Sallie B: Hampshire I: Blue, Edward B/P: 1/131 N: housewife

972 Frank, Fannie Mary - married white female D: Aug 11, 1917; 52y B/P: 2/34

973 Frank, Mary Ann - widow white female D: Dec 2, 1909; 73y 7m 10d N: 2/33

974 Frank, Mary E - white female D: Nov 15, 1880; 3y 6m; Hampshire F: Frank, A. M: Jackson, A. B: Hampshire DOI: father B/P: 1/27

975 Frank, William - white male D: Dec 28, 1896; 52y 4m; Capon District B: April 1848 DOI: friend B/P: 1/62

976 Fravel, Aldine S. - white male D: Mar 18, 1885; 7y; Hampshire F: Fravel, F.M. M: Fravel, Leah C. B: Hampshire DOI: father B/P: 1/41

977 Frazier, Edith M. - single white female D: Feb 15, 1922; 9y 10m 10d; Hampshire F: Frazier, Ira M: Fraizer, Minnie B: Logan County I: Griffey, M.F. B/P: 1/133

978 Frederick, Samuel A. - white male D: Feb 9, 1907; 47y 11m 8d B/P: 2/33 N: miller

979 French, Ann E. - white female D: Oct 8, 1880; 37y; Hampshire F: Pugh, B: Hampshire DOI: husband C: French, William B/P: 1/28

980 French, Chas. - married white male D: Mar 26, 1915; 74y B/P: 2/34

981 French, Florence - married white female D: Mar 31, 1907; 70y 10m B/P: 2/33

982 French, Hannah E - white female D: Dec 18, 1874; 41y 2m 19d; Hampshire F: Taylor, Joseph M: Taylor, Harriett B: Hampshire I: Gutherie, Wm Mrs. DOI: friend C: French, Charles B/P: 1/12

983 French, James - white male D: Mar 7, 1905; 77y B/P: 2/33

N: farmer

984 French, Rebecca - white female D: June 6, 1892; 55y; Hampshire B: Hampshire DOI: husband C: French, J. B/P: 1/57

985 French, Susan Ann - white female D: Feb 17, 1867; 64y 8m 3d; Mouth South Branch F: Taylor, John M: Taylor, Elizabeth B: near Springfield DOI: husband C: French, William B/P: 1/2

986 French, William T. - white male D: Dec 29, 1874; 41y 2m 19d; Hampshire F: French, William M: French, Susan B: Hampshire DOI: father C: French, Florence B/P: 1/12

987 French, William - white male D: Dec 29, 1881; 79y 10m 1d; Hampshire F: French, William M: French, Hester B: Hampshire I: French, Chas DOI: son C: French, Susan also Elizabeth B/P: 1/31 N: twice married; merchant

988 Friddle, Julia - white female D: Aug 14, 1896; 83y; Hampshire B: Aug 14, 1813 I: Friddle, Jno DOI: son B/P: 1/63

989 Friddle, Mary - white female D: July 3, 1878; 31y 2m 5d; Hampshire B: Hampshire DOI: husband C: Friddle, Sam'l B/P: 1/23

990 Friddle, Mrs. - widow white female D: Aug 15, 1896; abt 65y; near Slanesville B: WV BUR: church near Romney B/P: 1/91

991 Friddle, Sam'l - widower white male D: June 22, 1890; 70y; Romney District B/P: 1/52

992 Fry, Samuel V. - single white male D: Mar 28, 1922; 49y 6m 1d; Hampshire F: Fry, Benj. M: Fry, Mary B: Rio I: Fry, E.P. B/P: 1/133

993 Frye, B. Henson - married white male D: Dec 28, 1908; 58y 7m B/P: 2/33 N: farmer

994 Frye, Benj P. - white male D: Mar 31, 1889; 69y 6m 20d F: Frye, Benj. M: Frye, Mary B: Hampshire DOI: wife C: Frye, Mary J. B/P: 1/47

995 Frye, Eliza J. - white female D: Mar 29, 1908; 71y 9d B/P: 2/33

996 Frye, Elizabeth - white female D: Apr 7, 1892; 95y;

Hampshire B: Hampshire I: Frye, Geo. W. DOI: son B/P: 1/53

997 Frye, Elizabeth J. - white female D: Oct 29, 1885; 17y; Hampshire F: Frye, Geo. M. M: Frye, Mary Ann B: Hampshire DOI: father B/P: 1/41

998 Frye, Geo H. - white male D: Oct 5, 1877; Hampshire F: Frye, Geo W. M: Frye, Mary A. B: Hampshire DOI: father B/P: 1/22

999 Frye, H.G. - white male D: Jan 3, 1893; 12y 7m; Hampshire F: Frye, G.H. M: Frye, G.L. DOI: father B/P: 1/58

1000 Frye, Jacob - white male D: 26 July 1882; 82y; Capon District B: WV I: Frye, George W. DOI: son B/P: 1/33

1001 Frye, Mary I. - widow white female D: Oct 6, 1908; 75y 9m 20d B/P: 2/33

1002 Fuller, Wm. H. - white male D: Jan 25, 1881; Hampshire I: Poling, M.F. DOI: overseer of poor B/P: 1/30

1003 Furguson, Lucy White - widow white female D: Mar 9, 1917; 68y 7d B/P: 2/34

1004 Furr, Charlotte - white female D: Dec 23, 1900; 44y; Hampshire B: June 4, 1856 DOI: husband C: Furr, William B/P: 1/73

1005 Furr, Mary - widow white female D: Jan 14, 1909; 94y 4m 14d B/P: 2/33

1006 Ganoe, Campbell - single white male D: Dec 19, 1914; 8y 4m 17d B/P: 2/39

1007 Ganoe, Douglas G. - single white male D: Oct 1915; 3m B/P: 2/39

1008 Ganoe, Florence - white female D: Nov 30, 1914; 2m 16d B/P: 2/39

1009 Ganoe, Harold - married white male D: July 29, 1918; 28y 11m 18d; Hampshire B/P: 1/126 N: farm laboror

1010 Ganoe, Jno S. - white male D: Apr 11, 1889; 57y; Hampshire B: Hampshire I: Ganoe, C.E. DOI: son B/P: 1/51

1011 Ganoe, Julia B. - white female D: June 15, 1906; B/P: 2/39

1012 Ganoe, Margaret - white female D: Sept 10, 1910; 70y B/P: 2/39

1013 Ganoe, Minnie M. - white female D: Nov 5, 1898; 1y 3m; Romney F: Ganoe, James M. DOI: father B/P: 1/68

1014 Ganoe, Newa - white female D: July 28, 1906; 30y B/P: 2/39

1015 Ganoe, Robt A - white male D: Aug 11, 1886; 72y; Hampshire B: Hampshire I: Ganoe, John B/P: 1/44

1016 Ganoe, Virdie - married white female D: June 20, 1918; 35y; Hampshire B/P: 1/126 N: housewife

1017 Ganoe, Wilson - single white male D: May 3, 1918; stillborn; Hampshire B/P: 1/126

1018 Ganon, James P. - white male D: May 3, 1896; 70y 6m; Mill Creek District B: May 1826 B/P: 1/62

1019 Gardner, Amanda R. - married white female D: Oct 16, 1912; 63y 8m 4d B: Bloomery District B/P: 2/39

1020 Gardner, Edgar - single colored male D: June 14, 1895; 15y; Hampshire B: Hampshire B/P: 1/87

1021 Gardner, Jas. E. - white male D: June 26, 1890; 6m; Sherman District F: Gardner, Wm. H. M: Gardner, Frances B: Hampshire DOI: father B/P: 1/52

1022 Gardner, Margaret Ann - married white female D: July 6, 1910; 73y 5m 17d B/P: 2/39

1023 Gardner, Silas W. - white male D: Jan 27, 1885; 42y; Hampshire F: Gardner, John M: Gardner, S. B: Hampshire DOI: father C: 1/41

1024 Garland, E. P. - white male D: July 1, 1891; 1y; Hampshire F: Garland, Oliver M: Garland, A.M. B: Hampshire DOI: father B/P: 1/55

1025 Garr, Marion H. - single white male D: Sept 1, 1902; 9m 15d; Romney B: Hampshire BUR: Romney B/P: 1/116

1026 Garrett, Helena R.T. - single white female D: Aug 16, 1889; 1y 4m 25d; Doman B: near Doman BUR: near Doman B/P: 1/124

1027 Garvin, David J. - white male D: Mar 10, 1893; 82y 4m;

Hampshire F: Garvin, James B/P: 1/58

1028 Garvin, M.A.K. - white female D: Sept 6, 1897; 61y; Capon district F: Dunlap, William B: Capon District DOI: husband C: Garvin, Mahlon B/P: 1/64

1029 Garvin, Margaret - white female D: Jan 28, 1892; 81y; Hampshire B: Hampshire DOI: husband C: Garvin, David J. B/P: 1/53

1030 Gates, Haritte - white female D: Oct 22, 1872; 30y 6m; Hampshire B/P: 1/9

1031 Gaunan, Wille - white male D: Nov 6, 1867; 2m 23d; Mill C. Mountain F: Gaunan, James B: Mill C. Mountain DOI: father B/P: 1/2

1032 George, Colman - colored male D: Nov 4, 1867; 80y; Romney I: Jacob, J.J. B/P: 1/2

1033 Gess, Lina - single white female D: July 6, 1902; 19y 3m 6d; Hampshire B: Hampshire BUR: North River Mills B/P: 1/115

1034 Gets, Margt. L. - widow white female D: Apr 1, 1908; 53y B/P: 2/39

1035 Gibbons, Geo Allen - married white male D: Jan 4, 1917; 73y 4m 17d B/P: 2/40 N: clergyman, Episcopal

1036 Gibson, David D: Nov 10, 1870; 76y B/P: 1/5

1037 Gibson, Sarah E. - white female D: Nov 24, 1884; 38y; Hampshire F: Gilkeson, J.B. M: Gilkeson, Sarah B: Frederick Co., VA DOI: husband C: Gibson, Jas A. B/P: 1/38

1038 Giffin, Blanche - single white female D: Oct 2, 1908; 10y 2m 11d B/P: 2/39

1039 Giffin, Margaret C. - married white female D: Jan 16, 1908; 60y 4m 16d B/P: 2/39

1040 Giffin, Mary F. - white female D: Nov 13, 1886; 33y; Hampshire F: Simmons, Aaron M: Simmons, Mary B: Hampshire DOI: husband C: Giffin, J.J. B/P: 1/44

1041 Giffin, Robert - single white male D: Oct 10, 1873; 8m; Hampshire F: Giffin, David M: Giffin, Margaret B: Hampshire DOI: father B/P: 1/10

1042 Gilkeson, Robt W. - white male D: Oct 1890; 70y; Romney District B: Virginia I: Gilkeson, E.M. DOI: son B/P: 1/52 N: wife deceased

1043 Gill, Dolly - white female D: Oct 19, 1880; 77y; Hampshire F: Walker, Spencer B: Loudoun Co VA I: Gill, Sarah DOI: daughter in law B/P: 1/28

1044 Gill, Elizabeth - white female D: Jan 1885; 88y; Hampshire F: Gill, Thos. M: Gill, Elizabeth B: Hampshire I: Gill, James DOI: son B/P: 1/41

1045 Gill, Sarah C. - white female D: July 2, 1912; 7y 8m 11d B/P: 2/39

1046 Gill, Spencer - married white male D: Jan 9, 1900; 74y; Capon Bridge BUR: Bethel, VA B/P: 1/108

1047 Gilmore, S. - colored female D: Sept 6, 1892; 36y; Romney F: Collins, A.S. DOI: husband B/P: 1/56

1048 Ginevan, Ann V - single white female D: Dec 19, 1866; 14y 9m; Hampshire F: Ginevan, David M: Ginevan, Susan B: Hampshire DOI: parent B/P: 1/1

1049 Ginevan, Cecil - white male D: Nov 23, 1903; 4y; Levels B: Hampshire BUR: Levels B/P: 1/117

1050 Ginevan, David W. - white male D: Dec 18, 1884; 1y 8m; Hampshire F: Ginevan, Geo W. M: Ginevan, M.E. B: Hampshire DOI: father B/P: 1/39

1051 Ginevan, Elizabeth - white female D: May 29, 1883; 61y 3m 11d; Hampshire F: Ginevan, Mathias M: Ginevan, Catharine B: Hampshire I: Ginevan, Catharine DOI: sister B/P: 1/37

1052 Ginevan, Estella - white female D: Mar 27, 1903; 6y; Levels B: Hampshire BUR: Levels B/P: 1/117

1053 Ginevan, Harry - white male D: Mar 12, 1903; 10y; Levels B: Hampshire BUR: Levels B/P: 1/117

1054 Ginevan, Luther - white male D: Jan 5, 1882; 74y 1m 13d; Hampshire F: Ginnevan, M. M: Ginnevan, C. B: Ohio I: Ginnevan, Thos M. DOI: son C: Ginnevan, Ivy B/P: 1/34

1055 Ginevan, Raymond - white male D: Mar 6, 1912; 1y 4d B/P: 2/39

1056 Ginevan, Thos. - married white male D: Jan 27, 1910; 73y

B/P: 2/39 N: farmer

1057 Ginnevan, Catharine D: Feb 26, 1870; 84y 11m 6d; Hampshire F: Voke, C: Ginnevan, Mathias B/P: 1/5

1058 Ginnevan, Robt. - single white male D: June 30, 1921; stillborn; Hampshire B: WV B/P: 1/130

1059 Glaze, Joseph - white male D: Feb 3, 1889; 8m; Hampshire F: Glaze, C. M: Glaze, L. B: Hampshire DOI: father B/P: 1/51

1060 Glaze, M.E. - white female D: Dec 24, 1893; 20y; Hampshire F: Twigg, L.V. M: Twigg, M.J. B: Maryland DOI: father B/P: 1/58

1061 Godlove, Alonzo w. - white male D: Mar 14, 1892; 29d; Hampshire F: Godlove, J.C. M: Godlove, Eva J. B: Hampshire DOI: father B/P: 1/53

1062 Godlove, C.W. - single white male D: July 24, 1899; 17y 6m 23d; Capon Bridge B: Hampshire BUR: Capon Chapel B/P: 1/110

1063 Godlove, Chas W. - white male D: July 10, 1899; 17y; Capon F: Godlove, John A. B: Dec 31, 1883 B/P: 1/71

1064 Godlove, Daisy - single white female D: Feb 21, 1899; 17y 4m 21d; Sedan B: Hampshire BUR: Malicks B/P: 1/104

1065 Godlove, Emily M. - married white female D: Mar 27, 1899; 29y 8m 19d; Gore District B: Gore District BUR: Malicks B/P: 1/104

1066 Godlove, Jno. A. - white male D: June 8, 1915; 71y 1m 29d B/P: 2/39 N: undertaker

1067 Godlove, Lena - single white female D: Apr 4, 1907; 24d B/P: 2/39

1068 Godlove, Margarett - white female D: Dec 28, 1876; 19y 8m 6d; Hampshire F: Smith, Wesley M: Smith, Mary B: Hampshire DOI: father C: Godlove, Isaac B/P: 1/20

1069 Godlove, Mary A. - married white female D: May 24, 1894; 33y 3m 13d; Hampshire B: Hampshire B/P: 1/83

1070 Godlove, Miss - single white female D: Feb 16, 1900; 2y 3m 16d; Sedan B: Hampshire BUR: Malicks Graveyard B/P: 1/107

1071 Godlove, Peral - white female D: Feb 17, 1899; 2y 2m; Sherman District B/P: 1/72

1072 Godlove, Sevina S. - married white female D: June 10, 1897; 69y 7m 20d; Slanesville BUR: Malicks Yard B/P: 1/94

1073 Goldsborough, J. Waldo - single white male D: July 4, 1907; 11y 9m B/P: 2/39 N: drowned

1074 Goliday, Alina Lillie - single white female D: Nov 2, 1910; 4y 6m B/P: 2/39

1075 Goliday, William E. - white male D: Dec 13, 1904; B/P: 2/39

1076 Gooding, George H. - white male D: Aug 4, 1874; 6m 4d; Hampshire F: Gooding, George M: Gooding, Margaret B: Hampshire DOI: father B/P: 1/12

1077 Goshorn, Ella M. - single black female D: Dec 16, 1896; 5y 9m 9d; Romney B: Romney BUR: Romney B/P: 1/96

1078 Grabill, Louella - white female D: Oct 26, 1881; 13y 5m 14d; Hampshire F: Grabill, Dan'l M: Grabill, R.e. B: Hampshire DOI: father B/P: 1/31

1079 Grace, Catherine - white female D: May 16, 1878; 77y 16d; Hampshire I: Grace, Ephrem DOI: son C: Grace, John B/P: 1/24

1080 Grace, Edward T. - white male D: April 14, 1874; 49y; Hampshire F: Grace, John M: Grace, Catherine B: Hampshire I: Grace, John W. DOI: brother C: Grace, Roxanna N: 1/12

1081 Grace, Jno. - married white male D: May 17, 1897; 36y; Springfield B: Springfield BUR: Springfield B/P: 1/93

1082 Grace, Sydney - white female D: Nov 20, 1884; 58y 15d; Hampshire B: Hampshire DOI: husband C: Grace, Ephraim B/P: 1/39

1083 Grapes, Chodore Earl - single white male D: Oct 11, 1918; 9m 29d; Hampshire B/P: 1/126

1084 Grapes, Elizabeth - widow white female D: Nov 7, 1921; 82y 10m 6d; Hampshire F: Edwards, Robert B: Hampshire B/P: 1/131 N: housewife

1085 Grapes, Geo. Elbert - white male D: Apr 11, 1919;

stillborn B/P: 2/40

1086 Grapes, Geo. Wesley - married white male D: May 3, 1909; 45y 11m 28d B/P: 2/39 N: farmer

1087 Grapes, Isaac - married white male D: June 2, 1912; 74y 8m 11d B: Gore District B/P: 2/39 N: farmer

1088 Grapes, John Henry - white male D: Jan 4, 1908; 3y 10m 4d B/P: 2/39

1089 Grapes, M.C. - white female D: Sept 14, 1888; 89y; Hampshire B: Hampshire I: Edwards, F.F. B/P: 1/45

1090 Grapes, Mariah - white female D: June 29, 1881; 75y 11m 4d; Hampshire F: Bennett, Sylvanus B: Hampshire I: Grapes, Isaac DOI: son C: Grapes, Jno. B/P: 1/31

1091 Grapes, Martha D: Mar 1, 1869; 1y 10m 2d; Hampshire F: Grapes, I.A. M: Grapes, Elizabeth B/P: 1/4

1092 Grapes, Mary D: Apr 7, 1870; 26y 9d B/P: 1/5 N: father: ??? Thomas

1093 Grapes, Mary - white female D: June 1888; 60y; Hampshire F: Robinson, Moses B: Hampshire I: Carlyle, M.E. C: Grapes, Newton B/P: 1/46

1094 Grapes, Nancy Virginia - white female D: Nov 6, 1921; stillborn; Hampshire F: Grapes, Edward B: Hampshire B/P: 1/31

1095 Grapes, Newton - white male D: Apr 4, 1878; 61y 10m 27d; Hampshire F: Grapes, David M: Grapes, Hannah B: Hampshire I: Grapes, (young) DOI: son C: Grapes, Mary B/P: 1/24

1096 Grapes, Pearl - single white female D: Mar 31, 1920; 2y 3m 22d; Hampshire F: Grapes, Roy M: Grapes, Tilda B: Pleasant Dale B/P: 1/129

1097 Grapes, Robert Lee - single white male D: Nov 19, 1899; 3y 10m 29d; Romney B: Hampshire BUR: Romney B/P: 1/107

1098 Grapes, Russell Hyatt - white male D: Mar 11, 1912; 1m 13d B: Gore District B/P: 2/39

1099 Grapes, Sarah C. - colored female D: Jan 31, 1890; 50y; Sherman District F: Grapes, Uriah B: Sherman District DOI: father B/P: 1/49

1100 Grapes, Uriah - colored male D: May 15, 1890; 75y; Sherman District B: Hampshire I: Grapes, Ben DOI: son B/P: 1/52 N: wife deceased

1101 Grapes, Virginia - married white female D: July 20, 1907; 40y 1m 3d B/P: 2/39

1102 Grapes, Virginia - married white female D: May 13, 1908; 40y B/P: 2/39

1103 Grapes, Wm. H. - single colored male D: Jan 12, 1890; 34y; Sherman District F: Grapes, Uriah B: Sherman District DOI: father B/P: 1/49

1104 Gray, Barbara E. - white female D: May 25, 1875; 34y 10d; Hampshire F: Wise, Henry M: Wise, Catherine B: Hardy Co DOI: husband C: Gray, William B/P: 1/14

1105 Gray, Benj. F. D: July 15, 1870; 28y F: Gray, Spencer B/P: 1/5

1106 Gray, Edna - married white female D: Mar 24, 1912; 28y B: Springfield District B/P: 2/39

1107 Gray, Elias L. - white male D: June 16, 1872; 9m; Hampshire F: Gray, John M: Gray, Matilda B: Hampshire B/P: 1/9

1108 Gray, George - white male D: July 3, 1906; 35y 10m 20d B/P: 2/39 N: farmer

1109 Gray, George W. - white male D: May 17, 1872; 14y 20d; Hampshire F: Gray, John M: Gray, Matilda B: Hampshire B/P: 1/9

1110 Gray, Harry Bryan - single white male D: Nov 23, 1922; 3y 5m 7d; Hampshire F: Gray, H.B. M: Gray, Ida B: Hampshire County DOI: father B/P: 1/133

1111 Gray, John - widower white male D: Sept 4, 1908; 74y 9m 12d B/P: 2/39

1112 Gray, Jos. E. - white male D: Nov 3, 1884; 35y; Hampshire F: Gray, Spencer R. M: Gray, Sarah B: Hampshire DOI: wife C: Gray, Annie E. B/P: 1/39

1113 Gray, Rebecca - married white female D: Feb 18, 1899; 60y; Hanging Rock B: Hampshire BUR: Dillons Run B/P: 1/103

1114 Gray, Robert L. - married white male D: Feb 23, 1900;

35y 2m; Ruckman B: Hampshire BUR: Mt Zion B/P: 1/107

1115 Gray, Rueben D. - white male D: May 22, 1874; 10m; Hampshire F: Gray, Morgan M: Gray, Catherine B: Hampshire DOI: father B/P: 1/12

1116 Gray, Sallie - white female D: Mar 25, 1889; 23y; Sherman District F: Creswell, Abe M: Creswell, Eliz. B: Hampshire DOI: husband C: Gray, Henry N. B/P: 1/47

1117 Gray, Sam'l - single white male D: Nov 11, 1873; 19y 13d; Hampshire F: Gray, Spencer R. M: Gray, Sarah B: Hampshire DOI: father B/P: 1/10

1118 Gray, Sarah - married white female D: Mar 28, 1889; Hampshire B: Hampshire B/P: 1/124

1119 Gray, Sarah - married white female D: July 14, 1908; 53y B/P: 2/39

1120 Graybill, Dan H. - white male D: July 16, 1902; 77y; Hampshire B: Oct 1825 I: Graybill, H. DOI: son B/P: 1/79

1121 Green, Granville - colored male D: Feb 5, 1881; Hampshire I: Poling, M.F. DOI: overseer of poor B/P: 1/30

1122 Greybill, Sarah - single white female D: Dec 5, 1893; 57y 1m 29d; Hampshire B: Virginia I: Greybill, D.H. DOI: brother B/P: 1/58

1123 Greybill, Wm. S. - white male D: Feb 11, 1889; 7m 5d; Hampshire F: Greybill, Sam M: Greybill, L. B: Hampshire DOI: father B/P: 1/51

1124 Gritton, Debbie - single white female D: June 3, 1911; 73y B/P: 2/39

1125 Gross, Hattie - white female D: May 1886; 7y; Hampshire F: Gross, F.P. M: Gross, E.C. B: Hampshire DOI: father B/P: 1/44

1126 Gross, S. - white male D: June 10, 1888; 7m 17d; Hampshire F: Gross, F.P. M: Gross E.C. B: Hampshire DOI: father B/P: 1/45

1127 Grove, Soloman - white male D: Dec 13, 1872; 63y; Hampshire B: Frederick Co., VA DOI: wife C: Grove, Nancy B/P: 1/8

1128 Groves, Cyrus - white male D: Sept 17, 1889; 73y; Capon

District F: Groves, Peter W. M: Groves, Ala B: Capon District DOI: wife C: Groves, Eliza C. B/P: 1/49

1129 Groves, Sims S. - white male D: Sept 5, 1876; 21y 2m 10d; Hampshire F: Groves, Sims B: Hampshire I: Groves, Sarah DOI: step mother B/P: 1/18

1130 Gulick, Elmyra C. - married white female D: Dec 20, 1907; 65y B/P: 2/39

1131 Gulick, Foster - married white male D: Nov 12, 1902; 84y; Barnes Mills B: Hampshire BUR: Plesant Dale B/P: 1/116

1132 Gulick, Granville - white male D: Dec 10, 1905; 22y B/P: 2/39

1133 Gulick, Joseph W. - single white male D: Oct 22, 1881; 37y 4m 13d; Hampshire F: Gulick, N.F. M: Gulick, Jane A. B: Hampshire DOI: fatjer B/P: 131

1134 Gulick, Lacy A. - white female D: Apt 13, 1874; 14y; Hampshire F: Gulick, Nathaniel M: Gulick, Jane B: Hampshire DOI: father B/P: 1/12

1135 Gulick, Mrs. Foster - widow white female D: Feb 15, 1904; 80y B/P: 2/39

1136 Gulick, Sarah C. - white female D: Aug 28, 1906; 60y B/P: 2/39

1137 Guthrie, Newton B - white male D: May 12, 1885; 72y; Hampshire B: Hampshire I: Guthrie, W.N. DOI: son B/P: 1/42 N: merchant

1138 Guthrie, Newton B. - single white male D: Feb 19, 1899; 22y; Romney BUR: Romney B/P: 1/102

1139 Guthrie, Robert E. - married white male D: Aug 1, 1894; 29y 29d; Springfield B: Springfield BUR: Springfield B/P: 1/82

1140 Guthrie, Wm. F. - single white male D: Nov 18, 1907; 28y B/P: 2/39 N: merchant; gas explosion

1141 Haberlander, Minnie - widow white female D: Feb 23, 1908; 71y 4m 21d B/P: 2/45

1142 Haffer, Annie - white female D: Sept 17, 1888; 1m 2d; Romney District F: Haffer, W.H. M: Haffer, Kate B: Hampshire DOI: father B/P: 1/47

1143 Haffer, Otto - single white male D: Dec 5, 1912; 27y B: Romney B/P: 2/47

1144 Hagerty, Elizabeth J. - white female D: June 15, 1882; 43y; Mill Creek District B: WV DOI: husband C: Hagerty, Geo. W. B/P: 1/33

1145 Hagerty, Elizabeth - white female D: Dec 10, 1898; 29y 11m; Mill Creek District F: High, Alpheus M: High, Sarah I: High, Sarah B/P: 1/68

1146 Hagerty, Geo M - white male D: Nov 4, 1884; 53y; Hampshire B: Hampshire I: Hagerty, Daniel DOI: son C: Hagerty, Elizabeth B/P: 1/38

1147 Hahn, Becky E. - single white female D: Sept 26, 1922; 14y 9m 20d; Hampshire F: Hahn, A.W. M: Hahn, Cora B: Hampshire DOI: father B/P: 1/133

1148 Haines, A.C. - white female D: June 18, 1894; 3y; Hampshire F: Haines, G.M. M: Haines, A. B: Hampshire DOI: father B/P: 1/60

1149 Haines, Albert - white male D: Apr 29, 1912; 1d B: Sherman District B/P: 2/47

1150 Haines, Amanda - married white female D: Mar 9, 1904; 30y B/P: 2/55

1151 Haines, Anna S. - white female D: Nov 6, 1906; 40y B/P: 2/45

1152 Haines, Ashby, Jr. - white male D: July 6, 1906; 1y 6m B/P: 2/45

1153 Haines, Barbary - married white female D: May 12, 1899; 70y; Hampshire B: Hampshire BUR: Mouser's Ridge B/P: 1/106

1154 Haines, Benj. M. - married white male D: May 28, 1918; 78y 3m 6d; Hampshire B/P: 1/126 N: farmer

1155 Haines, Benjamin - white male D: July 26, 1913; 1y 1m B/P: 2/47

1156 Haines, Bessie - single white female D: Mar 12, 1895; 1m 14d; Near Haines' Mill B: Hampshire B/P: 1/82

1157 Haines, Caroline - widow white female D: Dec 12, 1911; 83y B: Gore District B/P: 2/47

1158 Haines, Carrie - married white female D: Dec 15, 1911; 22y B/P: 2/47

1159 Haines, Carrie - married white female D: Dec 16, 1911; 19y 3m 13d B: Gore District B/P: 2/47

1160 Haines, Carrie H. - white female D: Aug 27, 1912; B/P: 2/47

1161 Haines, Catharine - white female D: Dec 23, 1901; 84y; Hampshire I: Haines, A.C. B/P: 1/77

1162 Haines, Catherine - white female D: Dec 24, 1893; 72y; Hampshire B/P: 1/58

1163 Haines, Cora - single white female D: May 4, 1899; 16y; Capon Bridge B: Cold Stream BUR: Capon Chapel B/P: 1/102

1164 Haines, Cora A. - white female D: Jan 6, 1890; 13d; Sherman District F: Haines, Jno. H. M: Haines, Delila B: Sherman District DOI: father B/P: 1/49

1165 Haines, Cora Lee - white female D: May 4, 1899; 15y; Capon District F: Haines, Henry M: Haines, Elizabeth B: 1885 DOI: father B/P: 1/71

1166 Haines, Cordelia C - white female D: Sept 1, 1901; 50y; Capon District DOI: father B/P: 1/76

1167 Haines, David - white male D: Mar 20, 1883; 30y 3d; Hampshire F: Haines, William M: Haines, Mary B: Hampshire DOI: father C: Haines, Mary B/P: 1/36

1168 Haines, David W. - white male D: May 28, 1901; 28y; Sherman District B/P: 1/76

1169 Haines, Earl Clifton - single white male D: May 6, 1918; 3d; Hampshire B/P: 1/126

1170 Haines, Edward L - single white male D: Oct 13, 1873; 10m; Hampshire F: Haines, Jno. H.F. M: Haines, Delila B: Hampshire DOI: father B/P: 1/10

1171 Haines, Eliza Jane - married white female D: Oct 4, 1921; 70y 9m 18d; Hampshire F: Haines, Sam'l T. M: Haines, Eliza J. B: Hampshire I: Haines, Albert L. B/P: 1/131

1172 Haines, Elizabeth - married white female D: Dec 18, 1919; 63y; Gore District M: Wolford, Harietta B/P: 1/128 N:

housewife

1173 Haines, Elizabeth - white female D: Aug 12, 1875; 56y 3m 27d; Hampshire B: Rockingham Co VA DOI: husband C: Haines, Rhesa B/P: 1/14

1174 Haines, Elizabeth D: June 11, 1870; 44y; Hampshire F: Queen, Stephen M: Queen, May C: Haines, Silas B/P: 1/5

1175 Haines, Elmos H. - white male D: Mar 30, 1884; 3y; Hampshire F: Haines, Jas. H. M: Haines, Hannah B: Hampshire DOI: father B/P: 1/39

1176 Haines, Elyse W. - single white female D: Dec 21, 1922; 7y 7m 27d; Hampshire F: Haines, A.S. M: Haines, Virginia B: Augusta I: Haines, Salena B/P: 1/134

1177 Haines, Florence Belle - white female D: Nov 16, 1910; 30y B/P: 2/46

1178 Haines, Frank - white male D: Nov 18, 1906; 35y B/P: 2/45

1179 Haines, Geo - white male D: July 7, 1901; 1y; Hampshire F: Haines, T.L. M: Haines, A. DOI: father B/P: 1/77

1180 Haines, Geo - married white male D: May 8, 1912; 70y B: Springfield B/P: 2/47 N: farmer

1181 Haines, Granville - single white male D: Mar 22, 1910; 28y B/P: 2/46 N: killed by train

1182 Haines, Hampton - white male D: Nov 9, 1903; 23y; Cumberland, MD F: Haines, D.M. M: Haines, Catherine DOI: father B/P: 1/81

1183 Haines, I. Minor - married white male D: Dec 21, 1917; 71y; Hampshire B/P: 1/126 N: farmer

1184 Haines, Ida - married white female D: June 19, 1896; 27y; Romney B: West Virginia BUR: Jersey Mountain B/P: 1/96

1185 Haines, Ira A. - white male D: Feb 28, 1915; 36y 5m 26d B/P: 2/48

1186 Haines, Ira Albert - single white male D: Jan 25, 1920; stillborn F: Haines, Ira M: Haines, Mona B: Hampshire B/P: 1/129

1187 Haines, Ira C. - single white male D: Dec 7, 1922; 19y

2m 12d; Hampshire F: Haines, A.C. M: Haines, Chloe B: Hampshire DOI: father B/P: 1/134

1188 Haines, Irwin - white male D: July 7, 1906; 1y 6m 5d B/P: 2/45

1189 Haines, Irwin - white male D: July 6, 1906; 1y 6m 10d B/P: 2/45

1190 Haines, Isaac - widowed white male D: Sept 4, 1892; 80y 2m 29d; Haines Mill B: Little Capon I: Haines, Clayton DOI: son B/P: 1/56 N: farmer

1191 Haines, Isaac Henry - married white male D: Oct 4, 1898; 41y; near Romney B/P: 1/100

1192 Haines, Isaac Minor - white male D: Dec 26, 1917; 68y 10m 10d B/P: 2/48 N: farmer

1193 Haines, Isaac, Jr. - white male D: Aug 28, 1913; 8m 10d; B/P: 2/47

1194 Haines, Jacob - white male D: June 1, 1904; 86y B/P: 2/49

1195 Haines, James - white male D: Apr 3, 1891; 79y; Hampshire F: Haines, Isaac B: Hampshire DOI: wife C: Haines, Evaline B/P: 1/55

1196 Haines, Jas. H. - widowed white male D: July 21, 1920; 82y 7m 7d; Hampshire F: Haines, Isaac M: Haines, Sally B: Hampshire B/P: 1/129 N: farmer

1197 Haines, Jas. W. - white male D: Mar 1891; 4m; Romney District F: Haines, Jos M: Haines, Mary B: Hampshire B/P: 1/52

1198 Haines, John - married white male D: Feb 4, 1895; 37y; Hampshire B: Hampshire B/P: 1/89

1199 Haines, John H. - married white male D: Sept 27, 1909; 61y 17d B/P: 2/46 N: farmer

1200 Haines, John W. - married white male D: Dec 25, 1896; 53y; Green Spring Valley B: Little Capon BUR: Springfield B/P: 1/93

1201 Haines, Joseph - white male D: May 31, 1915; 68y 7m 13d B/P: 2/48

1202 Haines, Julia Ann - married white female D: Aug 30, 1913; 70y 4m B/P: 2/47

1203 Haines, Laura - single white female D: Dec 14, 1898; 15y; Hampshire B: Hampshire BUR: Hampshire B/P: 1/100

1204 Haines, Laura C. - white female D: Dec 25, 1898; 15y 1m 2d; Romney District F: Haines, Joseph E. DOI: father B/P: 1/68

1205 Haines, Lemuel H. - single white male D: Mar 23, 1899; 14y 3m 17d; Hanging Rock B: Hanging Rock BUR: Dillons Run B/P: 1/103

1206 Haines, Lizzie - white female D: May 26, 1917; 68y B/P: 2/48

1207 Haines, Lodena A. - white female D: Apr 3, 1881; 62y; Hampshire F: Ambler, Jno. B: Hampshire I: Haines, Noah W. DOI: son C: Haines, Jno B/P: 1/31

1208 Haines, Lou E. - married white female D: Aug 5, 1921; 39y 7m 9d; Hampshire F: Hines, G.R. M: Hines, Rebecca B: Hampshire B/P: 1/131 N: housewife

1209 Haines, M. - white male D: Feb 24, 1904; 1m B/P: 2/55

1210 Haines, Maggie - married white female D: Dec 11, 1913; 50y 4m 6d B/P: 2/47

1211 Haines, Margaret - white female D: May 8, 1884; 9m; Hampshire B/P: 1/39

1212 Haines, Marion J. - single white female D: Dec 25, 1922; 7m 15d; Hampshire F: Haines, Claud M: Haines, Anna B: Hampshire B/P: 1/133

1213 Haines, Martha E. - white female D: Oct 1889; 3y 3m; Sherman District F: Haines, Joseph M: Haines, Mary B: Sherman District DOI: father B/P: 1/49

1214 Haines, Martin - single white male D: Sept 24, 1918; 3m 28d; Hampshire B/P: 1/126

1215 Haines, Mary - widow white female D: Aug 2, 1899; 79y; Cold Stream B: Hampshire BUR: Capon Chapel B/P: 1/109

1216 Haines, Mary A. - widow white female D: Dec 23, 1916; 89y 2m 7d B: Romney B/P: 2/48

1217 Haines, Mary J. - white female D: May 5, 1900; 39y; Sherman District F: Abright, William B: July 20, 1861 I: Haines, Peter B/P: 1/72

1218 Haines, Mary Jane - married white female D: May 5, 1900; 35y; Romney B: Hampshire BUR: Mt Zion B/P: 1/110

1219 Haines, Mary M. - white female D: Dec 6, 1889; 34y 6m 20d; Hampshire F: Nealis, James M: Nealis, F. B: Hampshire DOI: husband C: Haines, Jno. B/P: 1/51

1220 Haines, Minnie L. - white female D: Sept 28, 1912; 32y B: Sherman District B/P: 2/47

1221 Haines, Miss - single white female D: Jan 1900, 5d; Pine Hill B: Hampshire BUR: Pine Hill B/P: 1/105

1222 Haines, Mrs. - married white female D: Mar 1, 1895; 76y; Hampshire B: Hampshire B/P: 1/89

1223 Haines, Myrtle - married white female D: Dec 6, 1918; 24y; Hampshire B/P: 1/126

1224 Haines, Noah - white male D: Dec 22, 1900; 44y; Hampshire B: 1856 I: Haines, Anna DOI: head of family B/P: 1/73

1225 Haines, Noah - white male D: Mar 14, 1905; 55y B/P: 2/45 N: farmer

1226 Haines, Nora Anna - married white female D: June 6, 1917; 29y 6m 5d B/P: 2/48

1227 Haines, Rachel - white female D: June 14, 1881; 67y 3m 4d; Hampshire B: Hampshire DOI: husband C: Haines, Joseph B/P: 1/29 N: parents: Benj. F. & Delila C.

1228 Haines, Reasin - married white male D: Dec 30, 1898; 78y; Hampshire B: Hampshire BUR: Grassy Lick B/P: 1/99 N: farmer

1229 Haines, Reazin - white male D: Dec 30, 1898; 79y; Gore District F: Haines, Dan M: Haines, Elizabeth DOI: wife C: Haines, Jennie B/P: 1/69

1230 Haines, Robt. - single white male D: Dec 26, 1910; 2y 9m 27d B/P: 2/46

1231 Haines, Rosa B. - single white female D: Oct 22, 1908; 21y 10m 27d B/P: 2/45 N: school teacher

1232 Haines, Rosa E. - white female D: Dec 7, 1888; 5y; Sherman District F: Haines, S.T. M: Haines E.J. B: Hampshire DOI: father B/P: 1/47

1233 Haines, Rose E. - white female D: Aug 28, 1899; 2y; Augusta F: Haines, Geo W. M: Haines, Susan B: 1898 DOI: mother B/P: 1/71

1234 Haines, Rosetta - white female D: May 12, 1901; 38y; Hampshire I: Haines, B.F. B/P: 1/77

1235 Haines, Rosie - white female D: Mar 11, 1895; 1m 16d; Sherman District F: Haines, W.L. B: Jan 1895 DOI: father B/P: 1/61

1236 Haines, Russel Wilco - white male D: Aug 26, 1916; 6y 3m B: Romney B/P: 2/48

1237 Haines, Sarah A. - married white female D: June 10, 1915; 61y 7m 26d B/P: 2/48

1238 Haines, Sarah Jane - white female D: Nov 8, 1902; 2y 9m; Sherman District F: Haines, B.F. M: Haines, Miranda C. B: Aug 10, 1900 DOI: father B/P: 1/78

1239 Haines, Stephen - white male D: Apr 10, 1894; 70y; Springfield B: Hampshire BUR: Springfield B/P: 1/82

1240 Haines, Stephen - white male D: Oct 5, 1893; 6y; Hampshire F: Haines, S. M: Haines, G. DOI: father B/P: 1/58

1241 Haines, Stephen - widower white male D: Nov 23, 1914; 69y 1m 7d B/P: 2/48

1242 Haines, Truman E. - white male D: Mar 28, 1884; 3y; Hampshire F: Haines, Jas. H. M: Haines, Hannah B: Hampshire DOI: father B/P: 1/39

1243 Haines, Ula - white female D: June 7, 1903; 2y; Hampshire F: Haines, G.K. M: Haines, Nettie B: June 3, 1901 DOI: father B/P: 1/80

1244 Haines, Wilda - white female D: Dec 30, 1915; 18y 4m 14d B/P: 2/48

1245 Haines, Wilda - white female D: Dec 31, 1915; 18y 6m 28d B/P: 2/48

1246 Haines, Wildie C. - white female D: Dec 31, 1914; 18m B/P: 2/48

1247 Haines, Wm. - white male D: May 21, 1888; 59y 1m 12d; Hampshire F: Haines, Dan M: Haines, E. B: Hampshire DOI: wife C: Haines, Catherine B/P: 1/45 N: farmer

1248 Haines, Wm. E. - white male D: Sept 28, 1881; 3m 11d; Hampshire F: Haines, L.B. M: Haines, Anna B. B: Hampshire DOI: father B/P: 1/31

1249 Hall, James L. - single white male D: Dec 22, 1880; 86y 6m 12d; Hampshire F: Hall, Rich M: Hall, Winiford B: Loudoun Co. VA I: Scanlan, Mariah DOI: friend B/P: 21/28

1250 Hambleton, Nannie - white female D: Apr 5, 1896; 69y 4m; Mill Creek District F: Grim, George B: Aug 5, 1827 DOI: husband B/P: 1/62

1251 Hamilton, Amos - married black male D: Feb 3, 1899; 27y; Cold Stream B: Capon District BUR: Capon Chapel B/P: 1/102

1252 Hamilton, Ida L. - white female D: Aug 8, 1896; 28y 6m; Mill Creek F: Barnes, T.P. B: Feb 1867 I: Hamilton, George B/P: 1/62

1253 Hamilton, Jas. Edw Taylor - single colored male D: Mar 4, 1907; 10y B/P: 2/45

1254 Hamilton, John - colored male D: Jan 26, 1874; 1y 3m 28d; Hampshire F: Hamilton, Amos M: Hamilton, Matilda B: Hampshire DOI: mother B/P: 1/12

1255 Hamilton, Paul McKinley - single colored male D: Mar 7, 1907; 7y B/P: 2/45

1256 Hamilton, S. - white female D: Apr 6, 1888; 19y; Hampshire F: Hamilton, A. M: Hamilton, M. B: Hampshire DOI: father B/P: 1/45

1257 Hamilton, Seamor - single colored male D: Aug 5, 1873; F: Hamilton, Gilbert M: Hamilton, Mariah B: Hampshire I: Hamilton, Amos DOI: brother B/P: 1/11

1258 Hammack, Jno W - single white male D: Dec 4, 1874; 27y 7m 29d; Hampshire F: Hammack, William M: Hammack, Barbara A B: Frederick Co VA DOI: father B/P: 1/12

1259 Hammack, William - white male D: Sept 1, 1899; 87y 4m 14d; Bloomery District B: Apr 17, 1812 I: Keiter, J.W. DOI:

grandson B/P: 1/70 N: farmer

1260 Hammock, Nayna - white female D: Feb 14, 1879; 4y 2m 10d; Hampshire F: Hammock, John M: Hammock, Nancy B: Hampshire DOI: father B/P: 1/25

1261 Hammock, William - widower white male D: Sept 21, 1899; 87y; Bloomery B: Virginia B/P: 1/108 N: farmer

1262 Hammon, Wesley - white male D: Feb 21, 1900; 60y; Romney B: Aug 1, 1840 DOI: son B/P: 1/72

1263 Hammond, Wesley - married white male D: Feb 21, 1900; 61y; Romney B: Virginia BUR: Frostburg, MD B/P: 1/110 N: preacher

1264 Hannahs, Hannah - white female D: Apr 2, 1876; 39y 6m 19d; Hampshire F: Lewis, Silas M: Lewis, Louisa B: Hampshire B/P: 1/20

1265 Hannahs, John W. - white male D: May 20, 1879; 50y; Hampshire F: Hannahs, John M: Hannahs, Mary B: Hampshire I: Seaders, Mary DOI: neighbor C: Hannahs, Emira B/P: 1/26

1266 Hannas, Deborah - white female D: Nov 19, 1893; 63y 3m 19d; Hampshire B/P: 1/58

1267 Hannas, James Woodrow - white male D: July 5, 1914; 8m 21d B/P: 2/48

1268 Hannas, Jno. S. - widower white D: June 23, 1911; 71y 5m 22d B: Gore District B/P: 2/47 N: farmer

1269 Hannas, John - white male D: May 10, 1867; 68y 1m 17d; Jersey Mountain B: Hampshire DOI: widow C: Hannas, Deborah B/P: 1/2

1270 Hannas, Laura F. - married white female D: Jan 31, 1909; 51y 10m 18d B/P: 2/46

1271 Hannas, Sarah - white female D: Dec 20, 1878; 5y 1m 2d; Hampshire B: Hampshire I: Hannas, Jack B/P: 1/23

1272 Hannas, Sarah M. - widowed white female D: Jun 10, 1920; 72y 5m 22d; Hampshire M: Carder, Susan B: Hampshire B/P: 1/129

1273 Hannas, Stephen - married white male D: Dec 29, 1913; 72y 5m 9d B/P: 2/47 N: farmer

1274 Hannum, Joseph - white male D: Nov 10, 1882; 78y; Capon District F: Hannum, Thomas M: Hannum, Jane B: WV I: Hannum, M.F. DOI: son B/P: 1/33

1275 Hannum, Rosa - married white female D: Oct 12, 1902; 25y 5m 4d; Levels B: Hampshire BUR: Levels B/P: 1/117

1276 Hannum, Wm E D: Aug 26, 1870; 31 y F: Hunnum, Joseph B/P: 1/5

1277 Hannun, Madison F. - white male D: Sept 4, 1904; 73y B/P: 2/49

1278 Hansborough, Nancy - white female D: Oct 3, 1879; 77y; Hampshire I: Hanns, Mar. DOI: grand daughter C: Hansborough, John B/P: 1/25

1279 Hanurus, Rosa Belle - white female D: Oct 12, 1902; 25y; Hampshire F: Pugh B: 1877 DOI: husband C: Hanurus, W.H. B/P: 1/79

1280 Harbaugh, O.W. - white male D: July 12, 1894; 7m; Romney F: Harbaugh, N. J. M: Harbaugh, Elizabeth B: Romney DOI: father B/P: 1/59

1281 Harbert, Thelma - single white female D: Nov 19, 1921; 12y; Hampshire F: Harbert, Harold B: Shinston B/P: 1/131

1282 Hardy, Charlotte J. - single white female D: Oct 9, 1920; 18m 9d; Hampshire F: Hardy, Dailey M: Hardy, Mary B: Hampshire B/P: 1/129

1283 Hardy, Daisy J. - single white female D: Nov 8, 1922; 9y 7m; Hampshire F: Hardy, Jno. M: Hardy, May B: Hampshire B/P: 1/134

1284 Hardy, E.B. - white female D: Mar 24, 1898; 88y; Bloomery District I: McCole, Jno. S. DOI: son in law C: Hardy, Israel B/P: 1/69

1285 Hardy, Elizabeth - white female D: Mar 6, 1897; 87y 11m 9d; Bloomery B: Mar 27, 1809 I: McCoole, J.S. DOI: son in law C: Hardy, Israel B/P: 1/66

1286 Hardy, Harriet - white female D: Aug 23, 1872; 40y 6m 8d; Hampshire F: Sneathen, Sam'l M: Sneathen, Elizabeth B: Hampshire DOI: father C: Hardy, Jeremiah B/P: 1/8

1287 Hardy, L.A. - single white male D: Nov 3, 1895; 23y 6m; Hampshire B: Hampshire B/P: 1/87 N: blacksmith

1288 Harlow, Catherine M. - white female D: May 17, 1875; 49y 10m; Hampshire B: New York State DOI: husband C: Harlow, Matthew B/P: 1/14

1289 Harlow, Matthew - white male D: Jan 6, 1885; 66y; Hampshire F: Harlow, Matthew M: Harlow, Catharine B: New York I: Harlow, William E. DOI: son C: Harlow, Catharine B/P: 1/41 N: merchant

1290 Harmison, Chas. Sr. - married white male D: Oct 31, 1896;Hampshire BUR: Romney B/P: 1/96

1291 Harmison, Elizabeth - married white female D: Mar 18, 1922; 41y 6m 3d; Hampshire F: Guthrie, Wm. M: Guthrie, Hannah B/P: 1/133 N: housewife

1292 Harmison, Hollie Lupton - white female D: Nov 14, 1914; 2y DOI: father B/P: 2/48

1293 Harmison, Sallie - white female D: Dec 1889; 74y; Romney District B: Romney District I: Harmison, J. DOI: son C: Harmison, Jonathan B/P: 1/49

1294 Harmison, Violet - white female D: Apr 6, 1904; 2m B/P: 2/55

1295 Harner, Jacob M. - white male D: Aug 3, 1904; 57y 6m 8d B/P: 2/55

1296 Harnum, Jos. Wm. - single white male D: Dec 24, 1919; 14y 1m 10d; Springfield District F: Harnum, W.H. M: Harnum, Marie B: Levels B/P: 1/128

1297 Harper, Florence A.V. - white female D: Aug 14, 1868; Hampshire F: Harper, J. R. B/P: 1/3

1298 Harriott, Susan M. - white female D: Nov 16, 1910; 63y 3m 9d B/P: 2/46

1299 Harris, Maria - white female D: Mar 1, 1904; 88y 7m 9d B/P: 2/49

1300 Harris, Susie - single colored female D: June 1895; 13y; Hampshire B: Hampshire B/P: 1/87

1301 Harrison, Jennie - single white female D: May 26, 1899; 19y; Winchester, VA F: Harrison, William M: Harrison, Alice B: May 26, 1880 DOI: father B/P: 1/70

1302 Harrison, Martha - white female D: Sept 6, 1894; 60y; Hampshire B: Hampshire I: Harrison, C. DOI: son B/P: 1/60

1303 Hartman, Annie E. - married white female D: Apr 3, 1897; 52y; Hampshire BUR: Home B/P: 1/96

1304 Hartman, Clara May - single white female D: June 13, 1918; 19y 5m; Hampshire B/P: 1/126 N: school teacher

1305 Hartman, James - white male D: May 26, 1881; 56y 3d; Hampshire B: Hampshire DOI: wife C: Hartman, H.A. B/P: 1.29

1306 Hartman, Josiah - single white male D: May 27, 1902; 27y; Mill Creek District F: Hartman, David M: Hartman, Bettie B: 1876 DOI: father B/P: 1/78

1307 Hartman, Mary S. D: Nov 19, 1866; Mill Creek F: Hartman, John M: Hartman, Susan B: Mill Creek DOI: mother B/P: 1/1

1308 Hartman, Rosa J. - white female D: Sept 26, 1881; 7m 16d; Hampshire F: Hartman, Ed. W. M: Hartman, Virginia B: Hampshire DOI: mother B/P: 1/29

1309 Hartman, Susan - married white female D: Mar 21, 1909; 71y 9m 21d B/P: 2/46

1310 Haslacker, Wm. - widowed white male D: Nov 25, 1921; 56y; Hampshire F: Haslacker, Wm. M: Haslacker, Mary E. B: WV B/P: 1/131 N: farmer

1311 Hass, Abram - white male D: Jan 1892; 83y; Hampshire B: Hampshire I: Pancake, Isaac DOI: son in law C: Hass, Nancy B/P: 1/54

1312 Hass, Ann M D: Oct 5, 1871; 48y 8m 22d B/P: 1/6

1313 Hass, John - white male D: Mar 16, 1910; 73y 3m B/P: 2/46 N: farmer

1314 Hass, Roberta - widow white female D: May 22, 1913; 69y 4m B/P: 2/47

1315 Hass, Thos. S. - white male D: Nov 22, 1881; 33y 5m 15d; Hampshire F: Hass, Abram M: Hass, Mary A. B: Hampshire I: Hass, Jno W. DOI: brother C: Hass, Hannah K. B/P: 1/31

1316 Hausell, May - white female D: May 1, 1886; 37y; Hampshire B: Hampshire DOI: husband C: Hausell, Joseph T.

B/P: 1/44

1317 Hawkins, Chas. - married white male D: Feb 17, 1907; 85y B/P: 2/45 N: wagon maker

1318 Hawkins, Dailey - white male D: Aug 11, 1907; 14y B/P: 2/45

1319 Hawkins, Dorly - single white male D: Aug 11, 1907; 14y B/P: 2/45

1320 Hawkins, James - white male D: Dec 7, 1872; 80y 4m 2d; Hampshire F: Hawkins, John M: Hawkins, Catherine B: Hampshire I: Hawkins, Henry DOI: Hawkins, Elizabeth B/P: 1/8

1321 Hawkins, John - white male D: Mar 2, 1874; 54y 5m 6d; Hampshire F: Hawkins, James M: Hawkins, Elizabeth B: Hampshire DOI: wife C: Hawkins, Elizabeth B/P: 1/12

1322 Hawkins, William A - white male D: Sept 17, 1875; 10m 23d; Hampshire F: Hawkins, David M: Hawkins, Elizabeth J. B: Hampshire DOI: father B/P: 1/16

1323 Haws, Mary - single white female D: May 24, 1877; Hampshire B: Hampshire I: Poling, M. F. DOI: overseer of poor B/P: 1/22

1324 Hawse, Fannie - married white female D: Dec 19, 1921; 41y 8m 18d; Hampshire F: Evans, Jacob M: Evans, Hannah B: Inkerman B/P: 1/131

1325 Hawse, Ruth J. - white female D: Nov 26, 1902; 3m 1d; Sherman district F: Hawse, Don M: Hawse, Mary E. B: 1902 DOI: father B/P: 1/78

1326 Haycock, Wade - married white male D: Nov 15, 1918; 45y; Hampshire B/P: 1/126 N: B & O track hand

1327 Hayden, Margaret W. - white female D: Dec 26, 1872; 31y 3m; Hampshire F: Hayden, D. M: Hayden, Eliza B: Hampshire DOI: father B/P: 1/9

1328 Heare S.B. - single white female D: Apr 7, 1896; 2m 14d; Kirby B: Kirby BUR: Mt. Zion M.E. Church B/P: 1/90

1329 Heare, Clara - white female D: Jan 12, 1908; 3y 1m 30d B/P: 2/45

1330 Heare, Cornwell W. - white male D: Apr 13, 1905; 5m

B/P: 2/45

1331 Heare, Elizabeth A. - white female D: Jan 3, 1888; 10y 9m; Sherman District F: Heare, Jno A. G. M: Heare, E. B: Hampshire DOI: father B/P: 1/47

1332 Heare, Francis - white male D: Feb 13, 1919; stillborn B/P: 2/48

1333 Heare, Gerald T. - white male D: July 15, 1888; 1y 2m 18d; Sherman District F: Heare, F. M: Heare, Ada B: Hampshire DOI: father B/P: 1/47

1334 Heare, Gladstone - single white male D: Jan 16, 1903; 2d; Hampshire B: Hampshire BUR: Mt Zion B/P: 1/114

1335 Heare, Hannah E D: Mar 6, 1866; Grassy Lick F: Heare, J.L. M: Heare, Hannah DOI: consort C: Heare, Isaiah J.F. B/P: 1/1

1336 Heare, Isaac - white male D: Aug 10, 1894; 61y; Sherman District B: Sherman District DOI: son B/P: 1/59

1337 Heare, Isaiah J. - married white male D: Aug 30, 1894; 70y 4m 13d; near Kirby B: Hampshire BUR: Grassy Lick Church B/P: 1/86

1338 Heare, James J. - white male D: Apr 30, 1873; 2y; Hampshire F: Heare, Jasper M: Heare, Mary B: Hampshire DOI: father B/P: 1/10

1339 Heare, Lina - single white female D: Feb 28, 1903; 5y 7m 3d; Hampshire B: Hampshire BUR: Mt Zion B/P: 1/114

1340 Heare, Mamie Lee - married white female D: Mar 24, 1907; 33y 7m 16d B/P: 2/45

1341 Heare, Mandie - white female D: Feb 13, 1919; 29y 1m 1d B/P: 2/48

1342 Heare, Margaret - single white female D: Oct 12, 1866; 3Y; Hampshire F: Heare, Benjamin M: Heare, Jane B: Hampshire DOI: parent B/P: 1/1

1343 Heare, Nora F. - white female D: July 7, 1904; 12y 10m 25d B/P: 2/55

1344 Heare, Nora F. - single white female D: Nov 13, 1902; 12y 10m 25d; Hampshire B: Hampshire B/P: 1/114

1345 Heare, Peter L. - white male D: June 1893; 29y; Hampshire F: Heare, J.A. M: Heare, B.A. DOI: father B/P: 1/58

1346 Heare, Ruban - white male D: Mar 10, 1866; Grassy Lick F: Heare, J.L. M: Heare, Hannah DOI: father B/P: 1/1

1347 Heare, Walter R. - white male D: May 19, 1878; 2m 19d; Hampshire F: Heare, J. M: Heare, S. B: Hampshire DOI: father B/P: 1/24

1348 Heath, David - white male D: Mar 26, 1915; 59y B/P: 2/48

1349 Heath, Mary - white female D: July 19, 1892; 66y 11m; Hampshire B: Hampshire DOI: husband C: Heath, William B/P: 1/57

1350 Heath, O.C. - white female D: Mar 26, 1892; 2y 3m 1d; Hampshire F: Heath, R.D. M: Heath, I.J. B: Hampshire DOI: father B/P: 1/57

1351 Heath, Sarah Jane - married white female D: Apr 25, 1913; 58y B/P: 2/47

1352 Heatwole, Barbara - white female D: May 5, 1884; 87y 8m 9d; Hampshire I: Heatwole, John DOI: son B/P: 1/39

1353 Heatwole, Charles - white male D: Apr 26, 1897; 45y 7m; Romney F: Heatwole, John E. M: Heatwole, Marthy J. B: Sherman District DOI: wife B/P: 1/64 N: Justice of the Peace

1354 Heatwole, Jno. E. - widower white male D: Jan 26, 1922; 93y; Hampshire B: Rockingham County I: Lupton, Geo. A. B/P: 1/134

1355 Heatwole, Margaret F. - married white female D: Aug 19, 1905; 52y 7m B/P: 2/45

1356 Heatwole, Robt. L. - married white male D: Dec 3, 1911; 31y 10m 17d B: Romney District B/P: 2/47 N: merchant

1357 Heckert, Ruby May - white female D: Oct 8, 1915; 1m 26d B/P: 2/48

1358 Heironoimus, Mariah B. - white female D: June 25, 1880; 70y 11m 15d; Hampshire F: Taylor, David M: Taylor, Martha B: Frederick Co, VA DOI: husband C: Heironoimus, O. F. B/P: 1/28

1359 Heironomius, Overton F. - white male D: Aug 31, 1881; 71y 1d; Hampshire F: Heironomius, Jacob M: Heironomius, E. B: Pennsylvania I: Heironomius, G. H. DOI: son C: Heironomius, B. B/P: 1/31

1360 Heiskell, Francis W. - white male D: Oct 1881; 59y 7m 13d; Hampshire F: Heiskell, Sam'l M: Heiskell, Sarah B: Hampshire I: Heiskell, E.S. DOI: son C: Heiskell, Elizabeth B/P: 1/31

1361 Helman, Aphir M. - single white male D: July 8, 1910; 1m 14d B/P: 2/46

1362 Helmick, Chas - single white male D: Mar 30, 1913; 53y 7m 4d B/P: 2/47 N: farmer

1363 Hemelright, Wilber H. - white male D: July 1, 1891; 3m; Hampshire F: Hemelright, J.H. M: Hemelright, M. B: Hampshire DOI: father B/P: 1/53

1364 Hemeright, L. R. - white male D: Nov 24, 1890; 6d; Romney District F: Hemeright, John M: Hemeright, Nora B: Hampshire DOI: father B/P: 1/52

1365 Hemeright, Louring - white male D: Nov 3, 1889; 3y 2m; Capon District F: Hemeright, John B: Capon District DOI: father B/P: 1/49

1366 Henderson, Eliza - white D: July 20, 1913; 88y B/P: 2/47

1367 Henderson, H.R. - white male D: Nov 30, 1898; 4y 6m 5d; Gore District F: Henderson, L.H.L. M: Henderson, S.V. DOI: father B/P: 1/69

1368 Henderson, J.L. - white male D: Sept 19, 1902; 28y; Hampshire B: Mar 23, 1874 DOI: sister B/P: 1/79

1369 Henderson, John - white male D: Aug 8, 1907; 1y 1m B/P: 2/45

1370 Henderson, Judson L. - single white male D: Sept 19, 1902; 28y; 6m 26d; Points B: Hampshire BUR: Wesley Chapel B/P: 1/117

1371 Henderson, Larkin D. - white male D: Dec 31, 1872; 82y 3m 3d; Hampshire F: Henderson, Thos M: Henderson, Mary B: Hampshire I: Henderson, Thos. DOI: son C: Henderson, Mary B/P: 1/8

1372 Henderson, Lottie - white female D: Oct 15, 1910; 14y B/P: 2/46

1373 Henderson, Maggie - single white female D: Nov 21, 1904; 36y B/P: 2/55

1374 Henderson, Matilda - single D: June 9, 1871; 77y 6m 6d F: Henderson, L.D. M: Henderson, Mary B/P: 1/6

1375 Henderson, May - white female D: Oct 18, 1910; 9y B/P: 2/46

1376 Henderson, Mrs. - married white female D: Oct 26, 1898; 56y; Hampshire B: Hampshire BUR: Hampshire B/P: 1/100

1377 Henderson, Mrs. - married white female D: Oct 25, 1898; 54y; Hampshire BUR: Hampshire B/P: 1/100

1378 Henderson, Nellie B. - white female D: Sept 14, 1911; 13y B: Gore district B/P: 2/47

1379 Henderson, Olive m. - white female D: Jan 25, 1902; 5y; Hampshire F: Henderson, L.H. M: Henderson, Sarah B: Feb 25, 1897 DOI: father B/P: 1/79

1380 Henderson, Raymond - wingle white male D: Dec 12, 1920; 64y 10m; Hampshire F: Henderson, Thos. M: Henderson, Elizabeth B: WV B/P: 1/129

1381 Henderson, T.R. - white male D: June 23, 1899; 54y 2m 6d; Springfield District F: Henderson, J.J. M: Henderson, Jane B: Apr 17, 1845 I: Henderson, J.L. DOI: son C: Henderson, M.J. B/P: 1/70 N: carpenter

1382 Henderson, Thomas - widower white male D: June 23, 1899; 55y; Higginsville B: Hampshire BUR: Wesley Chapel B/P: 1/106 N: farmer

1383 Henderson, Thos F. - white male D: Oct 3, 1878; 61y 6m 19d; Hampshire F: Henderson, L.D. M: Henderson, M. B: Hampshire DOI: wife C: Henderson, Eliza B/P: 1/24

1384 Henderson, Thos H. - white male D: Oct 1, 1884; 78y; Hampshire B: Hampshire I: Henderson, Thos J. DOI: son B/P: 1/39

1385 Hennerite, Mary E. - white female D: Apr 16, 1913; 68y B/P: 2/47

1386 Herbaugh, Harriett - white female D: Jan 28, 1877; Hampshire B: Rockingham VA DOI: husband C: Herbaugh, John B/P: 1/22

1387 Herbaugh, Roy - single white male D: July 27, 1913; 19y 2m 11d B/P: 2/47 N: farmer

1388 Herbaugh, Roy C. - white male D: July 27, 1912; 19y 8m 10d B: Gore District B/P: 2/47

1389 Herbough, Otis - single white male D: Aug 4, 1911; 2y B: Gore District B/P: 2/47

1390 Herriot, Geo. Silas - married white male D: Aug 8, 1919; 39y 11m 27d B/P: 2/48 N: farmer

1391 Herriott Ellen C. - white female D: Dec 5, 1878; 22y 7m 2d; Hampshire B: Hampshire DOI: husband C: Herriott, Wm. V. B/P: 1/23

1392 Herriott, Deborah E. - widow white female D: Sept 2, 1906; 71y B/P: 2/45

1393 Herriott, Eliza - white female D: Aug 6, 1892; 86y 4m 6d; Foxes Hollow F: Rees, William B: Patterson Creek I: Herriott, Isaac DOI: son B/P: 1/56

1394 Herriott, Ephriam - white male D: June 17, 1866; Foxes Hollow B: Foxes Hollow DOI: son B/P: 1/1

1395 Herriott, Franklin - widowed white male D: Sept 5, 1921; 76y 9m 3d; Hampshire F: Herriott, Ephriam M: Herriott, Eliza B: Hampshire B/P: 1/131 N: farmer

1396 Herriott, Isaac - married white male D: Jan 10, 1908; 67y B/P: 2/45 N: farmer

1397 Herriott, Susan E. - married white female D: July 28, 1921; 70y 8m 7d; Hampshire F: Reese, Jno. M: Reese, Susan B: Mineral County I: Herriott, Chas. B/P: 1/131 N: housewife

1398 Herriott, Susan M. - married white female D: Nov 16, 1909; 63y 3m 9d B/P: 2/46

1399 Herriott, William - white male D: Aug 3, 1892; 4m; Foxes Hollow F: Herriott, Franklin M: Herriott, Susan B: near Hanging Rock DOI: father B/P: 1/56

1400 Hers, Hannah Louise - widow white female D: Mar 27, 1915; 71y B/P: 2/48

1401 Hetrick, Mary - married white female D: Aug 1, 1912; 43y B: Springfield District B/P: 2/47

1402 Hetzel, Fred - white male D: Mar 20, 1907; 24y B/P: 2/45 N: mgr. grocery

1403 Hieskell, Bettie - widow white female D: Aug 27, 1909; 81y 3m B/P: 2/46

1404 Hieskell, D.H. - married white male D: Oct 7, 1904; 44y B/P: 2/55

1405 Hieskell, Edward - married white male D: Aug 16, 1911; 45y B: Bloomery District B/P: 2/47 N: farmer

1406 Hiett, Albert D: May 21, 1869; 11m; Hampshire F: Hiett, Jery M: Hiett, Sarah B: Hampshire B/P: 1/4

1407 Hiett, Ann - white female D: Jan 22, 1899; 81y 11m 18d; Bloomery District F: Park, Jacob B: Feb 4, 1817 DOI: husband C: Hiett, S.S. B/P: 1/70

1408 Hiett, Asa - single white male D: Dec 18, 1885; 73y; Hampshire F: Hiett, J. M: Hiett, Lucinda B: Hampshire I: Cowgill, A.C. DOI: nephew B/P: 1/42 N: politician

1409 Hiett, C.N. - widower white male D: Apr 30, 1912; 65y B: Gore District B/P: 2/47 N: Insurance Agent

1410 Hiett, Caroline - widow white female D: Nov 9, 1906; 95y B/P: 2/45

1411 Hiett, Edith - white female D: Oct 2, 1910; 6y 10m 11d B/P: 2/46

1412 Hiett, Elizabeth - white female D: June 25, 1872; 27y; Hampshire F: Wills, Deskin M: Wills, Susan B: Hampshire DOI: husband C: Hiett, John L. B/P: 1/8

1413 Hiett, Evan - white male D: July 22, 1902; 87y; Hampshire B: 1815 I: Hiett, S.L. DOI: son B/P: 1/79

1414 Hiett, Florence J. - single white female D: Mar 16, 1920; 16d; Hampshire F: Hiett, Shull M: Hiett, Leona B: Hampshire B/P: 1/129

1415 Hiett, Holmes - married white male D: Nov 24, 1908; 30y 8m 3d B/P: 2/45

1416 Hiett, Holmes - married white male D: Nov 24, 1909; 30y B/P: 2/46 N: Saw Mill

1417 Hiett, Ira - single white male D: Jan 30, 1907; 18y 7m 3d B/P: 2/45

1418 Hiett, Jeremiah - married white male D: Oct 9, 1893; 55y 11m 1d; Gore District B: Hampshire BUR: Family Burying Ground B/P: 1/83

1419 Hiett, Jno. S. - married white male D: June 28, 1906; 63y B/P: 2/45 N: farmer

1420 Hiett, John - white male D: July 30, 1883; 80y; Hampshire F: Hiett, Joseph M: Hiett, Alcinda B: Hampshire I: Hiett, Anna DOI: daughter C: Hiett, Julia B. B/P: 1/37

1421 Hiett, Jonathan - married white male D: Mar 7, 1907; 84y 5m 27d B/P: 2/45 N: farmer

1422 Hiett, Joseph - married white male D: Mar 8, 1900; 60y; Forks of Capon B: WV BUR: Forks of Capon B/P: 1/105

1423 Hiett, Joseph S. - married white male D: Aug 3, 1897; 82y; near N.River Mills B: Hampshire BUR: near N.R. Mills B/P: 1/92

1424 Hiett, Kenneth Warde - single white male D: Nov 27, 1921; stillborn; Hampshire F: Hiett, Hetzel M: Hiett, Elizabeth B: Hampshire B/P: 1/131

1425 Hiett, L.E. - white female D: July 1892; 3y; Hampshire F: Hiett, C.N. M: Hiett, R. B: Hampshire DOI: sister B/P: 1/57

1426 Hiett, Lillie Hendricks - married white female D: June 5, 1922; 36y 11m 27d; Hampshire F: Brathwait, O.B. M: Brathwait, Liddie B: Cross Junction, VA I: Hiett, J.P. B/P: 1/133 N: housewife

1427 Hiett, Loretta - white female D: Oct 15, 1872; 4m 2d; Hampshire F: Hiett, John M: Hiett, Elizabeth B: Hampshire DOI: father B/P: 1/9

1428 Hiett, Lucinda D: Sept 6, 1870; 83y; Hampshire F: Kidwell, John M: Kidwell, Ellen C: Hiett, Jeremiah B/P: 1/5

1429 Hiett, Lucy Jane - married white female D: Jan 6, 1908; 50y B/P: 2/45

1430 Hiett, Margaret - white female D: Aug 15, 1872; 58y; Hampshire F: McKee, Joseph M: McKee, Elizabeth B: Hampshire DOI: husband C: Hiett, Jonathan B/P: 1/8

1431 Hiett, Margaret - widow white female D: Mar 29, 1911; 65y B: Bloomery District B/P: 2/47

1432 Hiett, Montgomery - married white male D: Apr 15, 1898; 35y; North River B: Hampshire B/P: 1/99 N: farmer

1433 Hiett, Rosie - married white female D: Sept 16, 1895; 40y; Hampshire B: Hampshire B/P: 1/89

1434 Hiett, Sallie - single white female D: Mar 4, 1900; 85y; North River B: WV BUR: North River B/P: 1/105

1435 Hiett, Sarah - white female D: Mar 1900; 83y; Hampshire B: 1817 I: Hiett, Jonathan DOI: brother B/P: 1/73

1436 High, Alphus - white male D: Aug 5, 1894; 63y 2m; Mill Creek District B: Mill Creek DOI: wife B/P: 1/59

1437 High, Frederic S. - white male D: Jan 19, 1876; 63y 5m 24d; Hampshire F: High, F. B: Hampshire I: High, Alonzo DOI: son C: High, Hattie B/P: 1/18

1438 High, Frederick H. - white male D: Sept 10, 1875; 10y; Hampshire F: High, Warner M: High, Susan B: Hampshire DOI: father B/P: 1/14

1439 High, George - single white male D: Sept 24, 1872; 74y 2m 10d; Hampshire B: Loudoun Co., Va I: High, Alfred DOI: grandson B/P: 1/9

1440 High, George - white male D: Sept 18, 1892; 90y 9m 25d; Mill Creek B: Mill Creek I: High, William DOI: son B/P: 1/56 N: farmer

1441 High, Harriett - white female D: Dec 15, 1893; 75y 2m 5d; Hampshire B/P: 1/58

1442 High, Harriett - white female D: Mar 10, 1892; 64y 1d; Hampshire F: White, B: Hampshire I: High, Annie E. DOI: daughter C: High, H.M. B/P: 1/53

1443 High, Hays - single white male D: Apr 2, 1907; 30y 11m B/P: 2/45

1444 High, Henry M - white male D: Oct 21, 1876; 59y 3m 3d; Hampshire B: Hampshire DOI: wife C: High, Hannah B/P: 1/18

1445 High, James H. - white male D: Dec 18, 1898; 76y; Mill Creek District F: High, George I: High, Sarah B/P: 1/68

1446 High, James Slone - white male D: Sept 12, 1898; 5m 23d; Mill Creek District F: High, E.D. M: High, Annie DOI: father B/P: 1/68

1447 High, Lorenzo A. - white male D: Sept 26, 1875; 6y 3m; Hampshire F: High, Warner M: High, Susan B: Hampshire DOI: father B/P: 1/14

1448 High, Margaret Ann - white female D: Feb 14, 1887; 47y 11m 14d; Mill Creek District F: Liller, Henry M: Liller, Ann B: Hampshire DOI: husband C: High, William H. B/P: 1/43

1449 High, Mary Ellen - married white female D: July 7, 1907; 48y 12d B/P: 2/45

1450 High, Mary M. D: Nov 24, 1866; Mill Creek F: High, Alpheus M: High, Hannah B: Mill Creek DOI: father B/P: 1/1

1451 High, O.T. - white male D: Jan 3, 1890; 41y; Romney District F: High, John M: High, Rebecca B: Romney District DOI: wife C: High, Susie B/P: 1/49 N: merchant

1452 High, Susan - white female D: Sept 5, 1899; 67y 11m 8d; Romney B: Oct 13, 1832 DOI: niece B/P: 1/71

1453 High, Wm C.B. - white male D: Oct 15, 1866; Mill Creek F: High, Warner M: High, Hannah B: Mill Creek DOI: father B/P: 1/1

1454 Hines, Bertha A. - white female D: Aug 1, 1881; 85y; Hampshire B: Hampshire I: Hines, Jacob DOI: son C: Hines, Wm. B/P: 1/29

1455 Hines, George - white male D: Aug 4, 1912; 67y 7m 15d B: Sherman District B/P: 2/47

1456 Hines, Hannah A.A. - widow white female D: June 18, 1912; 63y B: Gore District B/P: 2/47

1457 Hines, Harvy - widower white male D: Mar 22, 1897; 69y; near Hanging Rock B: Hampshire BUR: Capon Chapel B/P: 1/97

1458 Hines, Minnie - white female D: June 23, 1909; 3m 1d B/P: 2/46

1459 Hines, Sarah - single white female D: Nov 14, 1873; 25y

8m 19d; Hampshire M: Hines, Susan B: Hampshire I: Lupton, S.R. DOI: physician B/P: 1/10

1460 Hines, William - white male D: Oct 1881; Hampshire F: Hines, Jas M: Hines, Sarah B: Hampshire I: Hines, Thos DOI: brother B/P: 1/30 N: blacksmith

1461 Hite, Virginia M. - white female D: June 15, 1915; 32y B/P: 2/48

1462 Hixon, Sarah - white female D: Mar 10, 1878; 31y 2m 17d; Hampshire F: Hixon, Timothy M: Hixon, Sarah B: Pennsylvania DOI: husband C: Hixon, Perry B/P: 1/23

1463 Hobert, Azarbah P. - white female D: Sept 1884; 92y; Hampshire B: Worster, MASS I: Hobert, Billings DOI: son C: deceased B/P: 1/38

1464 Hobert, Billings - married white male D: Sept 11, 1874; 77y 6m; Hampshire B: Ma?? DOI: wife B/P: 1/12

1465 Hockins, Anna - white female D: July 8, 1894; 16y; Hampshire F: Hockins, H. M: Hockins, M.J. B: Hampshire DOI: mother B/P: 1/60

1466 Hockins, Henry - white male D: July 8, 1894; 73y; Hampshire B: Virginia DOI: wife C: Hockins, J.M. B/P: 1/60

1467 Hockman, Caroline - widow white female D: Jan 25, 1910; 77y 3m 9d B/P: 2/46

1468 Hockman, Cora L. - white female D: Jan 21, 1882; 1y 4m 2d; Hampshire F: Hockman, J.W. M: Hockman, M.J. B: Hampshire DOI: father B/P: 1/34

1469 Hockman, Diadem - white female D: Jan 29, 1881; 60y; Hampshire F: Daughtery, Valentine M: Daughtery, Mary B: Rockingham Co., Va DOI: husband C: Hockman, Philip B/P: 1/31

1470 Hockman, Frank - white male D: Oct 2, 1914; stillborn B/P: 2/48

1471 Hockman, Homer - white male D: Sept 21, 1914; stillborn B/P: 2/48

1472 Hockman, Nellie - white female D: Oct 30, 1900; 2m; Hampshire F: Hockman, H.M. M: Hockman, Maggie B: Sept 10, 1900 DOI: father B/P: 1/73

1473 Hockman, Philip - white male D: July 1, 1904; 80y B/P: 2/49

1474 Hockman, Z. - single white female D: Jan 31, 1894; 6y; near Slanesville B: Hampshire BUR: near Slanesville B/P: 1/84

1475 Hoffman, Mary A - white female D: Aug 27, 1877; Hampshire B: Hampshire DOI: husband C: Hoffman, Daniel B/P: 1/22

1476 Hoffman, N.W. - white female D: Nov 19, 1893; 63y; Hampshire B: Maryland I: Dicken, M.L. DOI: son in law B/P: 1/58

1477 Hoffman, Otilia - white female D: Jan 5, 1894; 6m; Mill Creek F: Hoffman, W.S. B: Mill Creek District DOI: father B/P: 1/59

1478 Hoke, Solomon - white male D: Aug 10, 1886; 82y; Hampshire B: Pennsylvania I: Wolf, Joseph DOI: son in law C: Hoke, Lydia B/P: 1/41

1479 Holt, Caroline - colored female D: May 12, 1885; 37y; Hampshire F: Holt, Daniel M: Holt, K. B: Hampshire DOI: husband C: Holt, Daniel B/P: 1/41

1480 Holt, Emma - colored female D: Aug 12, 1885; 1y 6m; Hampshire F: Holt, Dan M: Holt, Caroline B: Hampshire DOI: father B/P: 1/41

1481 Holt, Lucinda - colored female D: Mar 7, 1884; 14y 6m 9d; Hampshire F: Holt, Daniel M: Holt, Caroline B: Hampshire DOI: father B/P: 1/38

1482 Holt, Sarah - single black female D: Sept 1, 1902; 23y; Romney B: WV BUR: Romney B/P: 1/116

1483 Homelwright, May - white female D: May 10, 1894; 2y 4m; Capon District F: Homelwright, J. B: Capon DOI: father B/P: 1/59

1484 Homer, Eliza - white female D: Feb 14, 1906; 62y B/P: 2/45

1485 Hoodley, David - white male D: Mar 1903; 47y; Hampshire B: 1856 I: Fralix, Joseph DOI: friend B/P: 1/80

1486 Hook, A.M. - white male D: Aug 15, 1903; 60y; Capon Bridge I: Hook, Marion B/P: 1/81

1487 Hook, Charles - single white male D: Aug 1, 1873; 1y; Hampshire F: Hook, George M: Hook, Eliza B: Hampshire DOI: father B/P: 1/10

1488 Hook, Elizabeth A - white female D: Feb 4, 1880; 51y; Hampshire F: Leath, William M: Leath, Mary B: Hampshire DOI: husband C: Hook, Wm. S. B/P: 1/28

1489 Hook, Ira C. - white male D: Aug 24, 1885; 11m; Hampshire F: Hook, H.P. M: Hook, Mary V. B: Hampshire DOI: father B/P: 1/41

1490 Hook, Isaiah - married white male D: Mar 29, 1912; 72y B/P: 2/47 N: farmer

1491 Hook, Leslie R. - white female D: Oct 9, 1879; 5m 28d; Hampshire F: Hook, L.C. M: Hook, Hettie M B: Hampshire DOI: father B/P: 1/25

1492 Hook, Mary - white female D: Aug 26, 1886; 71y 10m 7d; Capon District B: Hampshire DOI: husband C: Hook, Robert B/P: 1/43

1493 Hook, Mary A. - white female D: Feb 1901; 66y; Hampshire I: Hook, D. B/P: 1/77

1494 Hook, Mary V. - white female D: 1908 B/P: 2/45

1495 Hook, Mary Virginia - widowed white female D: Jan 7, 1922; 73y 1m 7d; Hampshire F: Creswell, Jas. B: Hampshire DOI: father B/P: 1/133

1496 Hook, Retta M. - married white female D: Apr 17, 1909; 55y 19m B/P: 2/46

1497 Hook, Robt. - widower white male D: Nov 10, 1907; 74y 6m 21d B/P: 2/45

1498 Hook, Robt. N.K. - white male D: May 27, 1878; 15y 11m 21d; Hampshire F: Hook, R.W. M: Hook, M. B: Hampshire DOI: father B/P: 1/24

1499 Hook, Samuel - married white male D: June 17, 1876; 85y; Hampshire F: Hook, William M: Hook, Mary B: Hampshire I: Hook, William DOI: son C: Hook, Elizabeth B/P: 1/20

1500 Hook, Walter B. - white male D: Dec 1888; 14y; Capon District F: Hook, H.P. M: Hook, Mary B: Hampshire I: Hook, Robert DOI: grandfather B/P: 1/47

1501 Hook, Wm. S. - white male D: Jan 19, 1882; 58y; Hampshire F: Hook, S. M: Hook, A. B: Hampshire I: Leath, Jas. F. DOI: brother in law C: Hook, Amanda B/P: 1/34 N: farmer

1502 Horn, John - single white male D: Oct 12, 1908; 4y B/P: 2/46

1503 Horn, Walter - white male D: 1908; 8y B/P: 2/45

1504 Horn, Walter - white male D: Oct 11, 1909; 8y B/P: 2/46

1505 Horner, Harry Lee - single white male D: 1922; 18y 3m 15d; Hampshire F: Horner, W.A. M: Horner, Martha B: WV I: Lupton, Geo. A. B/P: 1/136

1506 Horner, Mary B - white female D: Oct 18, 1874; 25y 6m; Hampshire F: Horner, William M: Horner, Isabel B: Washington Co PA DOI: mother B/P: 1/12

1507 Horner, T.R. - white male D: Dec 23, 1898; 51y; Bloomery District F: Horner, Wm. I: Riley, R.F. DOI: friend B/P: 1/69

1508 Horner, William - white male D: Feb 4, 1874; 22y 3m 10d; B & O R Road F: Horner, William M: Horner, Isabel B: Washington Co PA DOI: mother B/P: 1/12

1509 Horner, Wm. E. - white male D: Feb 28, 1884; 9m; Hampshire F: Horner, Jos. M: Horner, Annie B: Hampshire DOI: father B/P: 1/39

1510 Horseman, William - white male D: June 10, 1872; 88y 5m 14d; Hampshire B: Fred. Co., VA I: Lupton, Rachel DOI: friend B/P: 1/9

1511 Hoss, Ella - widow white female D: Sept 5, 1918; 67y 6m; Hampshire B/P: 1/126 N: housewife

1512 Hott, Aaron Burr - married white male D: Nov 2, 1918; 33y; Hampshire B/P: 1/126 N: farmer

1513 Hott, Abigail - widowed white female D: Jan 1, 1922; 65y 5m 24d; Hampshire F: Heare, Elisha M: Heare, Matilda B: Hampshire I: Hott, G.D. B/P: 1/133

1514 Hott, Agnes Odella - white female D: Sept 7, 1898; 1y 2m 10d; Kirby B: Kirby BUR: Mountain Dale B/P: 1/101

1515 Hott, Albertie - white male D: Sept 1874; Hampshire F: Hott, David M: Hott, Mary A. B: Hampshire DOI: father B/P: 1/12

1516 Hott, Bertha - white female D: Mar 25, 1910; 40y B/P: 2/46

1517 Hott, Clora Rosalie - single white female D: Nov 17, 1910; 27y 7m 14d B/P: 2/46

1518 Hott, Daid - white male D: Feb 27, 1881; 72y; Hampshire B: Hampshire I: Hott, John F. DOI: son C: Hott, Malinda B/P: 1/29

1519 Hott, David - white male D: Aug 1, 1900; 74y; Hampshire B: 1826 I: Hott, David DOI: son B/P: 1/73

1520 Hott, E. - white female D: Nov 3, 1899; 24y; Bloomery District F: Abrell, L. M: Abrell, Sallie B: Nov 3, 1875 DOI: husband C: Hott, K.G. B/P: 1/70

1521 Hott, Edith - married white female D: Nov 3, 1899; 24y; Bloomery district B: Hampshire BUR: Sandy Ridge B/P: 1/109

1522 Hott, Elizabeth - single white female D: Mar 25, 1910; 55y B/P: 2/46

1523 Hott, Frances H. - married white female D: May 25, 1885; 25y 11m 5d; Hampshire F: Patterson, Silas M: Patterson, Martha B: Hampshire I: Patterson, Jas. DOI: uncle B/P: 1/42

1524 Hott, George - white male D: May 1, 1867; 98y 7m 4d; Caudys Castle B: Frederick Co., VA I: Hott, William DOI: nephew B/P: 1/2 N: farmer

1525 Hott, Grace Ann - white female D: May 14, 1891; 42y; Hampshire F: Heare, E.P. M: Heare, Matilda J. B: Hampshire DOI: husband C: Hott, William T. B/P: 1/53

1526 Hott, Harold Warfield - white male D: Oct 13, 1912; 4d B: Sherman District B/P: 2/47

1527 Hott, Hetzel Jr. - single white male D: Mar 19, 1921; stillborn F: Hott, Hetzel M: Hott, Lucy B: Hampshire B/P: 1/130

1528 Hott, Hetzel Madison - white male D: Jan 25, 1904; 25d B/P: 2/55

1529 Hott, Hunter Bill Wm. - white male D: Feb 22, 1908; 36y 2m 7d B/P: 2/45 N: school teacher

1530 Hott, Isaac - widower white male D: Nov 27, 1918; 78y; Hampshire B/P: 1/126 N: farmer

1531 Hott, James H. - married white male D: Nov 18, 1914; 62y 9m 14d B/P: 2/48 N: farmer

1532 Hott, James Warner - white male D: Nov 2, 1917; 23y 3m 4d B/P: 2/48

1533 Hott, Jas. Benton - single white male D: Jan 25, 1920; stillborn; Hampshire M: Hott, Myrtle B: Hampshire B/P: 1/129

1534 Hott, John - white male D: Aug 17, 1883; 70y; Hampshire F: Hott, Sam'l M: Hott, Barbara B: Hampshire I: Hott, Jno W. DOI: son in law C: Hott, Caroline B/P: 1/37 N: wagonmaker

1535 Hott, Laura B. - white female D: Feb 10, 1890; 4d; Romney District F: Hott, Benj F. M: Hott, Martha B: Hampshire DOI: father B/P: 1/52

1536 Hott, Leona M. - white female D: Oct 20, 1914; 3y 5m 5d B/P: 2/48

1537 Hott, Levi - white male D: Dec 21, 1901; 85y; I: Hott, K.G. B/P: 1/77

1538 Hott, Lina E. - white female D: Nov 9, 1882; 4y 1m 24d; Hampshire F: Hott, J.W. M: Hott, J. B: Hampshire DOI: father B/P: 1/34

1539 Hott, Luanda Catharine - married white female D: Mar 12, 1909; 47y B/P: 2/46

1540 Hott, Lucy R - single white female D: Dec 31, 1874; 15y; Hampshire F: Hott, Levi M: Hott, Sarah B: Hampshire DOI: father B/P: 1/12

1541 Hott, Malinda - widow white female D: Jan 1, 1903; 67y 10m 14d; Hampshire B: Hampshire BUR: Grassy Lick Church B/P: 1/114

1542 Hott, Malinda Myrtle - white female D: Feb 24, 1912; 13y 5m 1d B: Sherman District B/P: 2/47

1543 Hott, Margaret - married white female D: Sept 25, 1917;

71y 19d B/P: 2/48

1544 Hott, Mary A. - white female D: Feb 21, 1875; 45y; Hampshire F: Shanholtzer, John M: Shanholtzer, Eva B: Hampshire DOI: husband C: Hott, David B/P: 1/16

1545 Hott, Mary E. - white female D: July 28, 1915; 11m 11d B/P: 2/48

1546 Hott, Mary Elizabeth - white female D: June 18, 1915; 11m B/P: 2/48

1547 Hott, Mary Ellen - white female D: Nov 20, 1867; 19y 3m 27d; Sandy Ridge F: Hott, Levi M: Hott, Sarah B: Sandy Ridge DOI: father B/P: 1/2

1548 Hott, Mary Ellen - white female D: Sept 20, 1893; 4m; Hampshire F: Hott, D.G. M: Hott, Ellen B/P: 1/58

1549 Hott, Matilda - white female D: June 15, 1875; 7m; Hampshire F: Hott, David M: Hott, Caroline B: Hampshire DOI: father B/P: 1/14

1550 Hott, Mona I. - single white female D: Jan 25, 1920; stillborn M: Hott, Mona B: Shanks B/P: 1/129

1551 Hott, Mrs. - widow white female D: Oct 4, 1899; 84y; Glebe B: WV BUR: Glebe B/P: 1/108

1552 Hott, Sarah - colored female D: Aug 5, 1902; 23y; Romney District F: Hott, Dan B: 1880 I: Johnson, Job B/P: 1/78

1553 Hott, Sarah Frances - white female D: May 14, 1912; 68y 1m 5d B: Sherman District B/P: 2/47

1554 Hott, Sarah Josephine - white female D: Dec 15, 1914; 5y B/P: 2/48

1555 Hott, Sarah M. D: June 4, 1866; Grassy Lick F: Hott, J.F. M: Hott, Susan DOI: father B/P: 1/1

1556 Hott, Susan - single white female D: April 10,1866; 23y 6m F: Hott, George M: Hott, Maria B: Hampshire DOI: parent B/P: 1/1

1557 Hott, Victoria - single white female D: Nov 3, 1918; 8y 9m; Hampshire B/P: 1/126

1558 Hott, Vienna - white female D: Sept 2, 1894; 12y; Hampshire F: Hott, G.A. M: Hott, C. B: Hampshire DOI:

father B/P: 1/60

1559 Hott, Walter H.S. - single white male D: Aug 10, 1907; 5m 22d B/P: 2/45

1560 Hott, William T. - married white male D: May 19, 1916; 68y 2m 5d B: Sherman District B/P: 2/48 N: farmer

1561 Hott, Willis - white male D: Mar 6, 1913; 19y 5m 22d B/P: 2/47 N: farmer

1562 Hottinger, Noah - married white male D: May 21, 1914; 60y 10d B/P: 2/48 N: farmer

1563 Houies, Grace - white female D: 1906 B/P: 2/45

1564 House, Geo W D: June 20, 1871; 1y 1m 8d; F: House, Samuel M: House, Eliza B/P: 1/6

1565 Householder, Minerva J. - white female D: July 23, 1882; 1m 23d; Hampshire F: Householder, Thomas W. M: Householder, M.J. B: Hampshire DOI: father B/P: 1/34

1566 Householder, Minerva J. - white female D: May 30, 1882; 24y 7m 15d; Hampshire F: Barnes, J.P. M: Barnes, M. B: Hampshire DOI: husband C: Householder, Thomas W. B/P: 1/34

1567 Householder, Mrs. - married white female D: Feb 19, 1896; 82y; Hampshire B: Hampshire B/P: 1/88

1568 Householder, Robt. - widower white male D: Apr 28, 1897; 89y; near Slanesville B: Hampshire BUR: near Romney B/P: 1/92

1569 Houser, Geo. P. - single white male D: Apr 5, 1888; 35y; Romney District F: Houser, Geo. P. B: Hampshire I: Poling, J.W. DOI: brother in law B/P: 1/47 N: saddler

1570 Houser, Henry - widowed white male D: Nov 30,, 1922; 82y 6m 21d; Hampshire F: Houser, Geo Y. B: Romney I: Houser, J. G. B/P: 1/133

1571 Houser, Louisa H. - married white female D: Dec 9, 1917; 78y 2m 21d B/P: 2/48

1572 Houser, Susan L. - white female D: Aug 12, 1881; 1m 19d; Hampshire F: Houser, H.G. M: Houser, Louisa H. B: Hampshire DOI: father B/P: 1/30

1573 Howard, Cornelea Bell - married colord female D: Feb 2,

1917; 45y B/P: 2/48

1574 Howard, Mary D: June 18, 1870; 11y 6m F: Miller, Robinson B/P: 1/5

1575 Howdyshell, Hattie - white female D: June 29, 1877; Hampshire M: Howdyshell, Rebecca B: Upshur, WV I: Howdyshell, Geo DOI: grandfather B/P: 1/22

1576 Howdyshell, Mary - white female D: Mar 8, 1881; 88y; Hampshire B: Maryland I: Howdyshell, Geo DOI: son C: Howdyshell, Adam B/P: 1/29

1577 Howse, Dallas O. - single white male D: Dec 9, 1902; 1y 1m 1d; Hampshire B: Hampshire BUR: Mountain Dale B/P: 1/114

1578 Howse, Ruth A. - single white female D: Nov 27, 1902; 3y 8m 6d; Hampshire B: Hampshire BUR: Mountain Dale B/P: 1/114

1579 Hudson, Charles S. - white male D: Jan 14, 1883; 4y 11m; Hampshire F: Hudson, Robt B. M: Hudson, Caroline B: Hampshire DOI: father B/P: 1/37

1580 Huffman, Amos - married white male D: May 24, 1896; 80y 7m 1d; Kirby B: Hampshire BUR: Quaker Graveyard B/P: 1/90

1581 Huffman, Carmon - white female D: Jan 4, 1909; 2y B/P: 2/46 N: drowned

1582 Huffman, Daniel - white male D: Oct 17, 1888; 81y; Mill Creek District F: Huffman, C. M: Huffman, C. B: Germany I: Huffman J.V. DOI: son B/P: 1/47 N: wife deceased

1583 Huffman, Elijah - white male D: Feb 2, 1890; 52y; Mill Creek F: Huffman, Daniel M: Huffman, E. B: Mill Creek DOI: wife B/P: 1/49 N: farmer

1584 Huffman, Sallie T. - white female D: Oct 20, 1883; 14y; Hampshire F: Huffman, Elijah M: Huffman, Sarah E. B: Hampshire DOI: father B/P: 1/36

1585 Huffman, Sarah - white female D: Feb 1887; 70y; Sherman District B: Hardy County I: Swisher, B.F. DOI: friend C: Huffman, Amos B/P: 1/43

1586 Hugh, Ella - white female D: Apr 12, 1909; 48y 4m 27d B/P: 2/46

1587 Hurd, Geo. E. - white male D: June 2, 1900; Sherman F: Hurd, Robt M: Hurd, Mary B: June 1, 1900 DOI: father B/P:

1/72

1588 Hushman, Bessie - white female D: Oct 14, 1895; 25y; Capon District F: Kline, Lemnel M: Kline, A.C. B: Oct 1870 DOI: father B/P: 1/61

1589 Huskins, Chas. G.F. - single black male D: July 19, 1899; Romney B: Philadelphia BUR: Romney B/P: 1/110

1590 Hustere, Andrew - married white male D: Oct 8, 1906; 50y B/P: 2/45

1591 Hutson, Greddy D. - white male D: Oct 1889; 7m; Romney District F: Hutson, Daniel M: Hutson, May B: Romney District DOI: father B/P: 1/49

1592 Ichelberger, I. - white male D: Dec 15, 1886; 52y; Capon District B: Jefferson County I: Billings, Hobart DOI: father in law C: Ichelberger, Maria B/P: 1/43 N: preacher

1593 Iden, Johnathan - white male D: Mar 1876; 90y 3m 27d; Hampshire F: Iden, Jacob M: Iden, Elizabeth B: Loudoun Co., VA I: Loy, Benjamin DOI: son in law C: Iden, Catherine B/P: 1/20

1594 Iliff, Elias Harrison - widowed white male D: Dec 24, 1921; 89y 9m 11d; Hampshire F: Iliff, Wm. Furr M: Iliff, Bettie B: Hampshire B/P: 1/131 N: farmer

1595 Iliff, Elizabeth - white female D: Nov 30, 1881; 93y; Hampshire F: Iliff, Stephen M: Iliff, Hannah B: Hampshire I: Seeders, Mary DOI: daughter B/P: 1/31

1596 Iliff, Ida A. - married white female D: Nov 20, 1914; 30y B/P: 2/56

1597 Iliff, Margaret - white female D: Feb 1904; 58y B/P: 2/56

1598 Inskeep, Elizabeth Ellen - widow white female D: Nov 26, 1911; 80y 8m 17d B: Romney District B/P: 2/56

1599 Inskeep, Henry - single white male D: May 4, 1899; 32y; Baltimore B: Hampshire BUR: Romney B/P: 1/106 N: farmer

1600 Inskeep, Henry M - white male D: May 4, 1899; 31y; Baltimore F: Inskeep, Foreman M: Inskeep, Alverda DOI: brother B/P: 1/71

1601 Inskeep, Jas. - white male D: Mar 1, 1888; 63y 6m;

Hampshire B: Hampshire DOI: wife C: Inskeep, E.E. B/P: 1/45

1602 Inskeep, Jno. J. - married white male D: Feb 15, 1918; 73y 10m 29d; Hampshire B/P: 1/126

1603 Inskeep, John - white male D: May 10, 1868; 72y; Great Capon B: Virginia DOI: widow B/P: 1/3

1604 Inskeep, Susan E. - white female D: Nov 25, 1877; Hampshire F: Vance, William B: Hampshire I: Vance, John T DOI: son in law C: Inskeep, Macker B/P: 1/22

1605 Inskeep, Wm. V. - white male D: June 4, 1866; South Branch F: Inskeep, H.M. M: Inskeep, Susan B: South Branch DOI: brother B/P: 1/1

1606 Isenburg, Mary M. - white female D: Dec 28, 1907; 3y 10m B/P: 2/56

1607 Isenburg, Verda L. - white female D: Dec 28, 1907; 6y 3m B/P: 2/56

1608 Iser, Chas B. - white male D: 1876; 4y; Hampshire F: Iser, Robert J. M: Iser, Mary B: Maryland DOI: father B/P: 1/20

1609 Iser, Daisy B. - white female D: Aug 14, 1900; 5y; Hampshire F: Iser, Robt. M: Iser, Amanda B: 1895 I: Hair, Zelenna DOI: friend B/P: 1/73

1610 Iser, Elizabeth - white female D: May 27, 1888; 77y; Hampshire B: Hampshire DOI: husband C: Iser, Wm. B/P: 1/45

1611 Iser, Isaac - white male D: Apr 29, 1915; 55y B/P: 2/56

1612 Iser, Isaac - married white male D: Apr 30, 1915; 55y 5m 1d B/P: 2/56

1613 Iser, Isaac - white male D: Sept 27, 1919; 40y B/P: 2/56 N: farmer

1614 Iser, Jedson - married white male D: Jan 29, 1911; 25y B: Springfield District B/P: 2/56 N: farm work

1615 Iser, Mammie - single white female D: Mar 14, 1913; 23y 6m 5d B/P: 2/56

1616 Iser, Nancy - white female D: Mar 28, 1886; 35y;

Hampshire F: Iser, Geo W. M: Iser, Elizabeth B: Hampshire DOI: father B/P: 1/44

1617 Iser, Robert - married white male D: Apr 28, 1905; 60y B/P: 2/56 N: farmer

1618 Iser, Silas - widow white male D: July 15, 1910; 84y B/P: 2/56 N: farmer

1619 Iser, Viola - white female D: Sept 29, 1907; 11m 25d B/P: 2/56

1620 Jackson, Ebenezer - white male D: May 26, 1873; 60 y; Hampshire B: Loudoun Co I: Jackson, James DOI: brother B/P: 1/10

1621 Jackson, Geraldine - white female D: Feb 26, 1913; 10m B/P: 2/59

1622 Jackson, Jane - black female D: Nov 12, 1896; 78y; Romney BUR: Romney B/P: 1/94

1623 Jackson, Lucy - white female D: May 15, 1896; 8y 2m; Romney F: Jackson, M: Clark, Margaret B: June 15, 1888 DOI: father B/P: 1/62

1624 Jackson, Luther Henry - white male D: Feb 18, 1912; B/P: 2/59

1625 Jackson, Mary - colored female D: Sept 1890; 98y; Capon District F: Jackson, Benj B: Hampshire I: Masson, Emily DOI: daughter B/P: 1/52

1626 Jackson, Mary E. - married white female D: Mar 27, 1895; 70y; Capon District B: 1824 I: Jackson, Luther DOI: son B/P: 1/61

1627 Jackson, Mattie - colored female D: Mar 1892; 1y 2m; Hampshire F: Jackson, Clark M: Jackson, Martha A. B: Hampshire DOI: father B/P: 1/53

1628 Jackson, Nannie - single black female D: Feb 19, 1898; 16y 2m 13d; Romney B: Romney BUR: Romney B/P: 1/98

1629 Jackson, Nannie - white female D: Mar 10, 1896; 13y 4m; Romney F: Jackson, M: Clark, Margaret B: Nov 8, 1882 DOI: father B/P: 1/62

1630 Jackson, Solomon - colored male D: Jan 7, 1904; 14y 8m 7d B/P: 2/62

1631 Jackson, William A - white male D: Aug 4, 1874; 1y 11m; Hampshire F: Jackson, H. M: Jackson, Mary B: Hampshire DOI: father B/P: 1/12

1632 Jacques, Nancy - widow white female D: Dec 21, 1916; 85y 4m 6d B: Augusta B/P: 2/59

1633 Jarboe, Francis M. - single white male D: Dec 3, 1894; 70y; Romney, WV B: Hampshire BUR: Romney B/P: 1/82

1634 Jarboe, Rachel E. - white female D: Aug 4, 1901; 58y; Romney F: Hines, James M: Hines, Sallie DOI: husband C: Jarboe, John B/P: 1/76

1635 Jeffries, Jane - single white female D: Jan 6, 1916; 65y B: Springfield B/P: 2/59

1636 Jeffries, Martha H.A. - single white female D: Sept 15, 1879; 15y; Hampshire F: Jeffries, Alexander M: Jeffries, Ann B: Hampshire I: Jeffries, William DOI: brother B/P: 1/26

1637 Jenkins, Bertella - single white female D: May 24, 1907; 1y 8m 11d B/P: 2/59

1638 Jenkins, Loura - white female D: Apr 26, 1902; 20y; Hampshire F: Cowgill, William M: Cowgill, E. B: 1882 DOI: husband C: Jenkins, E. B/P: 1/79

1639 Jenkins, Moe - white female D: July 6, 1915; 36y B/P: 2/59

1640 Jewel, Jackson B. - white male D: Nov 20, 1876; 2y 2m 6d; Hampshire F: Jewel, John M: Jewel, Mary B: Hampshire DOI: father B/P: 1/18

1641 Jewel, John N. - white male D: Oct 10, 1890; 57y; Mill Creek B: Hampshire DOI: wife C: Jewel, M.A. B/P: 1/52 N: shoemaker

1642 Jewell, Danger - single white male D: Apr 25, 1908; 24y B/P: 2/59

1643 Jewell, Sarah - widow white female D: Oct 22, 1904; 54y B: Bloomery B/P: 2/59

1644 Johnson, Betsey - white female D: Mar 10, 1906; 83y 9m B/P: 2/59

1645 Johnson, Chas. O. - white male D: Sept 8, 1881; 11y;

Hampshire F: Johnson, J.H. M: Johnson, E.R. B: Hampshire DOI: father B/P: 1/30

1646 Johnson, Chas. S. - white male D: Mar 14, 1913; 53y B/P: 2/59 N: mechanic

1647 Johnson, Cora B. - white female D: Aug 16, 1886; Hampshire F: Johnson, Zac. M: Johnson, Rebecca B: Hampshire DOI: father B/P: 1/44

1648 Johnson, Edna - white female D: July 15, 1900; 7m; Hampshire F: Johnson, Davis M: Johnson, Martha B: Dec 10, 1899 DOI: father B/P: 1/73

1649 Johnson, Edward B. - white male D: Feb 1887; 22y; Capon District F: Johnson, Wm. S. M: Johnson, Caroline B: Hampshire DOI: father B/P: 1/43

1650 Johnson, Elias D: Oct 15, 1869; 58y; Hampshire B/P: 1/4

1651 Johnson, Elmira G. - white female D: Aug 3, 1883; 1y 12d; Hampshire F: Johnson, Joseph E. M: Johnson, E. B: Hampshire DOI: father B/P: 1/37

1652 Johnson, Evaline - colored female D: Feb 1892; 14d; Hampshire F: Johnson, Thomas M: Johnson, Mary B: Hampshire DOI: father B/P: 1/53

1653 Johnson, Francis C. - white female D: Apr 5, 1879; 31y 1m 11d; Hampshire F: Fletcher, Isaac M: Fletcher, Elizabeth B: Frederick Co VA DOI: husband C: Johnson, John E. B/P: 1/26

1654 Johnson, George B. - white male D: Sept 28, 1900; 32y; Hampshire F: Johnson, Zackaria M: Johnson, Rebecca B: Jan 8, 1863 DOI: wife C: Johnson, Laura B/P: 1/74

1655 Johnson, Harriet A.E. - white female D: Aug 29, 1874; 6d; Hampshire F: Johnson, Joseph M: Johnson, Elizabeth B: Hampshire DOI: father B/P: 1/12

1656 Johnson, Hattie - married white female D: Aug 13, 1902; 27y; Hampshire B: Hampshire BUR: Wesley Chapel B/P: 1/116

1657 Johnson, Howard H. - married white male D: Feb 8, 1913; 67y B/P: 2/59 N: teacher

1658 Johnson, Jane Kelsoe - white female D: Nov 1, 1904; 63y B/P: 2/59

1659 Johnson, John W. - white male D: Mar 15, 1875; 73y; Hampshire F: Johnson, Thomas M: Johnson, Jane B: Hampshire DOI: wife C: Johnson, Ellen B/P: 1/16

1660 Johnson, John W.T. - white male D: July 19, 1872; Hampshire F: Johnson, Joseph M: Johnson, Elizabeth B: Hampshire I: Largent, Moses DOI: grandfather B/P: 1/8

1661 Johnson, Joseph - white male D: Sept 1896; 59y; Hampshire B: 1839 I: Kline, Jno R. DOI: friend C: Johnson, L. B/P: 1/63

1662 Johnson, Josephine - colored female D: Mar 15, 1881; 7y; Hampshire F: Johnson, Jas. M: Johnson, Emily B: Hampshire DOI: father B/P: 1/30

1663 Johnson, Lucy - colored female D: Mar 19, 1905; 76y B/P: 2/59

1664 Johnson, Maggie - colored female D: April 30, 1868; 9m 3d; Romney F: Johnson, James B: Romney DOI: father B/P: 1/3

1665 Johnson, Malinda E. - married white female D: Jan 12, 1908; 66y 6m B/P: 2/59

1666 Johnson, Martha J. - white female D: July 11, 1880; 1m; Hampshire F: Johnson, Joseph E. M: Johnson, Elizabeth B: Hampshire DOI: mother B/P: 1/28

1667 Johnson, Mary - white female D: Sept 29, 1880; 94y; Hampshire F: Johnson, Israel M: Johnson, Mary B: Pennsylvania I: Johnson, Zack DOI: son C: 1/28

1668 Johnson, Mary Hardy - female D: Oct 22, 1919; B/P: 2/59

1669 Johnson, R.M. - married white male D: Dec 10, 1909; 71y 6m 10d B/P: 2/59 N: farmer

1670 Johnson, Rebecca - married white female D: Feb 2, 1907; 65y B/P: 2/59

1671 Johnson, Sarah - colored female D: Nov 19, 1876; 32y; Hampshire B: Hampshire DOI: husband C: Johnson, Henry B/P: 1/18

1672 Johnson, William - colored male D: July 1872; 1y 2m; Hampshire F: Johnson, James M: Johnson, Mary B: Hampshire

DOI: mother B/P: 1/9

1673 Johnson, Z.E. - married white male D: Aug 3, 1910; 40y 11m 9d B/P: 2/59 N: farmer

1674 Jones, Elmira - colored female D: 1881; Hampshire F: Jones, Jesse M: Jones, Elly B: Hampshire DOI: father B/P: 1/30

1675 Jones, Mahala - colored female D: 1881; Hampshire F: Jones, Jesse M: Jones, Elly B: Hampshire DOI: father B/P: 1/30

1676 Kackley, John R. - single D: Sept 12, 1909; 20y 6m 9d B/P: 2/63

1677 Kalb, Chas. William - white male D: Oct 15, 1919; 1y 19d B/P: 2/64

1678 Kave, Charles - single white male D: white male F: Apr 1906; 35y B/P: 2/63

1679 Kayler, Nicholas - white male D: Feb 20, 1888; 80y; Hampshire B: Hampshire I: Kayler, J. DOI: nephew B/P: 1/45

1680 Kaylor, A.J. - white male D: May 25, 1899; 72y; Gore District F: Kaylor, J. M: Kaylor, M. B: May 25, 1827 I: Kaylor, J.Wesley DOI: son B/P: 1/70

1681 Kaylor, Adam - married white male D: Sept 24, 1910; 72y B/P: 2/63 N: killed by a horse; farmer

1682 Kaylor, Andy - widower white male D: May 26, 1899; 65y; Spring Gap B: Hampshire BUR: Big Capon B/P: 1/106

1683 Kaylor, Chester - single white male D: Jan 16, 1919; 18y B/P: 2/64 N: farmer

1684 Kaylor, Delsie Edith - married white female D: Apr 16, 1917; 30y 8m B/P: 2/64

1685 Kaylor, E.A. - white male D: Apr 6, 1889; 68y; Hampshire B: Hampshire DOI: husband C: Kaylor, A.D. B/P: 1/51

1686 Kaylor, Eliza - white female D: Sept 29, 1914; 16y 6m 19d B/P: 2/64

1687 Kaylor, Elizabeth - white female D: Feb 1901; 65y; Hampshire I: Kaylor, Jno. B/P: 1/77

1688 Kaylor, John - white male D: Sept 14,1893; 87y 6m 15d; Hampshire I: Kaylor, John DOI: son B/P: 1/58

1689 Kaylor, John - married white male D: Nov 16, 1913; 75y B/P: 2/64

1690 Kaylor, Joseph - single white male D: Aug 3, 1904; 58y B/P: 2/63

1691 Kaylor, Josiah - white male D: Dec 3, 1876; 72y 11m 23d; Hampshire F: Kaylor, Andrew M: Kaylor, Alice B: Hampshire I: Kaylor, Miss DOI: daughter C: Kaylor, Mary B/P: 1/20

1692 Kaylor, Lucy J.M. - white female D: July 1, 1875; 12d; Hampshire F: Kaylor, John M: Kaylor, Sarah B: Hampshire DOI: mother B/P: 1/16

1693 Kaylor, Mary - white female D: Mar 12, 1874; 74y; Hampshire F: Shade, Jacob M: Shade, Sophia B: Hampshire DOI: husband C: Kaylor, Josiah B/P: 1/13

1694 Kaylor, Mary - white female D: June 8, 1914; 22y B/P: 2/64

1695 Kaylor, Mary E. - widow white female D: Nov 24, 1914; 74y B/P: 2/64

1696 Kaylor, Mary Ellen - single white female D: Feb 11, 1898; 28y 7m 26d; BUR: Wesley Chapel B/P: 1/98

1697 Kaylor, Mary L.B. - white female D: Mar 26, 1880; 2y 22d; Hampshire F: Kaylor, Andrew M: Kaylor, Catherine B: Hampshire DOI: mother B/P: 1/28

1698 Kaylor, Mrs. - married white female D: May 16, 1894; 50y; Spring Gap Mt. B: Hampshire BUR: Little Capon B/P: 1/84

1699 Kaylor, Richard - white male D: Oct 14, 1888; 75y; Hampshire B: Hampshire I: Kaylor, J. DOI: nephew B/P: 1/45

1700 Kaylor, Richard - single white male D: July 12, 1899; 60y; Spring Gap B: Hampshire BUR: Big Capon B/P: 1/105

1701 Kaylor, Richard - single white male D: Dec 1889; Hampshire B: Virginia B/P: 1/125

1702 Kearn, Iley - white male D: June 10, 1910; 14d B/P: 2/63

1703 Keckley, Myrtle Leona - white female D: Aug, 1911; 1y 1m B/P: 2/63

1704 Keister, Jeremiah - white male D: Apr 6, 1901; 72y; Augusta I: Keister, J.W. B/P: 1/76

1705 Keiter, Geo - white male D: July 15, 1884; 18y; Hampshire F: Keiter, George M: Keiter, Margaret B: Hampshire DOI: mother B/P: 1/39

1706 Keiter, George - white male D: Mar 28, 1880; 89y 9m 15d; Hampshire F: Keiter, Geo M: Keiter, Hester B: Hampshire DOI: wife C: Keiter, Margaret A. B/P: 1/28

1707 Keller, Beula May - single white female D: May 16, 1921; stillborn; Hampshire F: Keller, Joe M: Keller, Blanche B: Hampshire B/P: 1/130

1708 Keller, Cora - white female D: Nov 30, 1881; 3y; Hampshire F: Keller, R.B. M: Keller, Jane B: Hampshire DOI: father B/P: 1/30

1709 Keller, John - white male D: Apr 17, 1883; 8d; Hampshire F: Keller, John F. M: Keller, Alice B: Hampshire DOI: father B/P: 1/36

1710 Keller, Lena - white female D: Aug 27, 1908; 9y B/P: 2/63

1711 Keller, Margt. Ann - widow white female D: Aug 10, 1914; 90y 4m 4d B/P: 2/64

1712 Keller, Ray Maynard - single white male D: May 28, 1911; 1y 3m 14d B/P: 2/63

1713 Keller, Thos. A. - white male D: Dec 8, 1885; 65y; Hampshire F: Keller, Daniel M: Keller, Margaret B: Hampshire DOI: wife C: Keller, M.A. B/P: 1/41 N: hotel keeper

1714 Keller, Thos. A. - white male D: Oct 5, 1889; 7m 27d; Romney District F: Keller, Jos. S. M: Keller, Louisa E. B: Romney District DOI: father B/P: 1/49

1715 Keller, Velma Rosella - single white female D: Aug 28, 1907; 2y 8m B/P: 2/63

1716 Kelley, C.D. - white male D: Sept 1, 1888; 8m; Hampshire F: Kelley, Isaac M: Kelley, Lydia B: Hampshire DOI: father B/P: 1/45

1717 Kelley, E.E. - married white female D: Mar 9, 1895; 55y 1m 7d; Hampshire B: Hampshire B/P: 1/90

1718 Kelley, Elizabeth - married white female D: Oct 24, 1895; 48y; Hampshire B: Hampshire B/P: 1/90

1719 Kelley, Henrietta D: Apr 14, 1866 F: Kelly, Henry M: Kelly, Delina B: Mill Creek B/P: 1/1 N: Drown

1720 Kelley, Henry - white male D: Apr 14, 1866; South Branch B: Mill Creek I: Kelley, Delina B/P: 1/1 N: Drown

1721 Kelley, Jos. A. - widowed white male D: Mar 25, 1922; 78y 5m 3d; Hampshire F: Kelley, Larken M: Kelley, Fannie B: Augusta, WV I: Racey, B.T. B/P: 1/134 N: farmer

1722 Kelley, Lucy - married white female D: Dec 15, 1921; 68y 7m 15d; Hampshire F: Shoemaker, Wm. M: Shoemaker, Sallie B: WV I: Funkhouser, Gertie B/P: 1/131 N: housewife

1723 Kelley, Mary M. - white female D: Feb 3, 1909; 68y B/P: 2/63 N: housekeeper

1724 Kelley, Thos - white male D: July 30, 1892; 82y; Hampshire B: Ireland I: Kelley, I.P. DOI: son B/P: 1/57

1725 Kelley, Thos W. - white male D: Feb 28, 1882; 33y; Hampshire F: Kelley, F. M: Kelley, R. B: Hampshire DOI: father B/P: 1/34

1726 Kelley, Wm. G. - white male D: Dec 15, 1908; 56y B/P: 2/63

1727 Kelly, Resina - white female D: May 5, 1878; 66y; Hampshire F: Smith, Peter M: Smith, Sarah DOI: husband C: Kelly, Thomas B/P: 1/24

1728 Kelly, Wade - white male D: Aug 18, 1894; 6m; Mill Creek District F: Kelly, George B: Mill Creek DOI: father B/P: 1/59

1729 Kelso, Cordelia J. - white female D: Nov 16, 1881; 15y 20d; Hampshire F: Kelso, Jas F. M: Kelso, Hannah B: Hampshire DOI: father B/P: 1/30

1730 Kelso, Eliza - single white female D: Dec 18, 1883; 59y; Hampshire F: Kelso, Jas. B: Hampshire I: Kelso, Jas. F. DOI: brother B/P: 1/36

1731 Kelso, Harvy - white male D: Nov 7, 1881; 8y; Hampshire

F: Kelso, Jas. F. M: Kelso, Hannah B: Hampshire DOI: father B/P: 1/30

1732 Kelso, Louella B. - white female D: Oct 30, 1881; 12y; Hampshire F: Kelso, Jas. F. M: Kelso, Hannah B: Hampshire DOI: father B/P: 1/30

1733 Kelsoe, James F. - white male D: Oct 31, 1904; 69y B/P: 2/63

1734 Kendall, Martha A - white female D: Mar 30, 1873; 52y; Hampshire F: Pattie, William M: Pattie, Elanor B: Farquier Co VA DOI: mother C: Kendall, Wm. R. B/P: 1/11

1735 Kendall, W.R. - widower white male D: Mar 19, 1888; 72y; Little Capon B: South Carolina BUR: Hampshire B/P: 1/123 N: Doctor

1736 Kenney, John - married white male D: Feb 4, 1908; 50y B/P: 2/63 N: farmer

1737 Kenney, Patrick - married white male D: Jan 8, 1913; 80y B/P: 2/64 N: farmer

1738 Kenny, Mrs. J.W. - married white female D: Mar 15, 1900; Springfield BUR: Springfield B/P: 1/109

1739 Kent, Paty - black female D: Feb 24, 1898; 90y; Romney B: VA BUR: Romney B/P: 1/95

1740 Kerfoot, Mattie - single black female D: Jan 20, 1900; 45y; North River B: Hampshire BUR: North River B/P: 1/105

1741 Kern, Geo W. - single D: Aug 4, 1871; 28y 2m F: Kern, Jas M: Kern, Eliza B/P: 1/6

1742 Kern, Jas P. - white male D: Nov 12, 1876; 1m 7d; Hampshire F: Kern, Stewart G M: Kern, Mary J. B: Hampshire DOI: father B/P: 1/20

1743 Kern, Jno R. - white male D: Sept 13, 1881; 35y 7m 26d; Hampshire F: Kern, Jonah M: Kern, Eliza B: Hampshire DOI: father B/P: 1/31

1744 Kern, Jno W. - white male D: July 9, 1883; 1y 3m 17d; Hampshire F: Kern, Jno S. M: Kern, Mary F. B: Hampshire DOI: father B/P: 1/37

1745 Kern, Mahlon H. - white male D: Dec 11, 1880; 16y 25d; Hampshire F: Kern, Stewart M: Kern, Mary B: Hampshire DOI:

father B/P: 1/28

1746 Kern, Nancy - white female D: May 23, 1881; 66y 8m; Hampshire F: Chilcott, Abner M: Chilcott, Priscilla B: Hampshire DOI: husband C: Kern, Edward B/P: 1/31

1747 Kern, Nellie F. - white female D: May 15, 1888; 10m 5d; Capon District F: Kern, J.M. M: Kern, Annie B: Hampshire DOI: father B/P: 1/47

1748 Kern, Verdie M. - white female D: 14 Aug 1878; 2d; Hampshire F: Kern, Jasper W. M: Kern, M.A. DOI: father B/P: 1/24

1749 Kernes, Rebecca - white female D: Nov 6, 1891; 54y; Hampshire F: Boxwell, Aron M: Boxwell, Diana B: Hampshire DOI: husband C: Kernes, Isaac B/P: 1/55

1750 Kerns, Albert - white male D: Mar 4, 1902; 23y; Hampshire F: Kerns, K. M: Kerns, Mary B: 1879 DOI: father B/P: 1/79

1751 Kerns, Anna - single white female D: May 4, 1918; stillborn; Hampshire B/P: 1/126

1752 Kerns, Elizabeth - married white female D: June 16, 1910; 106y B/P: 2/63

1753 Kerns, Ellen E. - white female D: Oct 28, 1899; 11m 10d; Bloomery District F: Kerns, S.E. M: Kerns, M.F. B: Nov 14, 1898 DOI: father B/P: 1/70

1754 Kerns, Ephraim - white male D: Jan 14, 1896; 84y; Hampshire B: 1812 I: Kerns, A. DOI: son C: Kerns, Sarah B/P: 1/63 N: veterinarian

1755 Kerns, Geo. W. - white male D: Dec 5, 1910; 77y B/P: 2/63

1756 Kerns, Geo. W. - white male D: Dec 26, 1913; 24y B/P: 2/64

1757 Kerns, George - white male D: Mar 24, 1885; 86y; Hampshire B: Hampshire DOI: wife B/P: 1/42

1758 Kerns, I.B. - white female D: June 15, 1915; 3m 7d B/P: 2/64

1759 Kerns, Isaac - white male D: July 16, 1872; 73y; Hampshire F: Kerns, John M: Kerns, Elizabeth B: Hampshire

I: Kerns, Sanford DOI: son C: Kerns, Elizabeth B/P: 1/8

1760 Kerns, James R. - white male D: Feb 27, 1915; 3d B/P: 2/64

1761 Kerns, Jasper W. - married white male D: May 19, 1911; 71y B: Bloomery District B/P: 2/64 N: farmer

1762 Kerns, John - married white male D: July 13, 1909; 77y B/P: 2/63 N: farmer

1763 Kerns, L.E. - white female D: July 4, 1889; 18d; Hampshire M: Kerns, Mary E. B: Hampshire DOI: mother B/P: 1/51

1764 Kerns, Leonard - single white male D: Feb 14, 1910; 14y B/P: 2/63

1765 Kerns, Lydia - married white female D: Dec 25, 1897; 42y; Bloomery B: Frederick County, VA BUR: Bloomery B/P: 1/97

1766 Kerns, Lydia - white female D: Dec 24, 1897; 42y 7m 14d; Bloomery F: Dailey B: May 10, 1853 DOI: husband C: Kerns, R.W. B/P: 1/66

1767 Kerns, Mary - married white female D: May 8, 1907; 75y B/P: 2/63

1768 Kerns, Mary E. - white female D: Apr 16, 1903; 70y; Hampshire F: Hartley B: 1833 DOI: husband C: Kerns, F. B/P: 1/80

1769 Kerns, Mary Louise - widowed white female D: Aug 19, 1917; 75y 2m 11d B/P: 2/64

1770 Kerns, Rebecca L - white female D: Jan 13, 1874; 73y; Hampshire B: VA I: Kern, Lou M DOI: daughter C: Kern, John Jr. B/P: 1/12

1771 Kerns, Rosetta - white female D: July 19, 1905; 21y B/P: 2/63

1772 Kerns, Sarah E. - white female D: Aug 1894; 3y; Hampshire F: Kerns, T.G. M: Kerns, F.A. B: Hampshire DOI: father B/P: 1/60

1773 Kerny, Chas. M. - white male D: Nov 13, 1922; 4m; Hampshire F: Kerny, Jno. M: Kerny, Mattie B: Maryland DOI: father B/P: 1/134

1774 Kessler, Mary - white female D: Jan 11, 1882; 82y 6m 9d; Hampshire F: Jennings, B: Pennsylvania I: Seaders, Charlotte DOI: daughter C: Kessler, Thomas B/P: 1/34

1775 Ketterman, S.A.O. - married white male D: Apr 14, 1922; 70y 3m 25d; Hampshire F: Ketterman, Evan M: Ketterman, Elsie B: Highland Co., VA I: Ketterman, Tabitha B/P: 1/134

1776 Keys, Foreman - single black male D: Sept 12 1897; 22y; Romney BUR: Romney B/P: 1/94

1777 Keys, Mattie - colored female D: April 1882; 13y; Romney F: Keys, Charles M: Keys, Sarah B: WV DOI: father B/P: 1/33

1778 Keys, Sarah - married colored female D: Aug 15, 1876; 40y 2m; Hampshire B: Hampshire DOI: husband C: Keys, Chas B/P: 1/18

1779 Keyser, Lillian - white female D: Oct 30, 1904; 11y 6m B: Bloomery District B/P: 2/63

1780 Kickley, Rumsey O. - white male D: Sept 1904; 2y B/P: 2/63

1781 Kickly, Elizabeth - single white female D: Oct 13, 1899; 65y 8m; Capon Bridge B: Hampshire BUR: Capon Chapel B/P: 1/110 N: school teacher

1782 Kidd, Sam'l B D: Apr 10, 1870; 28y F: Kidd, James B/P: 1/5

1783 Kidwell, A. - white male D: Dec 30, 1899; 6m 7d; Springfield District F: Kidwell, Wade M: Kidwell, M. B: June 23, 1899 DOI: father B/P: 1/70

1784 Kidwell, Anna - married white female D: Feb 16, 1908; 70y B/P: 2/63

1785 Kidwell, Belle - widow white female D: Aug 1, 1910; 50y B/P: 2/63

1786 Kidwell, Benj F. - white male D: Dec 25, 1883; 7y 8m; Hampshire F: Kidwell, Jos M. M: Kidwell, Cordelia B: Hampshire DOI: father B/P: 1/37

1787 Kidwell, Benjamin Frankli - white male D: Nov 1, 1867; 40y 9m 25d; Critton Valley F: Kidwell, Hawkins M: Kidwell, Nancy B: Hampshire DOI: wife C: Kidwell, Mahala B/P: 1/2

1788 Kidwell, Chas H. - white male D: Mar 6, 1884; 1m 16d; Hampshire F: Kidwell, R.S. M: Kidwell, Sarah B: Hampshire DOI: father B/P: 1/39

1789 Kidwell, Connard - single white male D: Nov 1, 1921; 3y 4m 25d; Hampshire F: Kidwell, Wade M: Kidwell, Margary B: Hampshire B/P: 1/131

1790 Kidwell, D.P. - white female D: Sept 30, 1899; 8y 10m 27d; Bloomery District F: Kidwell, R.H. M: Kidwell, R.F. B: Nov 3, 1890 DOI: father B/P: 1/70

1791 Kidwell, Elga - white male D: Jan 19, 1913; 27y B/P: 2/64

1792 Kidwell, Elizabeth - white female D: Dec 10, 1911; 80y 10m B/P: 2/63

1793 Kidwell, Ellen - widow white female D: Dec 7, 1909; B/P: 2/63

1794 Kidwell, Evan H. - single white male D: Feb 6, 1920; 73y 6m 22d; Hampshire F: Kidwell, Sam'l M: Kidwell, Nancy B: Sandy Ridge I: Kidwell, Julia B/P: 1/129 N: farmer

1795 Kidwell, F.M. - white male D: Aug 30, 1899; 53y 16d; Bloomery District F: Kidwell, J. M: Kidwell, R. B: Aug 14, 1846 DOI: wife C: Kidwell, Belle B/P: 1/70

1796 Kidwell, Frank - married white male D: Aug 28, 1899; 45y; Higginsville B: Hampshire BUR: Slanesville B/P: 1/105 N: farmer

1797 Kidwell, Guy E. - single white male D: Dec 17, 1902; 8d; Slanesville B: Hampshire BUR: North River B/P: 1/116

1798 Kidwell, Hawkins - married white male D: Feb 15, 1895; 65y; Sideling Hill B: Hampshire BUR: North River B/P: 1/83

1799 Kidwell, James - white male D: Sept 14, 1879; 76y; Hampshire B: Hampshire DOI: wife C: Kidwell, Elizabeth B/P: 1/26

1800 Kidwell, Jas - married white male D: June 13, 1895; 75y; Hampshire B: Hampshire B/P: 1/88

1801 Kidwell, Jno - married white male D: June 30, 1897; 70y; North River B: Hampshire BUR: North River at J. Kidwell B/P: 1/92

1802 Kidwell, John - white male D: June 30, 1897; 76y; Bloomery M: Hawkins, Nacy B: 1821 I: Kidwell, A. DOI: son C: Kidwell, M. B/P: 1/66

1803 Kidwell, Joseph E. - white male D: June 28, 1914; 3m 25d B/P: 2/64

1804 Kidwell, Mary - white female D: Jan 13, 1922; 70y 7m 26d; Hampshire F: Kidwell, Johnathan M: Kidwell, Ann B: WV I: Kaylor, Estella M. B/P: 1/134

1805 Kidwell, Mary - white female D: Sept 4, 1899; 67y; Bloomery District F: Duncan, Conrad M: Duncan, Money B: Sept 4, 1832 I: Kidwell, L.W. DOI: son B/P: 1/70

1806 Kidwell, Mary - widow white female D: May 8, 1907; 80y B/P: 2/63

1807 Kidwell, Mrs. - widow white female D: Sept 19, 1913; 93y B/P: 2/64

1808 Kidwell, Mrs. Jas. - widow white female D: Sept 4, 1899; 65y; Slanesville B: Hampshire BUR: Slanesville B/P: 1/105

1809 Kidwell, Nancy - white female D: Aug 23, 1879; 9d; Hampshire F: Kidwell, Joseph M: Kidwell, Cordelia B: Hampshire DOI: father B/P: 1/26

1810 Kidwell, Nancy - married white female D: Mar 12, 1903; 81y 6m; Hampshire B: Hampshire BUR: Slanesville B/P: 1/115

1811 Kidwell, Oscar - white male D: June 1900; 1y; Hampshire F: Kidwell, Wade M: Kidwell, Margary B: June 1899 I: Cudwell, G.B. DOI: grandfather B/P: 1/73

1812 Kidwell, Pauline - white female D: Jan 10, 1917; stillborn B/P: 2/64

1813 Kidwell, Porter - single white male D: Mar 29, 1897; 23y; near Higginsville B: Hampshire BUR: Union B/P: 1/92

1814 Kidwell, Rebecca - married white female D: May 17, 1963; 47y B/P: 2/63

1815 Kidwell, Sarah E. - white female D: June 20, 1900; 48y; Hampshire F: Kidwell, S.A. B: 1852 DOI: father B/P: 1/73

1816 Kidwell, Sarah E. - white female D: July 20, 1901; 48y; Hampshire F: Kidwell, S. DOI: father B/P: 1/77

1817 Kiester, Dailey W. - white male D: Sept 25, 1915; 5m 24d B/P: 2/64

1818 Kine, Freda - white female D: Nov 13, 1914; 14d B/P: 2/64

1819 King, M. - widower white male D: Nov 1, 1904; 75y B/P: 2/63 N: farmer

1820 King, Mary - white female D: Aug 13, 1892; 56y; Hampshire B: Hampshire DOI: husband C: King, M. B/P: 1/57

1821 King, Michael - white male D: Apr 23, 1913; 43y B/P: 2/64 N: killed by train

1822 King, Reasin D: June 12, 1871; 77y 6m 6d; F: King, William M: King, Susan C: King, Elizabeth B/P: 1/6

1823 King, Wm. - married white male D: June 24, 1897; 75y; Jersey Mt. B: Hampshire BUR: Jersey Mt. B/P: 1/92

1824 Kinkad, Martha - white female D: June 1, 1894; 57y; Hampshire B: England DOI: husband C: Kinkad, Hugh B/P: 1/60

1825 Kinkaid, Hugh - white male D: June 2, 1922; 89y; Hampshire F: Kinkaid, John B: Ireland I: Fields, Anna B/P: 1/134 N: farmer

1826 Kirby, Harriet J. - married white female D: July 4, 1896; 27y 5m 29d; Kirby B: Hardy County BUR: Grassy Lick Church B/P: 1/90

1827 Klienchalaw, Christina - white female D: Mar 11, 1882; 69y 10m 21d; Hampshire F: Mills, C. M: Mills, E. B: Maryland DOI: husband C: Kleinchalaw, Otto B/P: 1/34

1828 Kline, Abraham - single white male D: July 16, 1866; 4y 6m; Hampshire F: Kline, Joseph M: Kline, Rebecca B: Hampshire DOI: parent B/P: 1/1

1829 Kline, Benjamin - white male D: Oct 29, 1909; 60y 10m 5d B/P: 2/63 N: farmer

1830 Kline, Birdie R. - white female D: Apr 19, 1881; 10m; Hampshire F: Kline, Benj F. M: Kline, Susan J. B: Hampshire DOI: father B/P: 1/29

1831 Kline, Catherine - white female D: Feb 1887; 93y; Capon

District B: Hampshire I: Spaid, Wm. M. DOI: grandson C: Kline, Jacob B/P: 1/43

1832 Kline, Chas. W. - white male D: Oct 1886; 1y 5m 17d; Hampshire F: Kline, Steven M: Kline, Mary B: Hampshire DOI: father B/P: 1/44

1833 Kline, Christernia - white female D: Dec 13, 1872; 72 y; Hampshire B: Frederick Co VA I: Kline, George C: Kline, Wm. B/P: 1/9

1834 Kline, David W. - white male D: Jan 6, 1875; 3m 15d; Hampshire F: Kline, David W. M: Kline, Margaret B: Hampshire DOI: father B/P: 1/14

1835 Kline, Drusella D: May 25, 1870; 20m F: Kline, John B/P: 1/5

1836 Kline, Hannah - married white female D: Jan 26, 1908; 54y B/P: 2/63

1837 Kline, Henry - white male D: Aug 10, 1888; 74y; Hampshire B: Hampshire I: Kline, A.J. DOI: son C: Kline, C. B/P: 1/45

1838 Kline, Isaac N. - white male D: Mar 17, 1885; 17y; Hampshire F: Kline, S.F. M: Kline, Sarah B: Hampshire DOI: father B/P: 1/41

1839 Kline, Jacob - white male D: Oct 13, 1875; 67y; Hampshire F: Kline, Abraham M: Kline, Mary B: Hampshire I: Kline, Joseph DOI: son B/P: 1/14 N: farmer

1840 Kline, Jennings Bryan - white male D: Aug 19, 1897; 4m; Capon District F: Kline, Asa M: Kline, Jamima B: Capon District DOI: father B/P: 1/64

1841 Kline, Joseph - white male D: Apr 18, 1897; 67y; Gore F: Kline, B: 1830 DOI: wife C: Kline, Catherine B/P: 1/66

1842 Kline, Joseph - white male D: Nov 14, 1914; 88y B/P: 2/64

1843 Kline, Kate S. - white female D: June 1889; 22y; Piedmont, WV F: Rudolph, Jacob C. M: Rudolph, Cora E. B: Capon District DOI: father C: Kline, Frank B/P: 1/50

1844 Kline, Laura - white female D: July 12, 1889; 23y; Capon District F: Kline, Asa M: Kline, Rebecca B: Capon District DOI: father B/P: 1/49

1845 Kline, Margaret R. - white female D: Oct 17, 1881; 55y; Hampshire B: Hampshire DOI: husband C: Kline, Asa B/P: 1/30

1846 Kline, Margaret - white female D: June 8, 1914; 78y B/P: 2/64

1847 Kline, Matilda - white female D: May 19, 1911; B: Mill District B/P: 2/64

1848 Kline, Minnie M - white female D: Mar 7, 1880; 1y 9m 2d; Hampshire F: Kline, Evan B: Hampshire DOI: father B/P: 1/27

1849 Kline, Philip - white male D: June 19, 1890; 83y; Capon District B: Hampshire I: Creswell, C.W. DOI: grandson B/P: 1/52

1850 Kline, Philip - white male D: Feb 3, 1885; 9y; Hampshire F: Kline, S.F. M: Kline, Sarah B: Hampshire DOI: father B/P: 1/41

1851 Kline, Philip - white male D: June 22, 1901; 77y; Capon I: Kline, Ann R. B/P: 1/76

1852 Kline, Prudy - married white female D: Sept 10, 1909; 44y B/P: 2/63

1853 Kline, Rebecca - white female D: Nov 30, 1895; 67y; Sherman District B: Nov 1823 DOI: husband C: Kline, J.J. B/P: 1/61

1854 Kline, Stephen - married white male D: Feb 16, 1908; 88y 5m 28d B/P: 2/63 N: blacksmith

1855 Knippenberg, E. - white female D: Feb 23, 1888; 65y 4m 20d; Hampshire F: Heniebrick, Henry DOI: husband C: Knippenberg, H. B/P: 1/45

1856 Kremer, A.J. - white male D: Nov 27, 1908; 84y B/P: 2/63

1857 Kremer, Mary M - white female D: June 1872; 7 y; Hampshire F: Kremer, Andrew M: Kremer, Elizabeth B/P: 1/9

1858 Kremer, Susan - white female D: July 3, 1877; Hampshire I: Poling, M.T. DOI: overseer of poor B/P: 1/22

1859 Krouse, Gerty Belle - single white female D: Jan 29,

1922; 18y 10m 6d; Hampshire F: Drouse, C. M: Krouse, Ella B: Virginia I: Krouse, Lee B/P: 1/134

1860 Kump, Daisy B. - white female D: Nov 6, 1874; 10d; Hampshire F: Kump, Richard M: Kump, Mary C. B: Hampshire DOI: father B/P: 1/12

1861 Kump, Julia A. - white female D: Aug 8, 1891; 80y; Hampshire F: Earles, Jno. M: Earles, Mary B: Shenandoah County I: Kump, H. DOI: daughter B/P: 1/55

1862 Kump, Julia A. - white female D: June 26, 1890; 84y; Capon District B: Hampshire I: Kump, S.J. DOI: daughter in law B/P: 1/52

1863 Kump, Mary C.E. - white female D: Oct 13, 1889; 42y; Capon District F: Lineburg, Jno M: Lineburg, Barbara B: Capon District DOI: husband C: Kump, R.P. B/P: 1/49

1864 Kump, Samuel J. - white male D: Oct 18, 1896; 52y; Capon District F: Kump, Jacob B: Oct 13, 1843 I: Pugh, George B/P: 1/62

1865 Kuykendall Wm. V. D: Nov 14, 1869; 18y 2m; Hampshire F: Kuykendall, Wm B: Hampshire B/P: 1/4

1866 Kuykendall, Elizabeth D. - white female D: May 14, 1911; 2y 14d B/P: 2/64

1867 Kuykendall, H.L. - white female D: Apr 7, 1889; 73y; I: Kuykendall, J.L. DOI: friend B/P: 1/51

1868 Kuykendall, Hannah - widow white female D: Apr 7, 1889; 74y; South Branch Station B: Virginia BUR: Springfield B/P: 1/125

1869 Kuykendall, Isaac - white male D: Nov 29, 1909; 69y B/P: 2/63 N: farmer

1870 Kuykendall, James - white male D: Apr 8, 1873; 56y 5m 22d; Hampshire F: Kuykendall, Isaac M: Kuykendall, Jane B: Hampshire I: Taylor, Isaac DOI: son in law C: Kuykendall, Hannah L. B/P: 1/11 N: farmer

1871 Kuykendall, Tho. M. - white male D: Sept 5, 1886; 11m 5d; Hampshire F: Kuykendall, Thos. M: Kuykendall, Catherine B: Hampshire DOI: father B/P: 1/44

1872 Kuykendall, W.F. - white male D: Nov 1890; 1m; Romney District F: Kuykendall, Wm. M: Kuykendall, H.C. B: Hampshire

DOI: father B/P: 1/52

1873 Kuykendall, William - married white male D: Nov 9, 1898; 46y; Romney District F: Kuykendall, James I: Kuykendall, Michael DOI: son B/P: 1/68

1874 Kuykendall, William - married white male D: Nov 11, 1898; 42y; Glebe B: WV BUR: Burlington B/P: 1/100

1875 Laer, Sarah F. - single white female D: Feb 5, 1908; 19y 6m B/P: 2/68

1876 Lafollet, - female D: 1877 B/P: 1/22

1877 Lafollette, Amos - widower white male D: Feb 10, 1890; 79y; Capon District B: Capon District I: Lafollette, E.E. DOI: son B/P: 1/49

1878 Lafollette, Asbury C. - married white male D: Sept 5, 1908; 63y B/P: 2/68 N: farmer

1879 Lafollette, Caroline - white female D: July 5, 1893; 70y; Hampshire B/P: 1/58

1880 Lafollette, Elizabeth - white female D: May 29, 1882; 45y; Capon District F: Spaid, Hiram B: WV DOI: husband C: Lafollette, John B/P: 1/33

1881 Lafollette, Elra S - single white male D: Aug 30, 1917; 36y 10m 4d B/P: 2/69

1882 Lafollette, Even - single white male D: Apr 15, 1873; 18m; Hampshire F: Lafollette, E.E. M: Lafollette, Mary B: Hampshire DOI: father B/P: 1/10

1883 Lafollette, Mary E. - white female D: July 10, 1874; 31y 11m; Hampshire B: Hampshire DOI: husband C: Lafollette, E.E. B/P: 1/12

1884 Lambert, Adam H - white male D: Sept 24, 1877; Hampshire F: Lambert, Ben B: Pendleton DOI: father B/P: 1/22

1885 Lambert, Mary - widow white female D: Feb 24, 1907; 74y 6m 18d B/P: 2/68

1886 Lambert, Mary Jane - widow white female D: June 11, 1888; 48y; Romney BUR: Romney B/P: 1/122

1887 Landacre, Joseph - married white male D: Aug 14, 1888; 64y; Hardy County B: Hardy County BUR: Hardy County B/P:

1/123

1888 Landacre, Nora - white female D: July 4, 1909; 1y 3m B/P: 2/68

1889 Landes, Melvin - single white male D: Sept 11, 1922; 14y; Hampshire F: Landes, Abraham M: Landes, Mary B: Grant County DOI: father B/P: 1/134

1890 Largent, Ann M - white female D: July 18, 1873; 6y 1m 18d; Hampshire F: Largent, Thomas A M: Largent, Martha B: Hampshire DOI: father B/P: 1/11

1891 Largent, Asberry - married white male D: Sept 19, 1921; 75y 5m 10d; Hampshire F: Largent, Mose B: WV B/P: 1/131

1892 Largent, C.C. - white male D: Sept 5, 1899; 1y 3m; Gore District F: Largent, J.R. M: Largent, M.B. B: Sept 2, 1898 DOI: father B/P: 1/70

1893 Largent, Cassander - white female D: July 5, 1881; 64y 1m 22d; Hampshire F: Largent, Jno M: Largent, Margaret B: Hampshire DOI: husband C: Largent, Sam'l B/P: 1/31

1894 Largent, Chas B. - white male D: Apr 5, 1901; 12y; Hampshire F: Largent, T.S. DOI: father B/P: 1/77

1895 Largent, Chas. L. - married white male D: July 31, 1922; 54y 4m 25d; Hampshire F: Largent, Aaron M: Largent, Jane B: Frederick County, VA I: Largent, R.D. B/P: 1/134

1896 Largent, E.B. - white female D: Dec 22, 1899; 6y 2m 5d; Springfield District F: Largent, S.H. M: Largent, S.D. B: Oct 7, 1893 DOI: mother B/P: 1/70

1897 Largent, Elizabeth M. - white female D: July 12, 1881; 1y 1m 17d; Hampshire F: Largent, Arthur M: Largent, Ida V. B: Nebraska I: Largent, Elizabeth DOI: grandmother B/P: 1/31

1898 Largent, Etta B. - white female D: Nov 1879; 4m; Hampshire F: Largent, Geo W. M: Largent, Mary F. B: Hampshire DOI: father B/P: 1/26

1899 Largent, Frona - married white female D: June 12, 1910; 26y B/P: 2/68

1900 Largent, G.B. - white male D: Sept 22, 1892; 22y; Hampshire F: Largent, J.A. M: Largent, S.E. B: Hampshire DOI: father B/P: 1/57

1901 Largent, G.W. - white male D: Sept 27, 1892; 29y; Hampshire B: Hampshire DOI: wife C: Largent, M. B/P: 1/57

1902 Largent, George R. - white male D: Feb 14, 1874; 8m 14d; Hampshire F: Largent, Randolph M: Largent, Sarah E. B: Hampshire DOI: father B/P: 1/13

1903 Largent, Grover - single white male D: Feb 8, 1906; 18y B/P: 2/68

1904 Largent, Grover C. - white male D: Feb 8, 1905; 18y B/P: 2/72

1905 Largent, Ida V. - white female D: Nov 12, 1881; 22y; Hampshire F: Bannon, Bushrod M: Bannon, E. B: Frederick Co., VA I: Largent, Elizabeth DOI: mother in law C: Largent, Arthur B/P: 1/31

1906 Largent, J.W.C. - white male D: July 17, 1886; 59y 8m 20d; Hampshire B: Hampshire DOI: wife C: Largent, Sarah J. B/P: 1/44

1907 Largent, James - white male D: Sept 1888; 85y; Hampshire I: Largent, Jno. DOI: cousin B/P: 1/45

1908 Largent, James - white male D: Mar 30, 1899; 76y 6m 6d; Bloomery District F: Largent, J. M: Largent, M. B: Sept 24, 1822 I: Largent, John DOI: brother B/P: 1/70

1909 Largent, James - widower white male D: Mar 30, 1899; 75y; Forks of Capon B: Hampshire BUR: Forks of Capon B/P: 1/102 N: farmer

1910 Largent, Jas. S. - widower white male D: Aug 4, 1912; 70y B: Bloomery District B/P: 2/69 N: blacksmith

1911 Largent, Jerry - white male D: Aug 3, 1916; 49y B: Capon B/P: 2/69

1912 Largent, Jno H. - white male D: Nov 20, 1889; 16y 9m; Hampshire F: Largent, John M: Largent, S. B: Hampshire DOI: father B/P: 1/51

1913 Largent, John W - single D: Oct 26, 1870; 21y 7m; Hampshire F: Largent, William M: Largent, Catharine B/P: 1/5

1914 Largent, Joseph - white male D: June 18, 1872; 79y; Hampshire F: Largent, Lewis M: Largent, Keziah B: Hampshire

I: Largent, John DOI: son C: Largent, Mary B/P: 1/8

1915 Largent, Joseph P - white male D: Mar 29, 1875; 26d; Hampshire F: Largent, Randolph M: Largent, Sarah E. B: Hampshire I: Largent, Randolph B/P: 1/16

1916 Largent, Katharine - widow white female D: Feb 24, 1899; 75y; Cold Stream B: Virginia BUR: Cold Stream B/P: 1/101

1917 Largent, Lizzie - widow white female D: June 14, 1894; 68y; Hampshire B: Hampshire BUR: Forks of Capon B/P: 1/85

1918 Largent, Louisa Laonett - widowed white female D: Aug 8, 1921; 78y 7m 17d; Hampshire F: Schuler, Cornelius M: Schuler, Harriet B: Frederick Co., VA I: Schuler, Mary Jane B/P: 1/131

1919 Largent, Louisa - married white female D: Mar 23, 1899; 45y; Forks of Capon B: Hampshire BUR: Forks of Capon B/P: 1/102

1920 Largent, Lulu - white female D: Mar 23, 1899; 45y; Bloomery District F: Largent, J. M: Largent, E. B: Mar 23, 1854 I: Largent, Lydia C: Largent, D.H. B/P: 1/70

1921 Largent, Mary - white female D: Dec 6, 1875; 78y; Hampshire F: Alderton, William M: Alderton, Margaret B: Hampshire I: Allender, Thomas DOI: friend C: Largent, Thomas B/P: 1/16

1922 Largent, Mary - white female D: Oct 19, 1880; 90y 2m 18d; Hampshire F: Offord, John M: Offord, Ann B: Hampshire I: Largent, Silas DOI: son C: Largent, Sam'l B/P: 1/28

1923 Largent, Mary - white female D: Oct 25, 1881; 53y 6m 15d; Hampshire F: Moreland, Geo M: Moreland, Sarah B: Hampshire DOI: husband C: Largent, Jno J. B/P: 1/31

1924 Largent, Melvin - white male D: Aug 1912; 1y B: Bloomery District B/P: 2/69

1925 Largent, Mose - married white male D: Nov 9, 1918; 45y; Hampshire B/P: 1/126 N: farmer

1926 Largent, Samuel - white male D: Nov 17, 1879; 80y; Hampshire F: Largent, John M: Largent, Mary B: Hampshire I: Largent, Lem'l DOI: son C: Largent, Mahalah B/P: 1/26

1927 Largent, Samuel H. - white male D: Sept 17, 1881; 22y 11m; Hampshire F: Largent, Samuel M: Largent, Mahala B:

Hampshire DOI: mother B/P: 1/31

1928 Largent, Samuel - widower white male D: Nov 30, 1898; 81y; Bloomery District I: Largent, Lettie DOI: granddaughter B/P: 1/69

1929 Largent, Samuel H. - married white male D: Feb 25, 1908; 65y B/P: 2/68 N: farmer

1930 Largent, Thomas F - white male D: Nov 20, 1874; 61y 10m 24d; Hampshire F: Largent, Sam'l M: Largent, Mary B: Hampshire DOI: wife C: Largent, Sarah B/P: 1/13

1931 Largent, Thomas - white male D: June 4, 1896; 69y; Hampshire B: 1827 I: Largent, John R. DOI: son B/P: 1/63

1932 Largent, Wm. - white male D: Mar 25, 1889; 70y; Hampshire B: Hampshire I: Largent, Geo DOI: son C: Largent, C. B/P: 1/51

1933 Larick, Licragus - white male D: Oct 19, 1873; 9y; Hampshire F: Larick, John M: Larick, Margaret B: Hampshire DOI: father B/P: 1/10

1934 Larrick, Benj F. - married white male D: Oct 26, 1914; 40y 9m 26d B/P: 2/69

1935 Larrick, Hampton C. - white male D: Dec 1882; 2d; Capon District F: Larrick, Theo F. M: Larrick, Martha B: WV DOI: mother B/P: 1/33

1936 Larrick, Sarah - married white female D: Mar 3, 1906; 56y B/P: 2/68

1937 Larrie, Percenia - single white female D: Aug 9, 1878; 26y; Hampshire F: Larrie, John M: Larrie, Mary B: Hampshire DOI: father B/P: 1/23

1938 Lawless, Joseph - married white male D: Sept 11, 1916; 55y B: South Branch B/P: 2/69 N: farmer

1939 Lear, Andrew - white male D: Dec 5, 1908; 1y 6m B/P: 2/68

1940 Lear, Mary E. - widow white female D: Dec 25, 1913; 74y 10m B/P: 2/69

1941 Lear, Nancy - white D: Sept 6, 1868; 25y; Mill Creek B: Hampshire DOI: husband C: Lear, Thos. B/P: 1/3

1942 Lear, Thomas - married white male D: Mar 27, 1909; 72y B/P: 2/68 N: blacksmith

1943 Leath, Elmira - white female D: Mar 15, 1884; 2y 22d; Hampshire F: Leath, Walter M: Leath, Christena B: Hampshire DOI: father B/P: 1/39

1944 Leatherman, Carmen - single white female D: Jan 8, 1909; 4y B/P: 2/68

1945 Leatherman, Christina - single white female D: Dec 21, 1891; 84y 1m 5d; Hampshire F: Leatherman, B: Hampshire I: Ludwick, Fred DOI: nephew B/P: 1/53

1946 Leatherman, H.S. - white female D: June 20, 1884; 62y; Hampshire B: Hampshire DOI: husband C: Leatherman, Solomon B/P: 1/38

1947 Leatherman, James A - white male D: Oct 11, 1872; 21y 8m; Hampshire F: Leatherman, Dan'l M: Leatherman, Margaret B: Hampshire DOI: mother B/P: 1/9

1948 Leatherman, John - white male D: Apr 20, 1884; 85y; Hampshire F: Leatherman, Solomon B: Hampshire I: Leatherman, Sam DOI: nephew C: Leatherman, Rebecca B/P: 1/38

1949 Leatherman, Maude - white female D: Dec 27, 1893; 46y; Hampshire B/P: 1/58

1950 Leatherman, Robert - white male D: Aug 6, 1883; 6m; Hampshire F: Leatherman, Sam M: Leatherman, Hannah R. B: Hampshire DOI: father B/P: 1/36

1951 Leatherman, Sarah J. - white female D: July 15, 1875; 10m; Hampshire M: Leatherman, Mary B: Hampshire DOI: mother B/P: 1/14

1952 Leatherman, Tacey J. - widow white female D: Mar 28, 1911; 84y B: Romney District B/P: 2/68

1953 Lederer, Herman - white male D: June 19, 1905; B/P: 2/72

1954 Lederer, Susan - white female D: Dec 1902; Hampshire F: Lederer, H.T.L. B: Dec 1902 DOI: father B/P: 1/79

1955 Lee, Jacob D. - white male D: Nov 15, 1894; 72y; Sherman District B/P: 1/59

1956 Lee, Jasper Lee - married white male D: July 27, 1922;

72y 7m 27d; Hampshire F: Lee, Richard B: Hampshire Co. I: Lee, C.W. B/P: 1/134 N: farmer

1957 Lee, John David - married white male D: May 16, 1922; 72y 6m 10d; Hampshire F: Lee, Jackson M: Lee, Jane B: Hardy County I: Oates, E.F. B/P: 1/134 N: farmer

1958 Lee, Mamie - single white female D: Mar 4, 1905; 21y B/P: 2/68

1959 Lee, Martha - married white female D: July 8, 1908; 65y B/P: 2/68

1960 Lee, Mary A - white female D: Aug 15, 1877; Hampshire F: Swisher, Jacob M: Swisher, Emily B: Hampshire DOI: father B/P: 1/22

1961 Lee, Mr. - married white male D: Dec 20, 1896; 70y; near Slanesville B: Pennsylvania BUR: Salem Church B/P: 1/92

1962 Lee, Pauline Rachel - white female D: Sept 13, 1913; 1y 6m B/P: 2/69

1963 Leith, Chas. O. - single white male D: June 22, 1908; 19y B/P: 2/68

1964 Leith, James F. - white male D: Apr 28, 1889; 74y 10m 15d; Hampshire I: Leith, Philo DOI: nephew B/P: 1/51

1965 Leith, James W - white male D: Apr 14, 1874; 5m; Hampshire F: Leith, Edmund J. M: Leith, Sarah B: Hampshire DOI: father B/P: 1/13

1966 Leith, Mary - white female D: June 20, 1876; 68y 5m 7d; Hampshire F: McKee, Robert M: McKee, Mary B: Hampshire I: Leith, Edward DOI: son C: Leith, Joseph B/P: 1/20

1967 Lemon, Bessie - white female D: May 9, 1904; 13y B/P: 2/72

1968 Leonard, Edgar M. - single white male D: Jan 5, 1921; 11m; Hampshire F: Leonard, Henry M: Leonard, Mary B: Maryland DOI: father B/P: 1/130

1969 Leur, Malissa Belle - white female D: May 4, 1877; Hampshire M: Leur, Mary B: Hampshire DOI: mother B/P: 1/22

1970 Lewis, A.B. - white female D: July 14, 1889; 29y; Hampshire F: Brown, Ed. M: Brown, C. B: Hampshire DOI: husband C: Lewis, W.A. B/P: 1/51

1971 Lewis, Annie Laurie - white female D: Sept 17, 1882; 2y; Capon District F: Lewis, Wm. O. M: Lewis, M. S. B: WV DOI: father B/P: 1/33

1972 Lewis, Bell - married white female D: July 15, 1889; 31y 6m; near Springfield B: WV BUR: Three Churches B/P: 1/124

1973 Lewis, Benj F. - single D: July 15, 1871; 20y 1d F: Lewis, Silas M: Lewis, Abigail B/P: 1/6

1974 Lewis, Catharine - white female D: Mar 27, 1876; 43y; Hampshire F: Lewis, Malvin B: Hampshire DOI: mother B/P: 1/18

1975 Lewis, Daniel - white male D: Sept 13, 1873; 58y; Hampshire F: Lewis, Daniel M: Lewis, Martha B: Hampshire DOI: wife C: Lewis, Martha B/P: 1/11

1976 Lewis, Edward Lee - married white male D: Mar 9, 1907; 32y B/P: 2/68

1977 Lewis, Griffith - married white male D: Oct 1, 1916; 28y B: Springfield B/P: 2/69

1978 Lewis, John W. - white male D: Apr 21, 1908; 14d B/P: 2/68

1979 Lewis, Mahlon D: June 20, 1869; 64y; Hampshire C: Lewis, Mary B/P: 1/4

1980 Lewis, Martha - white female D: Oct 13, 1894; 73y 6m 15d; Hampshire B: Virginia I: Lewis, S.E. DOI: son C: Lewis, Daniel B/P: 1/60

1981 Lewis, Mary Jane - married white female D: Sept 12, 1906; 63y B/P: 2/68

1982 Lewis, Middleton - widower white male D: Feb 6, 1909; 75y 11m 26d B/P: 2/68

1983 Lewis, Peter S. - white male D: Nov 19, 1872; 37y 11d; Hampshire F: Lewis, Mahlon M: Lewis, Isabella B: Hampshire DOI: mother B/P: 1/8

1984 Lewis, Samuel - single white male D: Sept 12, 1921; 62y 6m 3d; Hampshire F: Lewis, Daniel M: Lewis, Martha B: Hampshire B/P: 1/131 N: farmer

1985 Lewis, Silas - white male D: Sept 19, 1881; 69y 4m 24d;

Hampshire F: Lewis, Dan'l M: Lewis, Martha B: Hampshire DOI: wife C: Lewis, Abigail B/P: 1/31

1986 Lewis, Tacy - single white female D: Feb 1900; 60y; Barnes Mills B: Hampshire BUR: Three Churches B/P: 1/107

1987 Lewis, Thos. Jefferson - married white male D: Aug 19, 1915; 72y B/P: 2/69 N: farmer

1988 Lewis, W.O. - widower white male D: Dec 14, 1908; 70y 1m B/P: 2/68

1989 Lewis, Wilbert - single white male D: Apr 9, 1907; 9m B/P: 2/68

1990 Light, Agnes - white female D: Mar 24, 1885; 33y; Hampshire B: Hampshire DOI: husband C: Light, C.H. B/P: 1/42

1991 Light, Mariah - white female D: July 30, 1873; 56y 5m 8d; Hampshire F: Migalis, Godfrey M: Migalis, Mariah B: Chambersburg, PA DOI: husband C: Light, Willaim B/P: 1/11

1992 Light, William - married white male D: Feb 17, 1895; 76y; Branch Mountain B: Frederick Co, VA B/P: 1/82

1993 Light, William - married white male D: Feb 17, 1895; 70y; Branch Mountain B: Virginia BUR: Wesley Chapel B/P: 1/85

1994 Liller, Henry B. - married white male D: May 1, 1917; 61y 4m B/P: 2/69 N: watchman

1995 Liller, J.E.N. - white male D: June 26, 1890; 3m; Romney District F: Liller, H.B. M: Liller, Alverda B: Hampshire DOI: father B/P: 1/52

1996 Liller, Sarah P. - white female D: Mar 19, 1890; 6m; Mill Creek F: Liller, H.B. M: Liller, Alverda B: Mill Creek District DOI: father B/P: 1/49

1997 Link, Ida Virginia - married white female D: Apr 14, 1918; 20y 3m 13d; Hampshire B/P: 1/126 N: housewife

1998 Link, Zola E. - single white female D: Jan 10, 1907; 3m 3d B/P: 2/68

1999 Linthicum, Chas. M.H. - white male D: Mar 19, 1903; 2y; Springfield F: Linthicum, J.C. M: Linthicum, K.M. DOI: father B/P: 1/81

2000 Linthicum, Gertrude Estel - white female D: Nov 16, 1916; 4y 2m 19d B: Sherman district B/P: 2/69

2001 Linthicum, Kelly - married white male D: Aug 17, 1887; 36y; Hardy County B: Hampshire BUR: Hardy County B/P: 1/122

2002 Linthicum, Margaret A. - white female D: Mar 28, 1892; 14y; Hampshire F: Linthicum, J.K. M: Linthicum, Sarah K B: Hampshire DOI: mother B/P: 1/54

2003 Linthicum, Susan S. - white female D: Feb 16, 1881; 43y; Hampshire F: Bowman, And. M: Bowman, Eleanor B: Hampshire DOI: husband C: Linthicum, William K. B/P: 1/31

2004 Linthicum, Susan - single white female D: Sept 13, 1887; 10y; Hampshire B: Hardy County BUR: Hampshire B/P: 1/122

2005 Lloyd, Fannie - married black female D: Aug 5, 1889; 62y; Hampshire B: Virginia BUR: Springfield B/P: 1/125

2006 Lochinder, Elizabeth - married white female D: Mar 15, 1873; 67y 5m; Hampshire F: Hott, John M: Hott, Elizabeth B: Hampshire DOI: husband C: Lochinder, John B/P: 1/10

2007 Lockenger, John - white male D: June 4, 1881; 84y; Hampshire B: Germany I: Haines, D.M. DOI: son in law C: Lockenger, Betsy B/P: 1/29

2008 Loffer, Julia - widow white female D: Jan 24, 1896; 82y; Hampshire B: Hampshire B/P: 1/88

2009 Lofollette, Tilberry - single white male D: Oct 15, 1873; 5m 10d; Hampshire F: Lafollette, E.E. M: Lafollette, Mary B: Hampshire DOI: father B/P: 1/10

2010 Long, Conrad - white male D: Feb 1, 1888; 86y; Hampshire F: Long, John M: Long, Mary B: Hampshire I: Milleson, C.M. DOI: son in law C: Long, Elizabeth B/P: 1/45

2011 Long, Ella L. - white female D: Aug 15, 1889; 1m 22d; Hampshire F: Long, Wm. M: Long, H. B: Hampshire DOI: father B/P: 1/51

2012 Long, Geo. W. - white male D: Apr 25, 1888; 8d; Hampshire F: Long, A.H. M: Long, C. B: Hampshire DOI: father B/P: 1/45

2013 Long, Jas. - white male D: Mar 7, 1888; 2y 11m; Hampshire F: Long, A.H. M: Long, C. B: Hampshire DOI:

father B/P: 1/45

2014 Long, Wm. J. - white male D: Dec 8, 1905; 78y B/P: 2/72 N: farmer

2015 Lovett, Joshua - white male D: June 10, 1867; 34y 6m 10d; Cold Stream F: Lovett, Jonathan M: Lovett, Nancy B: Frederick Co., VA I: Lovett, Albert O. DOI: brother B/P: 1/2

2016 Lovett, Mary S - white female D: July 12, 1873; 26y; Hampshire F: Park, Harvey H M: Park, Hester B: Hampshire DOI: husband C: Lovett, Albert B/P: 1/11

2017 Lovett, Nettie - white female D: Feb 1889; 18y 5m; Hampshire F: Lovett, A.O. M: Lovett, M.S. B: Hampshire DOI: father B/P: 1/51

2018 Lovitt, Chas - white male D: Aug 10, 1878; 7d; Hampshire F: Lovitt, A. M: Lovitt, Margaret DOI: mother B/P: 1/24

2019 Loy, Alonzo - white male D: May 1, 1885; 1y 8m 21d; Hampshire F: Loy, Peter M: Loy, Laura B: Hampshire DOI: father B/P: 1/42

2020 Loy, Andrew - single white male D: Oct 7, 1896; 1y 7m; Hampshire B/P: 1/96

2021 Loy, Anna - white female D: Apr 7, 1905; 84y B/P: 2/72

2022 Loy, Camelia - white female D: Mar 26, 1876; 1y; Hampshire F: Loy, William M: Loy, P. B: Hampshire DOI: father B/P: 1/18

2023 Loy, Daniel - white male D: May 6, 1892; 82y; Sherman District F: Loy, William B: Little Capon I: Loy, William DOI: son B/P: 1/56

2024 Loy, Ed. M - white male D: Dec 14, 1881; 20y 11m 26d; Hampshire F: Loy, Wm. B: Hampshire DOI: father B/P: 1/29

2025 Loy, Edgar S. - white male D: Apr 10, 1912; 1d B: Sherman District B/P: 2/69

2026 Loy, Eliza J. - married white female D: Jan 1912; 63y B: Sherman District B/P: 2/69

2027 Loy, Elizabeth - widow white female D: Nov 22, 1911; 68y 11m 17d B: Sherman District B/P: 2/68

2028 Loy, Emma Malissa - single white female D: Oct 6, 1894; 19y 11m 27d; B: Hampshire BUR: Mt Zion Church B/P: 1/86

2029 Loy, Estella May - widow white female D: Sept 7, 1914; 21y 4m 8d B/P: 2/69

2030 Loy, Eugene Harrison - single white male D: Nov 11, 1914; 2y 2m B/P: 2/69

2031 Loy, Eugene Hartzel - white male D: Nov 11, 1914; 2y 2m 1d B/P: 2/69

2032 Loy, George - married white male D: Feb 12, 1873; 55y; Hampshire F: Loy, William M: Loy, Mary B: Hampshire I: Loy, William DOI: son C: Loy, Jane Ann B/P: 1/10 N: preaching

2033 Loy, Georgia - married white female D: Apr 16, 1908; 26y B/P: 2/68

2034 Loy, Harvey Clinton - single white male D: Feb 2, 1899; 9m 3d; Ruckman B: Ruckman BUR: Mt. Zion B/P: 1/101

2035 Loy, Ira Frank - single white male D: Feb 29, 1912; 11y 6m 11d B: Sherman District B/P: 2/69

2036 Loy, James W. - widower white male D: Jan 1, 1909; 68y 7m 7d B/P: 2/68 N: farmer

2037 Loy, Jane - white female D: Mar 15, 1895; 76y; Sherman District B: Mar 1819 I: Loy, William DOI: son B/P: 1/61

2038 Loy, Jennie - married white female D: Dec 5, 1908; 52y 20d B/P: 2/68

2039 Loy, Jonah D.S. - white female D: July 7, 1914; 1y 3m 20d B/P: 2/69

2040 Loy, Mary J. - white female D: July 1, 1898; 2y 6m; Sherman District F: Loy, Robt. DOI: father B/P: 1/68

2041 Loy, Melissa A. - married white female D: May 25, 1908; 38y 11m 20d B/P: 2/68

2042 Loy, Morgan R. - married white male D: May 29, 1913; 55y 9m 15d B/P: 2/69

2043 Loy, R.R. - white male D: Nov 18, 1899; 3m 10d; Gore District F: Loy, E.B. M: Loy, Sallie B: July 28, 1899 DOI: father B/P: 1/70

2044 Loy, Rebecca - white female D: July 4, 1886; 27y; Sherman District F: Timbrook, I. B: Hampshire DOI: husband C: Loy, William B/P: 1/43

2045 Loy, Samuel - white male D: June 1881; 84y; Hampshire B: Hampshire DOI: wife C: Loy, Rachel B/P: 1/30

2046 Loy, Samuel - white male D: Feb 27, 1899; 77y 8m 3d; Sherman District F: Loy, William B: Nov 18, 1822 DOI: son B/P: 1/71

2047 Loy, Samuel - married white male D: Feb 27, 1899; 76y 3m 9d; Ruckman B: Hampshire BUR: Mt Zion B/P: 1/107

2048 Loy, Sarah - widow white female D: Feb 20, 1907; 76y B/P: 2/68

2049 Loy, Sarah Ann - married white female D: Mar 17, 1907; 58y 1m 2d B/P: 2/68

2050 Loy, Sarah M - married white female D: Oct 19, 1866; 38y 5m; Hampshire F: Houdyshell, Adam B: Hampshire DOI: husband C: Loy, Samuel of Wm. B/P: 1/1

2051 Loy, Seymour Dick - married white male D: Aug 4, 1913; 29y 8m 8d B/P: 2/69

2052 Loy, Susan Jane - white female D: Dec 20, 1893; 67y; Hampshire B/P: 1/58

2053 Loy, Wallace Hiett - single white male D: Sept 21, 1922; 1y 7m; Hampshire F: Loy, Harry M: Loy, Iliff B: Forks of Capon I: Lupton, Geo A B/P: 1/136

2054 Loy, Warner H. - white male D: Oct 17, 1885; 11m; Hampshire F: Loy, Peter M: Loy, Laura B: Hampshire DOI: father B/P: 1/42

2055 Loy, William - widower white male D: Feb 12,, 1899; 80y 6m 6d; Ruckman B: Hampshire BUR: Mt. Zion B/P: 1/101

2056 Loy, William Jas. - white male D: Feb 12, 1899; 82y; Sherman District F: Loy, William B: Aug 6, 1818 DOI: son B/P: 1/71

2057 Ludwick, Christena - white female D: Oct 15, 1875; 85y 1m 10d; Hampshire B: Hampshire I: Ludwick, John DOI: son C: Ludwick, John B/P: 1/14

2058 Ludwick, Joseph - married white male D: Aug 8, 1877;

Hampshire I: Ludwick, Mary DOI: daughter B/P: 1/22

2059 Ludwick, Mary - white D: Sept 21, 1866 B/P: 1/2

2060 Ludwick, Simon P - white male D: Aug 14, 1866 B/P: 1/2

2061 Ludwick, Susan - white female D: Dec 2, 1893; 71y; Hampshire B/P: 1/58

2062 Ludwick, Thomas - married white male D: Sept 5, 1907; 82y B/P: 2/68 N: farmer

2063 Ludwick, Wm. Harvey - single white male D: Apr 16, 1911; 74y 6m 4d B: Mill Creek District B/P: 2/68 N: farmer

2064 Lupton, Leattie - white female D: Nov 8, 1903; 63y; Dillons Run B/P: 1/81

2065 Lupton, Lizzie R - white female D: April 12, 1868; 16y 1m 2d; Romney F: Lupton, S.R. B: Petersburg, PA DOI: father B/P: 1/3

2066 Lupton, S.R. - white male D: Sept 7, 1880; 53y; Romney B: Virginia DOI: wife C: Lupton, P.P. B/P: 1/27 N: doctor of medicine

2067 Lupton, Vernon P. - white male D: Aug 1, 1882; 10m 4d; Capon District F: Lupton, Jesse G. M: Lupton, Rachel B: WV DOI: father B/P: 1/33

2068 Luttrell, John Lee - married white male D: July 3, 1920; 82y 10m 10d; Hampshire F: Luttrell, Jno. B: Morgan County I: Luttrell, R. Perry B/P: 1/129 N: carpenter

2069 Luttrell, Lizzie - married white female D: Jan 18, 1894; 30y; Near North River Mills B: Hampshire BUR: Hampshire County B/P: 1/84

2070 Luttrell, May - married white female D: Feb 9, 1913; 40y B/P: 2/69

2071 Luttrell, Susan R.M. - married white female D: July 3, 1911; 76y 11m 18d B/P: 2/68

2072 Lyons, Hester A D: Jan 10, 1869; 20y 2m; Hampshire F: Lyons, Amos B: Hampshire B/P: 1/4

2073 Mahlen, Wm. - white male D: Feb 6, 1881; Hampshire I: Poling, M.F. DOI: overseer of poor B/P: 1/30

2074 Main, John - white male D: Aug 6, 1875; 1d; Hampshire F: Main, John M: Main, Margaret B: Maryland DOI: father B/P: 1/16

2075 Malcolm, Burr - single white male D: Aug 2, 1906; 25y B/P: 2/73 N: drowned; farmer

2076 Malcolm, David H. - single white male D: Oct 2, 1902; 35y; near Three Chruches B: Hampshire BUR: Three Churches B/P: 1/116

2077 Malcolm, Davis S. - white male D: Oct 28, 1902; 38y; Hampshire F: Malcolm, C.B. M: Malcolm, Rachel B: 1874 DOI: father B/P: 1/79

2078 Malcolm, Edith Delsie - white female D: Apr 4, 1917; 7m B/P: 2/76

2079 Malcolm, J.A. - white female D: Jan 29, 1893; 76y; Hampshire B/P: 1/58

2080 Malcolm, Jas B. - white male D: Mar 29, 1889; 4y 9m 2d; Hampshire F: Malcolm, N.H. M: Malcolm, L. B: Hampshire DOI: father B/P: 1/51

2081 Malcolm, Julia F. - white female D: Feb 26, 1878; 14m; Hampshire F: Malcolm, J.S. M: Malcolm, Sarah F. DOI: mother B/P: 1/24

2082 Malcolm, Lemuel - white male D: Nov 15, 1891; 2y 11m; Hampshire F: Malcolm, N. M: Malcolm, L. B: Hampshire DOI: father B/P: 1/55

2083 Malcolm, M. - white male D: Dec 5, 1904 B/P: 2/82

2084 Malcolm, Mrs. Chas. - white female D: Dec 5, 1904; 65y B/P: 2/82

2085 Malcolm, Mrs. Robt. - married white female D: May 10, 1895; 50y 3m 5d; Hampshire B: Hampshire B/P: 1/87

2086 Malcolm, Mrs. Robt. - married white female D: May 15, 1895; 50y; Hampshire B: Hampshire B/P: 1/88

2087 Malcolm, Nathan - white male D: Feb 14, 1913; 78y B/P: 2/75

2088 Malcolm, Robert - white male D: Feb 9, 1904; 70y B/P: 2/82 N: farmer

2089 Malcolm, Wm - white male D: Apr 8, 1876; 72y 2m 21d; Hampshire F: Malcolm, William M: Malcolm, Nancy B: Hampshire DOI: wife C: Malcolm, Julia B/P: 1/20

2090 Malcom, Emily L - white female D: Apr 9, 1874; 6y; Hampshire F: Malcom, Chas B. M: Malcom, Rachel F. B: Hampshire DOI: father B/P: 1/13

2091 Malcom, Jas. S. - white male D: July 7, 1875; 41y 8m 4d; Hampshire F: Malcom, William M: Malcom, Julia B: Hampshire DOI: wife C: Malcom, Sarah J. B/P: 1/16

2092 Malcom, Martha E. - white female D: May 28, 1874; 4y; Hampshire F: Malcom, Chas M: Malcom, Rachel B: Hampshire DOI: father B/P: 1/13

2093 Malcom, Susan C. - single white female D: Aug 1, 1873; 26y 5m 14d; Hampshire F: Malcom, Wm M: Malcom, Julia B: Hampshire DOI: father B/P: 1/11

2094 Malcome, Emily - white female D: Jan 11, 1876; 29y; Hampshire F: Slane, Hugh M: Slane, Malinda B: Hampshire DOI: Malcome, Jno A. C: husband B/P: 1/20

2095 Malcome, Joseph Beverly - white male D: Aug 11, 1867; 2y 1m 10d; Levels F: Malcome, James M: Malcome, Sarah B: Levels DOI: father B/P: 1/2

2096 Malick, Catharine - white female D: Aug 1889; 79y; Hampshire F: Saville, O. M: Saville, M. B: Hampshire I: Saville, Jno. DOI: brother C: Malick, Aron B/P: 1/51

2097 Malick, Elizabeth - white female D: Oct 24, 1891; 42y 3m 18d; Hampshire F: Haines, Jas. M: Haines, Evaline B: Hampshire DOI: husband C: Malick, Geo. B/P: 1/55

2098 Malick, Geo. - married white male D: July 13, 1913; 74y 2m 10d B/P: 2/75 N: farmer

2099 Malick, James - white male D: Oct 30, 1890; 79y; Sherman District F: Malick, Philip M: Malick, M. B: Hampshire I: Malick, P. DOI: son B/P: 1/52 N: wife deceased

2100 Malick, Malick - white female D: Mar 10, 1890; 81y; Sherman District F: Dyer, Chas. M: Dyer, N. B: Hampshire I: Malick, P. DOI: son C: Malick, James B/P: 1/52

2101 Malick, Phillip - white male D: Mar 9, 1914; 79y 5m 14d B/P: 2/75 N: farmer, miller

2102 Malick, Rebecca A. - single white female D: Jan 4, 1911; 83y 10m 13d B/P: 2/74

2103 Malick, Sarah - white female D: Aug 16, 1872; 74y 11m 26d; Hampshire F: Shafer, Martin B: Hampshire I: Malick, Geo DOI: son C: Malick, David B/P: 1/8

2104 Maloney, Chas. - married white male D: June 18, 1902; 26y; Hampshire B: Hampshire BUR: Central Church B/P: 1/115

2105 Maloney, Edith C. - white female D: Jan 1886; 3y; Hampshire F: Maloney, B.F. M: Maloney, Mary J. B: Hampshire DOI: father B/P: 1/41

2106 Maloney, Harriet - white female D: July 5, 1901; 70y; Mill Creek District I: Maphis, Ed DOI: son in law B/P: 1/76 N: Parents: J.J. & Susan

2107 Maphis, Ann E. - married white female D: Sept 2, 1901; 16y 10m 28d; Sherman District DOI: father B/P: 1/76 N: Parents: Nathan & Lucinda

2108 Maphis, Basil W. - white male D: Sept 29, 1906; 1y 2m B/P: 2/73

2109 Maphis, George - white male D: Jan 13, 1881; 79y; Hampshire B: Hampshire DOI: wife C: Maphis, Elizabeth B/P: 1/29

2110 Maphis, Luther - white male D: Sept 28, 1910; 28y 11m 6d B/P: 2/74 N: merchant

2111 Maphis, Mary M. - married white female D: Sept 10, 1916; 41y B: Sherman District B/P: 2/75

2112 Maphis, Sadie - white female D: July 29, 1906; 15y 11m 27d B/P: 2/73

2113 Maphis, Sarah C. - white female D: July 15, 1915; 74y B/P: 2/75

2114 Maphis, Willie - white male D: Apr 12, 1911; 17y 8m 17d B/P: 2/74

2115 Marcer, R.W. - married white male D: Dec 2, 1898; 28y; Springfield B: Springfield BUR: Taylor Burying Place B/P: 1/100 N: minister

2116 Mark, Margaret - colored female D: Mar 13, 1880; 1y 25d; Hampshire F: Mark, John B: Hampshire DOI: father B/P: 1/27

2117 Marks, Caroline - widow colored female D: Sept 2, 1911; 83y B/P: 2/74

2118 Marks, Clarence Boyd - colored male D: Nov 26, 1910; 11y 4m 2d B/P: 2/74

2119 Marpel, Jennie - white female D: Aug 1, 1894; 32y; Hampshire B: Hampshire DOI: father C: Marple, J.M. B/P: 1/60

2120 Marpel, M.V. - white female D: Aug 18, 1894; 4m 12d; Hampshire F: Marpel, J.M. M: Marpel, J.A. B: Hampshire I: Marpel, Simon DOI: grandfather B/P: 1/60

2121 Marpel, Simon - widower white male D: Mar 7, 1913; 84y B/P: 2/75 N: farmer

2122 Marple, Martha - white female D: July 2, 1903; 69y; Hampshire F: Elliett B: 1834 DOI: husband C: Marple, Simon B/P: 1/80

2123 Marshall, John W. - white male D: May 29, 1901; 80y; Romney I: Neel, John W. DOI: son in law B/P: 1/76

2124 Marshall. E. - colored male D: June 1886; 70y; Hampshire B: Hampshire I: Fairfax, DOI: daughter B/P: 1/44

2125 Martin, Benjamin - white male D: May 29, 1874; 73y 10m 27d; Hampshire M: Martin, Mary B: Shenandoah Co VA I: Martin, Mary J DOI: daughter C: Martin, Margaret B/P: 1/13

2126 Martin, Bertie - married black female D: Oct 6, 1899; 38y; Romney BUR: Romney B/P: 1/108

2127 Martin, Bettie - colored female D: Sept 10, 1899; 28y; Romney B: 1872 DOI: husband B/P: 1/71

2128 Martin, Flostina - white female D: Jan 18, 1908; 4y 7m 5d B/P: 2/73

2129 Martin, Jane - married white female D: Apr 9, 1909; 66y B/P: 2/74

2130 Martin, Joseph - white male D: Oct 10, 1868; 88y; North River B: North River DOI: widow B/P: 1/3

2131 Martin, Mary - white female D: Mar 23, 1914; 10m 15d B/P: 2/75

2132 Martin, Montgomery - white male D: May 13, 1880; 5m 1d; Hampshire F: Martin, Levi M: Martin, Margaret A. B: Hampshire DOI: father B/P: 1/28

2133 Martin, Tebith - white male D: Jan 8, 1908; 2y 5m 8d B/P: 2/73

2134 Martin, Wheeler - white male D: Bay 1, 1874; 6y 6m; Hampshire F: Martin, Benj M: Martin, Jane B: Hampshire DOI: father B/P: 1/13

2135 Mason, Emily - widow colored female D: Sept 2, 1908; 74y B/P: 2/73

2136 Mason, Grace - colored female D: April 1903; 20y; Paw Paw F: Edmonson, E.B. B: 1883 DOI: father B/P: 1/80

2137 Mason, Hiram L. - married white male D: July 17, 1912; 57y 2m 17d B: Capon District B/P: 2/75 N: carpenter

2138 Mason, Lanilla - single black female D: Dec 26, 1902; 38y; Hampshire B: Coldstream BUR: Capon Chapel B/P: 1/115

2139 Mason, Loring - white male D: Mar 10, 1893; 6m; Hampshire B/P: 1/58

2140 Mathew, John - single colored male D: Oct 10, 1894; 18y 6m; Romney F: Mathew, Dan B: Romney DOI: father B/P: 1/59

2141 Mathews, Harriett - colored female D: May 15, 1886; 38y; Romney B: Hampshire DOI: husband C: Mathews, Daniel B/P: 1/43

2142 Mathews, Hellen - colored female D: Sept 15, 1897; 6m; F: Mathews, Burr M: Fisher, B: Romney I: Fisher, Richard DOI: grandfather B/P: 1/64

2143 Mathews, Hoppie - single black female D: Nov 14, 1898; 20y; Romney B: WV BUR: Romney B/P: 1/99

2144 Mathews, R. - colored D: Mar 3, 1895; 14y 6m; Romney F: Mathews, Dan B: Oct 1882 DOI: father B/P: 1/61

2145 Matthews, Roxey - single colored female D: Mar 12, 1895; 14y; Hampshire B: Hampshire B/P: 1/89

2146 Mauck, Fred - white male D: June 17, 1874; Hampshire B: Frederick Co VA I: Mauck, Fred DOI: son C: Mauck, Eve B/P: 1/18

2147 Mauk, Geo. Frederick - white male D: Aug 19, 1916; 88y 9m 24d B: Sherman District B/P: 2/75 N: farmer

2148 Mauk, Vallie - single white female D: Oct 3, 1912; 10y B: Romney B/P: 2/75

2149 Mauzy, Martha L. - white female D: Sept 20, 1881; 7m 4d; Hampshire F: Mauzy, Sam'l A. M: Mauzy, Julia A. B: Hampshire DOI: father B/P: 1/31

2150 Mauzy, Mary B. - white female D: Dec 3, 1881; Hampshire F: Mauzy, Sam'l A. M: Mauzy, Julia A. B: Hampsire DOI: father B/P: 1/31

2151 Mayhew, Chas. - single white male D: June 22, 1918; Hampshire B/P: 1/126

2152 Mayhew, Eva F. - widow white female D: Feb 1, 1914; 87y 1m 27d B/P: 2/75

2153 Mayhew, Geo Riley - white male D: Sept 9, 1904; 2y B/P: 2/73

2154 Mayhew, Isaac W. - white male D: Aug 10, 1901; 22y; Mill Creek District B/P: 1/76

2155 McAboy, Anna E. - white female D: Oct 27, 1872; 27y 5m 26d; Hampshire F: Shipe, Moses M: Shipe, Malinda I: McAboy, Jas. DOI: brother in law B/P: 1/8

2156 McBride Jos. - married white female D: Apr 14, 1898; 60y; Higginsville B: Hampshire BUR: Chapel Church B/P: 1/98

2157 McBride, A.L. - single white male D: Feb 8, 1897; 3y 11m 25d; Tearcoat B: Hampshire BUR: Mt Zion Church B/P: 1/90

2158 McBride, Albert - single white male D: June 9, 1922; 75y; Hampshire F: McBride, Alexander M: McBride, Elizabeth B: Hampshire I: McBride, Minerva B/P: 1/134

2159 McBride, Arra - white female D: Mar 1902; 2y; Hampshire F: McBride, Shelton M: McBride, Sallie B: 1900 DOI: father B/P: 1/79

2160 McBride, Arthur L. - white male D: Apr 8, 1897; 4y; Sherman District F: McBride, William B: Sherman District DOI: father B/P: 1/64

2161 McBride, Benj H. - single white male D: Dec 24, 1881; 20y; Hampshire F: McBride, Silas M: McBride, Martha B:

Hampshire DOI: mother B/P: 1/32

2162 McBride, Benj. E. - white male D: Dec 31, 1900; 5m; Hampshire F: McBride, William B: Aug 30, DOI: father B/P: 1/73

2163 McBride, C.A.L. - white male D: Apr 26, 1906; 10m 6d B/P: 2/73

2164 McBride, C.R. - white male D: Jan 12, 1889; 40y; Hampshire B: Hampshire DOI: wife C: McBride, M.D. B/P: 1/51

2165 McBride, Charles - single white male D: Jan 11, 1919; 68y 1d B/P: 2/76 N: farmer

2166 McBride, Chas H. D: Feb 19, 1871; 26d F: McBride, Isaih M: McBride, Sarah B/P: 1/6

2167 McBride, Conda - single white male D: Jan 10, 1920; 7y; Hampshire F: McBride, Shull B: Slanesville I: Rannells, Mrs. H. B/P: 1/129

2168 McBride, Daniel - white amle D: May 13, 1907; 75y B/P: 2/73

2169 McBride, Edw. J. - single white male D: Dec 5, 1882; 57y 3m 18d; Hampshire F: McBride, A. M: McBride, N. B: Hampshire I: McBride, Jno H. DOI: brother B/P: 1/34 N: farmer

2170 McBride, George - white male D: Oct 17, 1911; 75y B/P: 2/74

2171 McBride, H.S. - single white male D: Dec 2, 1909; 21y 11m B/P: 2/74 N: railroad employee

2172 McBride, Jane - married white female D: Nov 23, 1919; 78y B/P: 2/76

2173 McBride, John H. - white male D: June 1883; Hampshire B: Hampshire I: McBride, Chas DOI: son C: McBride, Abby B/P: 1/37

2174 McBride, John W. - white male D: July 16, 1874; 1y 11m 21d; Hampshire F: McBride, Daniel B: Hampshire DOI: father B/P: 1/13

2175 McBride, Joseph - widower white male D: Mar 3, 1899; 65y; Higginsville B: Hampshire BUR: Three Churches B/P: 1/103

2176 McBride, Joseph - widower white male D: July 1, 1907; 77y B/P: 2/73 N: farmer

2177 McBride, Kirk Taylor - married white male D: Dec 13, 1922; 25y 8m 3d; Hampshire F: McBride, Ely M: McBride, Elizabeth B: Higginsville I: Watson, W. B/P: 1/134

2178 McBride, Margaret A.V. - married white female D: Dec 1, 1919; 61y 5m 21d; Gore District F: Sanda, Hugh M: Sanda, Elizabeth B: Hampshire B/P: 1/128

2179 McBride, Mary - widow white female D: Jan 4, 1898; 71y; Gore District F: Saville, A. I: McBride, L.B. DOI: son B/P: 1/69

2180 McBride, Mary - single white female D: Oct 10, 1895; 76y; Sherman District B: 1819 I: Davis, Farmer B/P: 161

2181 McBride, Mrs. - married white female D: Jan 3, 1899; 65y; Springfield BUR: Springfield B/P: 1/102

2182 McBride, Nancy - white female D: Dec 19, 1915; 29y B/P: 2/75

2183 McBride, Peter - white male D: May 7, 1884; 89y; Hampshire B: Hampshire B/P: 1/39 N: farmer

2184 McBride, Robt - white male D: Jan 25, 1876; 54y 23d; Hampshire F: McBride, John M: McBride, Nancy B: Hampshire DOI: wife C: McBride, Mary B/P: 1/20

2185 McBride, Rosa - white female D: Nov 21, 1906; 9y B/P: 2/73

2186 McBride, Rosy - white female D: Nov 27, 1906; 10y 4m 5d B/P: 2/73

2187 McBride, Sarah A. - white female D: Sept 28, 1891; 20y; Hampshire F: McBride, D. M: McBride, Evaline B: Hampshire DOI: father B/P: 1/55

2188 McBride, Sarah C. - white female D: Mar 27, 1878; 33y; Hampshire F: Smith, Peter M: Smith, Nancy I: McBride, Miss DOI: sister in law C: McBride, Eli B/P: 1/24

2189 McBride, Wannita - single white female D: Aug 30, 1918; 3y 4m 7d; Hampshire B/P: 1/126

2190 McBride, William - white male D: Mar 28, 1899; 77y;

Augusta F: McBride, Stephen M: McBride, Ruthy B: Mar 5, 1823 I: Ruckman, J.W. B/P: 1/71

2191 McBride, William - single white male D: Mar 28, 1899; 76y; BUR: Mt. Zion B/P: 1/103

2192 McBride, Wm. Bryan - white male D: June 1903; 3y; Hampshire F: McBride, Taylor M: McBride, R. B: June 19, 1900 DOI: father B/P: 1/80

2193 McCallion, Harriet J. - white female D: Sept 15, 1875; 40y; Hampshire F: Orndorff, John M: Orndorff, Elizabeth B: Frederick Co VA DOI: husband C: McCallion, Thomas B/P: 1/16

2194 McCarty, Arthur W. - married white male D: June 21, 1919; 79y 2m 19d B/P: 2/76 N: farmer

2195 McCarty, Daisy - white female D: Oct 15, 1919; 36y 8m 27d B/P: 2/76

2196 McCarty, Olai - single white female D: June 22, 1906; 26y 6m 1d B/P: 2/73

2197 McCauley, Addison - white male D: Mar 20, 1867; 82y; Tearcoat Creek B: Maryland B/P: 1/2 N: carpenter

2198 McCauley, Benj. - married white male D: Mar 27, 1895; 65y; near N. River Mills B: Hampshire BUR: near N.R. Mills B/P: 1/85

2199 McCauley, Delsie - married white female D: Feb 16, 1920; 28y; Hampshire F: Moreland, Newton B: Levels B/P: 1/129 N: housewife

2200 McCauley, Elias - married white male D: Dec 15, 1907; 72y 3m 15d B/P: 2/73 N: farmer

2201 McCauley, Geo - white male D: Feb 4, 1881; 87y 3m; Hampshire F: McCauley, Geo M: McCauley, P. B: Maryland DOI: wife C: McCauley, Julia A. B/P: 1/31

2202 McCauley, Geo. W. - white male D: Jan 12, 1875; 60y 18d; Hampshire F: McCauley, Adison M: McCauley, Mary B: Hampshire I: McCauley, Arthur DOI: nephew B/P: 1/16

2203 McCauley, Jane - widow white female D: Feb 14, 1920; 89y 8m 6d; Hampshire F: Engle, Jno. M: Engle, Sarah B: Hampshire B/P: 1/129

2204 McCauley, Jno Andrew Jack - married white male D: May

16, 1914; 42y 3m 18d B/P: 2/75 N: school teacher

2205 McCauley, Maggie B. - white female D: Apr 29, 1884; 17y 3m 17d; Hampshire F: McCauley, Benj M: McCauley, Mary J. B: Hampshire DOI: father B/P: 1/39

2206 McCleary, Alice - single white female D: Mar 26, 1908; 15y B/P: 2/73

2207 McCleary, John - white male D: Feb 28, 1914; 69y B/P: 2/75 N: lumberman

2208 McCleary, Wm. H. - married white male D: Mar 27, 1908; 49y B/P: 2/73

2209 McCool, Gertrude - white female D: Dec 28, 1900; 31y; Paw Paw F: Largent, S.H. M: Largent, Lucy B: Oct 26, 1889 DOI: mother B/P: 1/73

2210 McCool, Miss - single white female D: Feb 19, 1896; 18y; Hampshire B: Hampshire B/P: 1/88

2211 McCormick, Jno. E. - single white male D: May 24, 1922; 25y 8m 3d; Hampshire F: McCormick, Wm. M: McCormick, Johannah B: Washington County, MD DOI: father B/P: 1/134

2212 McDonal, George - white male D: Dec 11, 1889; 80y 5m 9d; Hampshire B: Hampshire I: McDonal, S. DOI: daughter B/P: 1/51

2213 McDonal, Jas. W. - white male D: Apr 1893; 22y; Hampshire B/P: 1/58

2214 McDonald, Alvin - married white male D: Feb 21, 1909; 45y B/P: 2/74 N: school teacher

2215 McDonald, Annie - white female D: Nov 27, 1913; 32y 2m 3d B/P: 2/75

2216 McDonald, Archibald - white male D: Oct 29, 1884; 9d; Hampshire F: McDonald, Benj M: McDonald, Sarah B: Hampshire DOI: father B/P: 1/38

2217 McDonald, Benj - white male D: May 20, 1874; 66y 8m; Hampshire F: McDonald, Benj M: McDonald, Mary B: Hampshire I: McDonald, Evan DOI: son C: McDonald, Amy B/P: 1/13

2218 McDonald, Bertie - married white female D: Dec 25, 1908; 35y 7m 6d B/P: 2/73

2219 McDonald, C.B. - white male D: Dec 6, 1908; 4y B/P: 2/73

2220 McDonald, Calvin - single white male D: Apr 27, 1894; 25y; Hampshire B: Hampshire BUR: N. River B/P: 1/84

2221 McDonald, Conrad - single white male D: Dec 6, 1909; 4y 6m B/P: 2/74

2222 McDonald, Cordelia A. - white female D: Aug 15, 1892; 11y 9m 19d; Sherman District F: McDonald, Chas B. M: McDonald, Eliza B: Short Mountain DOI: mother B/P: 1/56

2223 McDonald, Eugene - white male D: Sept 10, 1916; stillborn B: Three Churches B/P: 2/75

2224 McDonald, Eva Kate - single white female D: Oct 21, 1918; 20y 8m 4d; Hampshire B/P: 1/126

2225 McDonald, Hannah - single white female D: Nov 13, 1907; B/P: 2/73

2226 McDonald, Howard V. - white male D: Sept 30, 1904; 4m B/P: 2/82

2227 McDonald, Isaac H. - single white male D: Feb 6, 1884; 64y; Hampshire B: Hampshire I: Kidwell, Frank DOI: friend B/P: 1/39

2228 McDonald, J. - white male D: June 6, 1901; 43y; Romney District F: McDonald, James I: Bowman, John W. B/P: 1/76

2229 McDonald, James D: Aug 25, 1869; 10m; F: McDonald, Angus M: McDonald, Rebecca B: Hampshire B/P: 1/4

2230 McDonald, James - married white male D: Mar 6, 1910; 78y 5m 5d B/P: 2/74 N: farmer

2231 McDonald, James - widower white male D: Dec 2, 1907; 74y B/P: 2/73

2232 McDonald, James - white male D: Dec 7, 1908; 75y B/P: 2/73

2233 McDonald, Jas. - widower white male D: Feb 16, 1892; 82y 9m; Hampshire F: McDonald, William B: Hampshire I: McDonald, Thos. DOI: son B/P: 1/54

2234 McDonald, Johnny - white male D: June 11, 1907; 16y 4d B/P: 2/73

2235 McDonald, Lula May - white female D: Sept 3, 1892; 6y 11m 8d; Sherman District F: McDonald, Chas. B. M: McDonald, Eliza B: Short Mountain DOI: mother B/P: 1/56

2236 McDonald, M.S. - white female D: Apr 21, 1892; 40y; Hampshire B: Hampshire DOI: husband C: McDonald, G.W. B/P: 1/57

2237 McDonald, Malissa J. - white female D: Nov 22, 1902; 51y 7m; Sherman District F: Pownall, A.H. M: Pownall, Charlot B: 1852 I: McDonald, J.H. B/P: 1/78

2238 McDonald, Margaret - white female D: Jan 30, 1903; 56y; Hampshire F: Malcolm B: 1847 DOI: husband C: McDonald, P. B/P: 1/80

2239 McDonald, Maria - white female D: Jan 1882; 25y 4m; Sherman District M: Shingleton, Mary B: WV DOI: mother C: McDonald, Jared B/P: 1/33

2240 McDonald, Mary - white female D: Jan 3, 1884; 74y; Hampshire B: Hampshire I: McDonald, Jno. DOI: son C: McDonald, George B/P: 1/39

2241 McDonald, Mr. - single white male D: Apr 16, 1895; 1d; Hampshire B: Hampshire B/P: 1/88

2242 McDonald, Mrs. Zeb - white female D: Sept 13, 1912; 70y B/P: 2/75

2243 McDonald, Pheobe - widow white female D: Aug 25, 1894; 83y; Mill Creek DOI: son B/P: 1/59

2244 McDonald, Rebecca - white female D: Oct 2, 1886; 25y 12d; Hampshire F: McDonald, Samuel M: McDonald, Elizabeth B: Hampshire I: McDonald, Sam B/P: 1/44

2245 McDonald, Rebecca - white female D: Feb 10, 1892; 86y; Hampshire B: Hampshire I: McDonald, Thomas H. DOI: son C: McDonald, James B/P: 1/54

2246 McDonald, Robt. - white male D: Mar 22, 1892; 20y 5m 20d; Hampshire F: McDonald, Thos. H. M: McDonald, M. B: Hampshire DOI: father B/P: 1/54

2247 McDonald, Roy - single white male D: May 9, 1920; 1d; Hampshire F: McDonald, Wilbert M: McDonald, Virgie B: Hampshire B/P: 1/129

2248 McDonald, Roy W. - white male D: Dec 11, 1915; 10d B/P: 2/75

2249 McDonald, Sallie - single white female D: June 13, 1897; 68y; Sandy Ridge B: Hampshire BUR: Sandy Ridge B/P: 1/97

2250 McDonald, Sarah - white female D: Nov 17, 1884; 41y; Hampshire B: Hampshire DOI: husband C: McDonald, Jacob B/P: 1/38

2251 McDonald, V.E. - white male D: 1894; 26y; Hampshire F: McDonald Z.B. B: Hampshire DOI: father B/P: 1/60

2252 McDonald, Vernia R. - white female D: Feb 5, 1909; 8m 21d B/P: 2/74

2253 McDonald, Violet Pearl - white female D: Sept 28, 1916; 6d B: Sherman District B/P: 2/75

2254 McDonald, William - married white male D: Apr 30, 1893; 71y; near Three Churches B: Hampshire BUR: Three Churches B/P: 1/82

2255 McDonald, William - white male D: April 3, 1893; 71y; Hampshire B/P: 1/58

2256 McDowell, Fannie A. - white female D: Feb 25, 1899; 26y 3m 12d; Bloomery District F: McDowell, H. M: McDowell, Louisa B: Nov 13, 1872 DOI: mother B/P: 1/70

2257 McDowell, Fannie - single white female D: Feb 25, 1899; 22y; Forks of Capon B: Hampshire BUR: Forks of Capon B/P: 1/103

2258 McDowell, Mary M. - white female D: Aug 18, 1904; 18y B/P: 2/82

2259 McDowell, Mr. - single white male D: Apr 24, 1897; 5d; B: Hampshire BUR: Forks of Capon B/P: 1/92

2260 McDowell, Sidney - white female D: Jan 22, 1867; 53y 9m; Romney I: McDowell, John B/P: 1/2

2261 McDowell, Viola - white D: Apr 18, 1904; B/P: 2/82

2262 McElfish, Amos - white male D: Dec 25, 1909; 85y B/P: 2/74 N: farmer

2263 McElfish, Annie - single white female D: June 7, 1906; 73y B/P: 2/73

2264 McGee, Mary - widow white female D: Jan 6, 1909; 75y B/P: 2/74

2265 McGill, E.W., Sr. - white male D: Sept 25, 1891; 7y 6m 17d; Hampshire M: McGill, Mary B: Maryland DOI: mother B/P: 1/55

2266 McGill, W.H. - white male D: July 24, 1888; 15y 7m 1d; Hampshire F: McGill, Ed M: McGill, M.E. B: Hampshire DOI: father B/P: 1/45

2267 McGlathery, Sarah N. - white female D: May 20, 1874; 6y 6m; Hampshire F: McGlathery, Sam'l M: McGlathery, Susan B: Hampshire DOI: father B/P: 1/13

2268 McGlothery, Samuel - widower white male D: June 9, 1909; 75y B/P: 2/74 N: farmer

2269 McGranlin, Nellie - white female D: Apr 6, 1893; 6y; Hampshire B/P: 1/58

2270 McIhou, Augusta - married white female D: Aug 20, 1910; B/P: 2/74

2271 McIlwee, David - white male D: April 1, 1866 B/P: 1/2

2272 McIlwee, Jacob - white male D: Oct 24, 1899; 77y; Capon District I: McIlwee, A.L. B/P: 1/71

2273 McIlwee, Lizzie - white female D: Aug 28, 1900; 19y; Romney F: McIlwee, John D. M: McIlwee, Margaret B: July 1881 DOI: father B/P: 1/72

2274 McIlwee, Mrs. Jno. - white female D: Feb 1904; 65y B/P: 2/82

2275 McIntire, Ann E. - white female D: July 5, 1908; 9m B/P: 2/73

2276 McIntyre, Geo - married white male D: Mar 21, 1910; 40y B/P: 2/74

2277 McKee, Bertha R. - white female D: Dec 5, 1902; 22y; Capon district F: McKee, A.D. B: 1881 DOI: father B/P: 1/78

2278 McKee, Bessie - single white female D: Aug 29, 1896; 2y; Capon Bridge B: Capon Bridge BUR: Fairview, VA B/P: 1/95

2279 McKee, Bettie - white female D: Feb 5, 1903; 4y; Sherman District F: McKee, Welby M: McKee, Kate DOI: father B/P: 1/81

2280 McKee, D.J. - white female D: July 1, 1884; 43y; Hampshire F: Shoemaker, Arch B: Hampshire I: McKee, George S. DOI: son C: McKee, Chas J. B/P: 1/38

2281 McKee, David - white male D: Sept 11, 1882; 13y 7m 18d; Hampshire F: McKee, Hamilton A.J. M: McKee, Martha B: Hampshire DOI: mother B/P: 1/34

2282 McKee, Dorsey - widower white male D: Aug 31, 1899; 71y 10m 15d; Capon Bridge B: Virginia BUR: Fairview, VA B/P: 1/108

2283 McKee, Earnest Lee - white male D: Mar 4, 1907; 2m B/P: 2/73

2284 McKee, Fannie - white female D: Feb 1902; 27y; Hampshire F: Sirbough, L. M: Sirbough, Mary B: 1875 DOI: father C: McKee, J.R, B/P: 1/79

2285 McKee, Florence E. - white female D: June 19, 1904; 38y B/P: 2/73

2286 McKee, Howard - white female D: Oct 21, 1911; 14m B/P: 2/74

2287 McKee, Jasper - white male D: April 11, 1877; Hampshire B: Hampshire I: McKee, Anderson DOI: son C: McKee, C. B/P: 1/22

2288 McKee, John - married white male D: Dec 11, 1911; 78y 9m 14d B/P: 2/74

2289 McKee, Jonathan W.B. - white male D: Aug 4, 1874; 6y 2m 14d; Hampshire F: McKee, Dorsey M: McKee, Susan E. B: Hampshire DOI: father B/P: 1/13

2290 McKee, Joseph - married white male D: Mar 17, 1914; 87 9m 11d B/P: 2/75 N: farmer

2291 McKee, Lydia P - white male D: June 20, 1873; 19y 8m 3d; Hampshire F: McKee, Benjm. M: McKee, Elizabeth B: Hampshire I: McKee, Riley DOI: father B/P: 1/11

2292 McKee, Madison - white male D: Sept 25, 1911; 6m 24d B/P: 2/74

2293 McKee, Mary E.E.R.D. - white female D: May 23, 1875; 2y 9m 4d; Hampshire F: McKee, Smith M: McKee, Ann B: Hampshire DOI: father B/P: 1/16

2294 McKee, Perry E. - white male D: June 19, 1898; 25y; Bloomery District F: McKee, H.A.J. M: McKee, Martha DOI: father B/P: 1/69

2295 McKee, Sadie M. - white female D: Nov 2, 1889; 18d; Hampshire F: McKee, H. M: McKee, M. B: Hampshire DOI: father B/P: 1/51

2296 McKee, Susan E. - white female D: June 20, 1873; 27y; Hampshire F: Johnson, Amos M: Johnson, Eliza B: Hampshire DOI: husband C: McKee, Dorsey B/P: 1/11

2297 McKee, Thos. Carson - married white male D: Mar 4, 1922; 42y 11m 8d; Hampshire F: McKee, Frances M: McKee, Annie B: Virginia I: McKee, Maggie Mrs. B/P: 1/134 N: farmer

2298 McKee, V.D. - widower white male D: Aug 31, 1899; 71y 10m 15d; Capon Bridge B: Virginia BUR: Fairview B/P: 1/109

2299 McKee, Washington - white male D: June 28, 1881; 59y; Hampshire B: Hampshire I: McKee, Wilbur DOI: son B/P: 1/29

2300 McKee, Welby - white male D: Mar 21, 1914; 71y 8m 16d B/P: 2/75 N: cabinet maker

2301 McKeever, Albert D: Sept 15, 1871; 1y 2m F: McKeever, Wm. B/P: 1/6 N: see #235

2302 McKeever, Alphus D: Sept 15, 1871; 1y 2m F: McKeever, Wm. B/P: 1/6 N: see #236

2303 McKeever, Geo - single white male D: Sept 8, 1866; 10m 5d; Hampshire F: McKeever, Tilbury M: McKeever, Jane B: Hampshire DOI: parent B/P: 1/1

2304 McKeever, James - single white male D: Jan 5, 1922; 45y 8m 13d; Hampshire F: McKeever, Elias M: McKeever, Mary B: Capon Bridge I: McKeever, Katie B/P: 1/134

2305 McKeever, Jno W. - married white male D: Oct 11, 1911; 74y 10m 4d B/P: 2/74 N: farmer

2306 McLaughlin, Ann - single white female D: July 2, 1874; 82y 5m 13d; Hampshire F: McLaughlin, Dan'l M: McLaughlin, Mary B: Hampshire I: McLaughlin, Miss DOI: niece B/P: 1/13

2307 McLaughlin, Daniel G. - white male D: July 26, 1873; 70y 4m 8d; Hampshire F: McLaughlin, William M: McLaughlin, Lancy B: Alleghany Co MD I: McGlaughlin, Miss DOI: daughter C: McLaughlin, Julia A. B/P: 1/11 N: farmer

2308 Mellon, J.W. - white male D: Dec 18, 1899; 72y 2m 14d; Bloomery District B: Oct 24, 1827 I: Oates, Geo. W. DOI: son in law C: Mellon, Catherine B/P: 1/70

2309 Mellon, John - married white male D: Dec 18, 1900; 72y 1m 24d; Capon Bridge B: WV BUR: Fairview, VA B/P: 1/108 N: farmer

2310 Mencer, Maggie - white female D: Nov 29, 1912; 28y B: Bloomery B/P: 2/75

2311 Menson, Wm - white male D: Sept 23, 1904; 9m B/P: 2/82

2312 Meritte, Adam - single white male D: Jan 28, 1873; 43 y; Hampshire I: Pancake, Isaac DOI: friend B/P: 1/10 N: farmer

2313 Merrilat, J.C. - white male D: Sept 8, 1881; 70y; Hampshire B: Baltimore Co., MD I: Parson, G.W. DOI: friend C: Merrilat, Mary B/P: 1/30

2314 Merritt, Geo W. - white male D: Mar 24, 1890; 78y; Mill Creek B: Mill Creek I: Merritt, Geo W. DOI: son B/P: 1/49

2315 Merritt, William - married white male D: Sept 10, 1897; 80y; Gap BUR: Gap B/P: 1/94

2316 Messick, Bell - white female D: Feb 3, 1898; 43y 4m; Romney District F: Kees, Chas A. M: Kees, Sallie B/P: 1/68

2317 Messick, Belle - married white female D: Feb 3, 1898; 43y 5m 10d; BUR: Ebenezer B/P: 1/98

2318 Messick, Frank - white male D: Feb 27, 1917; 65y 9m B/P: 2/76 N: farmer

2319 Messick, Frank - white male D: Aug 25, 1919; 2y 6m B/P: 2/76

2320 Meyers, Louzee - white female D: Dec 1896; 3y; Hampshire F: Meyers, W. O. B: 1893 DOI: father B/P: 1/63

2321 Michael E D: Aug 3, 1870; 2y 6m F: Michael, Robert B/P: 1/5

2322 Michael, Amanda - white female D: Sept 1886; 23y; Hampshire F: Michael, John M: Michael, Eliza B: Hampshire DOI: father B/P: 1/41

2323 Michael, Benjamin F. - white male D: Dec 18, 1868; 8m 8d; Dutch Hollow F: Michael, John B: Hampshire DOI: grandfather B/P: 1/3

2324 Michael, Christena - white female D: Feb 26, 1882; 75y; Capton District B: Virginia I: Michael, John DOI: son C: Michael, John B/P: 1/33

2325 Michael, Cleaveland - white male D: May 7, 1886; 3m; Hampshire F: Michael, John M: Michael, Eliza B: Hampshire DOI: father B/P: 1/41

2326 Michael, Cora A. - white female D: Feb 1881; 6m; Hampshire F: Michael, John M: Michael, Louiza B: Hampshire DOI: father B/P: 1/30

2327 Michael, Eliza J. - white female D: Sept 1886; 41y; Hampshire B: Hampshire DOI: husband C: Michael, John B/P: 1/41

2328 Michael, Frances V. - white female D: Sept 1886; 16y; Hampshire F: Michael, John M: Michael, Eliza J. B: Hampshire DOI: father B/P: 1/41

2329 Michael, H - white male D: Dec 1, 1874; 6d; Hampshire F: Michael, John M: Michael, Susan J B: Hampshire DOI: father B/P: 1/12

2330 Michael, Hiram - white male D: May 26, 1891; 75y 5m 16d; Hampshire F: Michael, Adam M: Michael, E. B: Hampshire I: Michael, F. DOI: son C: Michael, Nancy B/P: 1/55

2331 Michael, Ira Wm. - white male D: Feb 2, 1914; 3y 3d B/P: 2/75

2332 Michael, Jacob - white male D: June 15, 1882; 74y; Capon District B: Virginia DOI: wife C: Michael, Sarah B/P: 1/33

2333 Michael, John - white male D: May 22, 1882; 80y; Capon District B: Virginia I: Michael, John DOI: son C: Michael, Christena B/P: 1/33

2334 Michael, John I - white male D: June 20, 1876; 4m 15d; Hampshire F: Michael, Stephen M: Michael, Laura E. B: Hampshire DOI: father B/P: 1/20

2335 Michael, Minnie Belle - married white female D: Mar 28, 1922; 44y 2m 12d; Hampshire F: Kline, Jas. M: Kline, Prudy B: Hampshire B/P: 1/134

2336 Michael, Nancy M. - widower white female D: Oct 22, 1915; 80y 9m 17d B/P: 2/75

2337 Michael, Philip - white male D: Mar 8, 1904; 79y 11m B/P: 2/82

2338 Michael, Rachael D: June 22, 1869; 66y; Hampshire B: Shenandoah Co B/P: 1/4

2339 Michael, Robt. Cyril - single white male D: Mar 22, 1922; 3d; Hampshire F: Michael, Noah M: Michael, Minnie B: WV I: Ruckman, Benj. B/P: 1/134

2340 Michael, Sarah - white female D: Nov 18, 1882; 94y 1m 28d; Sherman District B: Virginia I: Michael, Mrs. P. Jr. DOI: daughter in law C: Michael, Philip B/P: 1/33

2341 Michael, W.H. - white male D: June 23, 1897; 59y 7m 4d; Bloomery F: Michael, Isaac M: Michael, Susan B: Nov 19, 1837 I: Michael, Everett DOI: son C: Michael, M. B/P: 1/66 N: merchant

2342 Michael, William H. - married white male D: June 26, 1897; 65y; Bloomery B: Morgan County BUR: Bloomery B/P: 1/97

2343 Middleton, J.B. - white male D: July 19, 1888; 35y; Hampshire M: Middleton, Nevel S. DOI: mother B/P: 1/45

2344 Milburn, Minnie - white female D: July 16, 1903; 26y; Hampshire F: Bohrer B: 1877 I: Milburn, W.F. DOI: husband B/P: 1/80

2345 Milburn, Nellie - white female D: May 1903; 2m; Hampshire F: Milburn, W.F. M: Milburn, M. B: Nov 28 DOI: father B/P: 1/80

2346 Miles, Elizabeth J. - white female D: Oct 8, 1878; 43y 6d; Hampshire F: Powell, Jas M: Powell, Rosanna DOI: husband C: Miles, John B/P: 1/24

2347 Miles, Ida M - white female D: Sept 15, 1875; 5m 13d; Hampshire M: Miles, Sarah A B: Hampshire I: Miles, Joseph DOI: grandfather B/P: 1/16

2348 Miles, Margaret - white female D: Mar 12, 1904; 77y

B/P: 2/82

2349 Miles, Peter - single white male D: Jan 8, 1899; 50y; Cold Stream B: WV BUR: Cold Stream B/P: 1/101

2350 Milison, Mary H. - white female D: Apr 16, 1876; 60y 3m 18d; Hampshire F: Offutt, Soloman M: Offutt, Elizabeth B: Hampshire I: Milison, Jas M. DOI: son C: Millison, Geo B/P: 1/21

2351 Millar, John D. - white male D: Dec 3, 1904; 79y 8m B/P: 2/82 N: farmer

2352 Miller, Albert - white male D: Apr 25, 1891; 3m 20d; Hampshire F: Miller, Lark M: Miller, A. B: Hampshire DOI: father B/P: 1/55

2353 Miller, Alice - single white female D: Aug 15, 1866; 5y 6m; Hampshire F: Miller, Moses M: Miller, Elmira B: Hampshire DOI: parent B/P: 1/1

2354 Miller, Arthur D. - white male D: Mar 22, 1911; 13y 11m B/P: 2/74

2355 Miller, Clara E. - white female D: Feb 23, 1911; 27y B: Bloomery B/P: 2/74

2356 Miller, David - white male D: June 24, 1910; 14y B/P: 2/74

2357 Miller, David A - white male D: Nov 13, 1885; 17y 8m; Hampshire F: Miller, Eli M: Miller, Frances B: Hampshire DOI: mother B/P: 1/42

2358 Miller, E.V. - white female D: June 17, 1894; 26y; Hampshire DOI: husband C: Miller, J.W. B/P: 1/60

2359 Miller, Emma - married white female D: Feb 4, 1894; 35y; near Slanesville B: Hampshire BUR: near Slanesville B/P: 1/84

2360 Miller, Geo. W. - white male D: apr 28, 1886; 61y; Hampshire B: Hampshire DOI: wife C: Miller, Eliza J. B/P: 1/41

2361 Miller, Hilda - single white female D: July 15, 1906; 10y 6m B/P: 2/73

2362 Miller, Ira B. - white male D: Jan 11, 1911; 2y 3m B/P: 2/74

2363 Miller, J.A. - white D: Nov 7, 1899; 34y 17d; Baltimore F: Miller, O.J. M: Miller, E. B: Nov 20, 1865 I: Miller, W.R. DOI: brother C: Miller, Ida B/P: 1/70

2364 Miller, J.W. - white male D: Sept 14, 1898; 33y; Gore District F: Miller, Washington M: Miller, Jane I: Miller, William R. DOI: brother B/P: 1/69

2365 Miller, Jacob - white male D: May 20, 1886; 83y 1m 6d; Mill Creek District B: Virginia I: Miller, Ephriam DOI: son C: Miller, Ann B/P: 1/43

2366 Miller, Jacob - married white male D: Nov 7, 1899; 35y; Baltimore, MD Hospital B: Hampshire BUR: Lost City B/P: 1/106

2367 Miller, Jas. - single white male D: Sept 14, 1898; 30y; Higginsville B: Hampshire BUR: Hampshire B/P: 1/101 N: merchant

2368 Miller, Jas. T. - white male D: Oct 9, 1885; 25y 2m; Hampshire F: Miller, Eli M: Miller, Frances B: Hampshire DOI: mother B/P: 1/42

2369 Miller, Jno L. - white male D: Sept 25, 1881; 5m 2d; Hampshire F: Miller, Joseph M M: Miller, Bertha C. B: Hampshire DOI: father B/P: 1/29

2370 Miller, Joseph - single white male D: Oct 1891; 20y; Hampshire F: Miller, A. M: Miller, H. B: Hampshire DOI: father B/P: 1/55

2371 Miller, Lane - white female D: Dec 16, 1910; 50y B/P: 2/74

2372 Miller, Larken D. - married white male D: Apr 16, 1921; 66y 5m 11d; Hampshire F: Miller, Hiett M: Miller, Mary B: WV B/P: 1/130 N: farmer

2373 Miller, Lena A. - married white female D: June 16, 1910; 53y B/P: 2/74

2374 Miller, Lilly L. - white female D: Mar 4, 1888; 22y 1m 3d; Hampshire F: Miller, J.D. B: Pennsylvania DOI: father B/P: 1/45

2375 Miller, Luther D. - white male D: Aug 6, 1894; 3m; Capon F: Miller, Wm M: Miller, Sarah B: Capon DOI: father B/P: 1/59

2376 Miller, Margaret Jane - married white female D: Feb 9, 1917; 69y 11m 20d B/P: 2/76

2377 Miller, Mary - white female D: Sept 22, 1893; 70y; Hampshire B/P: 1/58

2378 Miller, Mary E. - married white female D: Sept 9, 1909; 32y 6m B/P: 2/74

2379 Miller, Michael - married white male D: Nov 10, 1872; 87y 1m; Hampshire B: Hampshire DOI: son B/P: 1/9

2380 Miller, Moses - widower white male D: June 19, 1899; 84y 8m 9d; Sherman District B: Hampshire BUR: Mt Zion B/P: 1/107

2381 Miller, Part Wm. - white male D: Jan 7, 1910; 1y 11m 28d B/P: 2/74

2382 Miller, Patience P. - single white female D: Jan 28, 1868; 21y; Fred. Co., VA F: Miller, Robert B: Frederick Co, VA DOI: father B/P: 1/3

2383 Miller, Peter - married white male D: Oct 28, 1908; 84y B/P: 2/73 N: plasterer

2384 Miller, Rachael Lock - white D: Jan 7, 1866 B/P: 1/2

2385 Miller, Rebecca - single white female D: Aug 30, 1881; 80y; Hampshire I: Miller, Wm. L. DOI: nephew B/P: 1/31

2386 Miller, Richard A - white male D: June 18, 1901; 23y; Capon F: Miller, W.T. DOI: father B/P: 1/76

2387 Miller, Robt E. - married white male D: June 29, 1914; 42y 11m 10d B/P: 2/75 N: farmer

2388 Miller, Sallie - white female D: Mar 7, 1886; 56y 6m 6d; Hampshire F: Stump, Adam M: Stump, Parthenia B: Hampshire DOI: husband C: Miller, John D. B/P: 1/41

2389 Miller, Sarah A. - white female D: Jan 28, 1872; 54y 1m 16d; Hampshire F: Wills, B M: Wills, Charity B: Hampshire I: Miller, William DOI: son C: Miller, John B/P: 1/8

2390 Miller, Stephen - white male D: Sept 16, 1894; 16y 11m; Hampshire F: Miller, W.L. B: Hampshire DOI: father B/P: 1/60

2391 Miller, W.H. - white male D: Jan 23, 1899; 1y 6m 17d; Bloomery District F: Miller, William M: Miller, Lucy B: June 6, 1892 I: McCoole, James D. DOI: frandfather B/P: 1/70

2392 Miller, Washington - white male D: Dec 31, 1892; 66y 11m 8d; Hampshire B: Pennsylvania DOI: wife C: Miller, C. B/P: 1/57

2393 Miller, William - white male D: Mar 1900; 8m; Hampshire F: Miller, William M: Miller, Lucy B: Oct 1899 I: McCool, J.D. DOI: grandfather B/P: 1/73

2394 Milleson, Benj. - married white male D: Sept 6, 1895; 65y; Hampshire B: Hampshire B/P: 1/89

2395 Milleson, Chas. M. - married white male D: Feb 20, 1912; 70y B: Springfield B/P: 2/75 N: merchant

2396 Milleson, E.L. - white female D: May 26, 1897; 2m 10d; Cumberland F: Milleson, J.W. M: Milleson, S.F. B: Feb 6, 1897 DOI: father B/P: 1/66

2397 Milleson, Elizabeth R. - widow white female D: Nov 2, 1922; 81y 10m 17d; Hampshire F: Engle, Jno. M: Engle, Sarah B: Hampshire Co I: Milleson, J.C. B/P: 1/134

2398 Milleson, George - white male D: Dec 19, 1873; 61y 5m 13d; Hampshire F: Milleson, John M: Milleson, Ann B: Hampshire I: Milleson, Benj DOI: son C: Milleson, Mary H. B/P: 1/11 N: Deputy Sheriff

2399 Milleson, George - single white male D: Feb 28, 1895; 25y; near Slanesville B: Hampshire BUR: Salem Church B/P: 1/85

2400 Milleson, Harriett - married white female D: May 11, 1885; 76y 6m; Hampshire B: Hampshire I: Light, S.S. DOI: friend B/P: 1/42

2401 Milleson, James - white male D: Apr 8, 1904; 28y B/P: 2/82 N: clerk

2402 Milleson, James - married white male D: Apr 8, 1905; 28y B/P: 2/73 N: merchant

2403 Milleson, John - widower white male D: Feb 25, 1908; 76y B/P: 2/73

2404 Milleson, Johnson - white male D: Dec 29, 1874; 61y 9m 27d; Hampshire F: Milleson, Isaac B: Hampshire I: Milleson,

Peter DOI: son C: Milleson, Phoebe B/P: 1/13

2405 Milleson, Kate - white female D: Apr 9, 1912; 73y B/P: 2/75

2406 Milleson, Mary - single white female D: May 18, 1909; 70y B/P: 2/74

2407 Milleson, Mary E. - single white female D: Dec 23, 1872; 25y 9m 19d; Hampshire F: Milleson, George M: Milleson, Mary B: Hampshire DOI: mother B/P: 1/8

2408 Milleson, Mary H. - white female D: Feb 6, 1884; 25y; Hampshire M: Milleson, Phoebe DOI: mother B/P: 1/39

2409 Milleson, Sallie - white female D: Mar 16, 1904; 66y B/P: 2/82

2410 Milleson, Sarah - white female D: June 27, 1881; 75y; Hampshire F: Henderson, C: Milleson, Wm. B/P: 1/32

2411 Milleson, Silas - married white male D: May 23, 1885; 78y; Hampshire B: Hampshire I: Light, S.S. DOI: friend B/P: 1/42

2412 Milleson, Thos. S. - white male D: Apr 12, 1884; 1y; Hampshire F: Milleson, Chas. M: Milleson, Mary B: Hampshire DOI: father B/P: 1/39

2413 Milleson, Wm. J. - married white male D: Feb 25, 1920; 50y 4m 25d; Hampshire F: Milleson, Chas. M: Milleson, Mary B: WV B/P: 1/129 N: merchant

2414 Mills, C. - widower white male D: Mar 28, 1899; 88y; Cold Stream B: Hampshire BUR: Cold Stream B/P: 1/102

2415 Mills, Effie - white female D: Aug 1882, 3m; Mill Creek District F: Mills, John M. M: Mills, Mary M. B: WV DOI: father B/P: 1/33

2416 Mills, Effie D. - white female D: Aug 1883; 5m; Hampshire F: Mills, John M: Mills, Mary B: Hampshire DOI: father B/P: 1/36

2417 Mills, Elizabeth - white female D: July 8, 1901; 62y; Glebe DOI: father B/P: 1/76

2418 Mills, Emily J - white female D: Jan 1880; 6y 10m; Hampshire F: Mills, John B: Hampshire DOI: father B/P: 1/27

2419 Mills, I.K. - married white male D: Dec 15, 1904; 40y B/P: 2/82

2420 Mills, Jno. - married white male D: July 1, 1897; 59y; Jersey Mountain BUR: Jersey Mt. B/P: 1/92

2421 Mills, Manerva - white female D: June 15, 1908; 82y B/P: 2/74

2422 Mills, Sarah - white female D: Apr 10, 1898; 83y; Romney District F: Hartman, Isaac I: Oates, T.K. B/P: 1/68

2423 Mills, T. - married white female D: Feb 4, 1903; 34y; Hampshire B: Maryland BUR: Romney B/P: 1/114 N: seamstress

2424 Milslagle, George - single white male D: Oct 9, 1866; 81y 2m; Hampshire B: Hampshire B/P: 1/1

2425 Milslagle, Jacob - white male D: Feb 29, 1884; 68y; Hampshire B: Hampshire DOI: wife C: Milslagle, Margaret B/P: 1/38

2426 Milslagle, Jane - white female D: Mar 1, 1873; 66y; Hampshire F: Milslagle, Sam'l M: Milslagle, Sarah B: Hampshire I: Kelsoe, Joseph DOI: son in law C: Milslagle, Sam'l B/P: 1/10

2427 Milslagle, Samuel - white male D: Aug 30, 1868; 65y; Big Capon F: Milslagle, Jacob B: Hampshire DOI: son in law B/P: 1/3

2428 Monroe, Alexander - white male D: Mar 16, 1904; 87y B/P: 2/82 N: farmer

2429 Monroe, J.T. - white male D: May 27, 1908; 40y 1m 10d B/P: 2/73

2430 Monroe, Jeremiah - single white male D: Apt 14, 1875; 43y 11m 24d; Hampshire F: Monroe, James M: Monroe, Margaret B: Hampshire I: Monroe, John DOI: brother B/P: 1/14 N: farmer

2431 Monroe, John Garrett - widower white male D: Jan 5, 1913; 80y 1m 2d B/P: 2/75

2432 Monroe, Mary - married white female D: Feb 22, 1909; 75y 11m 15d B/P: 2/74

2433 Montgomery, Alie - white female D: July 15, 1876; 72y 8m

2d; Hampshire F: Wilson, William M: Wilson, Elizabeth B: Allegany Co MD I: Montgomery, William DOI: son C: Montgomery, Hugh B/P: 1/20

2434 Montgomery, Caroline - married white female D: Oct 9, 1913; 85y 2m 9d B/P: 2/75

2435 Montgomery, E.E. - single white male D: June 24, 1908; 8m 7d B/P: 2/73

2436 Montgomery, Edward - white male D: May 14, 1867; 35y 4m 3d; Middle Ridge F: Montgomery, Hugh M: Montgomery, Alice B: Middle Ridge DOI: father B/P: 1/3

2437 Montgomery, James - widower white male D: Feb 16, 1900; 80y; Spring Gap B: WV BUR: Salem B/P: 1/105

2438 Montgomery, John - colored male D: June 9, 1883; 80y; Hampshire B: Hampshire DOI: wife C: Montgomery, Rachel Ann B/P: 1/37

2439 Montgomery, Lory - married white female D: Jan 2, 1913; 36y B/P: 2/75

2440 Montgomery, Mary - white female D: 1894; 12y; Hampshire F: Montgomery, J. M: Montgomery, N. B: Pennsylvania DOI: father B/P: 1/60

2441 Montgomery, May - single white female D: Apr 2, 1894; 9y; Spring Gap B: Hampshire BUR: Salem Church B/P: 1/84

2442 Montgomery, Priscilla - married white female D: July 6, 1895; 70y; Hampshire B: Hampshire B/P: 1/89

2443 Montgomery, Thomas J D: May 1, 1870; 1m 5d; Hampshire F: Montgomery, William M: Montgomery, Caroline B/P: 1/5

2444 Moore, Abraham - white male D: Oct 10, 1881; 80y 8m 2d; Hampshire F: Moore, Henry M: Moore, E. B: Loudoun Co., VA DOI: wife C: Moore, Sarah B/P: 1/31

2445 Moore, Ivy - white female D: Oct 22, 1880; 66y; Hampshire F: Vandagriff, Christopher M: Vandagriff, Ann B: Hampshire DOI: husband C: Moore, John B/P: 1/28

2446 Moore, Jno W. - white male D: Oct 7, 1881; 75y; Hampshire B: Front Royal, Virginia DOI: wife C: Moore, Mary J. B/P: 1/32 N: doctor

2447 Moore, Peter - single white male D: Oct 27, 1874; 60y;

Hampshire F: Moore, Henry M: Moore, Elizabeth B: Hampshire I: Moore, Wm. H. DOI: nephew B/P: 1/13

2448 Moore, Rebecca A. - white female D: Feb 10, 1876; 45y; Baltimore MD F: Brian, Thos M: Brian, Masser B: Hardy Co DOI: husband C: Moore, Dr. John W B/P: 1/20

2449 Moore, Reuben - single D: June 13, 1869; 33y; Hampshire F: Moore, John W M: Moore, Jemima B: Hampshire B/P: 1/4

2450 Moore, Sarah C. - single white female D: July 15, 1876; 26y 7m 8d; Hampshire F: Moore, John M: Moore, J. B: Hampshire I: Barr, Jas H. DOI: friend B/P: 1/21

2451 Moorehead, Edward D: Oct 26, 1870; 2y 6m; Hampshire F: Moorehead, Robert M: Moorehead, Sarah B/P: 1/5

2452 Moreland, Albert Victor - white male D: Jan 18, 1917; 2m 10d B/P: 2/76

2453 Moreland, Alex'd Thomas - white male D: April 15, 1863; 2y 1m 10d; Levels F: Moreland, George M: Moreland, Sarah B: Levels DOI: father B/P: 1/2

2454 Moreland, Annie - married white female D: Feb 29, 1904; 49y B/P: 2/73

2455 Moreland, Annie H. - white female D: July 29, 1904; 15d B/P: 2/82

2456 Moreland, Arthur - white male D: Sept 5, 1898; 1y 7m; Gore District F: Moreland, W.P. M: Moreland, M.C. DOI: father B/P: 1/69

2457 Moreland, Benjamin - white male D: Jan 15, 1897; 39y; Springfield B: 1858 DOI: wife C: Moreland, E. B/P: 1/66 N: carpenter

2458 Moreland, Dora - white male D: Jan 1, 1910; 37y B/P: 2/74

2459 Moreland, E.B. - white female D: Aug 8, 1888; 11m; Hampshire F: Moreland, W.E. M: Moreland, V. B: Hampshire DOI: father B/P: 1/45

2460 Moreland, Elizabeth - single white female D: Dec 8, 1894; 60y; N. River Mills B: Hampshire BUR: Salem Church B/P: 1/86 N: seamstress

2461 Moreland, Evan - widower white male D: Oct 22, 1913; 93y

B/P: 2/75 N: farmer

2462 Moreland, Floyd S. - white male D: Oct 24, 1891; 15m; Hampshire F: Moreland, Jas. M: Moreland, S. B: Hampshire DOI: father B/P: 1/55

2463 Moreland, Geo H. - widower white male D: May 27, 1899; 80y; Spring Gap B: Hampshire BUR: Forks of Capon B/P: 1/106

2464 Moreland, Geo. Wm. - married white male D: Dec 17, 1920; 86y; Hampshire B: WV I: Moreland, D.W. B/P: 1/129 N: farmer

2465 Moreland, George D: Aug 3, 1870; 35y 10m; Hampshire F: Moreland, Basil M: Moreland, Sarah C: Moreland, Rachel B/P: 1/5

2466 Moreland, George - white male D: May 7, 1914; 4m B/P: 2/75

2467 Moreland, James - married white male D: Apr 20, 1903; 89y; Levels B: Hampshire BUR: Shade Graveyard B/P: 1/117

2468 Moreland, Jas. S. - white male D: July 15, 1884; 1y 1m 1d; Hampshire F: Moreland, Jas M: Moreland, Mary C. B: Hampshire DOI: father B/P: 1/39

2469 Moreland, John W. - white male D: May 29, 1882; 12y; Capon District F: Moreland, L.T. M: Moreland, Mary C. B: WV DOI: father B/P: 1/33

2470 Moreland, L. - white male D: Oct 15, 1901; 73y; Capon District I: Moreland, George DOI: son B/P: 1/76

2471 Moreland, Margt. J. - white female D: Mar 9, 1874; 37y 4m 8d; Hampshire F: Martin, John M: Martin, Eleanor B: Hampshire DOI: husband C: Moreland, James N: 1/13

2472 Moreland, Mary - widow white female D: Dec 16, 1922; 89y 3m 28d; Hampshire F: Queen, Stephen M: Queen, Mary B: WV I: Dehaven, Lee Mrs. B/P: 1/134

2473 Moreland, Mary - married white female D: July 9, 1876; 23y; Hampshire F: Malcolm, William M: Malcolm, Julia B: Hampshire I: Moreland, Magira DOI: mother in law B/P: 1/20

2474 Moreland, Mary C. - married white female D: Oct 20, 1921; 48y 10d; Hampshire F: Largent, Jno. A. M: Largent, Sarah B: Hampshire I: Moreland, W.P. B/P: 1/132

2475 Moreland, Miss - single white female D: Mar 11, 1896; 5y; Hampshire B: Hampshire B/P: 1/88

2476 Moreland, Mrs. Jas. - married white female D: Jan 19, 1894; 45y; Town Hill B: Hampshire BUR: Town Hill B/P: 1/84

2477 Moreland, Rosa B. - white female D: Sept 1874; 2y 4m; Hampshire F: Moreland, George M: Moreland, Mary B: Hampshire DOI: father B/P: 1/13

2478 Moreland, Sarah - white female D: July 29, 1880; 79y; Hampshire F: Marpole, Thos. M: Marpole, Abigail B: Frederick Co., VA I: Largent, Mary DOI: daughter C: Moreland, Geo. B/P: 1/28

2479 Moreland, Tabitha B - white female D: Aug 17, 1884; 21y 11d; Hampshire F: Moreland, Jas M: Moreland, Mary C. B: Hampshire DOI: father B/P: 1/39

2480 Moreland, Verda - white female D: May 16, 1876; 2y 2m 7d; Hampshire F: Moreland, Jas M: Moreland, Margarete B: Hampshire I: Burker, Catharine DOI: aunt B/P: 1/20

2481 Moreland, Virginia L - white female D: June 22, 1874; 4y 28d; Hampshire F: Moreland, James M: Moreland, Margaret B: Hampshire DOI: father B/P: 1/13

2482 Moreland, Wilbert - white male D: Mar 9, 1896; 10y; Hampshire F: Moreland, W. M: Moreland, Mary DOI: father B/P: 1/63

2483 Moreland, William - widower white male D: Nov 19, 1917; 69y 2m 20d B/P: 2/76 N: merchant

2484 Moreland, Wycliff - single white male D: Aug 25, 1920; stillborn; Hampshire F: Moreland, Wycliff M: Moreland, Etta B: Hampshire B/P: 1/129

2485 Moriarty, Davis - single white male D: Feb 20, 1875; 19y; Hampshire F: Moriarty, Martin M: Moriarty, Ellen B: New York City I: Sneathen, Rubin DOI: friend B/P: 1/16

2486 Morris, Cora - white female D: Mar 1889; 7y; Capon District F: Morris, Alex M: Morris, Virginia B: Hampshire DOI: father B/P: 1/47

2487 Morris, Nicholas - white male D: Nov 7, 1894; 15y 9m; Mill Creek F: Morris, Bushrod B: Mill Creek DOI: father B/P: 1/59

2488 Mowry, James Edward - white male D: Jan 29, 1917; 26y B/P: 2/76

2489 Mulledy, Ada - single white female D: Jan 2, 1908; 19y 9m 15d B/P: 2/73

2490 Mulledy, J.P. - white male D: Jan 15, 1888; 1y 11m 26d; Hampshire F: Mulledy, Jas. M: Mulledy, M. B: Hampshire DOI: father B/P: 1/45

2491 Mulledy, Robt - white male D: Aug 1, 1892; 83y; Hampshire B: Hampshire I: Mulledy, J. DOI: son B/P: 1/57

2492 Murray, Ada - white female D: June 4, 1904; 17y B/P: 2/82

2493 Murray, Elizabeth - white female D: Dec 22, 1882; 75y; Hampshire F: Richmond, J. M: Richmond, J. B: Hampshire I: Foreman, Ann DOI: sister C: Murray, Michael B/P: 1/34

2494 Myers, Nicholas Glenn - single white male D: Nov 7, 1894; 15y 9m; Hampshire B: Hampshire BUR: Pine Hill B/P: 1/92

2495 Mytinger, Bessie - white female D: Dec 24, 1893; 8m; Hampshire B/P: 1/58

2496 Mytinger, Edward - white male D: Nov 29, 1883; 18y 3m; Hampshire F: Mytinger, Tobias M: Mytinger, Martha V. B: Hampshire DOI: father B/P: 1/36

2497 Mytinger, Martha Virginia - widow white female D: Jan 15, 1913; 82y 29d B/P: 2/75

2498 Mytinger, Tobias - married white male D: Jan 19, 1908; 82y 1m 26d B/P: 2/73 N: carpenter

2499 Nair, Margaret - white female D: June 21, 1911; 71y B/P: 2/86

2500 Naylor, John J. - single white male D: May 15, 1900; 39y; Springfield B: WV B/P: 1/108

2501 Nealis, Emma M - white female D: May 16, 1874; 1m 8d; Hampshire F: Nealis, James P. M: Nealis, Mary B: Hampshire DOI: father B/P: 1/13

2502 Nealis, Hugh - single white male D: Oct 10, 1918; 18y 6m 10d; Hampshire B/P: 1/126 N: farmer

2503 Nealis, John - married white male D: Apr 12, 1916; 62y 4m 9d B: Sherman Dist. B/P: 2/86 N: farmer

2504 Nealis, John A - white male D: May 8, 1874; 12y 3m 10d; Hampshire F: Nealis, James P, M: Nealis, Mary B: Hampshire DOI: father B/P: 1/13

2505 Nealis, Joseph E. - white male D: Nov 12, 1910; 43y 3m B/P: 2/86

2506 Nealis, Mary C. - white female D: July 8, 1891; 31y; Hampshire B: Hampshire DOI: husband C: Nealis, William L. B/P: 1/55

2507 Nealis, Mary D. - widow white female D: Mar 31, 1909; 75y 18d B/P: 2/86

2508 Nealis, Nancy - white female D: Jan 15, 1872; 59y; Hampshire F: Coyle, John M: Coyle, Margaret B: Ireland DOI: husband C: Nealis, Geo. B/P: 1/8

2509 Nealis, Rosa - white female D: Oct 27, 1910; 6y B/P: 2/86

2510 Neff, Florence V. - widow white female D: Jun 28, 1920; 62y; Hampshire F: Fowler, Elonza M: Fowler, Hannah B: Maryland B/P: 1/129

2511 Neiswainger, Ida - married white female D: Dec 21, 1887; 18y; Jersey Mountain B: United States BUR: Three Churches B/P: 1/122

2512 Nelson, Althe P. - white female D: July 1, 1897; 6m; Capon District F: Nelson, John E. M: Nelson, Frances C. B: Capon DOI: father B/P: 1/64

2513 Nelson, Evan A. - white male D: Jan 14, 1890; 54y; Capon District F: Nelson, Lorenza M: Nelson, Mary B: Capon District DOI: wife C: Nelson, Mary B/P: 1/49 N: farmer

2514 Nelson, Fitzhue L. - white male D: 1868; 1y 8m; Capon Bridge F: Nelson, Ely J B: Capon Bridge DOI: father B/P: 1/3

2515 Nelson, I.R.B. - white male D: Feb 21, 1894; 1y 4m; Hampshire F: Nelson, R.B. M: Nelson, V.E. B: Hampshire DOI: father B/P: 1/60

2516 Nelson, James E. - white male D: May 21, 1882; 51y 8m 27d; Hampshire F: Nelson, L. M: Nelson, M. B: Hampshire

DOI: wife C: Nelson, Susan M. B/P: 1/34

2517 Nelson, Olla M - white female D: Dec 20, 1875; 3m 17d; Hampshire F: Nelson, James M: Nelson, Susan B: Hampshire DOI: mother B/P: 1/16

2518 Nelson, R.J. - married white male D: June 27, 1892; 82y; Hampshire B: Pennsylvania DOI: physician B/P: 1/57

2519 Nelson, Susan - white female D: Nov 1882; 68y; Capon District B: Virginia DOI: husband C: Nelson, Warner W. B/P: 1/33

2520 Nelson, Susanna D: Dec 17, 1870; 84y 1m 10d F: Kiter, George B/P: 1/5

2521 Nesmith, Mary - white female D: Sept 5, 1901; 43y; Hampshire I: Nesmith, W.B. B/P: 1/77

2522 Newhouse, Ed Lee - white male D: Dec 25, 1892; 20y 16m 8d; Mill Creek F: Newhouse, Thomas M: Newhouse, Kate B: Near Purgitsville DOI: father B/P: 1/56

2523 Newhouse, Kate - married white female D: Sept 28, 1907; 54y 9m 28d B/P: 2/86

2524 Newhouse, Rebecca Jane - white female D: Mar 18, 1905; 70y B/P: 2/86

2525 Newman, John C. - white male D: Nov 26, 1883; 54y 12m; Hampshire F: Newman, Ralph M: Newman, Margaret B: Hampshire I: Parson, Elwood DOI: cousin B/P: 1/37

2526 Nichol, Noel S. - white male D: Sept 30, 1904; 11y 10d B: Birmingham, Alabama B/P: 2/89

2527 Nichols, Ellen - married white female D: July 22, 1902; 72y; B: USA BUR: Bethel B/P: 1/115

2528 Nichols, Isaac - white male D: Jan 8, 1892; 73y 8m 12d; Hampshire B: Hampshire DOI: wife C: Nichols, Ellen B/P: 1/54

2529 Nichols, Martha A. - white female D: Aug 29, 1883; 40y; Hampshire F: McDonald, William B: Hampshire DOI: husband C: Nichols, O.G. B/P: 1/36

2530 Nixon, David W. - white male D: May 13, 1886; 72y; Hampshire F: Nixon, D. M: Nixon, Harriet E. B: Hampshire I: Nixon, William E. DOI: son C: Nixon, Harriet B/P: 1/41

2531 Nixon, George F. - white male D: Oct 11, 1892; 18y; Capon Bridge F: Nixon, George B: Capon Bridge DOI: father B/P: 1/56

2532 Nixon, Glenard O. - white male D: Sept 14, 1914; 4m B/P: 2/86

2533 Nixon, L. - married white male D: Mar 12, 1900; 87y; North River B: WV BUR: Capon Bridge B/P: 1/105

2534 Nixon, Louisa Ann - white female D: June 23, 1914; 63y B/P: 2/86

2535 Nixon, Mary - widow white female D: Mar 2, 1911; 75y B: Gore B/P: 2/86

2536 Nixon, William Edward - married white male D: Dec 17, 1917; 69y 3m B/P: 2/86 N: farmer

2537 Noland, Elisha - single white male D: Oct 9, 1867; 19y 5m 12d; Great Capon F: Noland, Chas. M: Noland, Catherine B: Great Capon DOI: father B/P: 1/3

2538 Noland, Mary - white female D: Feb 22, 1872; 1d; Hampshire F: Noland, John M: Noland, Ann B: Hampshire DOI: mother B/P: 1/8

2539 Noland, Robert D. - married white male D: Nov 25, 1905; 65y B/P: 2/86 N: farmer

2540 Noland, Virgie - single white female D: June 1, 1906; 7y B/P: 2/86

2541 not maned - white female D: Apr 1889; 1d; Romney District F: Hines, Jas. M: Hines, Malissa B: Romney DOI: father B/P: 1/49

2542 not named - white male D: June 30, 1922; 1d; Hampshire F: Seeders, W.H. M: Seeders, Eula B: Hampshire DOI: father B/P: 1/135

2543 not named - single white female D: Mar 19, 1920; stillborn; Hampshire F: Fultz, Homer M: Fultz, Hattie B: Higginsville B/P: 1/129

2544 not named - single white male D: Mar 23, 1921; stillborn; Hampshire F: Martin, Herbert B: Slanesville B/P: 1/130

2545 not named - single white male D: July 8, 1922; stillborn; Hampshire F: Hott, Hetzel M: Hott, Lucy B: Hampshire DOI: father B/P: 1/133

2546 not named - single colored male D: Dec 17, 1921; 3d; Hampshire F: Johnson, Slvester M: Johnson, Phoebe B: Hampshire I: Green, Henry B/P: 1/131

2547 not named D: Oct 24, 1921; stillborn; Hampshire F: Combs, Chas. M: Combs, Cora B: Hampshire B/P: 1/131

2548 not named - white male D: Aug 20, 1918; stillborn; Hampshire F: Saville, B/P: 1/127

2549 not named - single white male D: Oct 21, 1922; 1y 4m 14d; Hampshire M: Hawse, Lulu B. I: Evans, J.W. B/P: 1/133

2550 not named - single white male D: Dec 3, 1921; stillborn; Hampshire M: Halterman, Marie B/P: 1/131

2551 not named - single white female D: Aug 31, 1920; stillborn; Hampshire M: Peer, Flossie B: Slanesville B/P: 1/129

2552 not named - white male D: Aug 30, 1918; stillborn; Hampshire F: Shingleton, B/P: 1/127

2553 not named - single white male D: Sept 1, 1921; stillborn; Hampshire F: Timbrook, Ephriam M: Timbrook, Ida B: Hampshire I: Young, Chas. B/P: 1/132

2554 not named - single white male D: Aug 25, 1921; 5d; Hampshire F: Lee, Alex M: Lee, Nannie B: Hampshire B/P: 1/131

2555 not named - single white female D: DEc 9, 1921; 2d; Hampshire F: Ruckman, Ira M: Ruckman, Edith B: Hampshire DOI: father B/P: 1/132

2556 not named - single white male D: Apr 1920; stillborn; Hampshire F: Poland, Jas. A. M: Poland, Cora B: Hampshire B/P: 1/129

2557 not named - single white male D: Feb 27, 1922; stillborn; Hampshire F: Davis, J.F. M: Davis, Anna T. B: Romney DOI: father B/P: 1/133

2558 not named - white male D: Mar 30, 1873; 20d; Hampshire F: Timbrook, G. M: Timbrook, Elizabeth B: Hampshire DOI: father B/P: 1/10

2559 not named - single white male D: Mar 6, 1877; Hampshire F: Barney, Jacob M: Barney, Amanda B: Hampshire DOI: mother B/P: 1/22

2560 not named D: May 11, 1869; 1d; Hampshire F: Abrel, Lemuel M: Abrel, Sarah B: Hampshire B/P: 1/4

2561 not named D: Oct 17, 1879; 2d; Hampshire F: Peer, Jas H. M: Peer, Rebecca B: Hampshire I: Peer, Elias DOI: grandfather B/P: 1/25

2562 not named - white female D: Nov 10, 1881; 3d; Hampshire F: Mayhue, Joshua M: Mayhue, Susan E. B: Hampshire DOI: father B/P: 1/29

2563 Not named - white male D: Dec 3, 1867; stillborn; Levels F: Snyder, Levi M: Snyder, Elizabeth Cath. B: Levels DOI: father B/P: 1/3

2564 not named - white female D: Dec 10, 1867; 7m 2d; Forks of Capon M: Yost, Sarah B: Spring Gap Mt. DOI: mother B/P: 1/3

2565 not named D: Feb 18, 1870; 2d F: Mills, Jno B/P: 1/5

2566 not named - white female D: Sept 10, 1880; 1d; Hampshire F: Haines, Levi M: Haines, Ann E. B: Hampshire DOI: father B/P: 1/28

2567 not named - white male D: Dec 5, 1877; Hampshire F: Brill, Lemuel M: Brill, Catherine B: Hampshire I: Kump, Benj DOI: neighbor B/P: 1/22

2568 not named - white female D: Feb 2, 1877; Hampshire F: Michael, A.J. M: Michael, Christianni B: Hampshire DOI: father B/P: 1/22

2569 not named - white female D: Aug 14, 1879; 1d; Hampshire F: Himeright, John H. M: Himeright, Mary M. B: Hampshire DOI: father B/P: 1/25

2570 not named - white female D: Nov 14, 1878; 1d; Hampshire F: McKeever, J. M: McKeever, Lucy A. DOI: mother B/P: 1/24

2571 not named - white female D: Apr 2, 1873; 2m; Hampshire F: Shoemaker, Jasper M: Shoemaker, Mary B: Hampshire DOI: father B/P: 1/10

2572 Not named - white male D: Jan 2, 1867; stillborn;

Powell's Mountain F: Powell, Jas. F. M: Powell, Elizabeth B: Powell's Mt. DOI: father B/P: 1/3

2573 not named - white female D: July 14, 1880; 9d; Hampshire F: Echart, Fredk M: Echart, Anna B. B: Hampshire DOI: father B/P: 1/28

2574 not named - white male D: Aug 21, 1874; 20d; Hampshire F: McBride, Eli M: McBride, Rebecca B: Hampshire DOI: mother B/P: 1/13

2575 not named - white male D: Nov 31, 1881; stillborn; West Va F: Coffman, Julius M: Coffman, Susan B: Hampshire DOI: father B/P: 1/29

2576 not named D: Dec 25, 1869; 1d; Hampshire F: McKee, Riley M: McKee, E. B: Hampshire B/P: 1/4

2577 not named - white female D: July 1, 1881; 1d; Hampshire F: Haines, David M: Haines, Catherine B: Hampshire DOI: father B/P: 1/29

2578 not named D: Aug 21, 1871; 1d F: Gonoe, John M: Gonoe, Maria B/P: 1/6

2579 not named - white male D: Nov 8, 1879; 1d; Hampshire F: Milles, William M: Milles, Sarah B: Hampshire DOI: father B/P: 1/25

2580 not named - white male D: June 26, 1880; 14d; Hampshire F: Sherwood, Levi M: Sherwood, Mary J. B: Hampshire DOI: father B/P: 1/28

2581 not named - white female D: Feb 1881; 1d; Hampshire F: Fleming, Ed. A. M: Fleming, Susan C. B: Hampshire DOI: father B/P: 1/29

2582 not named D: Nov 16, 1871; 1d F: Stagg, Jacob B/P: 1/7

2583 not named - white male D: Apr 10, 1878; Hampshire F: Barr, Jas. M: Barr, Margaret B: Hampshire DOI: father B/P: 1/24

2584 not named - white female D: May 25, 1877; Hampshire F: Dolflemey, David M: Dolflemey, D. B: Hampshire DOI: father B/P: 1/22

2585 not named - white male D: Jan 10, 1876; 1d; Hampshire F: Shanholtzer, John M M: Shanholtzer, Anna B: Hampshire

DOI: father B/P: 1/18

2586 not named - white male D: June 8, 1872; 1d; Hampshire F: Corbin, Joseph M: Corbin, Jane B: Hampshire DOI: mother B/P: 1/8

2587 not named - white male D: June 20, 1874; stillborn; Hampshire F: Carrier, Isaac M: Carrier, Sarah B: Hampshire DOI: father B/P: 1/12

2588 not named - white male D: Apr 8, 1878; Hampshire F: Hixon, Perry M: Hixon, Sarah B: Hampshire DOI: father B/P: 1/23

2589 not named D: Sept 1, 1869; 0d; Hampshire F: Bremur, James M: Bremur, Martha B: Hampshire B/P: 1/4

2590 not named D: Oct 22, 1869; 2d; Hampshire F: Cheshire, Elias M: Cheshire, Cath B: Hampshire B/P: 1/4

2591 not named - white male D: Jan 1, 1872; Hampshire F: Poling, James M: Poling, Mary B: Hampshire DOI: father B/P: 1/9

2592 not named - single white male D: Sept 5, 1876; 1d; Hampshire F: Davis, G.W. M: Davis, Anna B: Hampshire I: Davis, G.W. B/P: 1/18

2593 Not Named - single white male D: Feb 7, 1866; 3M F: Brill, Amos M: Brill, E. B: Hampshire DOI: parent B/P: 1/1

2594 not named D: Sept 10, 1869; 0d; Hampshire F: McCauley, Benj F M: McCauley, Ellen B: Hampshire B/P: 1/4

2595 not named - white male D: Aug 25, 1875; 3d; Hampshire M: Howdyshell, Rebecca B: Hampshire DOI: mother B/P: 1/14

2596 not named - white male D: Sept 12, 1873; Hampshire F: Moreland, James M: Moreland, Sarah B: Hampshire DOI: father B/P: 1/11

2597 not named - white, male D: Nov 25, 1874; 5m; Hampshire F: Spaid, Nicholas M: Spaid, Ann B: Hampshire DOI: father B/P: 1/12

2598 not named - white female D: July 28, 1868; stillborn; Grassy Lick F: Haines, Razin B: Hampshire DOI: mother B/P: 1/3

2599 not named D: Apr 4, 1870; 5d F: Brady, Isaac B/P: 1/5

2600 not named - white male D: Jan 27, 1879; 1 d; Hampshire F: Nichles, Isaac M: Nichles, Martha B: Hampshire DOI: father B/P: 1/25

2601 not named - white female D: July 30, 1874; 1d; Hampshire F: Arnold, Joshua M: Arnold, Mary B: Hampshire DOI: father B/P: 1/11

2602 not named - white male D: Apr 2, 1873; 15d; Hampshire F: Haggerty, George M: Haggerty, Jane B: Hampshire DOI: father B/P: 1/10

2603 not named D: Sept 9, 1871; 1d; Hampshire F: Croston, Jno W M: Croston, E. B/P: 1/6

2604 not named D: Oct 1, 1870; 12 d F: Himelright John B/P: 1/5

2605 not named - white female D: July 8, 1867; 4d; Mouth Little Capon F: Kerns, Geo W M: Kerns, Susanna B: mouth Little Capon DOI: father B/P: 1/2

2606 not named - white D: Jan 27, 1877; Hampshire F: Hartman, David M: Hartman, Henrietta B: Hampshire DOI: mother B/P: 1/22

2607 not named - white male D: Apr 18, 1875 F: Arnold, Robt M: Arnold, Mary B: Hampshire DOI: father B/P: 1/14

2608 not named - white male D: Mar 31, 1880; 2m; Hampshire F: Seders, Jacob R. M: Seders, Charlotte B: Hammpshire DOI: mother B/P: 1/28

2609 not named - white female D: Aug 26, 1880; 21d; Hampshire F: Pickering, John M: Pickering, Martha A. DOI: father B/P: 1/28

2610 not named - white male D: July 25, 1880; 14d; Hampshire F: Hemilright, Jno H. M: Hemilright, Margaret B: Hampshire DOI: father B/P: 1/27

2611 not named - single white female D: Aug 10, 1873; Hampshire F: Mills, William M: Mills, Sarah B: Hampshire DOI: father B/P: 1/10

2612 not named - white female D: Nov 9, 1880; 5m; Hampshire F: Didawick, John M: Didawick, Elizabeth B: Hampshire I: Perrill, Jas. W. DOI: grandfather B/P: 1/27

2613 not named - white male D: Mar 24, 1878; 2d; Hampshire F: Hixon, Perry M: Hixon, Sarah B: Hampshire DOI: father B/P: 1/23

2614 not named - white female D: Aug 1, 1872; 17d; Hampshire F: Pantors, Oliver M: Pantors, Mary B: Maryland DOI: father B/P: 1/8

2615 not named - white male D: July 22, 1876; 1d; Hampshire F: Mauzy, Sam'l M: Mauzy, Julia B: Hampshire DOI: father B/P: 1/20

2616 not named D: Feb 22, 1871; 1y 1d F: Hannas, John M: Hannas, Hannah B/P: 1/6

2617 not named D: June 15, 1871; 1d F: Brill, Jonathan B/P: 1/6

2618 not named - white male D: Dec 17, 1884; 2d; Hampshire F: Snyder, Jas. M: Snyder, Verdie B: Hampshire DOI: mother B/P: 1/38

2619 not named - white male D: Jan 6, 1881; 2d; Hampshire F: Hiett, Evan M: Hiett, Sarah B: Hampshire DOI: father B/P: 1/31

2620 not named - white female D: Feb 1883; 1d; Hampshire F: McDonald, B.F. M: McDonald, Sarah B: Hampshire DOI: father B/P: 1/36

2621 not named - white female D: Sept 1888; stillborn; Sherman District F: Howard, J.T. M: Howard, Anna B: Hampshire DOI: father B/P: 1/47

2622 not named - white female D: Mar 6, 1885; 1d; Hampshire F: Leatherman, J.N. M: Leatherman, M.A. B: Hampshire DOI: mother B/P: 1/41

2623 not named - white female D: Aug 10, 1883; 1d; Hampshire F: Haines, George M: Haines, Susan B: Hampshire DOI: father B/P: 1/36

2624 not named - white female D: Jan 1, 1888; 13d; Hampshire F: McDonald, E.M. B: Hampshire DOI: father B/P: 1/45

2625 not named - white female D: Feb 4, 1892; 1d; Hampshire F: Kline, H.P. M: Kline, Minnie F. B: Hampshire DOI: father B/P: 1/53

2626 not named - white female D: Dec 1886; 1d; Sherman

District F: Bean, Erasmus M: Bean, Mary B: Hampshire DOI: father B/P: 1/43

2627 not named - white male (twins) D: May 20, 1889; Hampshire F: Spiar, Jas. M: Spiar, E. B: Hampshire DOI: father B/P: 1/52

2628 not named - white male D: Oct 1889; 1d; Sherman District F: Combs, W.A. B: Sherman District DOI: father B/P: 1/49

2629 not named - white female D: Oct 1888; 1d; Hampshire F: Taylor K. M: Taylor, L. B: Hampshire DOI: father B/P: 1/46

2630 not named - white female D: Mar 11, 1891; 1d; Hampshire F: Leatherman, Nick M: Leatherman, Martha A. B: Hampshire DOI: father B/P: 1/53

2631 not named - white male D: Aug 15, 1884; 8d; Hampshire F: Roomsberg, Geo W. M: Roomsberg, Matilda J. B: Hampshire DOI: father B/P: 1/38

2632 not named - white male D: Nov 11, 1883; 1d; Hampshire F: Abrel, Edward M: Abrel, Sarah E. B: Hampshire DOI: father B/P: 1/37

2633 not named - white male D: June 1885; 4d; Hampshire F: Farmer, John W. M: Farmer, Alice R. B: Hampshire DOI: father B/P: 1/41

2634 not named - white male D: Mar 1891; 6m; Sherman District F: Poland, W.A. M: Poland, Malinda B: Hampshire I: Poland, Louisa DOI: grandmother B/P: 1/52

2635 not named - white male D: Apr 1882; 15d; Hampshire F: Moreland, W.E. M: Moreland, V.B. B: Hampshire DOI: father B/P: 1/34

2636 not named - white male D: Feb 1891; 1m; Hampshire F: Wolford, J.W. M: Wolford, Fannie B: Hampshire DOI: father B/P: 1/53

2637 not named - white female D: Jan 23, 1890; 2m; Sherman District F: Poland, W.A. M: Poland, Malinda M. B: Sherman District DOI: father B/P: 1/49

2638 not named - colored male D: Jan 14, 1889; 8d; Romney District F: Day, Ed M: Day, Eliza B: Hampshire DOI: father B/P: 1/47

2639 not named - white female D: July 1888; 2d; Sherman

District F: Haines, G.W. M: Haines, M. B: Hampshire DOI: father B/P: 1/47

2640 not named - white male D: May 20, 1891; 3d; Hampshire F: Smith, Chas M: Smith, A. B: Hampshire DOI: father B/P: 1/55

2641 not named - white female D: July 1889; 1d; Romney District F: Herriot, Ephriam M: Herriot, Susan M. B: Romney, District DOI: father B/P: 1/49

2642 not named - white male D: Jan 1, 1890; 1d; Romney District F: Hott, Benj. F. M: Hott, Martha E. B: Romney District DOI: father B/P: 1/49

2643 not named - white male D: Dec 31, 1884; 1m 20d; Hampshire F: Anderson, Thos. M: Anderson, Laura B: Hampshire DOI: father B/P: 1/38

2644 not named - white male D: May 11, 1881; stillborn; Hampshire F: Brown, Jas M: Brown, Mary J. B: Hampshire DOI: mother B/P: 1/30

2645 not named - white male D: Jan 19, 1890; 1d; Mill Creek F: High, Jno H. M: High, Sarah E. B: Mill Creek DOI: father B/P: 1/49

2646 not named - white female D: Oct 1882; 2d; Capon District F: Frank, William H. M: Frank, Rachel B: WV DOI: father B/P: 1/33

2647 not named - white female D: Dec 1889; 1m; Sherman District F: Poland, Ruben M: Poland, Mary B: Sherman District I: Poland, Richard DOI: grandfather B/P: 1/49

2648 not named - white male D: Dec 23, 1889; 1d; Hampshire F: Iliff, H. M: Iliff, H. B: Hampshire DOI: father B/P: 1/51

2649 not named - white female (twin) D: June 8, 1888; 1d; Hampshire F: Mercer, Rob M: Mercer, E. B: Hampshire DOI: father B/P: 1/45

2650 not named - white female D: June 6, 1892; 1d; Hampshire F: Powell, J.B. M: Powell, M.E. B: Hampshire DOI: father B/P: 1/57

2651 not named - white male D: Feb 28, 1892; Sherman District F: Saville, John M: Saville, Sarah B: Sherman District DOI: father B/P: 1/56

2652 not named - white female D: May 1891; 2d; Hampshire F: Mills, I.K. M: Mills, Sydney M B: Hampshire DOI: father B/P: 1/53

2653 not named - white female D: Apr 21, 1891; stillborn; Hampshire F: Roberson, Jno. M: Roberson, J. B: Hampshire DOI: father B/P: 1/55

2654 not named - white female D: June 26, 1886; 1d; Sherman District F: Haines, John M: Haines, Delilia B: Hampshire DOI: father B/P: 1/43

2655 not named - white female D: Nar 16, 1885; 2d; Hampshire F: Arnold, Robt M: Arnold, Margaret B: Hampshire I: Arnold, Jno R. DOI: uncle B/P: 1/41

2656 not named - white male D: May 10, 1883; 1d; Hampshire F: Baker, Jacob M: Baker, Hannah B: Hampshire DOI: father B/P: 1/36

2657 not named - white male D: June 19, 1884; 17d; Hampshire B/P: 1/40

2658 not named - white male D: Feb 19, 1892; 1d; Hampshire F: Veach, H.W. M: Veach, Margaret B: Hampshire DOI: father B/P: 1/54

2659 not named - white female D: Dec 25, 1891; 1d; Hampshire F: High, N.P. M: High, Mary E. B: Hampshire DOI: father B/P: 1/53

2660 not named - white male D: May 14, 1891; 1d; Hampshire F: Hott, Wm. T. M: Hott, Grace A. B: Hampshire DOI: father B/P: 1/53

2661 not named - white male D: May 23, 1885; 1d; Hampshire F: Albaugh, John W. M: Albaugh, Adaline B: Hampshire DOI: father B/P: 1/42

2662 not named - white female D: Aug 1889; 1d; Romney District F: Cheshire, Jas. M: Cheshire, Mary H. B: Romney District DOI: father B/P: 1/49

2663 not named - white male D: Nov 15, 1885; Hampshire F: Moreland, Oliver M: Moreland, Alice B: Hampshire DOI: father B/P: 1/42

2664 not named - white male D: Oct 1886; 2d; Mill Creek District F: See, V.A. M: See, Amanda B: Hampshire DOI:

father B/P: 1/43

2665 not named - white male D: June 5, 1892; 21d; Hampshire F: Henderson, R.A. M: Henderson, M. B: Hampshire DOI: mother B/P: 1/57

2666 not named - white male D: Nov 1882; 1d; Mill Creek District F: Minshall, Jno. M: Minshall, Mary B: WV DOI: father B/P: 1/33

2667 not named - white male D: Mar 6, 1891; 1d; Mill Creek F: Hottinger, Noah M: Hottinger, D. B: Hampshire DOI: father B/P: 1/52

2668 not named - colored male D: June 1884; 7d; Hampshire F: Holt, John M: Holt, Bettie B: Hampshire DOI: mother B/P: 1/38

2669 not named - white female D: Mar 12, 1889; stillborn; Hampshire F: Saville, R. M: Saville, B. B: Hampshire DOI: father B/P: 1/51

2670 not named - white female D: Feb 13, 1891; 4d; Capon District F: McKee, C.C. M: McKee, Florence B: Hampshire DOI: father B/P: 1/52

2671 not named - white female D: Nov 14, 1889; 1d; Sherman District F: Shank, John H. M: Shank, Julian B: Sherman District DOI: mother B/P: 1/50

2672 not named - white female D: June 15, 1883; 20m; Hampshire F: Albaugh, John W. M: Albaugh, Adaline B: Hampshire DOI: father B/P: 1/37

2673 not named - white female D: Apr 7, 1892; 2d; Hampshire F: Ullery, A.L. M: Ullery, M.E. B: Hampshire DOI: father B/P: 1/57

2674 not named - white female D: Sept 1891; 6d; Hampshire F: Poling, Jos. M. M: Poling, Margaret B: Hampshire DOI: father B/P: 1/54

2675 not named - white male D: Mar 22, 1892; 1d; Hampshire F: Combs, P.S. M: Combs, Malinda B: Hampshire DOI: father B/P: 1/53

2676 not named - colored female D: Apr 8, 1888; 1d; Hampshire F: Fairfax, D. M: Fairfax, M. B: Hampshire DOI: father B/P: 1/45

2677 not named - white male D: Oct 9, 1884; 1d; Hampshire F: Baker, Isaac N. M: Baker, Catharine B: Hampshire DOI: father B/P: 1/38

2678 not named - colored female D: Mar 1887; stillborn; Romney District F: Jones, Jesse M: Jones, Edith B: Hampshire DOI: father B/P: 1/43

2679 not named - white female D: Sept 15, 1892; 1m 1d; Sherman District F: Godlove, J.C. B: Kirby DOI: father B/P: 1/56

2680 not named - white male D: Feb 1887; stillborn; Capon District F: Kump, Richard M: Kump, Mary P. B: Hampshire DOI: father B/P: 1/43

2681 not named - white male (twin) D: June 8, 1888; 1d; Hampshire F: Mercer, Rob M: Mercer, E. B: Hampshire DOI: father B/P: 1/45

2682 not named - white male D: May 7, 1891; 1d; Hampshire F: Rinker, Sylvester M: Rinker, Emily B: Hampshire DOI: father B/P: 1/54

2683 not named - white male D: July 1, 1888; stillborn; Sherman District F: Poland, Jas. W. M: Poland, Jennie B: Hampshire DOI: father B/P: 1/47

2684 not named - white male D: July 27, 1891; stillborn; Hampshire F: Pownall, F.J. M: Pownall, M. B: Hampshire DOI: father B/P: 1/55

2685 not named - white male D: Dec 12, 1882; 14d; Hampshire F: Wolford, G.F. M: Wolford, L. B: Hampshire DOI: father B/P: 1/34

2686 not named - white male D: May 7, 1891; 1 d; Hampshire F: Simpson, H. B: Hampshire DOI: father B/P: 1/55

2687 not named - white male D: June 15, 1884; 1d; Hampshire F: Kelley, Thos M: Kelley, Lydia B: Hampshire DOI: father B/P: 1/40

2688 not named - white male D: Feb 15, 1890; 1d; Romney District F: Baird, W.N. M: Baird, Sallie B: Romney DOI: father B/P: 1/49

2689 not named - white female D: Oct 25, 1882; 1d; Hampshire F: Darr, J. M: Darr, Mary C. B: Hampshire DOI: mother B/P: 1/34

2690 not named - white female D: May 1886; Hampshire F: Reel, Jesse M: Reel, Ann R. B: Hampshire I: Racey, Morgan DOI: friend B/P: 1/41

2691 not named - white male D: Oct 25, 1893; 5m; Hampshire F: Hott, D.G. M: Hott, Ellen DOI: mother B/P: 1/58

2692 not named - white male D: June 25, 1885; 1d; Hampshire F: Davy, Wm. H. M: Davy, Sarah V. B: Hampshire DOI: mother B/P: 1/41

2693 not named - white female D: Nov 5, 1892; 10m; Great Capon F: Brill, Wm. A. B: Capon River DOI: father B/P: 1/56

2694 not named - white female D: Sept 21, 1889; stillborn; Hampshire F: Largent, S.H. M: Largent, S. B: Hampshire DOI: father B/P: 1/51

2695 not named - white female D: Sept 2, 1890; 2d; Capon District F: Farmer, Benj. M: Farmer, Sarah B: Hampshire DOI: father B/P: 1/52

2696 not named - white female D: Nov 1888; 1d; Hampshire F: Bidinger, Geo M: Bidinger, Rebecca B: Hampshire DOI: father B/P: 1/45 N: twin see #1402

2697 not named - white female D: July 12, 1888; 3m; Capon District F: Oats, Geoge B: Hampshire DOI: father B/P: 1/47

2698 not named - white female D: Feb 1889; stillborn; Capon District F: Miller, W.T. M: Miller, H. B: Hampshire DOI: father B/P: 1/47

2699 not named - white male D: Jan 4, 1889; 8d; Sherman District F: Brill, I.B. M: Brill, Ann M. B: Hampshire DOI: father B/P: 1/47

2700 not named - white female D: Dec 1889; stillborn; Romney District F: Kline, Jno A. M: Kline, Sallie B: Romney District DOI: father B/P: 1/49

2701 not named - white female D: Apr 15, 1884; 3d; Hampshire F: Effland, Geo W. M: Effland, Sarah B: Hampshire DOI: father B/P: 1/40

2702 not named - white female D: June 1, 1886; 1d; Hampshire F: Luttrell, Jas. M: Luttrell, Mat. B: Hampshire DOI: father B/P: 1/44

2703 not named - white male D: Oct 16, 1884; 15d; Hampshire F: Ziler, Josh M: Ziler, Emily B: Hampshire DOI: father B/P: 1/40

2704 not named - white male D: Dec 25, 1884; 1d; Hampshire F: Barnes, A.F. M: Barnes, Margaret B: Hampshire DOI: father B/P: 1/40

2705 not named - white female D: Feb 7, 1890; 1m 15d; Sherman District M: Simmons, Dorsie B: Sherman District DOI: mother B/P: 1/50

2706 not named - white male D: Dec 25, 1892; stillborn; Mill Creek F: Bowman, John C. B: Mill Creek DOI: father B/P: 1/56

2707 not named - white female D: May 21, 1888; 4d; Hampshire F: Smith, C M: Smith, V B: Hampshire DOI: father B/P: 1/46

2708 not named - colored female D: July 22, 1881; 1d; Hampshire F: Mason, L. M: Mason, Susan B: Hampshire DOI: mother B/P: 1/31

2709 not named - white female D: Jan 1882; stillborn; Sherman District F: McDonald, Jared M: McDonald, Maria B: WV I: Shingleton, Mary DOI: grandmother B/P: 1/33

2710 not named - white female D: Sept 15, 1885; stillborn; Hampshire F: Bean, Erasmus M: Bean, Elizabeth B: Hampshire DOI: father B/P: 1/41

2711 not named - white male D: Dec 3, 1900; 1m; Hampshire F: Oats, J.R. M: Oats, M.A. B: Nov 1, 1900 DOI: father B/P: 1/73

2712 not named - white female D: Apr 26, 1901; 6d; Capon Springs F: Miller, Peter M: Miller, Fannie DOI: father B/P: 1/76

2713 not named - white male D: Jan 18, 1903; 2d; Kirby F: Heare, J.S. M: Heare, M. B: Jan 16 DOI: father B/P: 1/81

2714 not named - white male D: July 1898; 1m; Bloomery District F: Harrison, Wm. M: Harrison, M.A. DOI: father B/P: 1/69

2715 not named - white male D: Sept 1903; Hampshire F: Henderson, L.H. M: Henderson, Sarah B: 1903 DOI: father B/P: 1/80

2716 not named - white female D: Sept 18, 1898; 6m 1d; Bloomery District B: Bloomery District BUR: Cold Stream B/P: 1/98

2717 not named - single white female D: Mar 20, 1898 F: Brown, Jeff B: Romney BUR: Romney B/P: 1/98

2718 not named - white male D: July 15, 1903; 6d; Capon district F: Zilor, S.C. B/P: 1/81

2719 not named - white male D: June 21, 1894; 6m; Romney M: Shears, Eliza I: Kelly, Geo B/P: 1/59

2720 not named - white male D: Dec 1900; 15d; Hampshire F: Steward, E.G. M: Steward, Cloe B: Dec 1900 DOI: father B/P: 1/74

2721 not named - white male D: Aug 8, 1901; 1d; Hampshire F: Ambrose, W.C. M: Ambrose, Mary DOI: father B/P: 1/77

2722 not named - white male D: June 3, 1900; 1d; Hampshire F: Shanholts, B.W. M: Shanholts, Elizabeth B: June 3, 1900 DOI: father B/P: 1/73

2723 not named - white female D: Mar 12, 1895; 14d; near Kirby B: Hampshire BUR: Mountain Dale B/P: 1/86

2724 not named - white male D: Sept 9, 1894; 5m; Hampshire F: Buckwater, N.S. M: Buckwater, N. B: Hampshire DOI: father B/P: 1/60

2725 not named - white male D: Dec 1903; 1d; Hampshire F: Wolford, J.W. M: Wolford, Margaret B: Dec 1903 DOI: father B/P: 1/80

2726 not named - white female D: Aug 1899; 3m; Hanging Rock F: Whitacre, Auther M: Whitacre, Oliva DOI: father B/P: 1/71

2727 not named - white male D: Nov 5, 1900; 1d; Hampshire F: Shanholts, L. M: Shanholts, Liza B: Nov 5 DOI: father B/P: 1/73

2728 not named - white male D: Nov 12, 1894; Near North River Mills M: Short, Nannie B: Hampshire B/P: 1/83

2729 not named - white male D: June 12, 1898; 75y; Gore District F: Shanholtzer, S.J. DOI: father B/P: 1/69

2730 not named - white female D: Nov 17, 1894; 34d; near Slanesville B: Hampshire BUR: 1/85

2731 not named - single white male D: June 15, 1897; 5d; Spring Gap F: Fishell B: Hampshire BUR: Spring Gap B/P: 1/91

2732 not named - white male D: July 1901; 1d; Hampshire F: Lewis, L. M: Lewis, Emma I: Lewis, J. B/P: 1/77

2733 not named - white female D: Oct 1, 1903; 1m; Hampshire F: McDonald, J.A. M: McDonald, Martha B: Aug 22, 1903 DOI: mother B/P: 1/80

2734 not named - white female D: Nov 12, 1902; 7d; Romney District F: Howdyshell, T.B. M: Howdyshell, Ella B: Nov 5, 1902 DOI: father B/P: 1/78

2735 not named - single colored male D: June 20, 1897; 2y; Gap BUR: Gap B/P: 1/95

2736 not named - white female D: July 14, 1899; 9m 5d; Winchester F: Sloneaker, J.W.D. M: Sloneaker, E.E. B: Sept 9, 1898 DOI: father B/P: 1/70

2737 not named - white female D: June 5, 1901; 2m; Sherman District F: McCauley, George M: McCauley, Lura DOI: father B/P: 1/76

2738 not named - white male D: Aug 18, 1902; Hampshire F: McCauley, J.A. M: McCauley, Clara B: Aug 18, 1802 DOI: father B/P: 1/79

2739 not named - white male D: Dec 7, 1900; 1m; Hampshire F: Oats, J.R. M: Oats, M.A. B: Nov 1, 1900 DOI: father B/P: 1/73

2740 not named - white male D: Feb 1900; 1m; Hampshire F: Long, William M: Long, Hattie B: Jan 1900 DOI: father B/P: 1/74

2741 not named - white male D: May 10, 1898; 1d; Gore District F: Ganoe, Burr M: Ganoe, A.B. DOI: mother B/P: 1/69

2742 not named - white male D: July 14, 1900; 6m; Hampshire F: Slonaker, J.W.D. M: Slonaker, Emma B: Jan 2, 1900 DOI: father B/P: 1/73

2743 not named - white female D: Oct 14, 1895; 1m 1d; Capon

District F: Jackson, Luther B: Oct 28, 1895 DOI: father B/P: 1/61

2744 not named - single white male D: Dec 17, 1898; Hampshire BUR: Hampshire B/P: 1/99

2745 not named - white male D: Oct 19, 1900; 1d; Hampshire I: Yost, Rachel DOI: grandmother B/P: 1/73

2746 not named - white male D: July 10, 1901; 8m; Capon District F: Munroe, J.T. M: Munroe, M.F. DOI: father B/P: 1/76

2747 not named - single white male D: Jan 2, 1897; 15d; near Higginsville F: Bowen B: WV BUR: Salem Church B/P: 1/91

2748 not named - white male D: Oct 10, 1897; 4m; Hampshire F: Fields, William M: Fields, Mary B: June 10, 1896 DOI: father B/P: 1/63

2749 not named - white male D: Nov 17, 1899; 1d; Gore District F: Godlove, W.T. M: Godlove, Mary C. B: Nov 17, 1899 DOI: father B/P: 1/70

2750 not named - white male D: July 1, 1897; 4m 8d; Cold Stream B: Bloomery District BUR: Ebenezer B/P: 1/96

2751 not named - white female D: Dec 20, 1902; 6d; Romney District F: Davis, Jas. M. M: Davis, Emma B: Nov 10, 1892 DOI: father B/P: 1/78

2752 not named - single white female D: Apr 5, 1895; 29d; Hampshire F: Kenny B: Hampshire BUR: Hampshire B/P: 1/87

2753 not named - white male D: May 15, 1894; 18d; Slanesville F: Robinson B: Hampshire BUR: Salem Church B/P: 1/84

2754 not named - white male D: Sept 1899; 24d; Purgittsville F: George, William M: George, Maggie B: Sept 1899 DOI: father B/P: 1/71

2755 not named - white male D: Aug 15, 1899; 15d; Bloomery District F: Alabaugh, J.M. M: Alabaugh, A.M. B: Aug 1, 1899 DOI: father B/P: 1/70

2756 not named - white female D: Nov 15, 1894; 1m; Hampshire F: Haines, L. T. M: Haines, L. B: Hampshire DOI: mother B/P: 1/60

2757 not named - white male D: Aug 1902; Hampshire F:

Saville, R.W. M: Saville, Belle B: Aug 1902 DOI: father B/P: 1/79

2758 not named - white D: Feb 6, 1897; 1d; Hampshire F: Lovett, A.O. B: Hampshire B/P: 1/97

2759 not named - white female D: Dec 26, 1896; 13y; Hampshire F: Abrel, William M: Abrel, Angenina B: Dec 26, 1883 DOI: father B/P: 1/63

2760 not named - white female D: Feb 11, 1896; 3y 11m 11d; Hampshire F: Kline, John M: Kline, Amanda B: Mar 1892 DOI: father B/P: 1/63

2761 not named - white male D: Aug 3, 1898; 29d; Cold Stream B: Cold Stream BUR: Cold Stream B/P: 1/98

2762 not named - white male D: Dec 29, 1894; 5m; Hampshire F: Carder, L.A. M: Carder, M.S. B: Hampshire DOI: father B/P: 1/60

2763 not named - single white male D: Feb 21, 1897; 1d; near Highview B/P: 1/96

2764 not named - white male D: Jan 2, 1897; 7d; Bloomery F: Lovett, A.O. M: Lovett, Anna B: Dec 26, 1896 DOI: father B/P: 1/66

2765 not named - white female D: Jan 18, 1897; 2d; Springfield F: Lewis, C. M: Lewis, C. B: Jan 16, 1897 I: Mulledy, DOI: grandfather B/P: 1/66

2766 not named - white male D: July 18, 1894; 1d; F: Kidwell B: Hampshire B/P: 1/85

2767 not named - white female D: Aug 1894; 1d; Hampshire F: Kidwell, J.M. M: Kidwell, C. B: Hampshire DOI: father B/P: 1/60

2768 not named - white male D: Jan 3, 1894; 1 d; Near Slanesville M: Miller, Emma B: Hampshire BUR: Salem Church B/P: 1/84

2769 not named - white male D: Feb 9, 1902; 9d; Hampshire F: Whitacre, Arch M: Whitacre, Alice B: Feb 1, 1902 DOI: father B/P: 1/79

2770 not named - white male D: Aug 7, 1897; 1d; Gore F: Foltz, J.W. M: Foltz, Ida B: Aug 7, 1897 DOI: mother B/P: 1/66

2771 not named - white female D: July 4, 1902; 2m; Capon District F: Whitlock, D.M. M: Whitlock, Florence B: 1902 DOI: father B/P: 1/78

2772 not named - white male D: May 5, 1903; 27d; Hampshire F: Whitacre, J.W. M: Whitacre, E. B: Apr 18, 1903 DOI: father B/P: 1/80

2773 not named - white male D: Feb 15, 1898; 6d; Romney District F: Lewis, Chas K. M: Lewis, Otelia DOI: father B/P: 1/68

2774 not named - white male D: May 1902; Hampshire F: Stump, S.D. M: Stump, Jennie B: May DOI: father B/P: 1/79

2775 not named - white female D: May 8, 1903; 2m; Romney F: Johnson, Jas. S. M: Johnson, Bertha DOI: father B/P: 1/81

2776 not named - white male D: Nov 3, 1897; 2d; Bloomery F: Hott, K.G. M: Hott, E.V. B: Nov 1, 1897 DOI: father B/P: 1/66

2777 not named - white male D: May 15, 1894; 13d; Hampshire F: Robison, J.A. M: Robison, J.E. B: Hampshire DOI: father B/P: 1/60

2778 not named - white male D: May 1, 1896; stillborn; Hampshire F: Kerns, R.W. B: May 1, 1896 DOI: father B/P: 1/63

2779 not named - white male D: April 1902; 1d; Hampshire F: Roach, David M: Roach, Daisy B: Apr 1902 I: Simpson, Wm. DOI: friend B/P: 1/79

2780 not named - white female D: Dec 16, 1895; 10m; Sherman District F: Davidson, Thomas A. M: Davidson, Hallie B: Mar 16, 1895 DOI: father B/P: 1/61

2781 not named - white male D: Nov 1902; 1m; Hampshire F: Milleson, J.W. M: Milleson, S.L. B: Sept DOI: father B/P: 1/79

2782 not named - white male D: Jan 17, 1902; 1d; Hampshire F: Brelsford, M.F. M: Brelsford, Vernia B: Jan 17, 1902 DOI: father B/P: 1/79

2783 not named - white male D: Oct 15, 1898; 1m; Mill Creek F: Hamilton, Geo M: Hamilton, Fannie DOI: father B/P: 1/68

2784 not named - white male D: Apr 11, 1913; 2d F: Hockman, B/P: 2/47

2785 not named - single white male D: Dec 19, 1887; 8d; Jersey Mountain B: Hampshire BUR: Three Churches B/P: 1/122

2786 not named - white male D: May 31, 1913; stillborn F: Harold, B/P: 2/47

2787 not named - white male D: Apr 9, 1913; stillborn F: Hockman B/P: 2/47

2788 not named - white female D: Sept 8, 1912; stillborn F: Dorsey, B/P: 2/23

2789 not named - white male D: Nov 1, 1907; stillborn F: Hiett B/P: 2/45

2790 not named - white female D: Oct 3, 1904; 1m 4d; B/P: 2/3

2791 not named - white male D: May 17, 1911; F: Bradfield, B: Bloomery B/P: 2/6

2792 not named - single white male D: Aug 15, 1917; stillborn F: Carlyle B/P: 2/16

2793 not named - white female D: July 23, 1912; stillborn F: Henderson B: Gore District B/P: 2/47

2794 not named - single white male D: Jan 18, 1911; stillborn F: Beatty B/P: 2/6

2795 not named - white female D: July 13, 1915; stillborn F: Curry B/P: 2/16

2796 not named - white male D: Aug 1905; 1d F: Iser, B/P: 2/56

2797 not named - white female D: June 20, 1911; stillborn F: Haines, B: Gore District B/P: 2/47

2798 not named - single white male D: Sept 8, 1888; 12d; Okonoko F: Alderton, C. B: WV B/P: 1/123

2799 not named - white female D: June 20, 1911; stillborn F: Haines, B: Gore District B/P: 2/47

2800 not named - white female D: Nov 8, 1910; stillborn F: Day, B/P: 2/22

2801 not named - white male D: Apr 29, 1914; 13d F: Baker B/P: 2/6

2802 not named - white male D: Apr 3, 1913; stillborn F: Hawse B/P: 2/47

2803 not named - white female D: Feb 19, 1913; 5d F: Fishel B/P: 2/34

2804 not named - white male D: Apr 1, 1911; stillborn F: Doman, B/P: 2/23

2805 not named - white female D: Oct 15, 1906; 3m 1d F: Haines, B/P: 2/45

2806 not named - white male D: Aug 17, 1913; stillborn F: Henderson, B/P: 2/47

2807 not named - white male D: May 4, 1912; 24d F: Dorsey B/P: 2/23

2808 not named - white male D: July 18, 1915; stillborn F: Doman, B/P: 2/23

2809 not named - white male D: Mar 14, 1909; 4m 12d F: Hott, B/P: 2/46

2810 not named - white male D: Mar 22, 1907; 2y F: Burton, B/P: 2/4

2811 not named - white female D: Dec 8, 1907; 2d F: Everett, B/P: 2/29

2812 not named - white female D: Nov 7, 1914; 3d F: Haines, B/P: 2/48

2813 not named - single white male D: Dec 17, 1899; Ruckman B: Hampshire BUR: Mt Zion B/P: 1/107

2814 not named - white female D: Dec 1, 1913; stillborn F: Hoke, B/P: 2/47

2815 not named - white D: Oct 25, 1904; 2m F: Godlove, B/P: 2/39

2816 not named - single white male D: Mar 2, 1888 F: Wagoner, John B: Hampshire BUR: Little Capon B/P: 1/123

2817 not named - single white male D: Sept 5, 1898; 20 m;

Spring Gap F: Moreland, B: Spring Gap BUR: Hampshire B/P: 1/101

2818 not named - white male D: July 26, 1915; 1d F: Glaize, B/P: 2/39

2819 not named - single white male D: Dec 17, 1902; 4m 2d; Levels F: Milleson B: Hampshire BUR: Salem B/P: 1/117

2820 not named - white male D: Aug 9, 1911; 3y F: Day, B/P: 2/23

2821 not named - white female D: Oct 3, 1907; stillborn F: Haines, B/P: 2/45

2822 not named - white male D: Sept 8, 1908; F: Arnold, B: Hampshire B/P: 2/3

2823 not named - single white male D: Mar 20, 1899; stillborn; Higginsville F: Byrd, B: Hampshire BUR: Three Churches B/P: 1/102

2824 not named - white female D: Apr 7, 1903; 10d; Levels F: Cowgill B: Hampshire BUR: Levels B/P: 1/118

2825 not named - white male D: July 12, 1904; 1d F: Everett, B/P: 2/29

2826 not named - white male D: Nov 5, 1914; stillborn F: Haines, B/P: 2/48

2827 not named - white male D: Dec 26, 1904; 7y F: Fishel B/P: 2/33

2828 not named - single white male D: Mar 23, 1915; stillborn F: Bean, B/P: 2/6

2829 not named - white female D: Dec 9, 1914; F: Doman, B/P: 2/23

2830 not named - single white male D: July 5, 1889; 4d; near Springfield B: Springfield BUR: Springfield B/P: 1/124

2831 not named - white female D: Oct 9, 1909; stillborn F: Durst B/P: 2/22

2832 not named - white male D: June 2, 1912; 1d F: Fishel, B: Gore District B/P: 2/33

2833 not named - white male D: Sept 3, 1899; 10d; Bloomery

B: Hampshire BUR: Fairview B/P: 1/109

2834 not named - white male D: Dec 26, 1904; 9y F: Blue, B/P: 2/4

2835 not named - white female D: Dec 1, 1914; stillborn F: Hoke, B/P: 2/48

2836 not named - white male D: Oct 25, 1913; stillborn F: Bloom, B/P: 2/6

2837 not named - white female D: Nov 21, 1909; F: Haines, B/P: 2/46

2838 not named - white male D: Mar 21, 1907; 7d F: Foltz, B/P: 2/33

2839 not named - white female D: Mar 28, 1903; 1d; Levels F: Cowgill B: Hampshire BUR: Levels B/P: 1/118

2840 not named - white male D: Sept 11, 1912; 1m 14d F: Everett, B/P: 2/29

2841 not named - white male D: Dec 8, 1902 B: Hampshire BUR: Levels B/P: 1/117

2842 not named - single white male D: Feb 25, 1913; stillborn F: Collins, B/P: 2/16

2843 not named - single white female D: Aug 26, 1888; 6m; BUR: Gareduct B/P: 1/123

2844 not named - white male D: July 26, 1915; 1d F: Glaize, B/P: 2/39

2845 not named - white male D: June 8, 1914 F: Cowgill B/P: 2/16

2846 not named - white female D: 1914 F: Cowgill, B/P: 2/16

2847 not named - white male D: Aug 20, 1914; stillborn F: Dougherty, B/P: 2/23

2848 not named - white male D: Aug 1905; 3d F: Iser, B/P: 2/56

2849 not named - single white male D: Sept 21, 1908; 1d F: Abe, B: Hampshire B/P: 2/3

2850 not named - white female D: Mar 5, 1913; stillborn F: Foltz B/P: 2/34

2851 not named - white female D: Apr 22, 1909; 1d F: Johnson, B/P: 2/59

2852 not named - white male D: Jan 18, 1909; stillborn F: McDonald, B/P: 2/74

2853 not named - white male D: May 24, 1919; F: McBride, B/P: 2/76

2854 not named - white male D: Nov 30, 1909; stillborn F: Malcolm, B/P: 2/74

2855 not named - white male D: June 28, 1913; 3m 28d F: Kidwell, B/P: 2/64

2856 not named - white female D: June 16; 1914; F: Moreland, B/P: 2/75

2857 not named - white male D: Oct 21, 1906; 1d F: Montgomery, B/P: 2/73

2858 not named - white female D: May 25, 1911; 1d F: Leith, B: Springfield District B/P: 2/68

2859 not named - white male D: July 7, 1908; 6m F: Lewis, B/P: 2/68

2860 not named - white female D: Sept 6, 1909; stillborn F: Kerns, B/P: 2/63

2861 not named - white male D: Oct 28, 1904; 1d F: Malcolm, B/P: 2/82

2862 not named - white male D: Mar 4, 1914; 20d F: Moreland, B/P: 2/75

2863 not named - white male D: June 6, 1914; stillborn F: Karns, B/P: 2/64

2864 not named - white male D: Feb 1, 1915; stillborn F: Lewis, B/P: 2/69

2865 not named - white male D: Sept 8, 1914; stillborn F: Kidwell B/P: 2/64

2866 not named - white female D: Dec 27, 1915; stillborn F: Kerns, B/P: 2/64

2867 not named - white male D: Dec 25, 1908; 1d F: McDonald, B/P: 2/73

2868 not named - white male D: July 4, 1910; F: Kidwell, B/P: 2/63

2869 not named - white male D: July 5, 1913; stillborn F: McBride B/P: 2/75

2870 not named - white male D: May 10, 1908; F: Newcomer, B/P: 2/86

2871 not named - white female D: July 2, 1913; 6m F: McBride, B/P: 2/75

2872 not named - white female D: May 20, 1909; stillborn F: Lewis, B/P: 2/68

2873 not named - white female D: Mar 5, 1915; stillborn F: Merritt, B/P: 2/75

2874 not named - white female D: Feb 20, 1914; 2m 12d F: Milleson, B/P: 2/75

2875 not named - white male D: Jan 10, 1914; 1m 17d F: McBride B/P: 2/75

2876 not named - white male D: Oct 10, 1910; stillborn F: Nealis, B/P: 2/86

2877 not named - white female D: Sept 10, 1914; stillborn F: Moreland, B/P: 2/75

2878 not named - white male D: Sept 14, 1914; stillborn F: Kidwell B/P: 2/64

2879 not named - white female D: May 25, 1911; 1d F: Lewis, B/P: 2/69

2880 not named - white male D: Apr 2, 1911; 3y 1m F: Kline B: Gore District B/P: 2/64

2881 not named - white male D: Sept 27,1907; stillborn F: Lewis, B/P: 2/68

2882 not named - white female D: July 28, 1909; stillborn F: Shank, B/P: 2/109

2883 not named - white male D: 1905 F: Oates, B/P: 2/90

2884 not named - white female D: Apr 12, 1913; stillborn F: Wolford, B/P: 2/133

2885 not named - white male D: Jan 10, 1913; stillborn F: Wisner, B/P: 2/133

2886 not named - white male D: Oct 11, 1905; 1d F: Shank, B/P: 2/108

2887 not named - white female D: Apr 5, 1910; B/P: 2/98

2888 not named - white male D: Sept 6, 1914; stillborn F: Wolf, B/P: 2/133

2889 not named - white male D: July 19, 1908; F: Shanholtz, B/P: 2/109

2890 not named - white male D: Feb 9, 1913; 3d F: Shanholtz, B/P: 2/111

2891 not named - white male D: Jan 20, 1913; stillborn F: Shanholtz, B/P: 2/111

2892 not named - white male D: May 19, 1915; stillborn F: Shank, B/P: 2/112

2893 not named - white male D: Mar 12, 1909 F: Sirbaugh B/P: 2/110

2894 not named - white male D: Dec 2, 1913; 1d F: Shank, B/P: 2/111

2895 not named - white male D: Apr 19, 1911; 1d F: Kidwell B: Gore District B/P: 2/64

2896 not named - white male D: May 21, 1916; F: Wilkins, B: Sherman District B/P: 2/133

2897 not named - white male D: Dec 5, 1904; 1d F: Malcolm, B/P: 2/73

2898 not named - white male D: Jan 3, 1914; stillborn F: Shank, B/P: 2/111

2899 not named - white female D: July 28, 1906; 2m F: Richmond, B/P: 2/100

2900 not named - white male D: June 5, 1914; F: Straw, B/P: 2/112

2901 not named - white male D: Feb 1904; 16m F: Wolford, Ben B/P: 2/146

2902 not named - white female D: 1906 F: Ullery B/P: 2/129

2903 not named - white male D: Apr 8, 1909; F: Petit, B/P: 2/95

2904 not named - white female D: Aug 8, 1907; 2m F: Puffinberger, B/P: 2/94

2905 not named - white female D: Dec 14, 1907; stillborn F: Shank, B/P: 2/108

2906 not named - white male D: Oct 8, 1912; F: Speaks, B/P: 2/111

2907 not named - white male D: Feb 9, 1910; F: Moreland, B/P: 2/74

2908 not named - white male D: Jan 15, 1919; stillborn F: Morgan, B/P: 2/76

2909 not named - white male D: May 21, 1914; stillborn F: Miller, B/P: 2/75

2910 not named - white male D: May 17, 1914; stillborn F: Smith, B/P: 2/112

2911 not named - white male D: Feb 23, 1907; stillborn F: Kerns, B/P: 2/63

2912 not named - white male D: Nov 30, 1911; 16d F: Wolford, B: Romney District B/P: 2/132

2913 not named - white female D: May 1, 1914; stillborn F: Starkey, B/P: 2/112

2914 not named - white female D: June 3, 1911; stillborn F: Roberson B/P: 2/100

2915 not named - white male D: Apr 10, 1913; F: Timbrook, B/P: 2/121

2916 not named - white male D: Mar 30, 1912; stillborn F: Snyder, B/P: 2/111

2917 not named - white female D: June 18, 1911; stillborn F: Shank, B: Gore District B/P: 2/111

2918 not named - white female D: May 17, 1911; 1d F: Sapp, B/P: 2/111

2919 not named - white male D: Feb 18, 1908; 7d F: Poland, B/P: 2/94

2920 not named - white female D: July 23, 1909; 1m 25d F: Walker, B/P: 2/131

2921 not named - white female D: Feb 27, 1907; 1d F: Peters, B/P: 2/94

2922 not named - white female D: June 21, 1911; 1m 14d F: Sneathen, B/P: 2/111

2923 not named - white male D: Mar 18, 1914; stillborn F: Timbrook, B/P: 2/121

2924 not named - white male D: Nov 16, 1907; stillborn F: Pugh, B/P: 2/94

2925 not named - white male D: Apr 26, 1906; 1m F: Ullery, B/P: 2/129

2926 not named - white female D: July 21, 1906; stillborn F: Shank, B/P: 2/108

2927 not named - white male D: Jan 5, 1912; 10d F: Wagoner, B/P: 2/133

2928 not named - white female D: Jan 27, 1914; stillborn F: Palmer, B/P: 2/95

2929 not named - white female D: Feb 18, 1910; F: Peer, B/P: 2/98

2930 not named - white female D: Sept 24, 1908; 7m 16d F: Piles, B/P: 2/94

2931 not named - white male D: June 24, 1910; 12d F: Riggleman, B/P: 2/100

2932 not named - white male D: Apr 5, 1908; F: Roberson, B/P: 2/100

2933 not named - white male D: Oct 12, 1914; stillborn F: Piles, B/P: 2/95

2934 not named - white female D: July 28, 1906; 2m F:

Richmond, B/P: 2/107

2935 Oates, Annie R. - white female D: Feb 10, 1909; 7m 4d B/P: 2/90

2936 Oates, Emma Virginia - married white female D: May 19, 1910; 46y B/P: 2/90

2937 Oates, Ethel - white female D: Apr 25, 1897; 3m 7d; Bloomery F: Oates, J.R. M: Oates, E.S. B: Jan 18, 1897 DOI: mother B/P: 1/66

2938 Oates, Gertie - single white female D: Oct 25, 1898; 22y 8m 2d; Capon Bridge B: Capon Bridge BUR: Fairview, VA B/P: 1/100

2939 Oates, Gladys - white female D: Dec 11, 1906; 1m 1d B/P: 2/90

2940 Oates, Granville - single white male D: Oct 28, 1902; 2m 15d; Hampshire B: Hampshire BUR: Capon Bridge B/P: 1/115

2941 Oates, Janie P. - white female D: Nov 1905; 17y B/P: 2/90

2942 Oates, John - white male D: Dec 13, 1915; 65y 3m 17d B/P: 2/90 N: farmer

2943 Oates, Kate - married white female D: July 17, 1911; 30y B/P: 2/90

2944 Oates, Laura Bell - married white female D: Oct 23, 1908; 25y 1m B/P: 2/90

2945 Oates, Mary - widow white female D: Jan 13, 1899; 83y; Capon District B: Capon district BUR: Family Burying Ground B/P: 1/101

2946 Oates, Myrtle - single white female D: July 3, 1897; 10d; Capon Bridge B: Capon Bridge BUR: Fairview VA B/P: 1/95

2947 Oates, Robt. - widower white male D: Apr 19, 1908; 79y B/P: 2/90 N: stonemason

2948 Oates, Robt. W. - married white male D: Sept 17, 1921; 80y 7m 1d; Hampshire F: Oates, Wm. M: Oates, Mary B: Hampshire B/P: 1/132 N: farmer

2949 Oates, Ruth - single white female D: Feb 10, 1909; 7m 5d

B/P: 2/90

2950 Oates, Texas - single white female D: Nov 30, 1909; 69y 3m B/P: 2/90

2951 Oates, Uloselia - white female D: July 20, 1905; 52y B/P: 2/90

2952 Oates, Virginia Ann - married white female D: Jan 30, 1922; 72y; Hampshire B: Hampshire Co. I: Lupton, Geo. A. B/P: 1/134

2953 Oates, Virginia - married white female D: Dec 5, 1909; 58y 8m 4d B/P: 2/90

2954 Oates, Wesley - married white male D: Mar 21, 1914; 68y B/P: 2/90 N: farmer

2955 Oates, Wm. J. - married white male D: Jan 16, 1922; 76y; Hampshire B: Hampshire I: Lupton, Geo. A. B/P: 1/134

2956 Oats, Bertha - white female D: July 20, 1902; 1y 2m; Capon District F: Oats, J.F. B: July 20, 1902 DOI: father B/P: 1/78

2957 Oats, Christopher - white male D: Mar 1886; 67y; Capon District B: Hampshire I: Gray, Geo W DOI: friend B/P: 1/43

2958 Oats, Emma - white female D: July 12, 1888; 30y; Capon District B: Hampshire DOI: husband C: Oats, George B/P: 1/47

2959 Oats, George - white male D: Feb 11, 1890; 81y; Capon District F: Oats, Geo. B: Capon District I: Lupton, Geo DOI: nephew B/P: 1/49

2960 Oats, Granville - white male D: Nov 28, 1902; 2m 14d; Capon Bridge F: Oats, R.J. M: Oats, E.V. B: July 12, 1902 DOI: father B/P: 1/78

2961 Oats, Harman - white male D: Feb 11, 1874; 57y 2m 2d; Hampshire F: Oats, John M: Oats, Mary B: Frederick Co VA I: Oats, William DOI: son C: Oats, Sarah E. B/P: 1/13 N: farmer

2962 Oats, Henson - single white male D: Mar 13, 1922; 69y; Hampshire F: Oates, Wm. M: Oates, Mary B: Hardy County I: Poland, T.W. B/P: 1/134

2963 Oats, Ida - white female D: Aug 21, 1903; 31y; Hampshire

F: Haines, William M: Haines, Harriett I: Oats, J.D. B/P: 1/81

2964 Oats, Izatis - white male D: Aug 31, 1882; 10y; Capon District F: Oats, Samuel M: Oats, Mary J. B: WV DOI: father B/P: 1/33

2965 Oats, Jacob - married white male D: Aug 3, 1878; 62y; Hampshire B: Hampshire I: Oats, Daniel DOI: son B/P: 1/23

2966 Oats, Jacob - white male D: Feb 21, 1976; 85y; Hampshire F: Oats, Christopher M: Oats, Mary I: Oats, Dan'l P. DOI: son C: Oats, Mary B/P: 1/21

2967 Oats, Jettie Belle - single white female D: May 10, 1911; 2m 23d B/P: 2/90

2968 Oats, Lane - single white female D: June 24, 1876; 50y; Hampshire F: Oats, Jacob M: Oats, Mary I: Oats, Dan'l DOI: brother B/P: 1/21

2969 Oats, Reather - white male D: July 18, 1901; 2y; Yellow Spring F: Oates, James M: Oates, Vera DOI: father B/P: 1/76

2970 Obrien, Annie - white female D: Mar 8, 1890; 63y; Romney District B: Romney District DOI: husband C: Obrien, James B/P: 1/49

2971 Odely, Rufus - white female D: Oct 3, 1899; 2y 4m 6d; Maryland F: Odely, David M: Odely, Emma B: May 27, 1897 DOI: mother B/P: 1/70

2972 Offner, John E. - married white male D: Oct 29, 1914; 63y 10m B/P: 2/90 N: contractor

2973 Offner, Reuben - married white male D: Apr 21, 1889; 84y 6m; Hampshire B: Hampshire BUR: Romney B/P: 1/125

2974 Offutt, Howard G. - single white male D: Mar 5, 1890; 9m; Sherman District F: Offutt, Robert J. M: Offutt, Elizabeth B: Sherman District DOI: father B/P: 1/49

2975 Offutt, John P. - white male D: May 16, 1875; 17y 11m 17d; Cass Co., MO F: Offutt, Thornton W. M: Offutt, Sarah B: Hampshire DOI: father B/P: 1/16

2976 Offutt, Jonathan - white male D: July 3, 1902; 65y; Capon District F: Offutt, Nathaniel I: Ward, J.M. B/P: 1/78

2977 Offutt, Robt. - white male D: Nov 1, 1891; 27y 7m 26d; Hampshire F: Offutt, T.W. M: Offutt, S. B: Hampshire DOI: father B/P: 1/55

2978 Offutt, Sarah C. D: Dec 4, 1871; 39y F: Snapp, John H. M: Snapp, Hannah C: Offutt, Thornton W. B/P: 1/6

2979 Offutt, Sarah O. - white female D: Aug 5, 1882; 55y; Capon District B: WV DOI: husband C: Offutt, J.J.F. B/P: 1/33

2980 Offutt, Thornton W. - widower white male D: May 12, 1907; 77y 17m B/P: 2/90 N: farmer

2981 Oglesbee, Herbert - white male D: June 3, 1886; 6m; Hampshire F: Oglesbee, D.W. M: Oglesbee, Matilda B: Hampshire DOI: father B/P: 1/44

2982 Oglesby, Hillary - white male D: Mar 28, 1884; 57y; Hampshire B: Hampshire DOI: wife C: Oglesby, Sarah B/P: 1/38

2983 Oliver, W.R. - white male D: July 13, 1914; 57y B/P: 2/90

2984 Orendorff, Rachel - white female D: May 11, 1879; 22y; Hampshire B: Hampshire DOI: husband C: Orendorff, Joseph B/P: 1/25

2985 Orndoff, Levi D. D: Apr 27, 1869; 1m 10d; Hampshire F: Orndoff, Joseph B: Hampshire B/P: 1/4

2986 Orndorff, Bettie - married white female D: June 20, 1914; 48y 7m 13d B/P: 2/90

2987 Orndorff, David M. - white male D: Aug 7, 1901; 1y 6m; Yellow Spring B/P: 1/76 N: Parents: W.B. & Bertha

2988 Orndorff, Edward - white male D: June 1886; 1d; Hampshire F: Orndorff, Jos. A. M: Orndorff, Sarah B: Hampshire DOI: father B/P: 1/41

2989 Orndorff, Edward - single white male D: Sept 17, 1894; 20y 2m 28d; Hampshire B: Hampshire B/P: 1/87

2990 Orndorff, Eliza - widow white female D: June 20, 1907; 79y 5m 19d B/P: 2/90

2991 Orndorff, George F - white male D: Mar 6, 1867; 11y; Capon Springs F: Orndorff, Philip S. B: Capon Springs B/P:

1/2

2992 Orndorff, James C. - married white male D: Apr 24, 1906; 61y B/P: 2/90

2993 Orndorff, Joseph A - white male D: Aug 22, 1868; 1y 6m 2d; Capon Spring F: Orndorff, Joseph A B: Capon Spring DOI: father B/P: 1/3

2994 Orndorff, Julia A. - white female D: Apr 23, 1879; 45y; Hampshire F: Hanes, Dan'l M: Hanes, Elizabeth B: Hampshire DOI: father C: Orndorff, Mordia B/P: 1/26

2995 Orndorff, Lenora - single white female D: Apr 3, 1907; 9y 5m B/P: 2/90

2996 Orndorff, Lydia B. - white female D: Feb 7, 1867; near Capon Springs B/P: 1/2

2997 Orndorff, Mary - white female D: Sept 30, 1875; 37y 9m 4d; Hampshire B: Hampshire DOI: husband C: Orndorff, J.A. B/P: 1/14

2998 Orndorff, Philip H. - white male D: Oct 24, 1918; 66y 8m 27d; Hampshire B/P: 1/126 N: farmer

2999 Orndorff, Sallie - white female D: Mar 14, 1900; 30y; Hampshire B: June 11, 1870 I: Maiset, Simon DOI: friend B/P: 1/73

3000 Orndorff; Sallie - single white femlae D: Mar 14, 1900; 30y; Cold Stream B: Virginia BUR: Cold Stream B/P: 1/108

3001 Orndorff, Sarah - white famale D: Mar 1886; 35y; Hampshire B: Hampshire DOI: husband C: Orndorff, Jos. A. B/P: 1/41

3002 Orndorff, Theodore - white male D: Mar 28, 1900; 1m; Hampshire M: Orndorff, Sallie B: Feb 14, 1900 I: Maiset, Simon DOI: friend B/P: 1/73

3003 Orndorff, Thornton Wesley - married white male D: Apr 6, 1917; 93y 3m 26d B/P: 2/90 N: farmer

3004 Orndorff, Thornton W. - widower white male D: May 12, 1907; 80y B/P: 2/90

3005 Orndorff, Victoria - white female D: Dec 1, 1888; 28y; Capon District F: Wilson, John M: Wilson, Pernelia B: Hampshire DOI: husband C: Orndorff, P.H. B/P: 1/47

3006 Orndorff, Virginia - white female D: Sept 12, 1892; 10y 1m 10d; Capon Springs F: Orndorff, Henry M: Orndorff, V. B: Capon Springs DOI: father B/P: 1/56

3007 Orndorff, W.M. - white male D: Oct 6, 1892; 2y 6m; Capon Springs F: Orndorff, Jos. A. M: Orndorff, Virginia B: Capon Springs DOI: father B/P: 1/56

3008 Pain, Sarah L.A. - white female D: Dec 15, 1883; 42y; Hampshire F: Whitlock, Alonzo L.M. M: Whitlock, Cath. B: Hampshire DOI: husband C: Pain, And. B/P: 1/37

3009 Palmer, Frank - widower white male D: Aug 31, 1921; 67y 6m 8d; Hampshire F: Palmer, Joe M: Palmer, Fannie B: WV I: Palmer, Jas. W. B/P: 1/132

3010 Palmer, Mary - married white female D: Apr 8, 1908; 60y B/P: 2/94

3011 Palmer, Silas - white male D: Dec 8, 1881; 7m 22d; Hampshire F: Palmer, Albert M: Palmer, Mary B: Hampshire DOI: father B/P: 1/32

3012 Pancake, C - white male D: Sept 23, 1868; 1y; South Branch F: Pancake, Isaac B: South Branch DOI: father B/P: 1/3

3013 Pancake, I.H.C. - married white male D: Mar 30, 1911; 66y 4m 26d B: Romney District B/P: 2/95

3014 Pancake, Irvin F. - single white male D: Dec 21, 1896; 1m 17d; Hampshire B: Hampshire BUR: Family Burying Ground B/P: 1/96

3015 Pancake, John M - white male D: May 30, 1866 B/P: 1/2

3016 Pancake, Kate B. - white female D: Dec 25, 1881; 3y; Hampshire F: Pancake, J.A. M: Pancake, Susan B: Hampshire DOI: father B/P: 1/30

3017 Pancake, Mariah S. D: Mar 23, 1871; 2y F: Pancake, Isaac B/P: 1/6

3018 Pane, Jack - widower white male D: Sept 21, 1894; 56y; Haines Mill B: Hampshire BUR: Bethel Ch. B/P: 1/82

3019 Park, Cath. D: Mar 27, 1871; 26y F: Poland, Amos C: Park, Geo. B/P: 1/6

3020 Park, George - single white male D: Feb 9, 1875; 68y; Hampshire F: Park, George M: Park, Hannah B: Hampshire I: Park, William DOI: brother B/P: 1/16

3021 Park, Harriett A. - married white female D: Nov 24, 1902; 73y 2m 25d; Hampshire B: Hampshire BUR: Mt Zion B/P: 1/116

3022 Park, Jacob - white male D: May 23, 1866 B/P: 1/2

3023 Park, Jno. G. - single white male D: Mar 12, 1921; 29d; Hampshire F: Park, Dennis M: Park, Bessie B: Hampshire B/P: 1/130

3024 Park, Martha E. - white female D: Feb 10, 1890; 24y; Sherman District F: Cool, Jas. B: Sherman District DOI: husband C: Park, Jas. A. B/P: 1/49

3025 Park, Rebecca - single white female D: Sept 1, 1873; 55y; Hampshire F: Park, Jacob M: Park, Eve B: Hampshire I: Stickley, Tobias DOI: friend B/P: 1/10

3026 Park, Sam'l - white male D: May 29, 1866 B/P: 1/2

3027 Park, Samuel - white male D: July 12, 1905; 85y B/P: 2/94

3028 Park, Sarah Catherine - white female D: Aug 16, 1910; 65y 11m 19d B/P: 2/98

3029 Park, Susan Ann - widowed white female D: Nov 18, 1921; 80y 7m; Hampshire F: Brill, Jno. M: Brill, Cinderella B: WV I: Park, J.H. B/P: 1/132

3030 Park, W.B. - white male D: May 13, 1905; 26y B/P: 2/94

3031 Parker, Catharine - white female D: Aug 21, 1909; 85y B/P: 2/95

3032 Parker, Edgar S. - married white male D: Oct 17, 1898; 31y; Springfield B: Springfield BUR: Springfield B/P: 1/100 N: merchant

3033 Parker, Eleanor - married white female D: Nov 26, 1913; 33y B/P: 2/95

3034 Parker, Eliza J. - white female D: July 13, 1903; 67y; Mill Creek District I: Parker, A.V. DOI: son B/P: 1/81

3035 Parker, Elizabeth - white female D: Sept 2, 1881; 72y;

Hampshire B: Hampshire DOI: husband C: Parker, Jno. R. B/P: 1/29

3036 Parker, Geo. S. - white male D: Oct 31, 1904; 10y 7m 16d B/P: 2/98

3037 Parker, Hannibol - widower white male D: Sept 25, 1907; 73y 10m 22d B/P: 2/94 N: farmer

3038 Parker, Isaac P. - white male D: June 9, 1901; 86y; Hampshire B/P: 1/77

3039 Parker, Jacob - single white male D: July 1889; 72y; Mill Creek District F: Parker, Jacob M: Parker, Sallie B: Mill Creek District I: Parker, S.B. DOI: nephew B/P: 1/49

3040 Parker, James - married white male D: May 1, 1898; 83y 1m 12d; B: Hampshire County BUR: Family Burying B/P: 1/97

3041 Parker, John R. - married white male D: Oct 31, 1889; 77y; Mill Creek District F: Parker, Jacob M: Parker, Sallie B: Mill Creek District I: Parker, Jno E. DOI: son B/P: 1/49 N: farmer

3042 Parker, Lee - white male D: July 2, 1897; 7y 1m; Mill Creek District F: Parker, Thornton B: Mill Creek District DOI: mother B/P: 1/64

3043 Parker, Lydia - white female D: June 5, 1912; 76y B: Bloomery B/P: 2/95

3044 Parker, Robt. W. - married white male D: Apr 19, 1898; Springfield District B: Hampshire BUR: Home Farm B/P: 1/93

3045 Parker, T.R. - white male D: Oct 31, 1890; 40y; Mill Creek F: Parker, John R. M: Parker, E. B: Hampshire I: Parker, Jno DOI: brother C: Parker, Sallie B/P: 1/52

3046 Parks, Dennis A. - white male D: Oct 9, 1916; 6d B: Ford Hill B/P: 2/96

3047 Parks, Harriett A. - white female D: Dec 25, 1902; 72y; Sherman District F: Ruckman, Sam M: Ruckman, Betsy B: 1831 DOI: husband B/P: 1/78

3048 Parks, Mrs. - married white female D: Sept 27, 1887; 36y; Hampshire B: Hampshire BUR: Hampshire B/P: 1/122

3049 Parks, Virginia - white female D: Feb 17, 1876; 5d; Hampshire F: Parks, Geo M: Parks, Henrietta B: Hampshire

DOI: father B/P: 1/18

3050 Parrell, James - widower white male D: Feb 18, 1899; 80y; Hanging Rock B: Hampshire BUR: Dillons Run B/P: 1/103

3051 Parrill, Albert - married white male D: Feb 1904; 28y B/P: 2/98 N: teamster

3052 Parrill, James William - white male D: Apr 11, 1910; 35y 1m 13d B/P: 2/98

3053 Parrill, Mrs. Jno. C. - white female D: Dec 30, 1907; 63y B/P: 2/94

3054 Parson, Isaac - single white male D: Oct 16, 1902; 28y; Hampshire B: Hampshire BUR: Pancake Farm B/P: 1/114 N: stockman

3055 Parson, Marg. Avery - white female D: Oct 14, 1913; 61y B/P: 2/95

3056 Parson, Mary - white female D: Nov 19, 1883; 82y 7m 15d; Hampshire F: Curlett, William M: Curlett, Mary B: Hampshire I: Parson, Elwood DOI: grandson B/P: 1/37

3057 Parson, William B. - single white male D: Apr 21, 1900; 21y; New York City B: Hampshire BUR: Mrs. Ellen Pancake farm B/P: 1/110

3058 Parson, William C. - widower white male D: Aug 19, 1899; 71y 14d; Springfield B: Hampshire BUR: Springfield B/P: 1/109

3059 Parsons, Emma E. - widow white female D: Nov 17, 1898; 47y; Springfield F: Julius, C. M: Julius, M.J. I: Parsons, Isaac B. DOI: son B/P: 1/69

3060 Parsons, Isaac - white male D: Sept 11, 1891; 52y 10m 20d; Hampshire F: Parsons, Isaac M: Parsons, Susan B: Hampshire DOI: wife C: Parsons, Emma B/P: 1/55

3061 Parsons, James D: Aug 22, 1871; 37y F: Parsons, James M: Parsons, Mary B/P: 1/6

3062 Parsons, Mary - white female D: Aug 28, 1872; 14y; Hampshire F: Parsons, Wm M: Parson, Louisa B: Hampshire DOI: father B/P: 1/8

3063 Parsons, Mildred - white female D: Mar 19, 1884; 83y; Hampshire B/P: 1/39

3064 Parsons, Susan - white famale D: Oct 2, 1889; 72y; Romney District F: Blue, B: Romney District I: Parsons, G.W. DOI: son C: Parson, Isaac P. B/P: 1/49

3065 Paskel, Sarah - white female D: Feb 3, 1896; 79y 10m; Hampshire B: 1817 I: Strother, R.F. DOI: son in law B/P: 1/63

3066 Paterson, Clandella - white female D: Apr 1, 1879; 2y 4m 26d; Hampshire F: Paterson, Silas B. M: Paterson, Martha A. B: Hampshire DOI: mother B/P: 1/26

3067 Patterson, Ann - white female D: May 4, 1873; 81y 3m 14d; Hampshire F: Starn, Jacob M: Starn, Catherine B: Hampshire I: Shanholtzer, Mrs. DOI: daughter C: Patterson, Alexander B/P: 1/11

3068 Patterson, E. - white male D: Apr 3, 1892; 3m; Hampshire F: Patterson, T.C. M: Patterson V. B: Hampshire DOI: father B/P: 1/57

3069 Patterson, Isabell - white female D: July 15, 1872; 39y; Hampshire F: Patterson, Thomas M: Patterson, Sarah B: Hampshire I: Patterson, Jas. DOI: brother B/P: 1/8

3070 Patterson, James - white male D: Sept 14, 1891; 75y; Hampshire F: Patterson, Alex M: Patterson, A. B: Hampshire I: Patterson, A. DOI: son B/P: 1/55

3071 Patterson, Jas. H.F. - white male D: May 17, 1886; 57y 4m 12d; Hampshire F: Patterson, Thos. M: Patterson, Sarah B: Hampshire DOI: wife C: Patterson, M.V. B/P: 1/44

3072 Patterson, Jno - married white male D: July 3, 1899; 88y; Pine Hill B: Hampshire BUR: Pine Hill B/P: 1/106

3073 Patterson, John - white male D: July 3, 1899; 91y 6m 22d; Gore District F: Patterson, J. M: Patterson, M. B: Dec 12, 1807 DOI: wife C: Patterson, Margaret B/P: 1/70

3074 Patterson, M.E. - white female D: June 15, 1894; 64y; Hampshire B: Virginia DOI: husband C: Patterson, C.R. B/P: 1/60

3075 Patterson, Maria - white female D: Jan 30, 1913; 68y B/P: 2/95

3076 Patterson, Mariah E. - white female D: Jan 3, 1913; B/P: 2/95

3077 Patterson, Mrs. - married white female D: June 15, 1894; 50y; North River B: Hampshire BUR: North River B/P: 1/85

3078 Patterson, Nancy - white female D: Jan 2, 1872; 66y 11m 17d; Hampshire F: Offutt, Solomon M: Offutt, Elizabeth B: Berkeley Co DOI: husband C: Patterson, John B/P: 1/8

3079 Patterson, Robt - white male D: Dec 21, 1876; 86y 9m 16d; Hampshire F: Patterson, Jas M: Patterson Jane B: Hampshire I: Patterson, Jas H DOI: nephew B/P: 1/21

3080 Patterson, Silas B. - white male D: Oct 17, 1897; 69y; Romney B: Gore District B/P: 1/64

3081 Patterson, Wm. - single white male D: Mar 14, 1903; 9d; Hampshire B: Hampshire BUR: Slanesville B/P: 1/115

3082 Pattie, Nannie D: Sept 1, 1870; F: Pattie C.W. B/P: 1/5

3083 Payne, Edith Francis - white female D: May 10, 1897; 8m 24d; Sherman District DOI: father B/P: 1/64

3084 Payne, Minnie - married white female D: Sept 20, 1907; 36y 5m 14d B/P: 2/94

3085 Payne, Minnie B. - white female D: Sept 20, 1907; 33y 4m 13d B/P: 2/94

3086 Peacemaker, C. - white female D: Mar 12, 1892; 75y; Hampshire B: Hampshire I: Peacemaker, S. DOI: brother B/P: 1/57

3087 Peacemaker, C.E. - white female D: Feb 16, 1892; 5m; Hampshire F: Peacemaker, J.N. M: Peacemaker, Lucy B: Hampshire DOI: father B/P: 1/54

3088 Peacemaker, Jacob D: July 9, 1871; 77y 6d; F: Peacemaker, John C: Peasemaker, Margaret B/P: 1/6

3089 Peacemaker, Mary E. - white female D: Nov 22, 1881; 88y 9m 3d; Hampshire F: Smith, Conrad B: Pennsylvania I: Peacemaker, Simeon DOI: son C: Peacemaker, David B/P: 1/32

3090 Peacemaker, W.W. - white male D: Oct 26, 1878; 53y; Hampshire F: Peacemaker, D. M: Peacemaker, M. B: Fred. Co, VA DOI: wife C: Peacemaker, Mary B/P: 1/24

3091 Pearl, Voilet - white female D: Sept 29, 1916; 7d B:

Romney B/P: 2/96

3092 Peasemaker, Elizabeth C. - widowed white female D: Nov 29, 1921; 84y 1m 29d; Hampshire F: Johnson, Richard M: Johnson, Hannah B: Licking Co., Ohio I: Peasemaker, Offutt B/P: 1/132

3093 Peasmaker, Elizabeth C. - widowed white female D: Nov 29, 1921; 84y 1m 29d; Hampshire F: Johnson, Richard M: Johnson, Hannah B: Licking County Ohio I: Peasmaker, Offutt B/P: 1/134

3094 Peasmaker, Geo. - single white male D: Apr 20, 1889; 68y; Hampshire B: Frederick VA I: Peasmaker, J. DOI: brother B/P: 1/51

3095 Peasmaker, Isaac - white male D: Oct 4, 1914; 60y B/P: 2/96

3096 Peasmaker, Margt. J. - widow white female D: May 30, 1908; 82y B/P: 2/94

3097 Peasmaker, Rumsey - single white male D: Sept 17, 1910; 22y B/P: 2/98

3098 Peasmaker, Wm. P. - white male D: Jan 29, 1914; 61y 5m 20d DOI: brother B/P: 2/95

3099 Peer, Elizabeth - married white female D: June 10, 1912; 45y 6m 7d B: Bloomery District B/P: 2/95

3100 Peer, Hampton W. - white male D: Apr 19, 1899; 56y; Sherman District F: Peer, Elias M: Peer, Rachel B: Mar 4 DOI: son B/P: 1/71

3101 Peer, Jacob - single white male D: July 25, 1911; 66y B/P: 2/95

3102 Peer, Jacob - single white male D: July 22, 1911; 66y 8m 12d B/P: 2/95

3103 Peer, Jettie Marie - single white female D: Oct 10, 1918; 1y 1m; Hampshire DOI: father B/P: 1/127

3104 Pennington, Asby M - single white male D: Aug 15, 1866; 2y 5m; Hampshire F: Pennington, Enoch H M: Pennington, Mary B: Hampshire DOI: parent B/P: 1/1

3105 Pennington, Enock H. - white male D: Aug 17, 1912; 87y 1m 2d I: Pennington, Victor B/P: 2/95 N: farmer

3106 Pennington, Julia A - single white female D: Aug 20, 1866; 4y 7m; Hampshire F: Pennington, Enoch H M: Pennington, Mary B: Hampshire DOI: parent B/P: 1/1

3107 Pennington, Lydia E. - white female D: Mar 7, 1875; 12 d; Hampshire F: Pennington, E.H. M: Pennington, Mary B: Hampshire DOI: father B/P: 1/14

3108 Pennington, Mary A. - white female D: Jan 17, 1886; 55y; Hampshire B: Hampshire I: Pennington, Elijah DOI: brother B/P: 1/41

3109 Pennington, Mary E. - white female D: Mar 2, 1899; 9m; Capon DOI: father B/P: 1/71

3110 Pennington, Mary E. - single white female D: Mar 12, 1899; 9y; Dillons Run B: Parks Hollow BUR: Dillons Run B/P: 1/102

3111 Pennington, Mary - married white female D: Dec 18, 1917; 83y 10m B/P: 2/96

3112 Pennington, Oliver R. - white male D: Aug 18, 1906; 1y 15m B/P: 2/94

3113 Pennington, Ruth E. - white female D: Apr 8, 1908; 12y 9m 29d B/P: 2/94

3114 Pepper, A.E. - single white female D: Sept 27, 1895; 10m 17d; Hampshire B: Hampshire B/P: 1/87

3115 Pepper, Ann C. - married white female D: Apr 16, 1916; 73y 11m 16d B: Sherman District B/P: 2/96

3116 Pepper, Chas. A. - white male D: Sept 14, 1881; 4m; Hampshire F: Pepper, J.F. M: Pepper, Lucy M. B: Hampshire DOI: father B/P: 1/32

3117 Pepper, Edna R. - white female D: Sept 14, 1881; 14y; F: Pepper, Wm H. M: Pepper, Sarah E. B: Hampshire DOI: father B/P: 1/29

3118 Pepper, Ida M. - white female D: Sept 17, 1882; 4y; Hampshire F: Pepper, J.F. M: Pepper, L. B: Hampshire I: Patterson, Jno DOI: friend B/P: 1/34

3119 Pepper, Jacob - white male D: Oct 15, 1866 B/P: 1/2

3120 Pepper, Jno. Wm. - married white male D: Apr 22, 1895;

59y 3m 10d; Hampshire B: Hampshire BUR: Mt Zion Church B/P: 1/86

3121 Pepper, Joseph F. - single white male D: Aug 4, 1876; 41y; F: Pepper, Henry M: Pepper, Rachael B: Hampshire I: Pepper, Rachael DOI: sister B/P: 1/21

3122 Pepper, Lucy M. - white female D: Sept 10, 1881; 27y 1m 10d; Hampshire F: Pugh, Arthur H. M: Pugh, J. B: Hampshire DOI: husband C: Pepper, Joseph F. B/P: 1/32

3123 Pepper, Martha - white female D: Oct 24, 1886; 84y; Sherman District B: Hampshire I: Powell, S.D. DOI: son in law C: Pepper, Jacob, Sr. B/P: 1/43

3124 Pepper, Mrs. Jacob - widow white female D: June 21, 1902; 78y 21d; Hampshire B: Pleasant Dale B/P: 1/115

3125 Pepper, Rachael - white female D: Apr 16, 1876; 68y; Hampshire F: Late, John M: Late, Hannah B: Berkeley Co I: Pepper, Rachael DOI: daughter C: Pepper, Henry B/P: 1/21

3126 Pepper, Rachel J. - single white female D: Aug 4, 1882; 37y 8m 1d; Hampshire F: Pepper, H. M: Pepper, R. B: Hampshire I: Wolf, Jno DOI: friend B/P: 1/34

3127 Pepper, Sarah E. - white female D: Oct 6, 1881; 37y; Hampshire F: Dye, John R. B: Hampshire DOI: husband C: Pepper, Wm.H. B/P: 1/29

3128 Pepper, Stella V. - white female D: May 19, 1890; 10d; Sherman District F: Pepper, J.W. M: Pepper, Rebecca B: Hampshire DOI: father B/P: 1/52

3129 Pepper, Walker - single white male D: Dec 9, 1910; 67y 1m 3d B/P: 2/98

3130 Peppers, Isaac - single white male D: Apr 1, 1897; 64y 6m; Sherman District F: Peppers, Frederick M: Peppers, Debora I: Hiett, F.B. DOI: friend B/P: 1/64

3131 Perrill, Clarinda - widow white female D: June 19, 1922; 79y 3m 13d; Hampshire F: Raynolds, Henry B: Hardy County I: Lupton, Geo. B/P: 1/136 N: housewife

3132 Perrill, Isaac P. - white male D: Mar 27, 1878; 52y 5m 16d; Hampshire F: Perrill, Joshua I. B: Hampshire I: Hook, Robt W. DOI: brother in law B/P: 1/24

3133 Perrill, Mary Ann - white female D: Feb 25, 1880; 64y;

Hampshire B: Virginia DOI: husband C: Perrill, John W. B/P: 1/27

3134 Perry, Mary - white female D: Oct 4, 1905; 80y B/P: 2/94

3135 Peters, Ann Bille - colored female D: May 1, 1897; 57y; Romney District B: Romney I: Robinson, Jno DOI: friend B/P: 1/64

3136 Peters, Catharine - widow white female D: Feb 19, 1904; 83y 6m 11d B/P: 2/98

3137 Peters, Catherine - married white female D: Nov 7, 1915; 75y 8m 25d B/P: 2/96

3138 Peters, Catherine - married white female D: Nov 7, 1915; 75y 5m 20d I: Peters, Harrison B/P: 2/96

3139 Peters, J. - single white female D: Jan 1, 1908; 18y 10m 22d B/P: 2/94

3140 Peters, John - single white male D: Mar 24, 1877; Hampshire F: Peters, John M: Peters, L. B: Hampshire I: Poling, M.F. DOI: overseer of poor B/P: 1/22

3141 Peters, L.B. - white male D: Jan 10, 1891; 1y 10m 2d; Sherman District F: Peters, Jas. M: Peters, Mary B: Hampshire DOI: father B/P: 1/52

3142 Peters, Mary Ann - white female D: Jan 27, 1908; 55y 5m 1d B/P: 2/94

3143 Peters, Mrs. - married white female D: Jan 1, 1907; 24y B/P: 2/94

3144 Peters, Otelia Catherine - married white female D: Aug 21, 1909; 22y 5m 18d B/P: 2/94

3145 Peters, Sarah Amanda - white female D: Oct 3, 1907; 26y 10m 6d B/P: 2/94

3146 Peters, Woodrow Clarence - white male D: Dec 12, 1910; 1y 3m B/P: 2/98

3147 Philips, John W. - single white male D: Dec 26, 1904; 86y B/P: 2/94

3148 Pickering, Chas H - white male D: July 3, 1875; 1y 3m; Hampshire F: Pickering, John M: Pickering, Martha B:

Hampshire DOI: father B/P: 1/16

3149 Pickering, Timothy - single white male D: June 8, 1872; 26y 3m 2d; Hampshire F: Pickering, Hiram M: Pickering, Sophia B: Hampshire I: Thayler, And. DOI: brother in law B/P: 1/8

3150 Pierre - single white male D: Mar 18, 1895; 9 m; near Slanesville B: Hampshire B/P: 1/85

3151 Piles, Benj. - white male D: Dec 15, 1902; 86y; Romney District B: 1816 I: Messick, O. B/P: 1/78

3152 Piles, Catharine A. - married white female D: Feb 8, 1908; 33y 7m 1d B/P: 2/94

3153 Piles, Clara - white female D: Mar 12, 1910; 1y 5m 15d B/P: 2/98

3154 Piles, John H. - widow white male D: Dec 5, 1910; 73y 3m 19d B/P: 2/98

3155 Piles, Martha - white female D: Sept 30, 1886; 68y; Hampshire B: Hampshire DOI: husband C: Piles, Benjamin B/P: 1/41

3156 Piles, Mary V. - white female D: Dec 19, 1886; 21y; Hampshire F: Piles, J. H. M: Piles, Martha J. B: Hampshire DOI: father B/P: 1/41

3157 Piles, Matilda - white female D: May 24, 1900; 35y; Sherman B: 1865 B/P: 1/72

3158 Piper, John Ed - white male D: July 17, 1884; 1y; Hampshire F: Piper, J.C. B: Penn? DOI: father B/P: 1/39

3159 Poland, A.E. - white female D: July 6, 1890; 9m 6d; Romney District F: Poland, J. M: Poland, H. B: Hampshire DOI: father B/P: 1/52

3160 Poland, Abner N. - married white male D: Mar 7, 1906; 47y 10m B/P: 2/94

3161 Poland, Albert S.J. - white male D: Sept 8, 1882; 20y; Sherman District F: Poland, J.C. M: Poland, Martha B: WV DOI: father B/P: 1/33

3162 Poland, Amos - married white male D: May 21, 1904; 87y 5m 2d B/P: 2/98 N: farmer

3163 Poland, Anna J. - white female D: Jan 1901; 33y;

Hampshire I: Arnold, J.F. B/P: 1/77

3164 Poland, Audry Arnold - white female D: Sept 19, 1918; 3m 7d; Hampshire B/P: 1/127

3165 Poland, Belle - white female D: Dec 14, 1914; 4y DOI: father B/P: 2/96

3166 Poland, Eliza E. - white female D: Sept 26, 1902; 65y 2m 15d; Sherman District F: Bean, Marsham M: Bean, Elizabeth B: July 11, 1837 DOI: husband B/P: 1/78

3167 Poland, Eliza E. - married white female D: Sept 27, 1902; 64y 2m 16d; Hampshire B: Hampshire BUR: Mt Zion B/P: 1/114

3168 Poland, Geo. E. - white male D: Sept 3, 1904; 3m B/P: 2/98

3169 Poland, Geo. Edward - white male D: Nov 14, 1904; 4m B/P: 2/95

3170 Poland, Geo. Edward - white male D: Nov 14, 1904; 4y 11d B/P: 2/94

3171 Poland, James - white male D: Oct 13, 1892; 84y; Hampshire B: Hampshire DOI: wife C: Poland, J. B/P: 1/57

3172 Poland, James F. - white male D: Nov 24, 1875; 12y 9m 2d; Hampshire F: Poland, William M: Poland, Achsah B: Hampshire DOI: father B/P: 1/16

3173 Poland, James Wesley - married white male D: Aug 22, 1910; 59y 2m 23d B/P: 2/98 N: farmer

3174 Poland, Jane - widow white female D: Feb 21, 1912; 62y B/P: 2/95

3175 Poland, Jas - white male D: Nov 10, 1876; 12y 6m; Hampshire F: Poland, William M: Poland, Ayer B: Hampshire DOI: mother B/P: 1/18

3176 Poland, Jas. - white male D: Dec 7, 1905; 76y B/P: 2/94 N: farmer

3177 Poland, Jefferson - widower white male D: Nov 9, 1915; 81y B/P: 2/96 N: farmer

3178 Poland, John Wm. - married white male D: Aug 21, 1910; 32y B/P: 2/98 N: farmer

3179 Poland, Lillie Flossie - white female D: Dec 12, 1915; 1y 5m 5d B/P: 2/96

3180 Poland, Lillie Florence - married white female D: Aug 28, 1910; 26y 16d B/P: 2/98

3181 Poland, Lillie F. - white female D: Dec 15, 1914; 1y 5m 5d DOI: father B/P: 2/95

3182 Poland, Louisa - white female D: July 4, 1894; 73y 4m; Sherman District B: Sherman District DOI: husband C: Poland, Amos B/P: 1/59

3183 Poland, Malinda M. - white female D: Apr 18, 1903; 36y; Sherman District I: Poland, W.A. B/P: 1/81

3184 Poland, Martha - widowed white female D: Jan 10, 1921; 89y 4m 8d; Hampshire F: Heare, Jas. M: Heare, Mary B: Hampshire B/P: 1/130 N: housewife

3185 Poland, Mary Ann - white female D: Aug 12, 1905; 80y B/P: 2/94

3186 Poland, Matilda J. - white female D: 1872 M: Poland, Hannah B: Hampshire I: Poland, Deborah DOI: grandmother B/P: 1/8

3187 Poland, Mattie - married white female D: Oct 12, 1910; 21y B/P: 2/98 N: assistant clerk

3188 Poland, Maurice - single white male D: Mar 20, 1913; 6y B/P: 2/95

3189 Poland, Miss - single white female D: Apr 29, 1897; 4d; Ruckman F: Poland, C.L. M: Poland, S.F. B: Ruckman BUR: Ruckman B/P: 1/90

3190 Poland, Peter M. - white male D: July 6, 1882; 26y; Sherman District F: Poland, J.C. M: Poland, Martha L. B: WV DOI: father C: Poland, Rebecca F. B/P: 1/33 N: wagonmaker

3191 Poland, Roy A. - single white male D: Aug 22, 1909; 18y B/P: 2/95 N: drown

3192 Poland, Samuel - single white male D: Nov 17, 1894; 23y; Sherman District F: Poland, Peter M: Poland, Elizabeth B: Sherman District DOI: father B/P: 1/59

3193 Poland, Sarah E - white female D: Feb 7, 1876; 39y 3m

6d; Hampshire F: Hain, James M: Hain, Abigail B: Hampshire DOI: husband C: Poland, Richard B/P: 1/18

3194 Poland, Thos. F. - white male D: Dec 6, 1892; 6y 9m 22d; Mill Run F: Poland, Edward M: Poland, Mary B: Capon Springs DOI: father B/P: 1/56

3195 Poland, Wm. - married white male D: Dec 1, 1912; 71y B: Springfield B/P: 2/95 N: farmer

3196 Poling, Ellen D: Feb 22, 1869; 11m; Hampshire F: Poling, James B: Romney B/P: 1/4

3197 Poling, Fannie - white female D: Sept 12, 1881; 5m 2d; Hampshire F: Poling, J.W. M: Poling, E. B: Hampshire DOI: father B/P: 1/30

3198 Poling, Joseph M. - married white male D: Mar 9, 1922; 71y 2m 9d; Hampshire F: Poling, Jos. M: Poling, Elizabeth B: Romney I: Racey, B.T. B/P: 1/134 N: plasterer

3199 Poling, Mary I. - married white female D: Dec 22, 1887; 49y 2m 13d; Romney B: Romney BUR: Romney B/P: 1/122

3200 Poling, Percy C. - white male D: Aug 19, 1892; 8m; Romney F: Poling, Harry M: Poling, Hannah B: Capon Springs DOI: father B/P: 1/56

3201 Poling, Violet Cora - single white female D: Nov 7, 1922; 2m 6d; Hampshire F: Poling, Daniel M: Poling, Mollie B: Hampshire DOI: father B/P: 1/134

3202 Pool, Ann - single white female D: Aug 28, 1916; 59y 9m 16d B: Capon Bridge B/P: 2/96

3203 Pool, Joseph - white male D: Aug 22, 1909; 85y B/P: 2/95 N: farmer

3204 Pool, Joseph - married white male D: Feb 5, 1909; 85y B/P: 2/95

3205 Pool, Nancy - widow white female D: Sept 9, 1895; 77y; Capon District B: Oct 1818 I: Davis, Farmer B/P: 1/61

3206 Pool, Sarah E. - white female D: Feb 16, 1909; 65y 10m 19d B/P: 2/94

3207 Poola, Policastro - single white male D: June 1, 1913; B/P: 2/95 N: killed by train

3208 Porter, Abrose V D: Dec 29, 1871; 53y F: Porter, Robert M: Porter, Martha C: Porter, Sarah J. B/P: 1/6

3209 Porter, Mary A.E. - single white female D: Oct 3, 1878; 20y 2m; Hampshire M: Porter, June B: Hampshire DOI: mother B/P: 1/23

3210 Portmess, Addie - married white female D: Sept 13, 1902; 48y; Little Capon B: Hampshire BUR: L. Capon B/P: 1/116

3211 Portmess, B.J. - white male D: Nov 4, 1893; 1y 6m; Hampshire F: Portmess, J. M: Portmess, S.V. DOI: father B/P: 1/58

3212 Portmess, M. - white female D: Aug 9, 1902; 27y; Hampshire F: Milleson, Benj M: Milleson, Elizabeth B: 1875 DOI: husband C: Portmess, J.T. B/P: 1/79

3213 Portmess, Mauice - married white female D: Aug 30, 1902; 30y; Hampshire B: Hampshire BUR: L. Capon B/P: 1/116

3214 Portmess, Sarah J. - white female D: Apr 5, 1885; 59y; Hampshire F: Boxwell, William M: Boxwell, Rebecca B: Hampshire DOI: husband C: Portmess, W. B/P: 1/42

3215 Portmess, Washington - white male D: Nov 11, 1895; 60y; Hampshire B: Hampshire B/P: 1/89

3216 Potter, Harley E. - white male D: Nov 1888; 6m; Romney District F: Potter, H. M: Potter, M.V. B: Hampshire DOI: father B/P: 1/47

3217 Powell, Albt - white male D: Sept 10, 1885; 7m 4d; Hampshire F: Powell, A.P. M: Powell, Mary V. B: Hampshire DOI: father B/P: 1/42

3218 Powell, Audra - single white female D: Dec 5, 1912; 22y B: Bloomery B/P: 2/95

3219 Powell, Bertha - white female D: Jan 13, 1892; 10d; Hampshire F: Powell, John V. M: Powell, Bertha B: Hampshire DOI: father B/P: 1/54

3220 Powell, David S. - widower white male D: Jan 27, 1909; 71y B/P: 2/95 N: farmer

3221 Powell, Edward A - single white male D: Mar 8, 1875; 40y; Hampshire F: Powell, Dade M: Powell, Mary B: Hampshire I: Leith, E DOI: friend B/P: 1/16

3222 Powell, Jno. V. - white male D: Dec 31, 1903; 20y; Hampshire F: Powell, W.J. M: Powell, Mary B: 1883 DOI: father B/P: 1/80

3223 Powell, Lizzie - married white female D: Aug 5, 1909; 55y B/P: 2/95

3224 Powell, Lorena - white female D: Apr 7, 1891; 16y; Hampshire F: Powell, B.J. M: Powell, S. B: Hampshire DOI: father B/P: 1/55

3225 Powell, M. - white female D: Sept 17, 1898; Gore District DOI: husband C: Powell, D.S. B/P: 1/69 N: Parents: Silas & Harriett

3226 Powell, Martha - married white female D: Sept 17, 1898; 30y; Higginsville B: Hampshire BUR: Salem Church B/P: 1/101

3227 Powell, Mary - widow white female D: Jan 18, 1895; 89y; Forks of Capon B: Hampshire B/P: 1/85

3228 Powell, Ora Bell - white female D: Mar 25, 1887; 4y 6m; Sherman District F: Powell, S.D. M: Powell, Martha B: Hampshire DOI: father B/P: 1/43

3229 Powell, Pratt - white male D: May 22, 1900; 1y; Hampshire F: Powell, L.J. M: Powell, Mollie B: Dec 26, 1898 DOI: mother B/P: 1/73

3230 Powell, Robert M. - white male D: Oct 3, 1903; 33y; Hampshire F: Powell, D.S. M: Powell, Martha B: 1870 DOI: father B/P: 1/80

3231 Powell, Sarah A. - married white female D: Apr 5, 1896; 56y 9m 17d; Hampshire B: Hampshire B/P: 1/87

3232 Powell, Winnie - single white female D: 1892; 74y; Hampshire B: Hampshire I: Leath, J.W. DOI: friend B/P: 1/57

3233 Powelson, Alvin - married white male D: Mar 25, 1910; 32y 5m 8d B/P: 2/98 N: farmer

3234 Powelson, Benj. - widower white male D: Jan 26, 1921; 70y; Hampshire B: Virginia B/P: 1/130 N: farmer

3235 Powelson, Caroline - widow white female D: Sept 30, 1910; 86y 4m 13d B/P: 2/98

3236 Powelson, Catherine - married white female D: Feb 10,

1873; 59y; Hampshire F: French, Robert M: French, Sarah B: Hampshire I: Everett, Charles DOI: friend C: Powelson, John B/P: 1/10

3237 Powelson, Elizabeth - single white female D: Mar 5, 1872; 31y; Hampshire F: Powelson, John B: Hampshire I: Powelson, Isaih DOI: brother B/P: 1/8

3238 Powelson, Hannah - married white female D: Apr 5, 1911; 69y 8m 29d B/P: 2/95

3239 Powelson, James W.L. - white male D: July 1874; 5m; Hampshire F: Powelson, John W. M: Powelson, Matilda B: Hampshire DOI: father B/P: 1/13

3240 Powelson, John - white male D: Feb 2, 1873; 64y; Hampshire F: Powelson, John M: Powelson, Cloe B: Hammpshire I: Everett, Charles DOI: friend C: Powelson, Catherine B/P: 1/10

3241 Powelson, Lester A. D: Aug 13, 1871; 2y 2m 8d F: Powelson, John W. B/P: 1/6

3242 Powelson, Sarah - white female D: Sept 25, 1878; 25y 2m 10d; Hampshire B: Hampshire DOI: husband C: Powelson, Benj. B/P: 1/23

3243 Power, Annie - single white female D: Oct 8, 1898; 18y; Hampshire B: Ohio BUR: Baptist Church, Capon Br. B/P: 1/101

3244 Power, Truman Lynn - single white male D: Oct 15, 1921; 2m 16d; Hampshire F: Powers, Melvin M: Powers, Minnie B: WV I: Alkire, Edith B/P: 1/132

3245 Powers, Amie B. - white female D: Aug 8, 1898; 18y; Gore District F: Powers, Burr M: Powers, M.J. DOI: father B/P: 1/69

3246 Powers, Wallice - white male D: Aug 18, 1916; 17y B: L. Capon B/P: 2/96

3247 Pownall, Alice - white female D: May 30, 1901; 40y; Romney District F: Lewis, Jas. N. M: Lewis, Mary DOI: father B/P: 1/76

3248 Pownall, Ann Matilda - widow white female D: July 25, 1910; 68y 1m 14d B/P: 2/98

3249 Pownall, Arch - white male D: June 24, 1908; 20y 5m B/P: 2/94

3250 Pownall, Charles - married white male D: Apr 26, 1919; 44y 1m 2d B/P: 2/98 N: farmer

3251 Pownall, Cloe E. - white female D: Dec 15, 1888; 11d; Sherman District F: Pownall, D.G. M: Pownall, A.M. B: Hampshire DOI: father B/P: 1/47

3252 Pownall, Eliza - widow white female D: May 17, 1912; 64y 3m B: Bloomery B/P: 2/95

3253 Pownall, Elizabeth J. - white female D: June 28, 1886; 2y 6m; Sherman District F: Pownall, J.C. M: Pownall, Martha B: Hampshire DOI: father B/P: 1/43

3254 Pownall, Elizabeth - married white female D: Nov 1885; 65y 10m; Hampshire B: Hampshire I: Pownall, I.P. B/P: 1/42

3255 Pownall, F.J. - white male D: Mar 11, 1898; 52y; Gore District I: Pownall, J.W. DOI: son B/P: 1/69

3256 Pownall, J.M. - white male D: Dec 11, 1900; 54y; Sherman B: June 1847 DOI: son B/P: 1/72

3257 Pownall, Jno. D. - married white male D: Sept 22, 1912; 55y 7m 22d B: Springfield B/P: 2/95 N: B & O Railroad agent

3258 Pownall, Jno. D. - married white male D: Aug 22, 1911; 59y B: Springfield DOI: wife B/P: 2/95 N: express agent

3259 Pownall, John A. - white male D: Feb 28, 1891; 28y; Hampshire B: Hampshire DOI: wife C: Pownall, Alice B/P: 1/55

3260 Pownall, L.S. - white male D: June 30, 1894; 2m 6d; Hampshire F: Pownall, L.J. M: Pownall, M.C. B: Hampshire DOI: father B/P: 1/60

3261 Pownall, Orra - single white female D: May 18, 1895; 14y; Hampshire B: Hampshire B/P: 1/88

3262 Pownall, Rebecca - married white female D: July 14, 1894; 68y; Hampshire B: Virginia BUR: Three Churches B/P: 1/82

3263 Pownall, Sara - white female D: Feb 7, 1902; 87y; Sherman District B: 1815 I: Pownall, J.W. DOI: son B/P: 1/78 N: Parents: Jacob & Margaret

3264 Pownall, Susie - white female D: Feb 23, 1908; 9y B/P:

2/94

3265 Pownall, Virginia C. - white female D: June 25, 1897; 53y; Sherman District F: Baker, James E. M: Baker, Minna B: Sherman District DOI: husband C: Pownall, F.M. B/P: 1/64

3266 Pownall, Wm. J. - white male D: Apr 28, 1915; 80y 9m I: Pownall, Geo. W. B/P: 2/96

3267 Pownell, Chester - single white male D: June 15, 1922; 17y 28d; Hampshire F: Pownell, W.M. M: Pownell, Katherine B: Pennsylvania I: Pownell, Catherine B/P: 1/134

3268 Pownell, Granville D: Oct 1871 B/P: 1/6

3269 Pownell, Isaac W - single D: Sept 25, 1871; 18y 1m 25d F: Pownell, Isaac M: Pownell, Rebecca B/P: 1/6

3270 Pownell, Mary J. - single D: Oct 1871; F: Pownell, Joseph M: Pownell, Elizabeth B/P: 1/6

3271 Pownell, Mary V. - single white female D: Aug 12, 1881; 26y 11m 20d; Hampshire F: Pownall, Jno A. M: Pownall, Eliza A. B: Cumberland, MD DOI: father B/P: 1/32

3272 Pownell, Nancy E. - white female D: Feb 7, 1881; 35y; Hampshire F: Gulick, Nathaniel M: Gulick, Jane B: Hampshire DOI: husband C: Pownall, Jasper B/P: 1/32

3273 Pownell, Wm. Jr. - single white male D: Oct 21, 1921; 18y 8m 18d; Hampshire F: Pownell, Wm. M: Pownell, Kate B: Maryland B/P: 1/132

3274 Proctor, Adam - married white male D: Feb 26, 1898; 71y; Green Spring Valley B: Virginia BUR: Springfield B/P: 1/93

3275 Proctor, Kate - married white female D: Oct 15, 1907; 50y B/P: 2/94

3276 Proster, Mrs. Adam - widow white female D: Nov 20, 1909; 79y B/P: 2/95

3277 Proudfoot, John - white male D: Feb 1, 1914; 10d B/P: 2/95

3278 Puffenberger, Lucy - married white female D: May 25, 1907; 26y B/P: 2/94

3279 Puffenberger, Nora - white female D: May 10, 1907; 19y B/P: 2/94

3280 Puffinberger, Chas - widower male white D: Dec 11, 1899; 35y; Spring Gap BUR: Hampshire B/P: 1/106

3281 Puffinberger, Elizabeth - white female D: Aug 3, 1904; 60y B/P: 2/94

3282 Puffinberger, Mrs. - married white female D: Nov 25, 1899; 30y; Spring Gap BUR: Hampshire B/P: 1/106

3283 Pugh Ausker - white male D: Oct 17, 1899; 8y; Capon District B: Hampshire BUR: St. James B/P: 1/109

3284 Pugh, Ada M. - white female D: July 11, 1891; 9y 1m 23d; Hampshire F: Pugh, J.A. M: Pugh, M.V. B: Hampshire DOI: father B/P: 1/55

3285 Pugh, Benjm - white male D: Apr 12, 1876; 61y 6d; Hampshire B: Hampshire DOI: wife C: Pugh, Nancy B/P: 1/18

3286 Pugh, Bettie - single white female D: Apr 27, 1906; 77y B/P: 2/94

3287 Pugh, David - white male D: Mar 29, 1887; 85y 11m 5d; Capon District F: Pugh, Jos. B: Hampshire I: Pugh, George DOI: son in law C: Pugh, Hester Ann (dec'd) B/P: 1/43 N: David of Jos.

3288 Pugh, David C. - white male D: Aug 22, 1876; 20y; Hampshire F: Pugh, David M: Pugh, Elizabeth B: Hampshire DOI: father B/P: 1/18

3289 Pugh, Elizabeth - white female D: Mar 26, 1879; 57y 3m; Hampshire B: Hampshire I: Pugh, David DOI: son B/P: 1/25

3290 Pugh, Elizabeth - white female D: May 14, 1900; 80y; Hampshire B: 1820 I: Pugh, Anna Lee DOI: daughter B/P: 1/73

3291 Pugh, Elmira V - single white female D: Nov 20, 1866; 19y 6m 15d; Hampshire F: Pugh, David M: Pugh, Elizabeth B: Hampshire DOI: parent B/P: 1/1

3292 Pugh, Esther D: Aug 2, 1871; 68y 1m F: Hook, David C: Pugh, David B/P: 1/6

3293 Pugh, James N. - white male D: April 17, 1867; 24 y; Gr. Capon F: Pugh, D. B: Pleasant Dale I: Pugh, David DOI: cousin B/P: 1/2

3294 Pugh, Jane - white female D: Dec 18, 1886; 77y; Capon District B: Hampshire DOI: husband C: Pugh, Robert B/P: 1/43

3295 Pugh, Jas B. - white male D: Oct 1881; 4y 8m 18d; Hampshire F: Pugh, Geo M: Pugh, Louiza B: Hampshire DOI: father B/P: 1/30

3296 Pugh, Jesse J. - white male D: July 9, 1882; 72y; Capon District B: WV I: Pugh, Thomas DOI: son C: Pugh, Elizabeth B/P: 1/33

3297 Pugh, Jno - single white male D: Mar 6, 1866; 27y; Hampshire F: Pugh, David M: Pugh, Elizabeth B: Hampshire DOI: parent B/P: 1/1

3298 Pugh, Jonathan - single white male D: Feb 12, 1914; 82y 3m 17d B/P: 2/95 N: farmer

3299 Pugh, Julanna - white female D: Jan 5, 1866 B/P: 1/2

3300 Pugh, L.M. - white female D: July 10, 1897; 3m 10d; Bloomery F: Pugh, A.D. M: Pugh, M. B: Mar 30, 1897 DOI: father B/P: 1/66

3301 Pugh, Lemuel - white male D: Oct 28, 1877; Hampshire B: Hampshire I: Pugh, Amos L DOI: son C: Pugh, Elizabeth B/P: 1/22

3302 Pugh, Lizzie - married white female D: Mar 12, 1910; 70y B/P: 2/98

3303 Pugh, Lucile - single white female D: Sept 11, 1897; 5m 11d; Capon Bridge B: Capon Bridge BUR: Highview B/P: 1/95

3304 Pugh, Lucy A. - white female D: June 10, 1896; 46y; Capon District F: Carpenter, Louis B: June 1850 DOI: father B/P: 1/62

3305 Pugh, Margaret - white female D: Sept 26, 1908; 64y B/P: 2/94

3306 Pugh, Martha - married white female D: Dec 11, 1914; 73y 3m 10d B/P: 2/95

3307 Pugh, Mary - single white female D: Dec 30, 1878; 32y 3m 24d; Hampshire B: Hampshire I: Pugh, Geo DOI: brother B/P: 1/23

3308 Pugh, Mary M. - white female D: Oct 18, 1899; 68y;

Romney F: McKee, Joe M: McKee, Rebecca B: 1832 DOI: son B/P: 1/71

3309 Pugh, Nimrod - white male D: Oct 1882; 81y; Hampshire F: Pugh, J. M: Pugh, E. B: Hampshire I: Day, Jos DOI: son in law C: Pugh, Elizabeth B/P: 1/34 N: blacksmith

3310 Pugh, Oscar T. - white male D: Oct 15, 1899; 8y 11m 27d; Capon F: Pugh Z.T. B: 1892 B/P: 1/71

3311 Pugh, Robert - white male D: Oct 15, 1894; 81y 1m; Capon F: Pugh, Joseph B: Capon DOI: son B/P: 1/59

3312 Pugh, Robt. O. - white male D: Mar 30, 1908; 56y B/P: 2/94 N: farmer

3313 Pugh, Tanzin A. - single white male D: Apr 16, 1908; 24y 9m 25d B/P: 2/94 N: expressman

3314 Pugh, Thomas W. - white male D: Oct 17, 1880; 4d; Hampshire F: Pugh, Joseph A. M: Pugh, Martha V. B: Hampshire DOI: father B/P: 1/28

3315 Pugh, W.A. - white male D: Aug 26, 1894; 4y 8m 13d; Hampshire F: Pugh, D.W. M: Pugh, S.J. B: Hampshire DOI: father B/P: 1/60

3316 Pugh, William A. - white male D: Aug 28, 1894; 4y 8m 13d; Pleasant Dale B: Pleasant Dale BUR: Salem Church B/P: 1/83

3317 Puller, Mary S - white female D: July 10, 1876; 39y; Hampshire F: Ritter, Henry M: Ritter, Margaret B: Frederick Co VA DOI: husband C: Puller, Calvina B/P: 1/21

3318 Pultz, Frances - single female D: Apr 30, 1888; 10m; Hampshire B: Hampshire BUR: Hampshire B/P: 1/122

3319 Pultz, Isaac - white male D: Aug 14, 1905; 80y 10m B/P: 2/94 N: farmer

3320 Pultz, Jane - single white female D: Dec 31, 1887; 30y; Hampshire B: Hampshire BUR: Hampshire B/P: 1/122

3321 Pultz, Rebecca - white female D: May 12, 1897; 71y 10m 8d; Gore B: July 4, 1825 DOI: husband C: Pultz, Jacob B/P: 1/66

3322 Pultz, Sarah E. - white female D: Sept 29, 1886; 30y 8m 15d; Sherman District F: Pultz, Isaac M: Pultz, Mary B:

Hampshire DOI: father B/P: 1/43

3323 Purget, L.D. - white male D: May 11, 1896; 44y 8m 22d; Mill Creek District F: Purget, W.S. B: Mar 1859 DOI: father B/P: 1/62

3324 Purgett, Jas. S. - single white male D: June 6, 1879; 19y; Hampshire F: Purgett, Wm M: Purgett, Ann B: Hampshire DOI: father B/P: 1/25

3325 Purgit, A.A. - white female D: Aug 1888; 60y; Mill Creek District B: Hampshire DOI: husband C: Purgit, Wm. S. B/P: 1/47

3326 Purgit, Statton - single white male D: Apr 13, 1895; 1y 8m 5d; Hampshire B: Hampshire B/P: 1/89

3327 Purgit, William - white male D: May 8, 1886; 83y 11m 25d; Mill Creek District B: Hampshire I: Purgit, Wm. S. DOI: son B/P: 1/43

3328 Putz, Eliza - widow white female D: Nov 25, 1911; 79y 9m 17d B/P: 2/95

3329 Pyles, John - single white male D: May 24, 1918; 19y 5m 24d; Hampshire B/P: 1/127

3330 Pyles, Josephine Francis - white female D: Oct 1, 1919; 4y 3m 19d B/P: 2/98

3331 Pyles, Lucretia V. - white female D: Mar 21, 1914; 3m 25d B/P: 2/95

3332 Qualls, Susan - colored female D: Mar 1, 1902; 10m; Romney District F: Qualls, Joe M: Qualls, Maria B: Jan 2, 1902 DOI: father B/P: 1/78

3333 Queen, George - white male D: Aug 22, 1872; 5y 11m 25d; Hampshire F: Queen, John M: Queen, Mary B: Hampshire DOI: father B/P: 1/8

3334 Queen, Jane - married white female D: Jan 15,1913; 60y B/P: 2/99

3335 Queen, Stephen D: Dec 7, 1870; 23y; Hampshire F: Queen, Stephen M: Queen, May B/P: 1/5

3336 Racey, Hannah - widow white female D: Apr 3, 1921; 64y 1m 18d; Hampshire F: Groves, Jno. M: Groves, Hannah B: Shenandoah Co., VA I: Racey, Edward B/P: 1/130 N: housewife

3337 Racey, John - white male D: Oct 26, 1886; 71y; Sherman District B: Hampshire DOI: wife C: Racey, Eleanor B/P: 1/43

3338 Racey, Martha K. - white female D: Aug 5, 1917; 70y B/P: 2/101

3339 Racey, William D: Nov 28, 1870; 84y 5m B/P: 1/5

3340 Raigner, Mary J. - white D: Jan 21, 1905; 45y B/P: 2/101

3341 Ramsey, Kate - white female D: Apr 5, 1910; 60y B/P: 2/100

3342 Raney, Lydia J. - white female D: Mar 6, 1888; 38y; Hampshire F: Miller, J.D. B: Pennsylvania DOI: father B/P: 1/46

3343 Rannells, Doyle Wm. - white male D: Sept 23, 1914; 1d B/P: 2/100

3344 Rannells, Geo. - white male D: Feb 28, 1901; 34y; Hampshire I: Taylor, W.F.J. B/P: 1/77

3345 Rannells, H.A. - white female D: Jan 18, 1899; 65y; Gore District F: Burkett, J. M: Burkett, K.B. B: Jan 18, 1834 I: Rannells, J.B. DOI: son B/P: 1/70

3346 Rannells, Hester - widow white female D: Jan 18, 1899; 64y; Three Churches B: Hampshire BUR: Three Churches B/P: 1/103

3347 Rannells, J.N. - white male D: Nov 13, 1901; 65y; Hampshire I: Taylor, Mrs. E.F. B/P: 1/77

3348 Rannells, Keziah - white D: Feb 6, 1882; 78y; Hampshire F: Miller, W. M: Miller, C. B: Hampshire I: Burket, Ella DOI: daughter C: Rannells, Jno B/P: 1/34

3349 Rannells, Silas M. - married white male D: Apr 25, 1895; 70y; Hampshire B: Hampshire B/P: 1/88

3350 Rannells, W.E. - married white male D: Dec 12, 1912; B: Romney B/P: 2/100 N: carpenter

3351 Raymond, Moses - white male D: May 19, 1875; 77y; Hampshire F: Raymond, Moses M: Raymond, Rebecca B: Connecticut I: Raymond, Bell DOI: daughter C: Raymond, Sarah

B/P: 1/16

3352 Raymond, Sarah - white female D: May 21, 1884; 87y; Hampshire I: McGlothery, S.R. DOI: friend B/P: 1/39

3353 Rayner, Elizabeth - married white female D: Dec 2, 1905; 49y B/P: 2/101

3354 Rease, Anne E. - white female D: Apr 29, 1879;57y 11m 14d; Hampshire F: Knise, Valentine M: Knise, Anna E B: Germany DOI: husband C: Rease, John B/P: 1/26

3355 Redman, Mary - colored female D: May 8, 1913; 60y B/P: 2/100

3356 Reed, Hattie - widow white female D: Jan 15, 1911; 60y 7m 20d B: Gore District B/P: 2/100

3357 Reed, J. Smith - white male D: Dec 3, 1903; 21y; Capon District B/P: 1/81

3358 Reid, Cornelius - single white male D: Aug 27, 1866; 4y 7m F: Reid, Dorsey M: Reid, Louisa B: Hampshire DOI: parent B/P: 1/1

3359 Reiver, B.A. - white female D: May 6, 1899; 57y 9m 18d; Gore District F: Alkire, S. B: July 18, 1841 DOI: husband C: Reiver, R.W. B/P: 1/70

3360 Rennells, Pet - white female D: Dec 1, 1879; 10y; Hampshire F: Rennells, John M: Rennells, Hannah B: Hampshire DOI: father B/P: 1/26

3361 Reuse, John Jr. - white male D: Mar 14, 1922; Hampshire I: Lupton, Geo. A. B/P: 1/135

3362 Reynor, Myrtle - widow white female D: Apr 6, 1904; 22y B/P: 2/100

3363 Rice, Jno. R. - married white male D: 1906; 59y B/P: 2/100 N: accident

3364 Richards, B.F. - white male D: Mar 25, 1887; 3m; Sherman District F: Richards, B.F. M: Richards, Mary B: Hampshire DOI: father B/P: 1/43

3365 Richards, Henry S. - white male D: Mar 25, 1867; 39y 10m 13d; North River F: Richards, Henry B: Frederick Co. Va DOI: consort C: Richards, Martha B/P: 1/2

3366 Richmond, Elza - white female D: 21 May 1878; 60y; Hampshire F: McDougan, Wm M: McDougan, Mary DOI: husband C: Richmond, Wm. B/P: 1/24

3367 Richmond, Jane D: Apr 20, 1870; 83y; Hampshire F: Allen, John M: Allen, Ann C: Richmond, James B/P: 1/5

3368 Richmond, Johannah - single white female D: Oct 27, 1881; 60y; Hampshire F: Richmond, Jas M: Richmond, Jane B: Hampshire I: Foreman, Ann DOI: sister B/P: 1/32

3369 Ridgeway, Mary C. - widow white female D: Aug 27, 1910; 79y 11m B/P: 2/100

3370 Ridgeway, Rebecca - white female D: Oct 13, 1900; 78y; Hampshire I: Riley, R.F. DOI: friend B/P: 1/73

3371 Ridgeway, Sarah E - white female D: Aug 1, 1868; 3y 8m; Timber Ridge F: Ridgeway, William B: Hampshire DOI: father B/P: 1/3

3372 Ridgeway, Wm. G. - white male D: Feb 19, 1907; 88y 6m 8d B/P: 2/100

3373 Ridgway, John - white male D: Apr 6, 1867; 96y 4d; Timber Ridge I: Ridgway, William DOI: son B/P: 1/2 N: farmer

3374 Riggleman, A. - married white female D: Mar 24, 1896; 42y 1m 4d; Hampshire B: Hampshire B/P: 1/87

3375 Riley, C.A. - white male D: Nov 6, 1896; 27y 2m; Hampshire F: Riley, William C M: Riley, Susan B: Sept 7, 1869 I: Riley, R.F. DOI: brother B/P: 1/63 N: merchant

3376 Riley, Clark - single white male D: Nov 18, 1897; abt 25y; B: Bloomery BUR: Sandy Ridge B/P: 1/97

3377 Riley, Elmer, - white male D: Oct 4, 1882; 4y 11m 24d; Hampshire F: Riley, W.T. M: Riley, Susan A. B: Hampshire DOI: mother B/P: 1/34

3378 Riley, Garnet - white female D: 1903; 8y; Hampshire F: Riley, J.W. M: Riley, Rosie DOI: father B/P: 1/80

3379 Riley, Jane - white female D: Aug 27, 1902; 100y; Hampshire B: 1802 I: Rowzee, Sam DOI: son in law B/P: 1/79

3380 Riley, Mrs. - widow white female D: Aug 16, 1902; 100y; Points B: Hampshire BUR: Wesley Chapel B/P: 1/116

3381 Riley, Thomas - white male D: Apr 9, 1874; 59y 5m 12d; Hampshire F: Riley, Thomas M: Riley, Sarah B: Loudoun Co VA I: Riley, James DOI: son C: Riley, Margaret B/P: 1/13 N: blacksmith

3382 Riley, W. - white male D: Oct 29, 1896; 60y; Hampshire F: Riley, Thomas M: Riley, Margaret B: May 23, 1836 I: Riley, C.E. DOI: son C: Riley, S.A. B/P: 1/63

3383 Rinehart, Christena - white female D: Sept 20, 1868; 75y; North River DOI: son in law B/P: 1/3

3384 Rinehart, Mary C. - widowed white female D: Sept 30, 1922; 87y 3m 22d; Hampshire F: Stewart, Jno. M: Stewart, Lucinda B: Hampshire I: Moreland, Edw. B/P: 1/134

3385 Rinehart, Silas - white male D: Nov 10, 1879; 70y; Hampshire B: Hampshire I: Rinehart, Thos DOI: son C: Rinehart, Mary B/P: 1/26

3386 Rinker, Elizabeth - white female D: Oct 23, 1873; 83y 4m; Hampshire I: Rinker, Sam'l DOI: son C: Rinker, John B/P: 1/10

3387 Rinker, Frederick - white male D: Sept 29, 1909; 80y 6m B/P: 2/100 N: farmer

3388 Rinker, Geo. Sam'l - white male D: Aug 16, 1921 48y 4m 17d; Hampshire F: Rinker, Joshua M: Rinker, Susan B: Hampshire B/P: 1/132

3389 Rinker, Ira Dailey - single white male D: Aug 4, 1921; Hampshire F: Rinker, Jas. W. M: Rinker, Annie B/P: 1/132

3390 Rinker, J.R. - white male D: July 2, 1890; 59y 3m; Mill Creek District F: Rinker, S. M: Rinker, E. B: Hampshire DOI: wife C: Rinker, Susan E. B/P: 1/52

3391 Rinker, Samuel - white male D: May 16, 1905; 74y B/P: 2/100 N: farmer

3392 Ritchie, Albert Lee - white male D: Jan 7, 1922; 7d; Hampshire F: Ritchie, Perry M: Ritchie, Catherine B: Hampshire I: Day, Nelson B/P: 1/135

3393 Roach, Margarete - widowed white female D: Jan 18, 1922; 80y 23d; Hampshire F: Orndorff, Joe M: Orndorff, Mary B: WV I: Roach, H.S. B/P: 1/135

3394 Roberson, Caroline - white female D: Aug 28, 1914; 80y 6m 7d B/P: 2/100

3395 Roberson, Chester Lester - white male D: Dec 6, 1919; 2m 13d B/P: 2/101

3396 Roberson, Elizabeth - white female D: Apr 8, 1875; 73y; Hampshire F: Shanholtzer, Jacob M: Shanholtzer, Mary B: Hampshire DOI: husband C: Roberson, Moses B/P: 1/16

3397 Roberson, M.J. - white female D: June 1899; 71y; Gore District F: Roberson, J. M: Roberson, E. B: 1828 I: Roberson, R.T. DOI: brother B/P: 1/70

3398 Robinson, A. - white male D: Oct 4, 1889; 1m; Mill Creek F: Robinson, W.C. M: Robinson, Florence E. B: Mill Creek District DOI: father B/P: 1/49

3399 Robinson, Jno. R. - single white male D: Nov 14, 1921; 10d; Hampshire M: Robinson, Verna B: Augusta B/P: 1/130

3400 Robinson, John - married white male D: Mar 20, 1878; 62y 2m 22d; Hampshire B: Hampshire DOI: son B/P: 1/23

3401 Robinson, John - white male D: Feb 26, 1907; 73y 7m 14d B/P: 2/100 N: farmer

3402 Robinson, Martha - single white female D: Feb 22, 1904; 35y B/P: 2/100

3403 Robinson, P. - married black female D: June 20, 1897; 72y; Romney BUR: Romney B/P: 1/94

3404 Robinson, Philis - colored female D: Mar 15, 1897; 55y; Sherman District B: Romney District I: Hott, Jno. DOI: son C: Robinson, John B/P: 1/64

3405 Robison, Frances V - single white female D: Dec 10, 1873; 2y 7m 14d; Hampshire F: Robison, Joel M: Robison, Margaret B: Hampshire DOI: father B/P: 1/10

3406 Robison, Winfred - white male D: Feb 19, 1908; 3m B/P: 2/100

3407 Roby, Minnie Edith - married white female D: May 15, 1916; 31y 6m 15d B: Capon District B/P: 2/100

3408 Rockwell, Laura Mary - white female D: Jan 22, 1917; 2y 11m B/P: 2/101

3409 Rogers, Clayton - married white male D: June 5, 1912; 30y B/P: 2/100 N: farmer

3410 Rogers, Dallas Foster - married white male D: Oct 7, 1918; 32y 15d B/P: 2/101 N: farmer

3411 Rogers, Daniel - married white male D: July 31, 1921; 68y 10m 18d; Hampshire B: Frederick Co., VA B/P: 1/132 N: farmer

3412 Rogers, Elsie - widow white female D: Apr 28, 1919; 37y 20d B/P: 2/101

3413 Rogers, W.L. - white male D: Aug 24, 1907; 64y B/P: 2/100 N: farmer

3414 Roice, John - white male D: Feb 27, 1907; 65y B/P: 2/100 N: fruit tree agent; struck by engine

3415 Roigner, Myrtle - white female D: Mar 1903; 25y; Hampshire F: Crock B: 1876 I: Roigner, Thos. DOI: friend B/P: 1/80

3416 Roigner, Preston - white male D: Feb 17, 1903; 26y; Hampshire F: Roigner, William B: 1877 I: Roigner, Thomas DOI: uncle B/P: 1/80

3417 Roler, Willie - colored male D: Oct 15, 1874; 1y 1m; Hampshire F: Roler, Chas M: Roler, Sine B: Hampshire DOI: father B/P: 1/12

3418 Rolls, Chas - colored male D: Dec 19, 1881; 78y; Hampshire F: Rolls, Joshua M: Rolls, Philis B: Virginia I: Rolls, D.W. DOI: son B/P: 1/30

3419 Rolls, Guss - single black male D: Dec 12, 1898; 14y; Romney B: WV BUR: Romney B/P: 1/99

3420 Rolls, Harry R. - single black male D: Dec 27, 1898; 12y 3m 10d; Romney BUR: Romney B/P: 1/99

3421 Rolls, Henry - widower colored male D: Feb 1, 1911; 58y B: Romney District B/P: 2/100

3422 Rolls, Lucy - colored female D: Sept 14, 1905; 52y B/P: 2/100

3423 Rolls, Mary - married black female D: Jan 4, 1899; Romney BUR: Romney B/P: 1/102

3424 Rolls, Otie - colored female D: May 15, 1904; 3m B/P: 2/107

3425 Rolls, Susie - colored female D: May 6, 1905; 71y B/P: 2/100

3426 Roomsberg, Matilda J. - white female D: Aug 9, 1884; 28y; Hampshire B: Hampshire DOI: husband C: Roomsberg, Geo. W. B/P: 1/38

3427 Rose, Annie - married white female D: Sept 23, 1895; 23y; Hampshire B: Hampshire B/P: 1/90

3428 Rosebrock, Hannah - single white female D: Apr 20, 1877; Hampshire F: Rosebrock, Solomon M: Rosebrock, Rhoda B: Hampshire DOI: mother B/P: 1/22

3429 Rosebrock, Joan - single white female D: Feb 20, 1866; 25y 6m 20d; Hampshire F: Rosebrock, Moses M: Rosebrock, Rebecca B: Hampshire DOI: parent B/P: 1/1

3430 Rosebrock, S. F. D: May 21, 1870; 41y 1m F: Rosebrock, Moses B/P: 1/5

3431 Rosebrough, John M. - white male D: Feb 22, 1899; 76y; Capon I: Rosebrough, Marie B/P: 1/71

3432 Rosebrough, Parthena - white female D: Nov 8, 1874; 14m; Hampshire M: Rosebrough, Mary B: Hampshire DOI: mother B/P: 1/12

3433 Rosebrough, Rebecca - white female D: Nov 9, 1883; 79y; Hampshire B: Hampshire I: Rosebrough, Jas L. DOI: son C: Rosebrough, Mose B/P: 1/36

3434 Ross, Anna - married black female D: Oct 21, 1902; 40y 9m 28d; Springfield B: Hampshire BUR: Springfield B/P: 1/117

3435 Ross, Malinda - colored female D: Nov 3, 1912; B: Romney B/P: 2/100

3436 Rotruck, Bertie B. - white female D: 1885; Hampshire F: Rotruck, J.P. M: Rotruck, Ellen B: Hampshire DOI: father B/P: 1/42

3437 Rouzee, Ann J. - white female D: Dec 20, 1881; 41y 5m 10d; Hampshire F: Riley, Peter M: Riley, Jane B: Allegany Co., MD DOI: husband C: Rouzee, S.A. B/P: 1/32

3438 Rouzee, Lillian - white female D: June 29, 1916; 13y B: Points B/P: 2/100

3439 Rouzee, M.J. - white female D: July 8, 1892; 50y 4m 4d; Hampshire F: Malcolm, J. M: Malcolm, M. B: Hampshire DOI: husband C: Rouzee, S.A. B/P: 1/57

3440 Rouzee, S.H. - white male D: July 1889; 11m; Hampshire F: Rouzee, Jno W. M: Rouzee, V.B. B: Hampshire I: Rouzee, S. DOI: grandfather B/P: 1/51

3441 Rouzee, V.B. - white female D: Oct 1889; 24y; Hampshire F: Day, Alex M: Day, C. B: Hampshire I: Rouzee, S. DOI: father in law C: Rouzee, Jno W. B/P: 1/51

3442 Rowzee, Frank, Wm. - single white male D: May 8, 1922; 9m 15d; Hampshire F: Rowzee, Oscar B: Hampshire I: Kaylor, Estella B/P: 1/135

3443 Rowzee, Jas. - single white male D: July 30, 1918; stillborn; Hampshire B/P: 1/127

3444 Rowzee, S.A. - married white male D: Dec 6, 1908; 75y B/P: 2/100 N: farmer

3445 Royce, Hazel - white female D: Aug 17, 1917; 1y 2m B/P: 2/101

3446 Ruckman, Albert Middleton - married white male D: May 15, 1919; 58y 4m 23d B/P: 2/101

3447 Ruckman, Aloni S. - white male D: Sept 23, 1908; 2m 11d B/P: 2/100

3448 Ruckman, Alverda - white female D: Jan 18, 1886; Hampshire B: Hampshire DOI: husband C: Ruckman, Albert M. B/P: 1/41

3449 Ruckman, Arthur J. - white male D: Oct 12, 1915; 44y 5m B/P: 2/100

3450 Ruckman, Bertha Jane - white female D: July 4, 1876; 34y 6m; Hampshire F: Ruckman, Samuel M: Ruckman, Elizabeth B: Hampshire DOI: father B/P: 1/18

3451 Ruckman, Caroline - white female D: Apr 26, 1904; 66y; Augusta F: Phohs, Philip B: 1838 B/P: 1/81

3452 Ruckman, Catharine - white female D: Aug 6, 1866 B/P: 1/2

3453 Ruckman, Cyrus D: Jan 4, 1871; 1m 16d F: Ruckman, I G B/P: 1/6

3454 Ruckman, Elizabeth C. - white female D: Jan 1, 1884; 50y; Hampshire B: Hampshire DOI: husband C: Ruckman, Gibson B/P: 1/38

3455 Ruckman, Herman - white male D: Mar 23, 1902; 13y; Sherman District F: Ruckman, A. M. M: Ruckman A.M. B: 1889 DOI: father B/P: 1/78

3456 Ruckman, Jno. W. - married white male D: Jan 29, 1922; 72y 2m 18d; Hampshire F: Ruckman, Samuel B: Hampshire I: Ruckman, R.J. B/P: 1/134 N: farmer

3457 Ruckman, Juanita Enid - white female D: July 11, 1916; 1y 11m 12d B: Sherman District B/P: 2/100

3458 Ruckman, Margaret - white female D: July 13, 1908; 59y 11m 4d B/P: 2/100

3459 Ruckman, Minnie I. - married white female D: Feb 23, 1903; 27y 9m 3d; Hampshire B: Hampshire BUR: Mt Zion B/P: 1/114

3460 Ruckman, Rhoda E. - single white female D: Feb 4, 1899; 65y; Hampshire B: Hampsire BUR: Delaplanes' C. B/P: 1/104

3461 Ruckman, Sam'l C. - widower D: Sept 21, 1869; 62y 1m 15d; Hampshire F: Ruckman, Jacob B: Hampshire B/P: 1/4

3462 Ruckman, Wm J. - white male D: Aug 22, 1879; 13y 10m 20d; Hampshire F: Ruckman, Jas M: Ruckman, Caroline B: Hampshire DOI: father B/P: 1/25

3463 Rudolph E. - white female D: Feb 14, 1891; 65y; Sherman District B: Hampshire DOI: husband C: Rudolph, Henry B/P: 1/51

3464 Rudolph, Adam - white male D: Jan 16, 1874; 77y 6d; Hampshire B: Shenandoah DOI: wife C: Rudolph, Sarah B/P: 1/12

3465 Rudolph, Anthrs - white male D: Sept 30, 1876; 5y; Hampshire F: Rudolph, Jacob M: Rudolph, C. B: Hampshire DOI: father B/P: 1/18

3466 Rudolph, Daisey - single white female D: May 4, 1889; 19y; Hampshire B: Hampshire BUR: Hebron B/P: 1/125

3467 Rudolph, Daisy D. - white female D: May 1889; 19y; Capon District F: Rudolph, Jacob C. M: Rudolph, Cora E. B: Capon District DOI: father B/P: 1/50

3468 Rudolph, Hezekial - white male D: Aug 6, 1866 B/P: 1/2

3469 Rudolph, John L. - white male D: Mar 7, 1867; 22y 5m 11d; Gr. Capon F: Rudolph, George B: G. Capon I: Rudolph, Jacob DOI: brother B/P: 1/2

3470 Rudolph, M. - white female D: June 10, 1890; 1y 10m; Capon District F: Rudolph, Nathen M: Rudolph, C. B: Hampshire DOI: father B/P: 1/52

3471 Rudolph, Nancy - married white female D: Aug 15, 1866; 42 y B: Hampshire DOI: husband C: Rudolph, Sylvester B/P: 1/1

3472 Rudolph, Nathan F. - white male D: Dec 29, 1904; 57y B/P: 2/100

3473 Rudolph, Walter - white male D: June 19,1878; 2m 12d; Hampshire F: Rudolph, Nathan M: Rudolph, Catherine B: Hampshire DOI: father B/P: 1/23

3474 Rusel, William - colored male D: March 8, 1867; 32y 2m 10d; Forks of Capon M: Johnson, Ann B: Paw Paw I: Hiett, Evan B/P: 1/3

3475 Russell, Ada - white female D: Dec 22, 1889; 1y 5m; Sherman District F: Russell, J.R. M: Russell, Elizabeth B: Sherman District DOI: father B/P: 1/50

3476 Russell, Ada - single white female D: Dec 21, 1889; 2y; Hampshire B: WV B/P: 1/125

3477 Russell, Catharine A. - white female D: June 6, 1883; 66y; Hampshire F: Russell, David M: Russell, Rachel B: Old Town, MD DOI: husband C: Russell, William B/P: 1/37

3478 Russell, Mahlon - married white male D: Aug 22, 1905; 74y B/P: 2/101 N: farmer

3479 Russell, Mary A. - married white female D: June 27, 1892; 84y; Hampshire B: Hampshire I: Adams, M.H. DOI: nephew B/P: 1/57

3480 Sager, Annie L. - white female D: Dec 19, 1891; 22y 7m 16d; Hampshire F: Sager, Jas M: Sager, Mary B: Hardy Co. I:

Bradfield, J. DOI: friend B/P: 1/55

3481 Sager, Lula M. - white female D: June 25, 1900; 6m; Hampshire F: Sager, Julius M: Sager, Emma B: Dec 9, 1899 DOI: mother B/P: 1/73

3482 Sagnbert, L.W. - married white male D: Dec 5, 1894; 66y 7m 4d; Sherman District B: Pendleton County B/P: 1/83

3483 Sallyards, Margaret - white female D: Nov 28, 1880; 80y; Hampshire B: Virginia I: Rudolph, Barbara DOI: daughter B/P: 1/27

3484 Salvadore, Braine - single white male D: Aug 26, 1913; 23y B/P: 2/111 N: killed by train

3485 Salyards, John - married white male D: Apr 30, 1872; 65y 3m 10d; Hampshire B: Hardy Co DOI: wife B/P: 1/9

3486 Sanders, Jno. H. - married white male D: Mar 7, 1914; 65y 4m 17d B/P: 2/112

3487 Sanders, Sarah A - white female D: Mar 15, 1873; 2y 6m; Hampshire F: Sanders, Alex M: Sanders, Mary B: Hampshire DOI: father B/P: 1/10

3488 Sanders, Wm. K. - single white male D: Mar 31, 1922; 67y 2m 22d; Hampshire F: Sanders, Alexander M: Sanders, Mary B: Hampshire I: Fisher, R.S. B/P: 1/135

3489 Sandy, Rumsey - single white male D: Dec 1, 1899; 17y; Augusta B: WV BUR: Augusta B/P: 1/110

3490 Sandy, Samuel R. - white male D: Dec 1, 1899; 16y; Augusta F: Sandy, William S. M: Sandy, Margaret B: 1884 DOI: father B/P: 1/71

3491 Santamire, Geo W. - white male D: Apr 9, 1872; 22y; Preston Co WV F: John Santamire B: Hampshire DOI: father B/P: 1/9 N: killed on railroad

3492 Santimyre, H.D. - white male D: Aug 1, 1886; 1y 10d; Hampshire F: Santimyre, Thomas M: Santimyre, Elizabeth B: Hampshire DOI: father B/P: 1/44

3493 Santymire, Alex - married white male D: Mar 22, 1908; 75y B/P: 2/109 N: farmer

3494 Sauders, Alexander - white male D: June 23, 1886; 65y; Romney District B: Hampshire I: Sauders, M.G. DOI: son C:

Sauders, Mary E. B/P: 1/43

3495 Saville, Belle Zury - married white female D: Mar 27, 1922; 60y; Hampshire F: Roberson, Jno. M: Roberson, Annie B: Hampshire I: Saville, R.W. B/P: 1/135

3496 Saville, Bessie M - white female D: Aug 1, 1894; 2m; Sherman District M: Saville, Malvina B: Sherman District DOI: mother B/P: 1/59

3497 Saville, Cora - single white female D: May 19, 1894; 19y; Near Slanesville B: Hampshire BUR: Hampshire B/P: 1/84

3498 Saville, Drisilla - white female D: Apr 1889; 33y; Sherman District F: Saville, Isaac M: Saville, Martha B: Sherman District DOI: father B/P: 1/50

3499 Saville, Edgar - white male D: Nov 12, 1882; 13y; Hampshire F: Saville, J.W. M: Saville, M.J. B: Hampshire DOI: father B/P: 1/34

3500 Saville, Elizabeth D: Mar 16, 1870; 25y; Hampshire F: Moreland, Jacob M: Moreland, Sarah C: Saville, William B/P: 1/5

3501 Saville, Ella V. - single white female D: Nov 13, 1910; 20y B/P: 2/110

3502 Saville, Emily C. - white female D: Aug 10, 1879; 16y; Hampshire F: Saville, Peter M: Saville, Mary C. B: Hampshire DOI: mother B/P: 1/25

3503 Saville, Ethel Grace - married white female D: Jan 29, 1912; 22y B/P: 2/111

3504 Saville, Etta M. - white female D: Sept 30, 1902; 17y 3m 6d; Sherman District F: Saville, J.A. M: Saville, S. B: 1886 DOI: father B/P: 1/78

3505 Saville, Fannie - white female D: June 1, 1898; 47y 8m; Sherman District F: Orndorff, Wesley I: Saville, A.M. B/P: 1/68

3506 Saville, Hannah - widow white female D: Mar 9, 1914; 82y 7m 11d B/P: 2/111

3507 Saville, J.W. - white male D: Aug 14, 1902; 63y; Hampshire F: Saville, Jacob M: Saville, Eliza B: Apr 15, 1839 I: Saville, Margaret DOI: wife B/P: 1/79

3508 Saville, Jacob - married white male D: Feb 3, 1897; 89y; near Levels X Roads B: Hampshire BUR: Levels Church B/P: 1/93

3509 Saville, James - white male D: Nov 8, 1914 B/P: 2/112

3510 Saville, James T. - single white male D: Feb 6, 1889; 3y 2m 10d; Green Spring Run B: WV B/P: 1/125

3511 Saville, Jas. Jr. - single white male D: Jan 20, 1921; 6d; Hampshire F: Saville, Jas. M: Saville, Lura B: Hampshire B/P: 1/130

3512 Saville, Jennie - married white female D: Dec 21, 1919; 76y 9d; Green Spring F: Malcolm, Jno. M: Malcolm, Eleanor B: Hampshire B/P: 1/128 N: housewife

3513 Saville, Jerry L. - widower white male D: Sept 9, 1912; 71y B/P: 2/111

3514 Saville, Jno. - single white male D: Jan 14, 1921; stillborn; Hampshire F: Saville, Jas. C. M: Saville, Lura B: Hampshire B/P: 1/130

3515 Saville, Joseph - single white male D: June 10, 1886; 84y 2m 4d; Hampshire B: Hampshire I: Saville, John B/P: 1/44

3516 Saville, Joseph - married white male D: Apr 20, 1914; 75y 7m 13d B/P: 2/112

3517 Saville, Lewis - white male D: Dec 12, 1917; 1y 5m 14d B/P: 2/113

3518 Saville, Lewis Arlo - white male D: Dec 2, 1917; 1y 5m 14d B/P: 2/113

3519 Saville, Loyd Edward - single white male D: Nov 11, 1919; 3m; Gore District F: Saville, Earl M: Saville, Lillian B: Okonoko B/P: 1/128

3520 Saville, Mabel - married white female D: Oct 10, 1918; 23y; Hampshire B/P: 1/127 N: housewife

3521 Saville, Madelene May - single white female D: Aug 1, 1922; 16d; Hampshire F: Saville, Jas. C. M: Saville, Lura B: Hampshire DOI: father B/P: 1/135

3522 Saville, Martha - white female D: Dec 8, 1899; 74y; Sherman District F: McBride, John B: 1826 I: Saville, James

B/P: 1/71

3523 Saville, Martha E. - married white female D: Feb 9, 1912; 61y B/P: 2/111

3524 Saville, Mary J. - white female D: Feb 25, 1909; 2y 11m 20d B/P: 2/110

3525 Saville, Minnie - white female D: Sept 30, 1898; 72y; Springfield F: Doman, Tom N. M: Doman, R. I: Saville, Mrs. J.A. DOI: mother in law C: Saville, C.H. B/P: 1/69

3526 Saville, Mrs. Jack - married white female D: Jan 5, 1911; 50y B: Gore District B/P: 2/111

3527 Saville, Oliver - white male D: Mar 12, 1888; 65y; Hampshire B: Hampshire I: Saville, Isaac DOI: son B/P: 1/46

3528 Saville, Peter A. - white male D: 1878; 46y; Hampshire B: Hampshire I: Tharp, Samuel DOI: friend B/P: 1/23

3529 Saville, Peter A. - white male D: Feb 1, 1879; 45y 2m 10d; Hampshire B: Hampshire DOI: wife C: Saville, Mary B/P: 1/25

3530 Saville, Philip - white male D: July 31, 1891; 75y 4m 8d; Hampshire F: Saville, O. M: Saville, Mary B: Hampshire I: Saville, M. DOI: sister B/P: 1/55

3531 Saville, Rachel - widowed white female D: June 13, 1922; 82y 4m; Hampshire F: Hott, David B: Hampshire I: Ruckman, B. B/P: 1/135

3532 Saville, Rebecca - white female D: July 27, 1891; 57y; Hampshire F: Shickle, Peter M: Shickle, Mary B: Rockingham, VA I: Saville, M. DOI: daughter C: Saville, John B/P: 1/55

3533 Saville, Rebecca - white female D: July 7, 1900; 89y; Hampshire B: 1812 I: Largent, J.L. DOI: friend B/P: 1/73

3534 Saville, Robert Lee - white male D: Nov 1881; 16y; Hampshire F: Saville, Isaac M: Saville, Martha B: Hampshire DOI: father B/P: 1/29

3535 Saville, Rose L. - single white female D: Oct 19, 1877; Hampshire F: Saville, James M: Saville, Caroline B: Hampshire DOI: father B/P: 1/22

3536 Saville, Sarah M - single white female D: Sept 29, 1877;

Hampshire F: Saville, Peter M: Saville, Margaret B: Hampshire DOI: father B/P: 1/22

3537 Saville, Virna - married white female D: Feb 5, 1895; 40y; Hampshire B: Hampshire B/P: 1/89

3538 Saville, William - white male D: July 31, 1899; 56y; Capon F: Saville, Peter B: 1875 DOI: wife B/P: 1/71

3539 Saville, William - white male D: Dec 12, 1903; 34y; Hampshire F: Largent, J.J. M: Largent, Mary B: 1869 I: Largent, Jerry DOI: brother B/P: 1/80

3540 Scanlan, Ida - white female D: Aug 26, 1872; 29d; Hampshire F: Scanlan, Michael M: Scanlan, Mary B: Hampshire DOI: mother B/P: 1/8

3541 Scanlen, Frederick K. - white male D: Aug 24, 1879; 6m 26d; Hampshire F: Scanlen, Michael M: Scanlen, Mary E. B: Hampshire DOI: father B/P: 1/26

3542 Scanlon, Mariah - widow white female D: Dec 17, 1913; 83y B/P: 2/111

3543 Scanlon, Mariah - white female D: Dec 29, 1914; 84y B/P: 2/111

3544 Scanlon, Mary E. - widow white female D: Sept 5, 1914; 75y B/P: 2/112

3545 Scanlon, Michael - married white male D: June 20, 1897; 69y; Three Chruches BUR: Three Churches B/P: 1/94

3546 Scanlon, Michael - white male D: June 24, 1897; 68y 8m 2d; Gore B: Sept 28, 1828 I: Scanlon, Frank DOI: son C: Scanlon, M.E. B/P: 1/66

3547 Scanlon, Robt. R. - white male D: Aug 23, 1903; 3y; Hampshire F: Scanlon, Maurier M: Scanlon, A. B: July 13, 1900 DOI: father B/P: 1/80

3548 Scanlon, Thomas - married white male D: Dec 12, 1907; 82y B/P: 2/108 N: farmer

3549 Scanlon, William D. - white male D: May 5, 1891; 25y; Hampshire F: Scanlon, Thomas M: Scanlon, Maria B: Hampshire DOI: father B/P: 1/55

3550 Schaffenaker, Cora E. - white female D: Jan 11, 1891; 2m 2d; Hampshire F: Schaffenaker, A. M: Schaffenaker, Emma B:

Hampshire DOI: father B/P: 1/53

3551 Schaffenaker, E.W. - white male D: Sept 22, 1888; 2m; Capon District F: Schaffenaker, A. M: Schaffenaker, E.A. B: Hampshire DOI: father B/P: 1/47

3552 Schaffenaker, Earl - single white male D: Mar 16, 1913; 19y B/P: 2/111

3553 Schaffenaker, N.L. - married white female D: Aug 2, 1895; 20y 7m 12d; Hampshire B: Hampshire B/P: 1/90

3554 Schaffmaker, Bertha - white female D: Dec 27, 1902; 8y; Hampshire F: Schaffmaker, Albert M: Schaffmaker, Emma B: Aug 28, 1895 DOI: father B/P: 1/79

3555 Schnibbe, Elizabeth - widowed white female D: July 14, 1922; 80y 9m 18d; Hampshire F: Albin, Wesley M: Albin, Dorothy B: Hampshire I: Lupton, Geo. B/P: 1/136 N: housewife

3556 Schnibbe, L.D. - white male D: Feb 17, 1890; 49y; Sherman District B: Sherman District DOI: wife C: Schnibbe, E. B/P: 1/50

3557 Schnibbe, Virginia - white female D: Jan 4, 1919; 8d B/P: 2/113

3558 Schnibbie, Chas W. - white male D: Jan 16, 1877; Hampshire F: Schnibbie, Louis M: Schnibbie, Elizabeth B: Hampshire DOI: father B/P: 1/22

3559 Schuller, Catherine - married white female D: Dec 6, 1921; 64y 23d; Hampshire M: Frye, Elly B: Virginia B/P: 1/132 N: housewife

3560 Seaton, K. - white male D: Oct 18, 1886; 76y; Hampshire B: Hampshire I: Hass, Wm. B/P: 1/44

3561 Seaton, Pat - widower white male D: Nov 24, 1898; 65y; Romney BUR: Romney B/P: 1/99 N: Nationality: Irish; Lived in Country: 22 yrs.

3562 Sechrist, Christinia - widow white female D: Dec 11, 1908; 84y 4m 19d B/P: 2/109

3563 Sechrist, Frederick - white male D: Feb 2, 1892; 70y; Hampshire B: Hampshire I: Sechrist, William DOI: son C: Sechrist, Elizabeth B/P: 1/54

3564 Sechrist, Frederick - white male D: Oct 6, 1892; 70y; Capon Springs B: Capon I: Sechrist, William DOI: son B/P: 1/56

3565 Sechrist, Leola J. - white female D: Apr 3, 1909; 20y B/P: 2/109

3566 Secrest, Valentine - white male D: Dec 16, 1879; 86y 1m 9d; Hampshire I: Secrest, Mary DOI: daughter C: Secrest, Margaret B/P: 1/25

3567 Secrist, John - single white male D: June 17, 1866; 1m 10d; Hampshire F: Secrist, John M: Secrist, Letitia B: Hampshire DOI: parent B/P: 1/1

3568 Seders, Mary - married white female D: Apr 12, 1900; 35y; Donaldson B: WV BUR: Oldtown, MD B/P: 1/108

3569 See, A.M. - white male D: Dec 2, 1914; 55y 8m B/P: 2/112

3570 See, Amanda - single white female D: April 1891; 28y; Hampshire B: Hampshire I: See, Adam DOI: brother B/P: 1/54

3571 See, Anna R. - white female D: June 3, 1896; 1y 11m; Hampshire F: See, J.D. M: See, Sarah B: Jan 3, 1895 I: See, Sallie DOI: mother B/P: 1/63

3572 See, Galda Arabella - white female D: Apr 21, 1916; 1m 2d B/P: 2/112

3573 Seeders, Clarence - white male D: June 30, 1916; 40y B: Green Spring B/P: 2/112

3574 Seeders, Ida - white female D: Mar 5, 1882; 7m 3d; Hampshire F: Seeders, Jacob M: Seeders, C. B: Hampshire DOI: father B/P: 1/34

3575 Seeders, Jacob - married white male D: Mar 24, 1915; 80y B/P: 2/112 N: farmer

3576 Seeders, Mary J. - white female D: Apr 17, 1900; 34y; Hampshire F: Portmess, J.D. M: Portmess, Amanda B: Dec 1, 1866 DOI: husband C: Seeders, Robt. B/P: 1/74

3577 Seeders, Mary S. - widow white female D: Jan 12, 1913; 88y 8m B/P: 2/111

3578 Seeders, Robert - white male D: July 1, 1900; 3m; Hampshire F: Seeders, Robert M: Seeders, Mary B: Apr 12,

1900 DOI: father B/P: 1/74

3579 Seeders, Sally - single white female D: Feb 22, 1904; 73y B/P: 2/108

3580 Seeders, Wm. B. - single white male D: Oct 26, 1921; 1m 22d; Hampshire F: Seeders, Wm. M: Seeders, Eula B: Green Spring I: father B/P: 1/132

3581 Selby, Harrison - white male D: Sept 21, 1903; 38y; Hampshire F: Selby, William M: Selby, Luranor B: 1865 DOI: wife C: Selby, Susie B/P: 1/80

3582 Seldon, John - white male D: Feb 25, 1883; 43y; Hampshire F: Seldon, John M: Seldon, Eliza B: Germany DOI: wife C: Seldon, Jane B/P: 1/37 N: wagonmaker

3583 Seldon, Minnie - white female D: Sept 2, 1896; 1y 9m 2d; Capon Bridge B: Capon Bridge BUR: Capon Chapel B/P: 1/97

3584 Seldon, Minnie A. - white female D: Sept 1896; 1y; Hampshire F: Seldon, William M: Seldon, Christina B: Sept 1895 DOI: father B/P: 1/63

3585 Serbaugh, Elizabeth - white female D: Dec 5, 1883; 68y 8m 26d; Hampshire F: Oats, John M: Oats, Mary B: Hampshire I: Serbaugh, Sam'l DOI: son C: Serbaugh, Jacob B/P: 1/37

3586 Serbaugh, Florance - white female D: Aug 2, 1882; 1y 5m 20d; Hampshire F: Serbaugh, Harman M: Serbaugh, L.J. B: Hampshire DOI: father B/P: 1/34

3587 Serbaugh, Sarah E. - single D: Sept 7, 1871; 24y 4m 20d; F: Serbaugh, Jacob M: Serbaugh, Elizabeth B/P: 1/6

3588 Seton, C.A. - single white female D: Jan 10, 1888; 1y 9m 7d; Little Capon B: Hampshire BUR: No 12 Water Station* B/P: 1/122 N: *Paw Paw

3589 Settleton, Arch - married colored male D: July 21, 1922; 60y; Hampshire B: Virginia I: Jackson, Lucy B/P: 1/135

3590 Settleton, Arch - single colored male D: Feb 9, 1894; 2m 24d; Romney B: Romney B/P: 1/82

3591 Shade, Sophrona - widow white female D: Jan 30, 1906; 73y B/P: 2/108

3592 Shade, William - white male D: Apr 25, 1903; 59y; Levels B: Hampshire B/P: 1/118 N: Nationality: German

3593 Shadwell, Catharine - married white female D: Sept 19, 1887; 54y; Hampshire B: Hampshire BUR: Hampshire B/P: 1/122

3594 Shane, Chas - white male D: Mar 24, 1896; 1y; Hampshire F: Shane, Ed M: Shane, Marg B: 1895 DOI: father B/P: 1/63

3595 Shane, L.L. - white male D: Nov 24, 1894; 1y 2m; Hampshire F: Shane, E.F. M: Shane, L.M. B: Hampshire DOI: father B/P: 1/60

3596 Shanholtz, Bernice Onita - white female D: May 6, 1919; 12y 8m 22d B/P: 2/113

3597 Shanholtz, Cora - white female D: Apr 24, 1902; 15y; Hampshire F: Shanholtz, Philip M: Shanholtz, Mary B: July 16, 1886 DOI: mother B/P: 1/79

3598 Shanholtz, Harvey C. - single white male D: Feb 18, 1907; 10y B/P: 2/109

3599 Shanholtz, John H. - married white male D: June 7, 1895; 27y; Romney F: Shanholtz, Benj F. B: June 1868 DOI: father B/P: 1/61

3600 Shanholtz, Margaret - married white female D: July 28, 1912; 65y B/P: 2/111

3601 Shanholtz, Maria - white female D: Aug 27, 1902; 56y; Hampshire F: Watson, Jas. M: Watson, Catherine B: Jan 10, 1845 DOI: husband C: Shanholtz, Silas B/P: 1/79

3602 Shanholtz, Miss - single white female D: Mar 17, 1899; 1d; Slanesville B: Hampshire BUR: Salem B/P: 1/103

3603 Shanholtz, Pearl M. - single white female D: Jan 4, 1897; 1y 8m; Cold Stream B: Cold Stream BUR: Sandy Ridge B/P: 1/97

3604 Shanholtz, Pearl - single white female D: Nov 25, 1913; 17y 5m 7d B/P: 2/111

3605 Shanholtz, R. Fahs - white male D: Sept 1, 1895; 6m; Sherman District F: Shanholtz, John M: Shanholtz, Annie B: Apr 1895 DOI: father B/P: 1/61

3606 Shanholtz, Verna - white female D: June 1901; 19y; Hampshire F: Shanholtz, Philip M: Shanholtz, Mary I: McCauley, Frank B/P: 1/77

3607 Shanholtz, W.P.A. - white male D: Oct 2, 1897; 45y 7m 10d; Bloomery F: Shanholtz, Jas. M: Shanholtz, H. B: Feb 22, 1852 DOI: wife C: Shanholtz, M. B/P: 1/66

3608 Shanholtzer, A. - white female D: Mar 13, 1892; 77y; Hampshire B: Hampshire DOI: husband C: Shanholtzer, W. B/P: 1/57

3609 Shanholtzer, Alice - white female D: Apr 1, 1919; 1y 10m 24d B/P: 2/113

3610 Shanholtzer, Annie E. - white female D: Sept 28, 1886; 14 m; Sherman District F: Shanholtzer, Jacob M: Shanholtzer, Sarah B: Hampshire DOI: father B/P: 1/43

3611 Shanholtzer, Barbara A. - married white female D: Sept 15, 1904; 86y B/P: 2/108

3612 Shanholtzer, Benj F. - married white male D: Jan 19, 1917; 68y 2d B/P: 2/112

3613 Shanholtzer, Bertha Ellen - married white female D: Jan 20, 1917; 24y 10m 17d B/P: 2/112

3614 Shanholtzer, Bryd - white male D: July 6, 1898; 6m; Bloomery District F: Shanholtzer, Philip M: Shanholtzer, M.E. DOI: mother B/P: 1/69

3615 Shanholtzer, Carry E. - white female D: May 20, 1891; 2y; Hampshire F: Shanholtzer, Sol M: Shanholtzer, E. B: Hampshire DOI: father B/P: 1/55

3616 Shanholtzer, Chas. E. - married white male D: Nov 3, 1918; 39y 10m 2d; Hampshire B/P: 1/127

3617 Shanholtzer, Chas. I. - white male D: Apr 24, 1907; 7y 5m 18d B/P: 2/109

3618 Shanholtzer, Chester - white male D: Jan 21, 1891; 3y 8m 7d; Hampshire F: Shanholtzer, B.W. M: Shanholtzer, A. B: Hampshire DOI: father B/P: 1/55

3619 Shanholtzer, Christopher - white male D: Dec 30, 1897; 65y; Bloomery B: 1832 DOI: son C: Shanholtzer, M. B/P: 1/66

3620 Shanholtzer, Chris - married white male D: Dec 30, 1897; 60y; near Forks of Capon B: Hampshire BUR: Forks of Capon B/P: 1/92

3621 Shanholtzer, Clara B. - white female D: Jan 3, 1878; 3y; Hampshire F: Shanholtzer, J. M: Shanholtzer, M.J. DOI: father B/P: 1/24

3622 Shanholtzer, Edward - white male D: May 6, 1883; 1m 7d; Hampshire F: Shanholtzer, Joseph D.B. M: Shanholtzer, Harriett B: Hampshire DOI: father B/P: 1/37

3623 Shanholtzer, Eliza M. - married white female D: Mar 15, 1903; 29y 9m 14d; Hampshire B: Augusta B/P: 1/115

3624 Shanholtzer, Elizabeth - married white female D: Feb 4, 1910; 53y 3m 3d B/P: 2/110

3625 Shanholtzer, Elizabeth - married white female D: May 23, 1919; 67y B/P: 2/113

3626 Shanholtzer, Emily Susan - widow white female D: Jan 21, 1918; 72y 9m; Hampshire B/P: 1/127 N: housewife

3627 Shanholtzer, Etta V. - married white female D: Mar 31, 1909; 48y B/P: 2/110

3628 Shanholtzer, Ettie - married white female D: Jan 24, 1907; 27y B/P: 2/108

3629 Shanholtzer, Eva - white female D: Mar 19, 1879; 97y; Hampshire B: Frederick Co VA I: Shanholtzer, Henry DOI: son C: Shanholtzer, John B/P: 1/26

3630 Shanholtzer, Flora L. - white female D: Aug 30, 1904; 7m 21d B/P: 2/120

3631 Shanholtzer, Geo W. - white male D: June 19, 1899; 24y 9m; Romney F: Shanholtzer, Benj. F. B: June 6 DOI: father B/P: 1/71

3632 Shanholtzer, H.R. - white male D: Nov 1, 1899; 14y 10m 4d; Bloomery District F: Shanholtzer, D.T. M: Shanholtzer, R. B: Dec 27, 1884 DOI: father B/P: 1/70

3633 Shanholtzer, Harriet - single white female D: June 25, 1879; 22y 9m 9d; Hampshire F: Shanholtzer, James M: Shanholtzer, Harriet B: Hampshire I: Shanholtzer, Basil DOI: brother B/P: 1/26

3634 Shanholtzer, Harley - single white male D: Feb 18, 1908; 16y B/P: 2/109

3635 Shanholtzer, Henry - widower white male D: Feb 25, 1909;

89y 1m 24d B/P: 2/109

3636 Shanholtzer, Jacob - white male D: Mar 28, 1872; 90y 5m 19d; Hampshire F: Shanholtzer, Peter B: Hampshire I: Shanholtzer, W. DOI: son C: Shanholtzer, Mary Ann B/P: 1/8

3637 Shanholtzer, James D: Feb 15, 1871; 42y 2m F: Shanholtzer, Philip M: Shanholtzer, Z C: Shanholtzer, Harriet B/P: 1/6

3638 Shanholtzer, James C. - single white male D: Feb 6, 1880; 21y; Hampshire F: Shanholtzer, James M: Shanholtzer, Harriet B: Hampshire I: Shanholtzer, Basil DOI: brother B/P: 1/28 N: schoolteacher

3639 Shanholtzer, Jane - widow white female D: Sept 29, 1910; 81y 5m 2d B/P: 2/110

3640 Shanholtzer, Joanna - widow white female D: May 1, 1907; 89y 8m 24d B/P: 2/109

3641 Shanholtzer, Johnny - widower white male D: May 20, 1907; 86y 5m 13d B/P: 2/108

3642 Shanholtzer, Joseph - white male D: Nov 27, 1891; 83y; Hampshire B: Hampshire I: Thompson, R.J. DOI: son in law C: Shanholtzer, E. B/P: 1/55

3643 Shanholtzer, Lula - white female D: Oct 3, 1914; 9y 6m 2d B/P: 2/112

3644 Shanholtzer, Mary Ellen D: June 10, 1869; 2y 10m 11d F: Shanholtzer, James M: Shanholtzer, Harriett B: Hampshire B/P: 1/4

3645 Shanholtzer, Margaret - white female D: Mar 1890; 88y; Sherman District F: Saville, Isaac B: Sherman District I: Stickley, H. DOI: son in law C: Shanholtzer, Jos. B/P: 1/50

3646 Shanholtzer, Margaret - widow white female D: Dec 10, 1905; 82y 3m 25d B/P: 2/108

3647 Shanholtzer, Myrtle - white female D: Jan 1897; 8m; Bloomery F: Shanholtzer, T. M: Shanholtzer, A. B: May 10, 1896 DOI: father B/P: 1/66

3648 Shanholtzer, Paul - white male D: Apr 10, 1898; 78y; Bloomery District F: Shanholtzer, B.W. M: Shanholtzer, A.E. DOI: father B/P: 1/69 N: informant probably should read - son

3649 Shanholtzer, Paul - single white male D: Apr 10, 1898; 5m 3d; Augusta B: Hampshire B/P: 1/104

3650 Shanholtzer, Peter - white male D: Aug 20, 1882; 5m 26d; Hampshire F: Shanholtzer, P. M: Shanholtzer, Mary E. B: Hampshire DOI: mother B/P: 1/34

3651 Shanholtzer, Sallie E. - married white female D: Dec 31, 1920; 56y 5m 25d; Hampshire F: Davis, Jno. M: Davis, Matilda B: Hampshire I: Shanholtzer, Robt. B/P: 1/129 N: housewife

3652 Shanholtzer, Samuel - white male D: July 1, 1872; 71y; Hampshire F: Shanholtzer, Peter M: Shanholtzer, Matilda B: Hampshire DOI: son C: Shanholtzer, Phoebe B/P: 1/8

3653 Shanholtzer, Sarah J - white female D: Mar 29, 1881; 17y 4m 14d; Hampshire F: Shanholtzer, James M: Shanholtzer, Harriet B: Hampshire I: Shanholtzer, Basil DOI: brother B/P: 1/32

3654 Shanholtzer, Sarah A. - married white female D: Apr 9, 1915; 62y 7m B/P: 2/11

3655 Shanholtzer, Sylpha - married white female D: Dec 17, 1916; 92y 8m 20d B: Sherman District B/P: 2/112

3656 Shanholtzer, Vernie - white female D: June 25, 1902; Hampshire F: Shanholtzer, G.B. M: Shanholtzer, M. B: June 25, 1902 DOI: father B/P: 1/79

3657 Shank, Caroline Robts - single white female D: Mar 2, 1922; 2y 1m 15d; Hampshire F: Shank, Dougal M: Shank, Otie B: Romney I: Loy, E. B/P: 1/135

3658 Shank, Ida May - married white female D: Jun 6, 1917; 28y 11m 9d B/P: 2/113

3659 Shank, Jimima L. - white female D: Sept 1891; 5y 3m 6d; Hampshire F: Shank, Geo. W. M: Shank, Susan V. B: Hampshire DOI: father B/P: 1/54

3660 Shank, Margaret A - white female D: 1866 B/P: 1/2

3661 Shank, Margaret C. - single D: Mar 9, 1871; 15y F: Shank, Wm M: Shank, Mary B/P: 1/6

3662 Shank, Mary E. - white female D: Mar 1898; 29y; Gore District F: Hedrick, Goning DOI: husband C: Shank, W.G. B/P: 1/69

3663 Shank, Robt. F. - single white male D: Jan 15, 1898; 3m 18d; Romney B: Romney BUR: Ebenezer B/P: 1/98

3664 Shannon, Benjamin - white male D: Dec 22, 1898; 28y; Springfield F: Shannon, Andrew M: Shannon, Mary I: Shannon, J.C. DOI: grandson B/P: 1/69 N: blacksmith

3665 Shannon, Benjamin - married white male D: Dec 22, 1898; 77y; Springfield B: Hampshire BUR: Springfield B/P: 1/100

3666 Shannon, Chas. T. - white male D: Oct 7, 1886; 34y; Hampshire F: Shannon, Jas. M: Shannon, Elizabeth B: Hampshire DOI: wife C: Shannon, Mary B/P: 1/44 N: merchant

3667 Shannon, Jas. - widower white male D: July 25, 1907; 85y B/P: 2/108

3668 Shannon, Jeremiah C. - married white male D: May 19, 1876; 30y 4d; Hampshire F: Shannon, Benj. M: Shannon, Catherine B: Hampshire DOI: wife C: Shannon, Florence B/P: 1/21

3669 Shannon, Sallie Walker - single white female D: Oct 8, 1912; 18y B/P: 2/111 N: drown

3670 Shannon, Sarah R. - single white female D: July 25, 1876; 17y 5m 8d; Hampshire F: Shannon, Jas C. M: Shannon, Elizabeth B: Hampshire DOI: father B/P: 1/21

3671 Shannon, W.W. - white male D: Jun 12, 1897; 44y; Springfield F: Shannon, B. M: Shannon, H.C. B: 1853 DOI: father B/P: 1/66 N: blacksmith

3672 Shannon, Wm. W. - married white male D: abt 1898; Springfield B: Springfield BUR: Springfield B/P: 1/93

3673 Sharff, John H. - white male D: Jan 26, 1894; 1m; Romney F: Sharff, H.H. M: Sharff, Adda DOI: mother B/P: 1/59

3674 Sharff, John H. - white male D: Jan 16, 1895; 1m 15d; Romney F: Sharff, H. M: Sharff, Ada B: Nov 28, 1894 DOI: father B/P: 1/61

3675 Shawen, Alinza L - single white male D: Feb 15, 1866; 2y 3m 20d; Hampshire F: Shawen, Dan'l M: Shawen, Jane B: Hampshire DOI: parent B/P: 1/1

3676 Shawen, Elizabeth J. - married white female D: June 9, 1908; 75y 5m 14d B/P: 2/109

3677 Shawen, Florence - married white female D: Mar 10, 1915; 55y 9m 16d B/P: 2/112

3678 Shear, Henry - white male D: Aug 28, 1904; B/P: 2/108

3679 Shearer, Calie - white female D: Mar 31, 1910; 1m 2d B/P: 2/110

3680 Shearwood, F.C. - white female D: Mar 1888; 3d; Hampshire F: Shearwood, J.W. M: Shearwood, F. B: Hampshire DOI: mother B/P: 1/46

3681 Sheetz, Jacob - white male D: June 26, 1884; 71y 5m 3d; Hampshire B: Hampshire DOI: wife C: Sheetz, Sarah B/P: 1/39 N: gunsmith

3682 Sheetz, Jacob - married white male D: Oct 9, 1907; 59y B/P: 2/109

3683 Sheetz, Mahala - white female D: May 23 1868; 50y 10m; Romney B: Fairfax Co, Va DOI: husband C: Sheetz, James B/P: 1/3

3684 Shelby, Marnie - married white female D: Aug 28, 1920; 31y 5m 6d; Hampshire F: Nealis, Jno. M: Nealis, Mattie B: Hampshire B/P: 1/129 N: housewife

3685 Shelley, Clinton - single white male D: Jan 10, 1914; 20y 7m 15d B/P: 2/112

3686 Shelley, Hannah D - white female D: Mar 26, 1876; 48y 1m 10d; Hampshrie F: Shank, Jacob M: Shank, Margaret B: Hampshire DOI: husband C: Shelley, Philip B/P: 1/18

3687 Shelley, Philip - white male D: Apr 4, 1913; 81y 8m 13d B/P: 2/111

3688 Shelly, Daniel - white male D: Nov 9, 1876; 85y; Hampshire F: Shelly, Christianna B: Pennsylvania I: Shelly, David DOI: son C: Shelly, Catherine B/P: 1/21

3689 Shelly, David - married white male D: Nov 20, 1900; 78y; Romney B: 1832 I: Jackson, B. DOI: son in law B/P: 1/72

3690 Sherman, Ada - married white female D: Mar 15, 1906; B/P: 2/108

3691 Sherridan, Mary D: July 27, 1871; 27y F: McNewman, John M: McNewman, Margaret C: Sherridan, John B/P: 1/6

3692 Sherwood, Florence C. - white female D: June 11, 1880; 5y 3m 11d; Hampshrie F: Sherwood, John W. M: Sherwood, Frances C. B: Hampshire DOI: father B/P: 1/28

3693 Shilcott, Eliza - widow white female D: Mar 13, 1908; 75y B/P: 2/109

3694 Shingleton, Alexander - colored male D: Feb 18, 1906; 50y B/P: 2/108

3695 Shingleton, Catharine - white female D: May 16, 1882; 49y; Sherman District B: WV I: Shingleton, E.P. DOI: son C: Shingleton, William B/P: 1/33

3696 Shingleton, Catherine - white female D: Dec 12, 1892; 70y 1m; Hampshire B: Hampshire I: Shingleton, Jas. R. DOI: son C: Shingleton, John B/P: 1/54

3697 Shingleton, Fanny - single colored female D: Feb 11, 1906; 26y B/P: 2/108

3698 Shingleton, Francis M. - widower white male D: June 28, 1907; 69y 9m 8d B/P: 2/109 N: farmer

3699 Shingleton, Jacob L. - widower white male D: July 10, 1918; 63y 6m 6d; Hampshire B/P: 1/127 N: farmer

3700 Shingleton, Mary E. - single white female D: May 21, 1921; stillborn; Hampshire F: Shingleton, Riley M: Shingleton, Caren B: Augusta B/P: 1/130

3701 Shingleton, Melvin - white male D: Mar 14, 1914; 1y B/P: 2/112

3702 Shingleton, Wm A - married white male D: July 29, 1866; 52y 5m; Hampshire F: Shingleton, Absolom M: Shingleton, Martha B: Hampshire I: Shingleton, Catherine DOI: widow B/P: 1/1

3703 Shinlar, John - white male D: Nov 27, 1896; 1d; Sherman District B: 1896 B/P: 1/62

3704 Shirk, Austin - married white male D: Dec 2, 1921; 45y; Hampshire F: Shirk, Geo. M: Shirk, Elizabeth B: Pendleton Co. I: Teeter, R.L. B/P: 1/132

3705 Shoemaker, Annie Hoffman - white female D: June 6, 1880; 3y; Hampshire F: Shoemaker, Edward H. M: Shoemaker, Hester A. B: Hampshire DOI: father B/P: 1/27

3706 Shoemaker, Granville - white male D: Aug 23, 1901; 77y; Mill Creek District DOI: daughter B/P: 1/76

3707 Shoemaker, H.R. - married white female D: Dec 4, 1907; 55y 3m 8d B/P: 2/109

3708 Shoemaker, James H. - white male D: Sept 9, 1899; 14m; Purgittsville F: Shoemaker, James B: June 10, 1898 DOI: father B/P: 1/71

3709 Shoemaker, Jno. W. D: June 26, 1871; 4y 10m F: Shoemaker, John B/P: 1/7

3710 Shoemaker, John - white male D: July 27, 1891; 57y 8m; Hampshire B: Hampshire DOI: wife C: Shoemaker, Eliza B/P: 1/54

3711 Shoemaker, Joseph - married white male D: 1894; 71y 2d; Hampshire B: Virginia I: Saville, J.M. DOI: neighbor B/P: 1/60

3712 Shoemaker, M.C. - white female D: Feb 16, 1891; 37y; Hampshire F: Shockey, Sam M: Shockey, Mary J. B: Hampshire DOI: husband C: Shoemaker, George B/P: 1/53

3713 Shoemaker, S.E. - white female D: Feb 19, 1881; 37y; Hampshire B: Hampshire DOI: husband C: Shoemaker, Thomas B/P: 1/30

3714 Shoemaker, Sarah E. - white female D: 1880; Hampshire B/P: 1/27

3715 Shoemaker, Silva - white female D: Dec 11, 1880; 2y 9m; Hampshire F: Shoemaker, Edward H. M: Shoemaker, Hester A. B: Hampshire DOI: father B/P: 1/27

3716 Shoemaker, Susan - single white female D: June 13, 1908; 17y 10m 27d B/P: 2/109

3717 Shorb, Lon C. - white male D: July 31, 1911; 83y B/P: 2/111

3718 Shorb, Townsend C. - married white male D: July 31, 1911; 85y B/P: 2/111

3719 Short, Amanda D: Dec 1871; 31y F: Baker, Lewis M: Baker, Margaret B/P: 1/6

3720 Short, Bell - single white female D: Apr 13, 1898; 33y;

Springfield B: Springfield BUR: Springfield B/P: 1/93

3721 Short, Harriet A. - married white female D: Feb 20, 1900; 59y; Springfield B: Hampshire BUR: Springfield B/P: 1/109

3722 Short, Ira Z. - white male D: Aug 14, 1888; 2y 3m 14d; Hampshire F: Short J.C. M: Short, P. B: Hampshire DOI: father B/P: 1/46

3723 Short, J.C. - white male D: June 26, 1894; 37y 9m; Hampshire B: Hampshire DOI: wife C: Short, Bell B/P: 1/60

3724 Short, Jacob T. - white male D: Dec 1, 1886; 76y; Hampshire B: Hampshire I: Short, E. B/P: 1/44

3725 Short, James - married white male D: Oct 15, 1895; Hampshire B: Hampshire B/P: 1/87

3726 Short, Mary - single white female D: Mar 27, 1907; 8m B/P: 2/108

3727 Short, Nannie - married white female D: Nov 12, 1894; 44y; North River B: Hampshire BUR: North River B/P: 1/83

3728 Short, Nannie - married female D: Nov 13, 1894; 41y; North River B: Hampshire BUR: Stump Graveyard B/P: 1/83

3729 Short, Nannie V. - white female D: Nov 21, 1894; 40y; Hampshire B: Virginia DOI: husband C: Short, J.W. B/P: 1/60

3730 Short, O.E. - white male D: Jan 1, 1894; 3m; Hampshire F: Short, J.C. M: Short, Bell B: Hampshire DOI: mother B/P: 1/60

3731 Short, Pearl - single white female D: Mar 15, 1897; 16y; near Slanesville B: Hampshire BUR: Salem Church B/P: 1/92

3732 Short, Raymond C. - white male D: Oct 23, 1917; 9m 23d B/P: 2/113

3733 Short, S.A. - white female D: Apr 25, 1892; 70y; Hampshire B: Hampshire I: Crostin, Chas DOI: son in law B/P: 1/57

3734 Short, Walter - white male D: Mar 30, 1907; 35y B/P: 2/108

3735 Short, Wesley - widower white male D: Sept 4, 1917; 72y

27m 5d B/P: 2/113

3736 Shouse, Mary B. - single white female D: Feb 21, 1922; 66y 1m 23d; Hampshire F: Shouse, Jno. W. M: Shouse, Mary B: Hampshire I: Shannon, Edith B/P: 1/135

3737 Showalter, Elmyra - widow white female D: Sept 4, 1917; 77y 7m 5d B/P: 2/112

3738 Showalter, Jeremiah - white male D: Dec 6, 1884; 68y; Hampshire B: Rockingham Co., VA DOI: wife C: Showalter, Margaret B/P: 1/39 N: farmer

3739 Showalter, Samuel - married white male D: Oct 16, 1910; 78y B/P: 2/110 N: farmer

3740 Shrout, Rosa Lee - single white female D: Oct 10, 1922; 1m 5d; Hampshire F: Shrout, Herbert M: Shrout, Edna B: Hampshire DOI: father B/P: 1/135

3741 Shue, V.S.H. - white female D: Mar 18, 1877; Hampshire F: Daniel, Alpheus M: Daniel, Eliza B: Hampshire DOI: husband C: Shue, Jas. W. B/P: 1/22

3742 Shull, Etta V.B. - married white female D: Feb 5, 1888; 27y 6m 16d; Pleasant Dale B: WV BUR: Sherman District B/P: 1/123

3743 Shull, Maggie A. - white female D: Dec 10, 1909; 67y 7m 5d B/P: 2/109

3744 Shull, T.C. - single white male D: Oct 30, 1904; 74y 6m 20d B: Virginia B/P: 2/120 N: miller

3745 Simmons, Clarence E. - single white male D: Apr 27, 1894; 1y 11m 9d; Sherman District B: Hampshire B/P: 1/83

3746 Simmons, Daniel - white male D: Mar 4, 1905; 75y B/P: 2/108

3747 Simmons, John - married white male D: Feb 8 1906; 66y B/P: 2/108

3748 Simmons, John H. - white male D: Apr 26, 1891; 29y 3m; Hampshire F: Simmons, Jno. M: Simmons, Maria B: Hampshire DOI: wife C: Simmons, A.L. B/P: 1/55

3749 Simmons, Mary - white female D: Nov 3, 1875; 65y 4m 15d; Hampshire F: Cooper, John M: Cooper, Mary B: Hampshire DOI: husband C: Simmons, Aaron B/P: 1/14

3750 Simpson, H.S. - widowed white male D: June 28, 1922; 65y 3m 6d; Hampshire F: Simpson, Hugh M: Simpson, Mary B: PA I: Adams, W. Mrs. B/P: 1/135 N: farmer

3751 Simpson, Hugh - widower white male D: Oct 28, 1908; 84y B/P: 2/110

3752 Simpson, Hugh - white male D: Sept 23, 1908; 90y B/P: 2/109 N: farmer

3753 Simpson, Hugh S. - white male D: Dec 29, 1880; 1d; Hampshire F: Simpson, Hugh S. M: Simpson, Nancy A. B: Hampshire DOI: father B/P: 1/28

3754 Simpson, Lilly M - white female D: June 19, 1880; 7m 7d; Hampshire F: Simpson, J.W. M: Simpson, Mary B: Hampshire DOI: father B/P: 1/27

3755 Simpson, Mrs. S.H. - married white female D: Aug 1, 1902; 25y; Springfield B: Hampshire BUR: Springfield B/P: 1/117

3756 Simpson, N. - white female D: May 6, 1891; 35y; Hampshire F: Chaney, Robt. M: Chaney, L. B: Hampshire DOI: husband C: Simpson, H.F. B/P: 1/55

3757 Sine, Guy R. - white male D: Oct 17, 1898; 2y 5m; Sherman District DOI: father B/P: 1/68

3758 Sine, Jefferson D. - single white male D: Mar 26, 1913; 22y B/P: 2/111

3759 Sine, Robt. Washington - married white male D: Jan 17, 1913; 68y 8m 7d B/P: 2/111

3760 Sine, Tinie - married white female D: May 4, 1899; 42y; Bloomery B: Frederick County, VA BUR: Frederick Co., VA B/P: 1/109

3761 Singhass, Wm. Christian - married white male D: Dec 31, 1911; 50y B: Springfield B/P: 2/111

3762 Sirbaugh, Bulah - white female D: Dec 30, 1900; 2m; Hampshire F: Sirbaugh, Jas. M: Sirbaugh, Mary B: 1898 DOI: father B/P: 1/73

3763 Sirbaugh, George - married white male D: Feb 27, 1912; 70y B/P: 2/110

3764 Sirbaugh, Hester - widow white female D: Aug 28, 1914; 73y 4m B/P: 2/111

3765 Sirbaugh, Hilda - white female D: Jan 6, 1913; 2m B/P: 2/111

3766 Sirbaugh, Lohr - single white male D: Oct 17, 1907; 6d B/P: 2/109

3767 Sirbaugh, Maggie May - white female D: July 3, 1909; 1m 27d B/P: 2/110

3768 Sirbaugh, Maria - married white female D: Nov 26, 1898; 60y 8m 20d; Sandy Ridge B: Hampshire BUR: Sandy Ridge B/P: 1/100

3769 Sirbaugh, Mary - married white female D: Mar 15, 1900; 41y 3m 14d; Cold Stream B: Hampshire BUR: Cold Stream B/P: 1/108

3770 Sirbaugh, Mary C. - white female D: Dec 8, 1891; 50y; Hampshire F: McKee, David M: McKee, Mahala B: Frederick DOI: husband C: Sirbaugh, Jno. R. B/P: 1/55

3771 Sirbaugh, Mary E. - white female D: Mar 15, 1900; 42y; Hampshire F: Hawkins, Davis M: Hawkins, Lucinda B: June 1, 1855 DOI: husband C: Sirbaugh, J.A. B/P: 1/73

3772 Sirbaugh, Mary E. - married white female D: Dec 28, 1909; 27y 3m 10d B/P: 2/109

3773 Sirbaugh, Mary Elizabeth - white female D: Oct 7, 1917 B/P: 2/112

3774 Sirbaugh, Minnie B. - white female D: Apr 5, 1899; 31y 7m 10d; Bloomery District F: Keckley, Elias M: Keckley, M. B: Aug 25, 1867 DOI: husband C: Sirbaugh, S.H. B/P: 1/70

3775 Sirbaugh, Mrs. - married white female D: Nov 7, 1898; 70y; near Forks of Capon B: Hampshire BUR: Forks of Capon B/P: 1/99

3776 Sirbaugh, Ruth May - single white female D: July 19, 1910; 1y 5m 22d B/P: 2/110

3777 Sirbaugh, S. Marie - white female D: Nov 27, 1898; 17y; Bloomery District F: Riley, Thomas M: Riley, Margaret DOI: husband C: Sirbaugh, Isaac B/P: 1/69

3778 Sirbaugh, Susan E. - white female D: Mar 12, 1914; 8y 2d

B/P: 2/112

3779 Sirbaugh, Theodore - single white male D: Oct 6, 1908; 1y 8m B/P: 2/109

3780 Sirbaugh, Thos. - white male D: July 1, 1886; 6m; Hampshire F: Sirbaugh, Harmon M: Sirbaugh, Lucy B: Hampshire DOI: father B/P: 1/44

3781 Sirbaugh, William - single white male D: Feb 7, 1899; 23y; Forks of Capon B: Hampshire BUR: Camp Hill B/P: 1/103

3782 Sirbough, Lillian - white female D: Oct 5, 1906; 31y B/P: 2/108

3783 Sirbough, Luther J. - white male D: Feb 1902; 25y; Hampshire F: Sirbough, L. M: Sirbaugh, Mary B: 1877 DOI: father B/P: 1/79

3784 Sirk, Blanche - single white female D: Sept 22, 1912; 14y B: Springfield B/P: 2/110

3785 Sitour, John - single white male D: Aug 13, 1921; 4d; Hampshire F: Sitour, John M: Sitour, E. B: Green Spring B/P: 1/132

3786 Slane, Frank - single white male D: May 15, 1910; 56y B/P: 2/110

3787 Slane, Hugh - white male D: Apr 3, 1882; 62y 7m 9d; Hampshire F: Slane, B. M: Slane, D. B: Hampshire DOI: wife C: Slane, Malinda E. B/P: 1/34

3788 Slane, James - white male D: June 2, 1885; 63y; Hampshire B: Hampshire I: Slane, Frank DOI: son C: Slane, Elizabeth B/P: 1/42

3789 Slonaker, Alen N. - white male D: Feb 22, 1905; 11m B/P: 2/108

3790 Slonaker, Christopher - white male D: Dec 31, 1881; 53y 9m 23d; Hampshire F: Slonaker, Chris M: Slonaker, Mary B: Hampshire DOI: wife C: Slonaker, Sarah B/P: 1/32

3791 Slonaker, Edgar B. - white male D: Mar 2, 1882; 4m 2d; Hampshire F: Slonaker, Adam C. M: Slonaker, E.B. B: Hampshire DOI: father B/P: 1/34

3792 Slonaker, Harvey W. - white male D: June 4, 1873; 14y 6d; Hampshire F: Slonaker, Christopher M: Slonaker, Sarah J.

B: Hampshire I: Slonaker, Wesley DOI: uncle B/P: 1/11 N: drown

3793 Slonaker, Icie - single white female D: Sept 5, 1907; 16y B/P: 2/108

3794 Slonaker, James - married white male D: Mar 14, 1910; 37y B/P: 2/110

3795 Slonaker, John - married white male D: Nov 23, 1912; 83y B: Bloomery B/P: 2/111

3796 Slonaker, Wesley - white male D: Nov 16, 1914; 80y B/P: 2/112

3797 Slonaker, William - married white male D: Oct 6, 1906; 73y 6m 24d B/P: 2/108 N: farmer

3798 Smaltz, Amelia W. - white female D: Sept 22, 1882; 15y 10m 16d; Hampshire F: Smaltz, Wm. M: Smaltz, C. B: Hampshire DOI: father B/P: 1/34

3799 Smaltz, Emma - single white female D: Feb 1, 1899; 25y; North River Mills B: North River Mills BUR: North River Mills B/P: 1/103 N: school teacher

3800 Smaltz, Emma A. - single white female D: Jan 28, 1899; 25y 8m; Gore District F: Smaltz, William M: Smaltz, Cara B: May 28, 1873 DOI: father B/P: 1/70

3801 Smaltz, L.V. - white female D: Apr 13, 1897; 25y 7m; Gore F: Smaltz, Wm M: Smaltz C. B: Sept 13, 1871 DOI: father B/P: 1/66

3802 Smaltz, Mrs. - married white female D: May 9, 1904; 65y B/P: 2/108

3803 Smith, Abbie - widow white female D: July 29, 1910; 52y 7m 7d B/P: 2/110

3804 Smith, Albert - married white male D: May 27, 1915; 29y B/P: 2/112 N: farmer

3805 Smith, Amos A - white male D: Aug 9, 1876; 9y 10d; Hampshire F: Smith, Jacob M: Smith, Elizabeth B: Pennsylvania DOI: father B/P: 1/21

3806 Smith, Balelia May - single white female D: Oct 31, 1921; 2y 5m 1d; Hampshire F: Smith, Rumsey M: Smith, Flora B: Hampshire B/P: 1/132

3807 Smith, C.F. - white male D: Nov 13, 1896; 10m; Romney F: Smith, William M: Smith, Edith B: Feb 10, 1896 DOI: brother B/P: 1/62

3808 Smith, Cath. A. D: Oct 2, 1869; 49y 2m 14d B: Hampshire C: Smith, H. B/P: 1/4

3809 Smith, Charles F. - single black male D: Sept 13, 1896; 10y 9m; Romney B: Romney B/P: 1/96

3810 Smith, Chas. - white male D: June 25, 1910; 10m B/P: 2/110

3811 Smith, Chester - white male D: July 18, 1900; 3m; Hampshire F: Smith, William M: Smith, Anna B: Apr 13, 1900 DOI: father B/P: 1/73

3812 Smith, Edie - married black female D: Feb 1898; 28y; Romney BUR: Romney B/P: 1/100

3813 Smith, Edith - married black female D: Mar 25, 1898; 27y 6m 4d; Romney B: Romney BUR: Romney B/P: 1/97

3814 Smith, Edith Myrtle - colore female D: Mar 23, 1898; 27y 9m; Romney District I: Smith, W.B. B/P: 1/68

3815 Smith, Eleanor - white female D: Dec 21, 1916; stillborn B: South Branch B/P: 2/112

3816 Smith, Elizabeth - white female D: Jan 21, 1893; F: Steine, A.P. M: Steine, M.C. DOI: father B/P: 1/58

3817 Smith, Elizabeth - widow white female D: Aug 14, 1906; 83y B/P: 2/108

3818 Smith, Ephraim - married white male D: Mar 5, 1908; 50y B/P: 2/109

3819 Smith, Geo Washington D: Apr 29, 1870; 12y 8m 18d; Hampshire F: Smith, Nathan M: Smith, Rachel B/P: 1/5

3820 Smith, Geo. - white male D: Feb 12, 1912; 23y 8m 12d B: Springfield B/P: 2/110

3821 Smith, Geo. G. - single white male D: Oct 21, 1909; 26y 6m B/P: 2/110

3822 Smith, George R - white male D: July 13, 1873; 4y 3m 7d; Hampshire F: Smith, George M: Smith, Ann B: Hampshire DOI:

father B/P: 1/11

3823 Smith, Jacob D: Apr 31, 1871; 55y B/P: 1/6

3824 Smith, Jacob - married white male D: June 30, 1904; 63y 4m B/P: 2/120 N: farmer

3825 Smith, James W. - white male D: Apr 9, 1891; 26y; Hampshire F: Smith, Wesley M: Smith, Mary B: Hampshire DOI: father B/P: 1/55

3826 Smith, Jannie - white female D: Mar 14, 1917; 63y B/P: 2/112

3827 Smith, Jefferson - white male D: July 11, 1879; 59y 10m 28d; Hampshire F: Smith, Jacob M: Smith, Rachel B: Hampshire I: Smith, Jas F. DOI: son C: Smith, Mary B/P: 1/26

3828 Smith, John A. - white male D: Feb 8, 1891; 74y 6m; Hampshire F: Smith, Ben M: Smith, Emily B: Hampshire DOI: wife C: Smith, Elizabeth B/P: 1/55

3829 Smith, John H.H. - white male D: July 8, 1876; 5m 11d; Hampshire F: Smith, David M: Smith, Tabith B: Hampshire DOI: father B/P: 1/21

3830 Smith, Joseph - white male D: Jun 9, 1880; 87y; Hampshire B: Hampshire DOI: wife C: Smith, Mahala B/P: 1/27

3831 Smith, Kirk T. - single white male D: June 25, 1910; 9m B/P: 2/110

3832 Smith, Leo Cornwell - white male D: June 3, 1919; 2y 29d B/P: 2/113

3833 Smith, Lester - white male D: July 17, 1900; 3m; Hampshire F: Smith, William M: Smith, Anna B: Apr 13, 1900 DOI: father B/P: 1/73

3834 Smith, Lorena - widow white female D: Mar 5, 1907; 66y 11m 16d B/P: 2/109

3835 Smith, Mahala - white female D: June 20, 1902; 95y; Sherman District F: Bloxham, Thos. M: Bloxham, Nancy I: Bloxham, E. B/P: 1/78

3836 Smith, Margaret C. - white female D: Mar 12, 1881; 22y; Hampshire F: Haines, Silas M: Haines, E. B: Hampshire DOI: husband C: Smith, Benj. B/P: 1/32

3837 Smith, Mariah - white female D: Sept 12, 1875; 70y; Hampshire F: Pugh, Jonathan M: Pugh, Mary B: Hampshire I: Pugh, John DOI: brother C: Smith, Wm. L. B/P: 1/16

3838 Smith, Mary - widow white female D: Dec 26, 1907; 82y 2m 26d B/P: 2/108

3839 Smith, May - widow white female D: Nov 7, 1914; 84y B/P: 2/112

3840 Smith, Minnie S. - married white female D: Nov 15, 1922; 45y 4m 3d; Hampshire F: Schaffer, David M: Schaffer, Mary B: Hampshire I: Smith, J.W. B/P: 1/135

3841 Smith, Moody - white male D: July 1, 1902; 3y; Hampshire F: Smith, B.T. M: Smith, Evangeline B: 1899 DOI: father B/P: 1/79

3842 Smith, Moody - single white male D: June 18, 1903; 3y; Hampshire B: Pleasant Dale BUR: Malick Grave Yard B/P: 1/115

3843 Smith, Mrs. Wm. - married white female D: Nov 15, 1908; 35y B/P: 2/109

3844 Smith, N.L. - white female D: Jan 10, 1892; 4y 7m 4d; Hampshire F: Smith, J.S. M: Smith, E.V. B: Hampshire DOI: father B/P: 1/57

3845 Smith, N.L. - white female D: Jan 10, 1893; F: Smith, J.W. M: Smith, E.J. B/P: 1/58

3846 Smith, O.G. - white male D: Feb 12, 1897; 11m 3d; Gore F: Smith, J.W. M: Smith, M.A. B: Jan 15, 1896 DOI: father B/P: 1/66

3847 Smith, Polly - married white female D: Feb 3, 1899; 60y; North River Mills B: Hampshire BUR: North River B/P: 1/103

3848 Smith, Rachel - white female D: Dec 17, 1875; 80y; Hampshire F: Rinehart, Abraham M: Rinehart, Mary B: Hampshire I: Smith, Jefferson DOI: son C: Smith, Jacob B/P: 1/16

3849 Smith, Rebecca - white female D: Apr 1, 1904; 78y B/P: 2/108

3850 Smith, Rebecca - single white female D: May 3, 1915; 70y 8m 21d B/P: 2/112

3851 Smith, Sarah E. - married white female D: Jan 1, 1920; 82y 2m 5d; Hampshire F: Baker, Jas. M: Baker, Rebecca B: Hampshire B/P: 1/129

3852 Smith, Silas - white male D: Aug 22, 1916; 40y B: Green Spring B/P: 2/112

3853 Smith, Wesley - widower white male D: Sept 8, 1904; 77y B/P: 2/108

3854 Smith, Wm. - white male D: July 21, 1904; 11d B/P: 2/108

3855 Smoot, John - white male D: May 10, 1878; 70y; Hampshire F: Smoot, J M: Hott, C. DOI: wife C: Smoot, Sarah B/P: 1/24

3856 Smoot, Robt. - single white male D: Mar 4, 1921; 7y; Hampshire F: Smoot, Charley B: WV B/P: 1/130

3857 Smoot, Sarah - widow white female D: Feb 25, 1907; 95y B/P: 2/108

3858 Snan, Elizabeth - widow white female D: Feb 29, 1908; 76y 1m 9d B/P: 2/109

3859 Snapp, Alex - white male D: Dec 26, 1909; 45y B/P: 2/110

3860 Snapp, Alex - single white male D: Dec 26, 1908; 46y B/P: 2/109

3861 Snapp, Ellen - widow white female D: Oct 12, 1896; 85y; N.R. Mills B: Hampshire BUR: Salem Church B/P: 1/92

3862 Snapp, Hannah - white female D: Mar 14, 1876; 76y 8m 14d; Hampshire F: Milison, Benj. M: Milison, Phoebe B: Hampshire I: Snapp, John C: Snapp, John B/P: 1/21

3863 Snapp, Jas. W. - white male D: May 11, 1886; 74y 3m 9d; Hampshire F: Snapp, Jos. M: Snapp, Mary B: Hampshire DOI: wife C: Snapp, Malinda B/P: 1/44

3864 Snapp, Jos. C. - white male D: May 21, 1882; 77y 15d; Hampshire F: Snapp, J. M: Snapp, M. B: Augusta County VA DOI: wife C: Snapp, Ellen B/P: 1/34 N: miller

3865 Sneathen, Elizabeth - white female D: Apr 29, 1875; Hampshire F: Rinker, B: Hampshire I: Sneathen, Reubin DOI:

son C: Sneathen, Samuel B/P: 1/16

3866 Sneathen, Hester - married white female D: July 23, 1898; 60y; Three Churches B: Hampshire BUR: Three Churches B/P: 1/99

3867 Sneathen, Mary L. - married white female D: Sept 17, 1911; 69y 4m B: Springfield B/P: 2/111

3868 Sneathen, Mrs. Reuben - married white female D: Jan 13, 1906; 65y B/P: 2/108

3869 Sneathen, Reuben - widower white male D: May 25, 1911; 78y 11m 17d B/P: 2/111

3870 Sneathen, Sam'l - white male D: Apr 21, 1875; 67y; Hampshire F: Sneathen, Reubin B: Pennsylvania I: Sneathen, Reubin DOI: son C: Sneathen, Elizabeth B/P: 1/16

3871 Sneathen, Stanley - single white male D: Aug 13, 1922; 54y 2m 12d; Hampshire F: Sneathen, Amos M: Sneathen, Mary B: WV I: Racey, B.T. B/P: 1/135

3872 Sniggers, Polly - married colored female D: Mar 21, 1915; 78y B/P: 2/112

3873 Snook, Susan - white female D: Sept 6, 1905; 95y B/P: 2/108

3874 Snowberger, Lorena E. - married white female D: Jan 28, 1907; 40y B/P: 2/109

3875 Snyder, Algemon S. - married white male D: Mar 26, 1889; near Inkerman B: WV BUR: Asburry Church B/P: 1/125

3876 Snyder, Anna B. - white female D: Dec 9, 1889; 15y 10m 8d; Hampshire F: Snyder, F. M: Snyder, L. B: Hampshire DOI: father B/P: 1/51

3877 Snyder, Dock - married white male D: Nov 5, 1912; 50y B/P: 2/111 N: farmer

3878 Snyder, E.E. - white female D: Oct 20, 1899; 80y 11m 8d; Gore District F: Snyder, May M: Snyder, J. B: Nov 12, 1818 I: McBride, John A. DOI: son in law B/P: 1/70

3879 Snyder, Elizabeth - married white female D: August 19, 1867; 82y 5m; Levels B: Hardy Co, VA I: Snyder, Levi DOI: son B/P: 1/3

3880 Snyder, Ethel - white female D: Jan 4, 1912; 1m 13d B/P: 2/111

3881 Snyder, Fred M. - white male D: Aug 14, 1889; 19y 1m 10d; Hampshire F: Snyder, F. M: Snyder, L. B: Hampshire DOI: father B/P: 1/51

3882 Snyder, Frederick - widow white male D: May 12, 1908; 80y B/P: 2/109

3883 Snyder, Ira - white male D: Dec 30, 1910; 18y B/P: 2/110

3884 Snyder, Ira L. - single white male D: Dec 29, 1909; 18y 2m B/P: 2/110

3885 Snyder, John M - white male D: Oct 10, 1877; Hampshire B: Hampshire DOI: wife C: Snyder, Virginia B/P: 1/22 N: doctor

3886 Snyder, Joseph - single white male D: Nov 21, 1873; 49y; Hampshire B: Rockingham Co I: Everitt, Wilson DOI: friend B/P: 1/10 N: farmer

3887 Snyder, Kiah - white male D: Apr 2, 1914; 26y B/P: 2/112

3888 Snyder, Laura Belle - married white female D: Mar 29, 1922; 55y 7m; Hampshire F: Kerns, Stewart M: Kerns, Belle B: Hampshire I: Sirbaugh, Elizabeth B/P: 1/135 N: housewife

3889 Snyder, Louretta - married white female D: Jan 16, 1912; 20y 6m 3d B/P: 2/111

3890 Snyder, Lydia A. - white female D: Sept 1, 1886; 31y 5m 5d; Hampshire F: Snyder, John M: Snyder, Mary B: Hampshire DOI: husband C: Snyder, Fred B/P: 1/44

3891 Snyder, M.M. - single white female D: Aug 24, 1894; 24y 4m 24d; Hampshire B: Hampshire I: Shanholtzer, R. H. DOI: neighbor B/P: 1/60

3892 Snyder, Orean L. - white male D: Feb 18, 1913; 10y 6m 4d B/P: 2/111

3893 Snyder, Sarah C. - white female D: Nov 26, 1881; 14y 8m 5d; Hampshire F: Snyder, Frederick M: Snyder, Lydia B: Hampshire DOI: father B/P: 1/32

3894 Snyder, Vernia - married white female D: Aug 21, 1898;

39y 9m 15d; Kirby B: Shenandoah County, VA BUR: Mt Zion B/P: 1/101

3895 Snyder, Virginia Ida - white female D: Aug 13, 1911; 13m B/P: 2/111

3896 Sours, Rufus P. - white male D: Feb 13, 1902; 1y 2m; Hampshire F: Sours, J.R. M: Sours, Nora B: Dec 20, 1901 DOI: father B/P: 1/79

3897 Sowers, James Rufus - married white male D: Apr 1, 1904; 30y B/P: 2/108

3898 Sowers, John - white male D: Nov 1903 F: Sowers, Jos. M: Sowers, Rachel B: 1860 I: Hott, J.H. DOI: brother in law B/P: 1/80

3899 Sowers, M.E. - white female D: May 10, 1898; 4d; Gore District F: Smith, J. M: Smith, M. I: Sowers, Jno. N. - husband DOI: husband C: Sowers, Jno. N. B/P: 1/69 N: age 4d

3900 Sowers, Mrs. Jno. - married white female D: May 10, 1898; 34y; Pleasant Dale B: WV BUR: Haines Cemetery B/P: 1/98

3901 Sowers, Paul - single white male D: Feb 12, 1903; 15d; Hampshire B: Hampshire BUR: Slanesville B/P: 1/115

3902 Spade, S.B. - single white male D: May 27, 1877; Hampshire F: Spade, John M: Spade, Margaret B: Hampshire DOI: father B/P: 1/22

3903 Spaid, A.R. - white male D: Nov 24, 1902; 45y; Capon District F: Spaid, Michael M: Spaid, Mary B: 1858 I: Spaid, William B/P: 1/78

3904 Spaid, Amos D: Mar 23, 1871; 61y 6m F: Spaid, John B/P: 1/7

3905 Spaid, Cecil M. - single white male D: May 9, 1908; 4y 4m 2d B/P: 2/109

3906 Spaid, Fred - white male D: Jan 28, 1872; 86y 5m; Hampshire F: Spaid, John M: Spaid, Jemima B: Hampshire DOI: son C: Spaid, Mary B/P: 1/9

3907 Spaid, Frederick D: Dec 15, 1871; 86y 1m B/P: 1/7

3908 Spaid, Frederick - white male D: Aug 27, 1909; 66y 10d

B/P: 2/109

3909 Spaid, Geo - white male D: Mar 12, 1879; 67y 4m; Hampshire I: Spaid, Sam'l DOI: son C: Spaid, Rebecca B/P: 1/25

3910 Spaid, Geo - white male D: Mar 13, 1876; 14y; Hampshire F: Spaid, Hiram M: Spaid, Jemima B: Hampshire DOI: father B/P: 1/18

3911 Spaid, Hannah - white female D: 1866 B/P: 1/2

3912 Spaid, Hiram - white male D: Nov 13, 1876; 64y 6m 5d; Hampshire B: Hampshire I: Spaid, Fredk DOI: son B/P: 1/18

3913 Spaid, Jemimiah - white female D: Mar 19, 1876; 62y 5m; Hampshire B: Hampshire DOI: husband C: Spaid, Hiram B/P: 1/18

3914 Spaid, John - married white male D: Aug 6, 1976; 80y; Hampshire B: Hampshire I: Spaid, Joseph DOI: brother B/P: 1/18

3915 Spaid, John W. - married white male D: Apr 9, 1907; 66y 4m 23d B/P: 2/109

3916 Spaid, Joseph - white male D: Apr 1, 1900; 88y; Capon F: Spaid, Nicholas B: 1812 I: Spaid, Nicholas DOI: son B/P: 1/72

3917 Spaid, Margaret Catherine - married white female D: Nov 30, 1917; 74y 1m 24d B/P: 2/113

3918 Spaid, Margaret E. - widow white female D: Jan 6, 1910; 70y 3m 12d B/P: 2/110

3919 Spaid, Mariah C. - white female D: Apr 7, 1875; 67y 6m 10d; Hampshire B: Hampshire I: Spaid, Laflavius DOI: son B/P: 1/14

3920 Spaid, Mary E. - white female D: Sept 18, 1901; 80y; Capon DOI: son B/P: 1/76

3921 Spaid, Sarah - white female D: Oct 14, 1876; 24y 2m 10d; Hampshire F: Spaid, Hiram M: Spaid, Jemima B: Hampshire DOI: father B/P: 1/18

3922 Spaid, T.M. - white male D: Dec 1, 1903; 40y; Capon District B/P: 1/81

3923 Spaid, Tilberry - white male D: May 9, 1913; 1y B/P: 2/111

3924 Spaid, Willie L. - white male D: Apr 16, 1886; 7y; Hampshire F: Spaid, Jno W. M: Spaid, Margaret E. B: Hampshire DOI: father B/P: 1/41

3925 Spatts, Jane - white female D: Mar 6 1867; 74y 30d; H. Rock Run F: Sisson, Thomas B: Near Brucetown, Va I: Wilson, N. DOI: brother in law B/P: 1/2

3926 Speelman, John - single white male D: Mar 27, 1908; 7y B/P: 2/109

3927 Speelman, John Stanley - single white male D: May 17, 1906; 18y B/P: 2/108

3928 Speelman, William - married white male D: Oct 2, 1894; 25y 7m; Capon B: Fairfax Co., VA B/P: 1/59

3929 Spencer, Jno. N. - widower white male D: June 4, 1915; 75y B/P: 2/112

3930 Sperow, Edward Strother - married white male D: Feb 5, 1917; 57y 7m 18d B/P: 2/112

3931 Sperrow, Levi M. - white male D: Dec 15, 1884; 34y 11m 12d; Hampshire DOI: wife C: Sperrow, E. B/P: 1/39

3932 Spicer, Geo. Wm. - white male D: Nov 15, 1922; 2m 15d; Hampshire F: Spicer, Geo. W. M: Spicer, Nannie B: Hampshire DOI: father B/P: 1/135

3933 Spicer, Mary E. - white female D: May 12, 1883; 1m 7d; Hampshire F: Spicer, James M: Spicer, Annie B: Hampshire DOI: father B/P: 1/37

3934 Spier, Jas. - married white male D: Oct 2, 1895; 55y; Hampshire B: Hampshire B/P: 1/89

3935 Spier, Maria - single white female D: Mar 27, 1896; 80y; Hampshire B: Hampshire B/P: 1/88

3936 Spurling, Emma Shears - married white female D: May 2, 1918; 30y; Hampshire B/P: 1/127

3937 Spurling, Frank - white male D: Mar 10, 1894; 1y 6m; Mill Creek F: Spurling, Wm. M: Spurling, Nancy B: Mill Creek DOI: father B/P: 1/59

3938 Spurling, Luke - widowed white male D: Nov 27, 1922; 82y; Hampshire F: Spurling, Wm. M: Spurling, Martha B: Hampshire I: Shull, J.W. B/P: 1/135

3939 Spurling, Mary - white female D: Dec 1883; 39y; Hampshire B: Hampshire DOI: husband C: Spurling, Luke B/P: 1/36

3940 Spurling, Mary - white female D: Feb 28, 1894; 26y; Romney F: Lar, Thomas M: Lar, Nancy B: Mill Creek DOI: husband B/P: 1/59

3941 Staggs, Eliza J. - white female D: May 21, 1891; 37y 11m; Hampshire B: Hampshire DOI: husband C: Staggs, Jerry B/P: 1/54

3942 Starnes, Jno. W. - married white male D: May 23, 1922; 77y 8m 23d; Hampshire F: Starnes, Frederick M: Starnes, Anna B: WV I: Guthrie, N.B. B/P: 1/135 N: Justice of Peace

3943 Starnes, Macher I. - married white male D: Feb 28, 1922; 72y 3m; Hampshire F: Starnes, Frederick M: Starnes, Annie B: Hampshire I: Carder, J.F. B/P: 1/135 N: farmer

3944 Starnes, Matilda - white female D: Mar 5, 1893; B/P: 1/58

3945 Starns, James E. - single white male D: May 4, 1868; 30y; Romney F: Starns, Frederick B: Romney DOI: father B/P: 1/3

3946 Staub, Christian - married white male D: May 23, 1909; 74y 15d B/P: 2/109 N: farmer

3947 StClair, Myrtle - single white female D: Oct 11, 1918; Hampshire B/P: 1/127 N: pupil at Deaf & Blind School

3948 Steckman, Leah - white female D: May 9, 1884; 72y; Hampshire B: Penn I: Simmons, John DOI: son in law B/P: 1/39

3949 Steckman, Sarah - widow white female D: June 3, 1909; 79y 8m B/P: 2/109

3950 Stephens, Charles - white male D: Oct 28, 1894; 22y; Sherman District F: Stephens, Wm. B: Sherman District DOI: father B/P: 1/59

3951 Stephens, Lettie D: Oct 9, 1871; 79y F: Stephens, David M: Stephens, Susan B/P: 1/6

3952 Sterling, Edward - married white male D: Sept 6, 1911; 54y 6m 7d B/P: 2/111 N: engineer

3953 Stevens, John D: Aug 25, 1871; 70y C: Stevens, Leah B/P: 1/7

3954 Stevens, Leah D: Sept 25, 1871; 70y C: Stevens, John B/P: 1/7

3955 Steward, Chas. - white male D: Oct 7, 1892; 10m; Hampshire F: Steward, J.W. M: Steward, E. B: Hampshire DOI: father B/P: 1/57

3956 Steward, G.C. - white female D: Mar 25, 1893; B/P: 1/58

3957 Steward, Gracie - single white female D: Dec 18, 1907; 18y 7m 2d B/P: 2/109

3958 Steward, John - married white male D: Nov 22, 1914; 69y 9m 5d B/P: 2/112

3959 Steward, Sardinia - widow white female D: Apr 24, 1909; 85y B/P: 2/110

3960 Steward, William - married white male D: Jan 4, 1908; 45y B/P: 2/110 N: farmer

3961 Stewart, Charles - white male D: Jan 1887; 15y; Sherman District F: Stewart, Jas. H. M: Stewart, Jane B: Hampshire DOI: father B/P: 1/43

3962 Stewart, Geo - married white male D: Nov 26, 1896; South Branch B/P: 1/94

3963 Stewart, Geo W - white male D: 1866 B/P: 1/2

3964 Stewart, James - white male D: June 13, 1902; 84y; Sherman District I: Stewart, J. B/P: 1/78

3965 Stewart, Jessie - single white male D: Feb 3, 1914; 17y 4m 3d B/P: 2/112

3966 Stewart, Jno W. - white male D: Dec 21, 1913; 61y B/P: 2/111

3967 Stewart, Jno Wm. - married white male D: Dec 10, 1914; 64y 5m 13d B/P: 2/112

3968 Stewart, John W. - white male D: Mar 10, 1873; 63y 4m 9d; Hampshire B: Hardy Co I: Stewart, Wm J DOI: son C: Stewart, T. B/P: 1/10

3969 Stewart, Lucinda - white female D: Feb 1891; 79y; Hampshire B: Hampshire I: Stewart, Robt DOI: son B/P: 1/53

3970 Stewart, Lucinda - widow white female D: Jan 13, 1903; 76y 8m 24d; Hampshire B: Hampshire BUR: Mountain Dale B/P: 1/114

3971 Stewart, Wm. J. - white male D: Jan 21, 1907; 21d B/P: 2/109

3972 Stickley, Geo - white male D: July 21, 1901; 85y; Hampshire I: Stickley, A.F. B/P: 1/77

3973 Stickley, John - white male D: July 2, 1880; 73y 3m; Hampshire F: Stickley, Abram M: Stickley, Leah B: Shenandoah Co., VA I: Stickley, Miss DOI: daughter C: Stickley, Sarah B/P: 1/28

3974 Stickley, John R. - white male D: Sept 5, 1889; 19y; Mill Creek F: Stickley, John A. M: Stickley, Grace A. B: Mill Creek DOI: mother B/P: 1/50

3975 Stickley, Mrs. - married white female D: Nov 7, 1895; 75y; Hampshire B: Hampshire B/P: 1/89

3976 Stickley, Sarah M. - white female D: Mar 5, 1884; 38y 5m 11d; Hampshire DOI: husband C: Stickley, John B/P: 1/39

3977 Stickley, Tobias - white male D: Aug 17, 1889; 84y 5m 15d; Hampshire B: Virginia DOI: wife C: Stickley, M.A. B/P: 1/51

3978 Stickly, Elizabeth - white female D: Mar 12, 1872; 68y; Hampshire B: Hampshire I: Cookus, William B/P: 1/9

3979 Stonebraker, Clement S. - single white male D: Aug 4, 1921; 1y 4m 4d; Hampshire F: Stonebraker, Frederick M: Stonebraker, Bernice B: WV I: Shrout, W.L. B/P: 1/132

3980 Straw, Elizabeth - married white female D: Sept 14, 1919; 38y 8m 8d B/P: 2/113

3981 Streets, Jno W. - divorced colored male D: Oct 12, 1921; 54y; Hampshire B: Hampshire I: White, Robert B/P: 1/132 N: stonemason

3982 Streets, John - colored male D: 1873; Hampshire C: Streets, Emily B/P: 1/11

3983 Streits, Jane - single white female D: Jan 26, 1866; 9y 5d; Hampshire F: Streits, John M: Streits, Emily B: Hampshire DOI: parent B/P: 1/1

3984 Strieby, H.J. - white male D: Oct 1903; 69y; Hampshire F: Strieby, Jas. M: Strieby, Sarah B: 1834 I: Strieby, J.C. DOI: son B/P: 1/80

3985 Strieby, Rachel - widow white female D: Feb 2, 1907; 63y 3m B/P: 2/108

3986 Strother, Jno. H. - married white male D: Dec 1, 1922; 46y 4m 15d; Hampshire F: Strother, Robt. M: Strother, Rachel B: Hampshire I: Strother, J.A. B/P: 1/135 N: lumber dealer

3987 Stuckey, Hambleton - white male D: Apr 10, 1892; 67y; Sherman District B: Berkeley County, VA DOI: wife B/P: 1/56

3988 Stump, Adam - white male D: Oct 1866 B/P: 1/2

3989 Stump, Elizabeth D: June 29, 1871; 33y F: Sloan, James C: Stump, W.B. B/P: 1/7

3990 Stump, Geo - single white male D: Jan 3, 1881; 70y; Hampshire F: Stump, Benj M: Stump, Sarah B: Hampshire I: Moreland, Jane DOI: friend B/P: 1/32

3991 Stump, George F. - white male D: July 22, 1888; 14m; Romney District F: Stump, J.P. M: Stump, Belle B: Hampshire DOI: father B/P: 1/47

3992 Stump, James A. - married white male D: Jan 12, 1910; 49y 4m 19d B/P: 2/110

3993 Stump, John W. - white male D: June 9, 1885; 47y 8m 16d; Keyser Mineral Co B: Hampshire DOI: wife C: Stump, Jennie B/P: 1/42

3994 Stump, Joseph - white male D: Dec 19, 1872; 22y; Hampshire F: Stump, Jacob M: Stump, Rhoda B: Hampshire DOI: father B/P: 1/8

3995 Stump, Joseph - white male D: Nov 6, 1889; 80y 7m; Hampshire B: Hampshire DOI: wife C: Stump, N. B/P: 1/51

3996 Stump, Kirkbride - single white male D: Apr 5, 1911; 1y 8m B: Gore District B/P: 2/111

3997 Stump, Lilian P. - white female D: Aug 28, 1900; 5y; Hampshire F: Stump, S.D. M: Stump, Jennie B: Oct 17, 1885 I: Power, Jennie DOI: mother B/P: 1/73

3998 Stump, Margaret M - white female D: May 12, 1880; 80y; Hampshire F: Caudy, John M: Caudy, Rebecca B: Hampshire I: Stump, Rebecca DOI: sister C: Stump, Peter B/P: 1/28

3999 Stump, Margaret - single white female D: May 4, 1915; 86y B/P: 2/112

4000 Stump, R. - white male D: Feb 28, 1881; Hampshire I: Poling, M.F. DOI: overseer of poor B/P: 1/30

4001 Stump, Rebecca - white female D: Oct 1, 1888; 90y 11m 5d; Hampshire I: Stump, J. C: Stump, Wm. B/P: 1/46

4002 Stump, Rebecca - white female D: Feb 2, 1913; 75y B/P: 2/111

4003 Stump, Roda A D: Sept 7, 1871; 47y 7m 7d; F: Huff, Jacob M: Huff, Catherine C: Stump, Jacob B/P: 1/6

4004 Stump, S. D: Mar 30, 1869; 63y F: Stump, Jno M: Stump, Nancy B: Hampshire C: Stump, Rebecca B/P: 1/4

4005 Stump, Sarah J - single white female D: June 12, 1866; 3d; Hampshire F: Stump, Jacob M: Stump, Rhoda B: Hampshire DOI: parent B/P: 1/1

4006 Stump, William - white male D: Dec 27, 1879; 79y 9m 8d; Hampshire F: Stump, Joseph M: Stump, Elizabeth B: Loudoun Co., VA I: Stump, Jacob DOI: son C: Stump, Rebecca B/P: 1/26

4007 Sturgiss, J.W. - married white male D: Feb 27, 1907; 73y B/P: 2/109

4008 Suiter, Geo - single white male D: June 21, 1897; 7y 10m 11d; Springfield B: Springfield BUR: Springfield B/P: 1/94

4009 Suiter, Wayne - single white male D: June 19, 1897; 12y 3m 22d; Springfield B: Springfield BUR: Springfield B/P: 1/93

4010 Surbay, William - white male D: Nov 10, 1901; 54y; Capon B/P: 1/76

4011 Suter, G.R. - white male D: June 21, 1897; 7y 11m 19d;

Springfield F: Suter, W.S. M: Suter, M. B: Aug 10, 1889 DOI: father B/P: 1/66

4012 Suter, W.S. - white male D: June 19, 1897; 12y 3m 22d; Springfield F: Suter, W.S. M: Suter, M. B: Feb 28, 1885 DOI: father B/P: 1/66

4013 Sutton, Earl - white male D: Jan 15, 1894; 6m; Romney M: Sutton, Ann B: Romney DOI: mother B/P: 1/59

4014 Swaltz, Samuel - married white male D: Mar 19, 1910; 82y 2m 10d B/P: 2/110 N: farmer

4015 Swarts, Charles T. - single white male D: Sept 6, 1889; 4m; Hampshire B: Hampshire BUR: Hampshire B/P: 1/124

4016 Swarty, Charles T. - white male D: Sept 1889; 6m; Sherman District F: Swarty, Samuel M: Swarty, Mary B: Sherman District DOI: mother B/P: 1/50

4017 Swartz, Delila - white female D: Feb 14, 1892; 62y; Hampshire B: Hampshire DOI: husband C: Swartz, John B/P: 1/54

4018 Swartz, Lee Victor - white male D: Sept 15, 1914; 2y 2m B/P: 2/112

4019 Swisher, Arthur M. - white male D: Jan 15, 1917; 33y 7m 21d B/P: 2/113

4020 Swisher, Caudy S. - white male D: Oct 9, 1881; 1y 9m 2d; Hampshire F: Swisher, Perry M: Swisher, C. B: Hampshire DOI: father B/P: 1/30

4021 Swisher, Christiana A - white female D: 1866 B/P: 1/2

4022 Swisher, David - married white female D: Dec 30, 1905; 83y B/P: 2/108 N: farmer

4023 Swisher, Edmonia L. - white female D: April 6, 1873; 6d; Hampshire F: Swisher, Simon W M: Swisher, Mary B: Hampshire DOI: mother B/P: 1/11

4024 Swisher, Elizabeth J. D: Apr 19, 1870; 23y 4m; Hampshire F: Swisher, Jacob M: Swisher, Sarah B/P: 1/5

4025 Swisher, Ella May - white female D: May 30, 1892; 11y 11m 28d; Sherman District F: Swisher, P.M. M: Swisher, Ella M. B: Sherman District DOI: father B/P: 1/56

4026 Swisher, Fanny - married white female D: Aug 13, 1910; 31y 9m 16d B/P: 2/110

4027 Swisher, George D: Dec 6, 1871; 38y 3m 5d F: Swisher, Phil B/P: 1/7

4028 Swisher, H.C. - white male D: Sept 16, 1898; 68y; Springfield F: Swisher, John M: Swisher, Catherine I: Swisher, C.K. DOI: son C: Swisher, E.E. B/P: 1/69

4029 Swisher, Jacob - single white male D: Apr 13, 1886; 70y 11m 28d; Hampshire B: Hampshire I: Swisher, J. B/P: 1/44

4030 Swisher, Jane - married white female D: May 2, 1909; 64y 9m 2d B/P: 2/109

4031 Swisher, Leah D: May 26, 1869; 41y 10m 2d F: Fahs, Phillip M: Fahs, Rebecca B: Hampshire C: Swisher, Samuel B/P: 1/4

4032 Swisher, Louisa - single D: Sept 2, 1871; 21y F: Swisher, Jacob M: Swisher, Sarah B/P: 1/6

4033 Swisher, Louiza C. - white female D: Sept 3, 1881; 27y; Hampshire B: Hampshire DOI: husband C: Swisher, Phillip B/P: 1/29

4034 Swisher, Maranna - white female D: 1866 B/P: 1/2

4035 Swisher, Mattie - single white female D: Oct 8, 1897; 30y; Hampshire BUR: Three Churches B/P: 1/95

4036 Swisher, Mauise - white female D: Aug 10, 1903; 8m; Hampshire F: Swisher, D.C. M: Swisher, Agnes B: Dec 1902 DOI: father B/P: 1/80

4037 Swisher, Mrs Capt. - married white female D: Aug 20, 1904; 60y B/P: 2/108

4038 Swisher, Opal M - white female D: Dec 16, 1916; 5m 13d B/P: 2/112

4039 Swisher, Perry F. - married white male D: Jan 19, 1917; 65y 5m 11d B/P: 2/113

4040 Swisher, Philip D: Nov 29, 1870; 73y 5m 8d B/P: 1/5

4041 Swisher, Sarah - white female D: Jan 26, 1884; 67y; Hampshire B: Hampshire DOI: husband C: Swisher, Jacob B/P: 1/39

4042 Swisher, Sarah C. D: Aug 20, 1871; 28y F: Swisher, Jacob M: Swisher, Sarah B/P: 1/6

4043 Swisher, Sarah Jane - married white female D: Apr 15, 1913; 76y 8m 13d B/P: 2/111

4044 Swisher, Simon - widower white male D: Dec 18, 1910; 70y B/P: 2/110

4045 Swisher, Susan - married white female D: Aug 15, 1887; 20y; Hardy County B: Hardy County BUR: Hardy County B/P: 1/122

4046 Swisher, Waldo - white male D: Aug 31, 1907; 12d B/P: 2/109

4047 Swisher, Wilco - white male D: Sept 4, 1907; 12d B/P: 2/109

4048 Swisher, William F D: May 1870; 2y 11m; Hampshire F: Swisher, David M: Swisher, Mary B/P: 1/5

4049 Swisher, William F. - single white male D: Dec 31, 1880; 43y; Hampshire F: Swisher, Jacob M: Swisher, Sarah B: Rockingham Co., VA DOI: father B/P: 1/28

4050 Sword, Samuel - married white male D: Nov 6, 1913; 58y B/P: 2/111

4051 Tabb, D.C. - widower white male D: Dec 29, 1895; 65y; Hampshire B: Hampshire B/P: 1/89

4052 Tarr, Louis Henry - white male D: Oct 12, 1898; 5m 8d; Romney District F: Tarr, Oliver Henry M: Tarr, M.A. B/P: 1/68

4053 Taylor, Armita E. - single white female D: Apr 9, 1922; 61y 4m 22d; Hampshire F: Taylor, Wm. M: Taylor, Margaret B: Mechanicsburg I: Racey, B.T. B/P: 1/135

4054 Taylor, Atta M D: Mar 24, 1870; 30y 6m 5d; Hampshire F: Eastman, Simon M: Eastman, Matilda C: Taylor, Lemuel F. B/P: 1/5

4055 Taylor, D.K. - married white male D: Oct 9, 1914; 73y 2m 17d B/P: 2/121 N: physician

4056 Taylor, David - single white male D: May 20, 1912; 20y 7m 1d B: Mill Creek B/P: 2/121

4057 Taylor, Edward - white male D: June 1888; 1y 4m; Romney District F: Taylor, J.E. M: Taylor, Annie B: Hampshire DOI: father B/P: 1/47

4058 Taylor, Emma - widow white female D: Sept 17, 1912; 68y B/P: 2/121

4059 Taylor, Ettie G. - white female D: Dec 14, 1891; 2m; Hampshire F: Taylor, J.T. M: Taylor, Sarah B: Hampshire DOI: father B/P: 1/54

4060 Taylor, Fannie - married white female D: Sept 28, 1921; 80y 13d; Hampshire F: Kuykendall, Jas. M: Kuykendall, Hannah B: Maryland I: Blue, C.J. Mrs. B/P: 1/132

4061 Taylor, Foreman - widower white male D: May 4, 1917; 103y 10m 16d B/P: 2/121 N: farmer

4062 Taylor, Harriet A. - white female D: Nov 5, 1902; 79y; Hampshire F: Brady, Jno. M: Brady, Hannah B: Apr 2, 1823 I: Taylor, Sarah V. DOI: daughter B/P: 1/79

4063 Taylor, Herriett - widow white female D: Oct 5, 1902; 79y 7m 3d; Springfield B: Hampshire BUR: Springfield B/P: 1/117

4064 Taylor, J. Ann - white female D: June 24, 1889; 76y; Near Springfield B: WV BUR: Springfield B/P: 1/125

4065 Taylor, J.J. - single white male D: May 15, 1900; 38y; Hampshire F: Taylor, W.F.J. M: Taylor, Elizabeth B: 1862 DOI: mother B/P: 1/74

4066 Taylor, Jemima C. - white female D: Dec 22, 1897; 41y; Mill Creek District F: Thompson, Daniel B: Mill Creek District DOI: husband C: Taylor, Dora B/P: 1/64

4067 Taylor, Joseph H. - single white male D: Apr 26, 1880; 26y 5m 19d; Hampshire F: Taylor, William M: Taylor, Elizabeth A. B: Hampshire DOI: father B/P: 1/28

4068 Taylor, Joseph I. - white male D: Jan 11, 1886; 68y; Hampshire B: Hampshire DOI: wife C: Taylor, Harriet A. B/P: 1/44

4069 Taylor, L.A. - white female D: Dec 4, 1884; 58y; Hampshire B: Hampshire DOI: husband C: Taylor, Geo W. B/P: 1/39

4070 Taylor, Manasa - white male D: Dec 29, 1893; DOI: physician B/P: 1/58

4071 Taylor, Marvin E. - white male D: Mar 23, 1879; 1y 7m; Hampshire F: Taylor, Samuel M: Taylor, Rebecca B: Hampshire DOI: father B/P: 1/26

4072 Taylor, Mrs. Effie - married white female D: Sept 30, 1915; 41y B/P: 2/121

4073 Taylor, Mrs. James - married white female D: Mar 4, 1907; 55y B/P: 2/121

4074 Taylor, Nancy J. - white female D: Oct 5, 1890; 66y; Hampshire F: Statton, Jacob M: Statton, M. B: Hampshire I: Taylor, S.R. DOI: son B/P: 1/53

4075 Taylor, Simon H. - white male D: May 2, 1873; 57y 2m 6d; Hampshire F: Taylor, Jacob M: Taylor, Mary B: Oldtown, MD DOI: wife C: Taylor, Louisa B/P: 1/11 N: farmer

4076 Taylor, Susan Kuykendall D: Mar 8, 1869; 9m F: Taylor, Isaac M: Taylor, Fannie B: Hampshire B/P: 1/4

4077 Taylor, Thomas - white male D: Apr 4, 1891; 81y; Hampshire B: Hampshire I: Taylor, Geo. W. DOI: son B/P: 1/54

4078 Taylor, W.F.N. - white male D: Oct 25, 1900; 19y; Hampshire F: Taylor, W.F. M: Taylor, Susan B: May 3, 1881 DOI: father B/P: 1/74

4079 Taylor, W.G. - white male D: July 28, 1892; 1y 1m 2d; Hampshire F: Taylor, B. M: Taylor, E. B: Hampshire DOI: father B/P: 1/57

4080 Taylor, William - white male D: 1902; 84y; Mill Creek F: Taylor, Edward B: 1819 I: Taylor A.W. B/P: 1/78

4081 Taylor, Wm S. - white male D: 1866 B/P: 1/2

4082 Teters, William D: 1870; 1y 11m 20d; Hampshire F: Teters, Jno M: Teters, Hannah B/P: 1/5

4083 Tevolt, Virgy - white female D: July 29, 1913; 25y 5m B: Frederick Co., VA B/P: 2/121

4084 Tharp, Ann M. - white female D: May 17, 1883; 40y; Hampshire F: Pepper, Jas M: Pepper, Ann B: Hampshire I: Tharp, John DOI: brother in law C: Tharp, Sam B/P: 1/36

4085 Tharp, Samuel - married white male D: June 28, 1916; 77y 8m 10d B/P: 2/121

4086 Tharp, Solomon - white male D: Dec 27, 1881; 70y; Hampshire B: Hampshire I: Tharp, John DOI: son C: Tharp, Rebecca B/P: 1/29

4087 Thomas, Abram - married white male D: Dec 22, 1909; 73y 5m B/P: 2/121 N: farmer

4088 Thomas, Clemima - white female D: Aug 21, 1881; 9y; Hampshire F: Thomas, Abram M: Thomas, E. B: Pennsylvania DOI: father B/P: 1/32

4089 Thomas, D.H. - married white male D: Aug 11, 1910; 34y B/P: 2/121

4090 Thomas, Robert - single white male D: Dec 2, 1921; 5y 3m 7d; Hampshire F: Thomas, Oad M: Thomas, Lola B: WV I: Thomas, A.O. B/P: 1/132

4091 Thompson, Bell - colored female D: Dec 20, 1892; 23y; Romney F: Thompson, Benjamin B: Romney DOI: father B/P: 1/56

4092 Thompson, Benjamin - colored male D: Feb 5, 1917; 68y B/P: 2/121

4093 Thompson, Daniel - widower white male D: Feb 1890; 87y; Mill Creek B: Mill Creek I: Turley, Samuel DOI: friend B/P: 1/50

4094 Thompson, Elizabeth - white male D: Oct 1886; 91y; Sherman District B: Hampshire I: Coffman, Julius DOI: grandson B/P: 1/43

4095 Thompson, Emma - married white female D: June 24, 1906; 41y 7m 9d B/P: 2/121

4096 Thompson, Eva E. - white female D: Oct 26, 1888; 1y 7m; Hampshire F: Thompson, J. M: Thompson, C. B: Hampshire DOI: father B/P: 1/46

4097 Thompson, Holland D. - white male D: Aug 16, 1898; 60y; Bloomery District F: Thompson, Jas. W. M: Thompson, E. DOI: father B/P: 1/69 N: soldier; lawyer

4098 Thompson, James L. - white male D: Aug 14, 1873; 4y 12d; Hampshire F: Thompson, Jno H M: Thompson, Catherine B:

Hampshire DOI: father B/P: 1/11

4099 Thompson, Jno. T. - white male D: June 14, 1913; 81y B/P: 2/121

4100 Thompson, John - married white male D: Aug 20, 1902; 82y 7m 14d; Three Churches BUR: Three Churches B/P: 1/117

4101 Thompson, John Harris - married white male D: Apr 10, 1913; 68y 6m B/P: 2/121 N: farmer

4102 Thompson, Lucy A. - single white female D: Feb 6, 1897; 20y 10m 10d; Hampshire B: Hampshire BUR: Malicks Yard B/P: 1/94

4103 Thompson, Margaret - white female D: Dec 15, 1881; 67y; Hampshire B: Hampshire DOI: husband C: Thompson, Daniel B/P: 1/29

4104 Thompson, Martha - married white female D: Dec 7, 1908; 70 y 7m 24d B/P: 2/121

4105 Thompson, Mary - white female D: Oct 28, 1886; 87y; Hampshire B: Hampshire I: Thompson, Robt. C: Thompson, George B/P: 1/44

4106 Thompson, Mary - single white female D: Sept 2, 1894; 20y; Jersey Mountain B: Hampshire BUR: Three Churches B/P: 1/82

4107 Thompson, Mary M. - single white female D: Oct 25, 1902; 10m 21d; Hampshire B: Romney BUR: Romney B/P: 1/115

4108 Thompson, Millie - single white female D: Mar 26, 1909; 86y B/P: 2/121

4109 Thompson, N.B. - white female D: Feb 7, 1888; 3y 10m 26d; Hampshire F: Thompson, J. M: Thompson, C. B: Hampshire DOI: father B/P: 1/46

4110 Thompson, Robt - widower white male D: Mar 25, 1912; 79y 1d B: Romney District B/P: 2/121

4111 Thompson, Rosa M. - white female D: Sept 12, 1881; 1y 4m 25d; Hampshire F: Thompson, Robt J. M: Thompson, Martha B: Hampshire DOI: father B/P: 1/32

4112 Thompson, Willie - colored male D: Feb 10, 1892; 10m; Romney B: Romney DOI: grandfather B/P: 1/56

4113 Thompson, Wm - single white male D: Oct 19, 1866; 1y 11m 17d; Hampshire F: Thompson, Wm P. M: Thompson, Jemima B: Hampshire DOI: parent B/P: 1/1

4114 Thornton, Ellen - colored female D: Oct 31, 1876; 10y; Hampshire M: Thornton, Zolle B/P: 1/21

4115 Timbrook, Annie - married white female D: Jan 29, 1900; 25y; near Romney B: Hardy County BUR: Mill Run Cemetery B/P: 1/110

4116 Timbrook, Curtis - white male D: May 18, 1917; 25d B/P: 2/121

4117 Timbrook, Earl Gladston - white male D: Oct 20, 1915; 26d B/P: 2/121

4118 Timbrook, Edward - white male D: June 6, 1910; 90y B/P: 2/121

4119 Timbrook, Elizabeth - white female D: Mar 17, 1873; 40y; Hampshire F: Hott, David M: Hott, Melinda B: Hampshire DOI: husband C: Timbrook, Gibson B/P: 1/10

4120 Timbrook, Ellenor R. - single white female D: Jan 1, 1903; 4y 2m 27d; Hampshire B: Hampshire BUR: Bethel Church B/P: 1/114

4121 Timbrook, Emma R. - white female D: Jan 1, 1903; 14y; Sherman District F: Timbrook, Geo. W. B/P: 1/81

4122 Timbrook, Frank - married white male D: Dec 6, 1914; 69y 7m 10d B/P: 2/121 N: farmer

4123 Timbrook, G. - white male D: Jan 1, 1891; 6m; Hampshire F: Timbrook, Benj H. M: Timbrook, B. B: Hampshire DOI: father B/P: 1/53

4124 Timbrook, Gibson - married white male D: Jan 28, 1907; 77y 6m 6d B/P: 2/121 N: farmer

4125 Timbrook, John - white male D: Dec 10, 1872; 10m 5d; Hampshire F: Timbrook, William M: Timbrook, Susan B: Hampshire DOI: father B/P: 1/9

4126 Timbrook, Linda - widow white female D: Oct 26, 1907; 68y B/P: 2/121

4127 Timbrook, Lydia M. - married white female D: Oct 31, 1904; B/P: 2/128

4128 Timbrook, May - widow white female D: Dec 17, 1915; 74y 1m 7d B/P: 2/121

4129 Timbrook, Rebecca - married white female D: Feb 3, 1894; 25y 8m; Shèrman District F: Singleton, Absolen B: Sherman District I: Timbrook, Isaac B/P: 1/59

4130 Timbrook, Susan - widow white female D: Nov 3, 1904; 70y 8m B/P: 2/128

4131 Timbrook, Virgnia - single white female D: Oct 20, 1915; 25d B/P: 2/121

4132 Timbrook, Walter L - single white male D: Sept 14, 1866; 1m 15d; Hampshire F: Timbrook, William M: Timbrook, Susan B: Hampshire DOI: parent B/P: 1/1

4133 Timbrook, Wm - white male D: Mar 22, 1876; 55y; Hampshire F: Timbrook, John M: Timbrook, Sarah B: Hampshire DOI: wife C: Timbrook, Susan B/P: 1/18

4134 Timbrook, Wm. - white male D: Nov 27, 1878; 1m 14d; Hampshire F: Timbrook, Gibson M: Timbrook, Mary B: Hampshire DOI: father B/P: 1/23

4135 Timmerman, M.R. - white female D: Sept 9, 1896; 31y; Hampshire B: 1865 DOI: husband C: Timmerman, W.H. B/P: 1/63

4136 Topper, Belle - married white female D: May 28, 1906; 51y 6m 13d B/P: 2/121

4137 Topper, Belle - married white female D: Apr 29, 1906; 40y B/P: 2/121

4138 Topper, Carl - single white male D: May 29, 1912; 16y B: Gore District B/P: 2/121

4139 Topper, Sam'l L. - white male D: Dec 17, 1882; 71y 6m 10d; Hampshire F: Topper, H. M: Topper, M. B: Gettysburg, PA DOI: wife C: Topper, Julia A. B/P: 1/34

4140 Topper, Thomas - single white male D: Feb 25, 1907; 18y 7m 18d B/P: 2/121 N: farmer

4141 Torr, Marion - male D: Sept 2, 1902; 9m; Romney District F: Torr, O.H. M: Torr, Susan B: Dec 1, 1902 DOI: father B/P: 1/78

4142 Towers, Miss - single white female D: Jan 1899; 2y; Springfield BUR: Springfield B/P: 1/102

4143 Trenary, Helen Anna - single white female D: Dec 14, 1921; 1d; Hampshire F: Trenary, Carrol M: Trenary, Francies B: Green Spring DOI: father B/P: 1/132

4144 Triplett, Elizabeth - widow white female D: Apr 9, 1908; 87y 10m B/P: 2/121

4145 Troxwell, Susan - widow white female D: July 14, 1920; 90y 10m 19d; Hampshire F: Jenkins, Jno. B: Pennsylvania B/P: 1/129

4146 Truax, Alb - single white male D: Sept 24, 1885; 21y 9m; Hampshire F: Truax, Wm. B: Penn. DOI: father B/P: 1/42 N: father

4147 Truax, Andrew - white male D: Mar 26, 1884; Hampshire F: Truax, William M: Truax, Martha B: Hampshire DOI: father B/P: 1/39

4148 Truax, Martha - white female D: Nov 6, 1884; 40y; Hampshire F: Steckman, Jno. M: Steckman, Leah B: Penn DOI: husband C: Truax, William B/P: 1/39

4149 Turley, Charley - widower white male D: Nov 1898; 68y; Hampshire County BUR: Hampshire Co B/P: 1/99 N: Nationality: Irish

4150 Turner, John - white male D: Sept 24, 1873; Hampshire I: Shanholtzer, Mrs. DOI: friend B/P: 1/11

4151 Tusing, Michael - white male D: May 9, 1872; 87y; Hampshire B: Rockingham I: Shanholtzer, Barbara DOI: dauther C: Tusing, Susan B/P: 1/9

4152 Tutwiler, A.Bryon - white male D: July 10, 1897; 1y; Sherman District F: Tutwiler, Jonathan M: Tutwiler, M. B: Sherman District B/P: 1/64

4153 Tutwiler, Elveria - white female D: Dec 6, 1913; 5m 14d B/P: 2/121

4154 Tutwiler, Elvin - white male D: Dec 4, 1911; 5m 5d B/P: 2/121

4155 Tutwiler, Fannie - married white female D: Dec 10, 1913; 31y 4m 5d B/P: 2/121

4156 Tutwiler, Granville - single white male D: June 18, 1908; 29y 10m 6d B/P: 2/121 N: teacher

4157 Tutwiler, Harriet D: Feb 16, 1871; 44y F: Henderson, L.D. C: Tutwiler, M. B/P: 1/7

4158 Tutwiler, Martin - white male D: Dec 28, 1901; 87y; Sherman District DOI: son B/P: 1/76

4159 Tutwiler, Percilla F. - married white female D: Dec 10, 1911; 30y 2m 5d B/P: 2/121

4160 Ullery, Adaline - white female D: Aug 8, 1911; 11m B/P: 2/129

4161 Ullery, Anna B. - white female D: Aug 31, 1908; 1m 30d B/P: 2/129

4162 Ullery, Christina - single white female D: Nov 5, 1922; stillborn; Hampshire F: Ullery, Tilden M: Ullery Tula B: Okonoko DOI: father B/P: 1/135

4163 Ullery, Ellen - married white female D: Jan 9, 1908; 60y B/P: 2/129

4164 Ullery, Franklin - white male D: Apr 17, 1917; B/P: 2/129

4165 Ullery, Homer Lusby - married white male D: Nov 18, 1922; 29y 2m 7d; Hampshire F: Ullery, A.L. M: Ullery, Bettie B: Hampshire Co. I: Ullery, H.A. B/P: 1/135 N: farmer

4166 Ullery, Lemuel - married white D: Nov 30, 1911; 65y B/P: 2/129

4167 Ullery, Mary - single white female D: Nov 30, 1918; 15d; Hampshire B/P: 1/127

4168 Ullery, Mrs. - widow white female D: Oct 23, 1899; 68y; Spring Gap B: Hampshire BUR: Salem B/P: 1/106

4169 Ullery, Mrs. John - married white female D: Jan 21, 1911; 30y B/P: 2/129

4170 Umstot, Phil - single white male D: July 16, 1915; 67y 5m 5d B/P: 2/129 N: farmer

4171 Umstot, Sarah E. - white female D: June 23, 1880; 7m 8d; Hampshire F: Umstot, Philip M: Umstot, Mary B: Mineral Co. I: Seaders, John DOI: uncle B/P: 1/28

4172 Vanasdel, Isaac - white male D: Oct 30, 1867; Pine Hills M: Vanasdel, Anna B: Hampshire DOI: widow C: Vanasdel, Nancy B/P: 1/3

4173 Vance, Frank M. - white male D: Jan 29, 1892; 15y 11m; Hampshire F: Vance, John T. M: Vance, Elizabeth B: Hampshire DOI: father B/P: 1/54

4174 Vance, M.C. - widow white female D: Apr 8, 1904; 67y B/P: 2/130

4175 Vandagriff, Mary - white female D: June 14, 1872; 24y 11m 18d; Hampshire F: Watson, James M: Watson, Catherine B: Hampshire DOI: father C: Vandagriff, William B/P: 1/9

4176 Vandegrift, Wm. L. - white male D: Apr 20, 1919; 78y 4m 6d B/P: 2/130 N: farmer

4177 Vandragraft, Margaret - white female D: Apr 2, 1881; 2m; Hampshire F: Vandragraft, Jno M: Vandragraft, S.A. B: Hampshire I: Miles, Sarah DOI: grandmother B/P: 1/32

4178 Vanesdel, Catherine - white female D: Aug 8, 1874; 87y; Hampshire F: Huff, Cornelius M: Huff, Elizabeth B: Hampshire I: Heiskell, Francis W. DOI: son in law C: Vanesdel, Cornelius B/P: 1/13

4179 Vanmeter, Catherine - single white female D: Nov 20, 1907; 71y 11m 3d B/P: 2/130

4180 Vanosdall, Nancy - white female D: Oct 3, 1880; 73y; Hampshire F: Miller, Conrad M: Miller, Sarah B: Morgan Co I: Alderton, Wm. H. DOI: son in law C: Vanosdall, Isaac B/P: 1/28

4181 Varnasdal, Cornelius - white male D: Aug 5, 1876; 77y; Hampshire F: Varnasdal, Garrett M: Varnasdal, Sarah I: Hieskel, Elizabeth DOI: daughter B/P: 1/21

4182 Veach, Christinia - married white female D: Aug 16, 1909; 48y 5m 28d B/P: 2/130

4183 Veach, Kearrol Kole - white male D: Sept 13, 1905; 7m B/P: 2/130

4184 Voss, James E. D: Aug 17, 1870; 70y B/P: 1/5

4185 Waddle, Julius Randall - white male D: July 24, 1899; 1m; Romney F: Waddle, Julius M: Waddle, Edith B: June 24

DOI: father B/P: 1/71

4186 Wagner, Florence - married white female D: Dec 26, 1905; 29y B/P: 2/131

4187 Wagner, Margaret - widow white female D: Aug 3, 1916; 68y B: Cacapon B/P: 2/133

4188 Wagnor, Ida M. - white female D: Nov 19, 1896; 10y; Hampshire F: Wagnor, Jno. W. M: Wagnor, Sarah Jane B: 1886 DOI: father B/P: 1/63

4189 Wagoner, Dorothy - white female D: Jan 12, 1919; 18m B/P: 2/133

4190 Wagoner, Florence - white female D: Dec 27, 1905; 31y B/P: 2/131

4191 Wagoner, Georgia E. - white female D: Feb 10, 1903; 1y; Romney F: Wagoner, George H. DOI: father B/P: 1/81

4192 Wagoner, John - white male D: May 9, 1914; 69y B/P: 2/133

4193 Wagoner, Lucy L. - white female D: Mar 22, 1884; 9y 4m 11d; Hampshire F: Wagoner, Norman M: Wagoner, Mary B: Hampshire DOI: father B/P: 1/39

4194 Wagoner, Mary T.C. - white female D: Apr 15, 1909; 18d B/P: 2/131

4195 Wagoner, Sarah - white female D: Feb 14, 1901; 30y; Hampshire I: Wagoner, H.C. B/P: 1/77

4196 Wagoner, Wm. - white male D: Mar 1, 1888; 2m; Hampshire F: Wagoner, J.W. M: Wagoner, Jane B: Hampshire DOI: father B/P: 1/46

4197 Walker, E.H. - single white female D: Oct 8, 1889; 78y; Hampshire B: Hampshire I: Walker, J.W. DOI: nephew B/P: 1/52

4198 Walker, Isabell - single white female D: June 14, 1880; Hampshire F: Walker, James M: Walker, Susan B: Hampshire I: McGlothery, S. DOI: friend B/P: 1/28

4199 Wall, Susan - widow white female D: Apr 19, 1911; 80y B: Springfield B/P: 2/132

4200 Ward, Briget - white female D: Mar 14, 1874; 45y;

Hampshire B: Hampshire DOI: husband C: Ward, John B/P: 1/12

4201 Ward, James - white male D: Feb 9, 1873; 88y; Hampshire B: Ireland I: Ward, Sarah J DOI: daughter C: Ward, Mary B/P: 1/10 N: stonemason

4202 Ward, Mr. - white male D: Nov 4, 1905; 8y B/P: 2/131

4203 Ward, Simeon C D: Aug 17, 1870; 54y F: Ward Joel B/P: 1/5

4204 Warner, Ruben - colored male D: Nov 25, 1879; 3m 19d; Hampshire F: Warner, Wm M: Warner, Vilett B: Hampshire DOI: mother B/P: 1/25

4205 Washington, Anna N. - colored female D: Apr 26, 1882; 1m 25d; Hampshire F: Washington, J. M: Washington, M. B: Hampshire DOI: mother B/P: 1/34

4206 Washington, Bettie - single white female D: Mar 2, 1889; 18y 25d; Springfield B: WV BUR: near Springfield B/P: 1/125

4207 Washington, Chas. - colored male D: Feb 21, 1907; 17y B/P: 2/131

4208 Washington, Clarence - single black male D: Dec 27, 1898; 8y; North River Mills B: Slanesville BUR: Slanesville B/P: 1/100

4209 Washington, Edward - white male D: June 7, 1901; 66y; Hampshire I: Washington, W.L. B/P: 1/77

4210 Washington, G W - white male D: Feb 2, 1876; 68y; Hampshire F: Washington, Edward M: Washington, Margaret B: Fairfax Co VA I: Washington, R.M. DOI: son C: Washington, Sarah B/P: 1/21

4211 Washington, Jas. O. - single colored male D: Dec 30, 1922; 29y 11m 17d; Hampshire F: Washington, Jno. M: Washington, Martha B: WV I: Guthrie, N.B. B/P: 1/135 N: farmer

4212 Washington, Jennie - colored female D: Oct 1893; F: Edmonson, R. M: Edmonson, A. DOI: husband C: Washington, Joe B/P: 1/58

4213 Washington, John - colored male D: Dec 13, 1921; 66y 10m; Hampshire F: Washington, Geo. M: Washington, Mary B: WV I: Parson, E.E. B/P: 1/132

4214 Washington, Kate - widow black female D: Apr 20, 1899; Springfield B: Fairmont, WV B/P: 1/106

4215 Washington, L. - colored male D: Dec 13, 1894; 6m B: Hampshire B/P: 1/85

4216 Washington, L.E. - colored female D: Dec 13, 1894; 1m; Hampshire F: Washington, J.C. M: Washington, A. B: Hampshire DOI: father B/P: 1/60

4217 Washington, Lida - colored female D: May 11, 1911; 4y B: Springfield District B/P: 2/132

4218 Washington, Mauda - married colored female D: Feb 28, 1894; 25y; near Slanesville B: Hampshire BUR: Salem Church B/P: 1/84

4219 Washington, Miss - single colored female D: Feb 28, 1896; 4y; Hampshire B: Hampshire B/P: 1/88

4220 Washington, Rhode - colored female D: Dec 12, 1897; 50y 6m 11d; Bloomery B: June 1, 1847 DOI: husband C: Washington, John B/P: 1/66

4221 Washington, Robt C. - colored male D: Dec 28, 1898; 30y; Springfield F: Washington, Jo M: Washington, Amanda I: Edmondson, Robt DOI: grandfather B/P: 1/69

4222 Washington, Sallie A - white female D: Nov 25, 1886; 75y; Hampshire B: Loudoun Co, VA I: Washington, Ed C: Washington, George W. B/P: 1/44

4223 Watkins, Martha - married white female D: Mar 14, 1909; 58y 5m 1d B/P: 2/131

4224 Watson, Fannie - white female D: Sept 10, 1900; 6m; Hampshire F: Watson, J.W. M: Watson, Lydia B: Apr 2, 1900 DOI: father B/P: 1/74

4225 Watson, Gordon - married white male D: Aug 6, 1921; 71y 2m; Hampshire F: Watson, Jas. M: Watson, Katherine B: WV B/P: 1/132 N: farmer

4226 Watson, James - white male D: June 28, 1882; 63y 3m 14d; Hampshire F: Watson, J. M: Watson, M. B: Ireland I: Watson, Jethro DOI: son C: Watson, Cath E. B/P: 1/34

4227 Watson, Jas. Offutt - single white male D: Dec 23, 1921; 30y 2m 3d; Hampshire F: Watson, J.S. M: Watson, Augusta B:

Pleasant Dale I: Watson, Edgar B. B/P: 1/132 N: salesman

4228 Watson, Mrs. - widow white female D: July 1, 1904; 80y B/P: 2/131

4229 Watson, Rebecca A. - white female D: Aug 9, 1883; 41y; Hampshire F: Swisher, Jacob M: Swisher, Sarah B: Hampshire I: Burkett, Taylor DOI: friend C: Watson, Gordon G. B/P: 1/37

4230 Webster, Bruce - colored male D: Sept 30, 1907; 1y 6m B/P: 2/131

4231 Webster, Frances - colored female D: Mar 5, 1911; 2y 4m B/P: 2/132

4232 Webster, Jas. B. - colored male D: Sept 1875; 7m; Hampshire F: Webster, Jno M: Webster, Harriet B: Hampshire DOI: mother B/P: 1/16

4233 Webster, Joseph - colored male D: May 1901; 54y; Hampshire I: French, Florence B/P: 1/77

4234 West, Mr. - white male D: Sept 29, 1905; 31y B/P: 2/131

4235 Whitacre, Annie - white female D: Apr 15, 1899; 53y; Capon Bride B: 1847 I: Whitacre, Daniel B/P: 1/71

4236 Whitacre, Benna - white female D: June 25, 1910; B/P: 2/132 N: accident

4237 Whitacre, Benton - white male D: Aug 21, 1896; 26y 4m 10d; Capon District F: Whitacre, Adison B: May 1870 B/P: 1/62

4238 Whitacre, Benton - white male D: Sept 1, 1896; 27y; Hampshire F: Whitacre, Adam M: Whitacre, Ruth B: 1869 DOI: wife C: Whitacre, May B/P: 1/63

4239 Whitacre, Bessie - white female D: Feb 5, 1912; 22y B/P: 2/132

4240 Whitacre, Bettie Annie - widow white female D: Mar 5, 1898; 81y; Bloomery B: West Virginia BUR: Fairview B/P: 1/95

4241 Whitacre, Cecil - white male D: July 8, 1914; 1y 1d B/P: 2/133

4242 Whitacre, Chloe - white female D: Nov 24, 1907; 1y 20d B/P: 2/131

4243 Whitacre, Cora A. - white female D: Aug 20, 1911; 3y 7m B/P: 2/132

4244 Whitacre, George - single white male D: June 1, 1912; 72y B/P: 2/132

4245 Whitacre, Jno W. - married white male D: Dec 18, 1911; 74y 8m B/P: 2/132

4246 Whitacre, John W. - white male D: June 5, 1875; 6m; Hampshire F: Whitacre, Benj F. M: Whitacre, Margaret B: Hampshire DOI: father B/P: 1/16

4247 Whitacre, Jonah - married white male D: Dec 3, 1912; 40y B/P: 2/132

4248 Whitacre, Lebanon J. - white male D: June 26, 1876; 4m 9d; Hampshire F: Whitacre, Dorsey M: Whitacre, Nancy DOI: father B/P: 1/21

4249 Whitacre, Lola - single white female D: Aug 18, 1906; 9m 20d B/P: 2/131

4250 Whitacre, Mary - white female D: DEc 6, 1912; 13d B/P: 2/132

4251 Whitacre, Mary C. - white female D: May 19, 1922; 84y; Hampshire F: Sirbaugh, Jacob M: Sirbaugh, Elizabeth B: Frederick County, VA I: Whitacre, A.J. B/P: 1/135

4252 Whitacre, Myrtle - white female D: Aug 20, 1901; Capon Bridge DOI: father B/P: 1/76 N: Parents: Henry C. & Bell

4253 Whitacre, Nettie B. - white female D: Oct 22, 1899; 1d; Bloomery District F: Whitacre, A.C. M: Whitacre, Fannie B: Oct 21, 1899 DOI: mother B/P: 1/70

4254 Whitacre, Nola - white female D: Mar 23, 1906; 4m 24d B/P: 2/131

4255 Whitacre, Rachael - widow white female D: Feb 13, 1898; near Slanesville B: Hampshire BUR: Bloomery B/P: 1/92

4256 Whitacre, Rachel - widow white female D: Feb 4, 1898; 6y 6m; Gore District F: Kerns, Nathan I: Abrell, Lem. T. DOI: son in law B/P: 1/69

4257 Whitacre, Rilla Walker - white female D: Oct 29, 1899; 13y; Romney F: Whitacre, A.B.C. M: Whitacre, Lucy B: July 18, 1886 DOI: father B/P: 1/71

4258 Whitacre, Snowden - single white male D: Jan 2, 1903; 1y 10m 26d; Hampshire B: Hampshire B/P: 1/115

4259 Whitacre, Walter S. - single white male D: Feb 12, 1897; 16d; 5 mi. N of Capon Bridge B: Capon Bridge BUR: Ebenezer B/P: 1/95

4260 Whitacre, William - married white male D: Dec 19, 1912; 78y B/P: 2/132

4261 Whitaker, Nellie - white female D: Oct 21, 1899; 2d; Bloomery District B: Hampshire BUR: Cold Stream B/P: 1/109

4262 White, Bessie - white female D: May 28, 1888; 17y; Capon District F: White G.A. M: White, Bettie B: Hampshire DOI: father B/P: 1/48

4263 White, Bessie J. D: June 24, 1869; 30y; Hampshire C: White, C.S. B/P: 1/4

4264 White, Catherine S. - married white female D: 1911; 69y B: Romney District B/P: 2/132

4265 White, Christian Streit - widower white male D: Jan 28, 1917; 77y 10m 18d B/P: 2/133 N: lawyer

4266 White, Hester - married white female D: Apr 28, 1904; 65y B/P: 2/131

4267 White, Thomas - white male D: Oct 1, 1877; Hampshire DOI: wife C: White, Elizabeth B/P: 1/22 N: farmer

4268 Whiteman, Bertie - white female D: Feb 1, 1905; 16y 3m B/P: 2/131

4269 Whiteman, E. - white male D: May 12, 1874; 6m 5d; Hampshire F: Whiteman, E.F. M: Whiteman, Hannah B: Hampshire DOI: father B/P: 1/12

4270 Whiteman, Fannie - married white female D: Nov 24, 1922; 40y 3m 24d; Hampshire F: Martin, Isaac M: Martin, Susan B: Martin I: Whiteman, Walter B/P: 1/135

4271 Whiteman, Hannah C.V. - white female D: Nov 10, 1898; 50y 9m 13d; Mill Creek District F: Carrole, J. I: Whiteman, E.T. B/P: 1/68

4272 Whiteman, Jas - white male D: July 29, 1878; 64y; Hampshire B: Hampshire DOI: wife C: Whiteman, C. B/P: 1/23

4273 Whiteman, Jas. T. - white male D: Aug 15, 1894; 46y; Mill Creek F: Whiteman, Jas. B: Mill Creek DOI: wife B/P: 1/59

4274 Whiteman, Lena - white female D: Mar 1, 1889; 9m; Mill Creek District F: Whiteman, J.F. M: Whiteman, H. B: Hampshire DOI: father B/P: 1/48

4275 Whiteman, Rich - white male D: July 10, 1909; 2y 9m 6d B/P: 2/132

4276 Whiting, Alfred - widowed white male D: Mar 6, 1922; 98y 2m 5d; Hampshire F: Whiting, Saul M: Whiting, Jane B: Hampshire County B/P: 1/135

4277 Whitlock, Clara - white female D: July 23, 1909; 1m 5d B/P: 2/131

4278 Whitlock, Emma - white female D: Oct 18, 1882; 13y; Capon District F: Whitlock, Durino M. M: Whitlock, Lucy B: WV DOI: mother B/P: 1/33

4279 Whitlock, Franklin T - while male D: Oct 18, 1867; 1y 1m 3d; Parks Hollow F: Whitlock, Robert M: Whitlock, Mary C. B: Parks Hollow DOI: father B/P: 1/3

4280 Whitlock, Gay T. - white female D: Aug 30, 1907; 1y 6m 8d B/P: 2/131

4281 Whitlock, Gilbert - white male D: July 17, 1900; 1y; Hampshire F: Whitlock, W.B. M: Whitlock, Sophia B: June 18, 1898 DOI: mother B/P: 1/73

4282 Whitlock, Mary C. - white female D: May 8, 1911; 72y 3m 14d B: Bloomery District B/P: 2/132

4283 Whitlock, Theodocia - white female D: Oct 7, 1907; 60y B/P: 2/131

4284 Whitlock, Thursey - married white female D: Nov 7, 1907; 63y 5m 17d B/P: 2/131

4285 Whitlock, Walter - single white male D: Apr 12, 1915; 15y B/P: 2/133

4286 Wilkins, Sarah - married white female D: Jan 14, 1911;

50y 7m 12d B/P: 2/132

4287 Willer, Lucy - colored female D: Jan 1, 1881; Hampshire I: Poling, M.F. DOI: overseer of poor B/P: 1/30

4288 Williams, Catherine B - white female D: Apr 17, 1876; 49y; Hampshire B: South Carolina DOI: husband C: Williams, D.R. B/P: 1/18

4289 Williams, Mary A. - white female D: Nov 25, 1902; 84y; Romney District B: Feb 13, 1818 I: Williams, S.W. B/P: 1/78

4290 Williams, Mary A. - widow white female D: Nov 29, 1902; 83y 9m 16d; Romney B: WV BUR: Romney B/P: 1/116

4291 Williamson, G.W.D. - colored female D: Sept 23, 1886; 11y; Hampshire F: Williamson, Thos. M: Williamson, Amanda B: Hampshire DOI: father B/P: 1/44

4292 Williamson, Geo J. - widower white male D: Jan 21, 1917; 73y 5m B/P: 2/133

4293 Williamson, Mrs. Margt. - married white female D: May 7, 1912; 69y B/P: 2/133

4294 Williamson, Odus - white male D: Dec 23, 1898; 24y; AT SEA F: Williamson, S.W. M: Williamson, A.J. DOI: father C: Williamson, Ollie B/P: 1/69

4295 Williamson, Otis - married white male D: Dec 23, 1898; 24y; Cold Stream B: Bloomery District BUR: Sandy Ridge B/P: 1/99

4296 Williamson, Rebecca - married white female D: May 22, 1909; 65y B/P: 2/132

4297 Williamson, Silas - white male D: June 3, 1912; 73y 8m B/P: 2/132

4298 Willison, Eva - single white female D: Oct 9, 1911; 2y 5m 17d B/P: 2/132

4299 Wills, Ann - white female D: Apr 16, 1882; 76y 6m 2d; Hampshire F: Carmichael, Dan'l B: Hampshire DOI: husband C: Wills, Deskin B/P: 1/34

4300 Wills, Anna - white female D: May 5, 1881; 30y; Hampshire F: Taylor, William F.J. M: Taylor, E. B: Hampshire DOI: husband C: Wills, Silas B/P: 1/32

4301 Wills, Frank - white male D: Aug 29, 1905; 60y B/P: 2/131

4302 Wills, Mary F. - white female D: Aug 29, 1905; 64y 11m B/P: 2/131

4303 Wills, Rebecca A. - white female D: Mar 5, 1876; 46y 9d; Hampshire F: Milison, Silas M: Milison, Henrietta B: Hampshire DOI: husband C: Wills, Thos. B/P: 1/21

4304 Wills, Rolley - white male D: June 22, 1908; 11y B/P: 2/131 N: accident

4305 Wills, William - married white male D: Oct 25, 1912; 70y B/P: 2/132

4306 Wilson, Agnes C - white female D: July 24, 1874; 1y 6m; Hampshire F: Wilson, John M: Wilson, Elizabeth B: Hampshire DOI: father B/P: 1/12

4307 Wilson, Arthur - white male D: Sept 1878; 37y; Hampshire F: Wilson, Jno. B: Maryland I: Shannon, Benj DOI: friend C: Wilson, Mary B/P: 1/24 N: merchant

4308 Wilson, Carl - white male D: Mar 21, 1914; 2y 1m B/P: 2/133

4309 Wilson, Carl Francis - white female D: May 19, 1914; 2y 1m 22d B/P: 2/133

4310 Wilson, Classie L. - white female D: Aug 22, 1901; 5y; Rio F: Wilson, Cal M: Wilson, Virginia DOI: father B/P: 1/76

4311 Wilson, D. - white male D: June 27, 1872; 2y; Mineral County F: Wilson, N. M: Wilson May B: Mineral Co DOI: father B/P: 1/9

4312 Wilson, Elizabeth - white female D: June 14, 1884; 49y; Hampshire F: Gibsor, David M: Gibson, Ann B: Hampshire I: Gibson, J.A. DOI: brother C: Wilson, J.P. B/P: 1/38

4313 Wilson, Ella - white female D: Nov 20, 1903; 28y; Rio B/P: 1/81

4314 Wilson, Elyar - white D: Aug 11, 1872; 55y 6m 2d; Hampshire F: Davy, William M: Davy, Nancy B: Hampshire DOI: husband C:Wilson, N. B/P: 1/9

4315 Wilson, Geo B.M. - white male D: Nov 16, 1878; 9y 9m 3d;

Hampshire F: Wilson, J.C. M: Wilson, E. B: Bedford, PA DOI: father B/P: 1/24

4316 Wilson, Ivin - single white male D: Sept 11, 1911; 16y B: Springfield District B/P: 2/132 N: track hand; struck by train

4317 Wilson, John D: Sept 24, 1871; 69y 8m 11d B/P: 1/7

4318 Wilson, John - married white male D: Jan 5, 1895; 70y; near North River Mills B: Virginia B/P: 1/85

4319 Wilson, John - married white male D: Oct 24, 1912; 35y B/P: 2/132

4320 Wilson, John P. - white male D: Aug 2, 1875; 7m; Hampshire F: Wilson, John P. M: Wilson, Elizabeth B: Hampshire DOI: father B/P: 1/14

4321 Wilson, Lucinda - single white female D: Apr 3, 1876; 58y 9m 28d; Hampshire F: Wilson, Isaac M: Wilson, Rachel B: Hampshire I: Saville, Mrs. DOI: sister B/P: 1/18

4322 Wilson, Maria C. - white female D: Nov 6, 1881; 74y; Hampshire B: Hampshire I: Wilson, Zack DOI: son C: Wilson, John F. B/P: 1/29

4323 Wilson, Mary H. - white female D: July 1, 1874; 2y 11m; Hampshire F: Wilson, John M: Wilson, Elizabeth B: Hampshire DOI: father B/P: 1/12

4324 Wilson, Robt. Belle - married white male D: Mar 17, 1922; 33y 11m 18d; Hampshire F: Wilson, Calvin M: Wilson, Virginia B: Kirby I: Poland, T.W. BUR: 1/135

4325 Wilson, W.R. - white male D: Dec 18, 1898; 23y; Bloomery District F: Wilson, Nathan M: Wilson, Mary DOI: wife C: Wilson, E.B. B/P: 1/69 N: merchant

4326 Wilson, Winifred L. - white male D: June 6, 1910; 9m 4d B/P: 2/132

4327 Wilt, Gladys - single white female D: Dec 19, 1919; 5m; Gore District M: Wilt, Gladys B: WV B/P: 1/128

4328 Wince, John J. - white male D: May 2, 1899; 84y 3m 18d; Springfield District B: Jan 15, 1815 I: Wince, H.S. DOI: son B/P: 1/70

4329 Windall, John - single white male D: June 11, 1897;

Springfield BUR: Springfield B/P: 1/93

4330 Windle, Adam - white male D: Apr 13, 1876; 8m 17d; Hampshire F: Windle, Adam M: Windle, Hannah P. DOI: father B/P: 1/21

4331 Windle, Hannah - widow white female D: May 7, 1913; 75y B/P: 2/133

4332 Wingfield, Mr. - married white male D: Aug 29, 1894; 50y; Hampshire B: Maryland DOI: son B/P: 1/60

4333 Wirgman, Mary B. - white female D: Sept 1888; 22y; Romney District F: Wirgman, O.P. M: Wirgman, M.J. B: Hampshire I: Wirgman, W.F. DOI: brother B/P: 1/48

4334 Wirgman, O.P. - married white male D: Mar 19, 1890; 75y; Romney District B: Romney District I: Wirgman, W.F. DOI: son B/P: 1/50 N: minister

4335 Wise, Ida Lavina - single white female D: Aug 23, 1889; 7m 6d; near Doman WV B: near Doman WV BUR: Asberry Church B/P: 1/124

4336 Withers, Bessie E. - white female D: Nov 9, 1900; 17y; Hampshire F: Withers, Clay M: Withers, Annie B: July 24, 1883 DOI: mother B/P: 1/73

4337 Withers, Charles - married white male D: Apr 11, 1907; 35y B/P: 2/131

4338 Wolf, Jessie - single white male D: Dec 30, 1897; 1m 14d; Kirby B: Kirby BUR: Bethel Church, Kirby B/P: 1/90

4339 Wolf, Joseph - white male D: Jan 10, 1872; 7y 2m 10d; Hampshire F: Wolf, Joseph M: Wolf, Elizabeth B: Hampshire B/P: 1/9

4340 Wolf, Joseph - white male D: Dec 8, 1893; F: Wolf, John B/P: 1/58

4341 Wolf, Solomon H. - white male D: Nov 24, 1893; F: Wolf, J. M: Wolf, L. DOI: mother B/P: 1/58 N: blacksmith

4342 Wolfe, Eliza F. - white female D: June 4, 1884; 40y; Hampshire F: Wolfe, Geo M: Wolfe, Sarah B: Hampshire DOI: mother B/P: 1/38

4343 Wolfe, Jno. S. - married white male D: Mar 29, 1895; 33y 3m; Sherman District B: Penna. BUR: Home B/P: 1/83

4344 Wolfe, Lydia - widow white female D: Sept 5, 1918; 82y 3m; Hampshire B/P: 1/127 N: housewife

4345 Wolford, A.M. - white male D: Mar 1898; 6y; Gore District F: Wolford, J.W. M: Wolford, M.E. DOI: father B/P: 1/69

4346 Wolford, Amanda - white female D: Mar 13, 1889; 21y; Romney District F: Wolford, J. M: Wolford, Mary B: Hampshire DOI: father B/P: 1/48

4347 Wolford, Belle - white female D: June 1900; 9m; Hampshire F: Wolford, William M: Wolford, Mary B: Oct 1899 DOI: father B/P: 1/74

4348 Wolford, Cora R. - white female D: July 1876; 6m; Hampshire F: Wolford, Azariah M: Wolford, Nancy J. DOI: mother B/P: 1/21

4349 Wolford, Daniel - widower white male D: Dec 21, 1915; 85y 11m 10d B/P: 2/133 N: carpenter

4350 Wolford, David - white male D: Nov 7, 1890; 68y 1m 14d; Hampshire F: Wolford, Henry M: Wolford, Margaret B: Hampshire DOI: wife C: Wolford, Mary B/P: 1/53

4351 Wolford, Deborah - single white female D: Dec 28, 1914; 70y B/P: 2/133

4352 Wolford, Earnest - single white male D: Oct 17, 1909; 19y 9m 9d B/P: 2/132

4353 Wolford, Edith I. - white D: Feb 22, 1908; 15y 8m 21d B/P: 2/131

4354 Wolford, Elijah - white male D: June 14, 1884; 59y; Hampshire F: Wolford, Jacob M: Wolford, Catharine B: Hampshire DOI: wife C: Wolford, Lucinda B/P: 1/39

4355 Wolford, Elisabeth J. - widow white female D: Oct 30, 1896; B: Frederick County VA BUR: Augusta B/P: 1/94

4356 Wolford, Elizabeth J. - white female D: Oct 30, 1896; 73y 2m; Sherman District F: McKee, Joshua B: Aug 1823 DOI: son B/P: 1/62

4357 Wolford, Elsie - single white female D: Nov 24, 1905; 1y 2m 4d B/P: 2/131

4358 Wolford, Ethyl - single white female D: July 16, 1912; 2y 15m B/P: 2/132

4359 Wolford, Fannie L. - white female D: Sept 11, 1897; 25y; Sherman District F: Alamong, Christopher DOI: husband C: Wolford, John W. B/P: 1/64

4360 Wolford, Feby Jane - white female D: Dec 8, 1898; 65y; Sherman District I: Wolford, R.M. B/P: 1/68

4361 Wolford, Geo. W. - white male D: Aug 13, 1904; 9m 24d B/P: 2/146

4362 Wolford, J.E. - white male D: Sept 11, 1892; 8m; Hampshire F: Wolford, G.H. M: Wolford, S.C. B: Hampshire DOI: father B/P: 1/57

4363 Wolford, Jacob - white male D: July 10, 1874; 74y 4m 4d; Hampshire F: Wolford, John M: Wolford, Catherine B: Hampshire DOI: wife C: Wolfrod, Catherine B/P: 1/13 N: farmer

4364 Wolford, James M. - single white male D: Feb 15, 1880; 30y 1m 15d; Hampshire F: Wolford, William M: Wolford, Rebecca B: Hampshire DOI: father B/P: 1/28

4365 Wolford, John - white male D: Nov 29, 1906; B/P: 2/131

4366 Wolford, John J. - white male D: July 22, 1896; 80y 20d; Sherman District F: Wolford, Martin B: June 1816 DOI: son B/P: 1/62

4367 Wolford, John J. - married white male D: July 22, 1896; 80y; Augusta B: Hampshire BUR: Augusta B/P: 1/94

4368 Wolford, Josiah - white male D: July 8, 1874; 45y; Hampshire F: Wolford, Henry M: Wolford, Margaret B: Hampshire DOI: wife C: Wolford, Lydia B/P: 1/13 N: farmer

4369 Wolford, L. - white female D: Dec 16, 1893; B/P: 1/58

4370 Wolford, L.B. - white female D: Sept 1, 1892; 7m; Hampshire F: Wolford, B.N. M: Wolford, M. B: Hampshire DOI: father B/P: 1/57

4371 Wolford, L.M. - white male D: Apr 26, 1899; 8m 10d; Gore District F: Wolford, W.w. M: Wolford, M.E. B: Aug 16, 1898 DOI: father B/P: 1/70

4372 Wolford, Lillian - white female D: Jan 30, 1912; 9m 30d

B/P: 2/132

4373 Wolford, Lucinda - white female D: Feb 22, 1900; 68y; Hampshire I: McBride, William DOI: friend B/P: 1/73

4374 Wolford, Lula E. - white female D: Aug 12, 1891; 2m 4d; Hampshire M: Wolford, Lucy B: Hampshire DOI: mother B/P: 1/55

4375 Wolford, Lyda - white female D: June 24, 1896; 36y 6m; Sherman District F: Albright, William B: 1867 B/P: 1/62

4376 Wolford, Lydia A. - married white female D: June 24, 1896; Augusta B: Hampshire BUR: Augusta B/P: 1/94

4377 Wolford, Maggie - married white female D: Oct 14, 1911; 33y B: Gore District B/P: 2/132

4378 Wolford, Margaret E. - married white female D: May 4, 1922; 80y 4m 29d; Hampshire F: Shanholtzer, Philip B: Hampshire I: Smith, J.F. B/P: 1/135

4379 Wolford, Martha J. - white female D: Oct 6, 1868; 2m; Tearcoat F: Wolford, David B: Tearcoat DOI: mother B/P: 1/3

4380 Wolford, Martin - white male D: May 17, 1872; 78y 2m; Hampshire B: Hampshire DOI: wife C: Wolford, Mary B/P: 1/9 N: farmer

4381 Wolford, Mary - white female D: May 14, 1914; 2m B/P: 2/133

4382 Wolford, Michael C. - married white male D: Apr 18, 1894; 81y 2m 5d; Hampshire B: Hampshire BUR: Gore District B/P: 1/83

4383 Wolford, Milessa - white male D: June 4, 1913; 19d B/P: 2/133

4384 Wolford, Miss - single white female D: Feb 11, 1896; 10y; Hampshire B: Hampshire B/P: 1/88

4385 Wolford, Miss - single white female D: Apr 11, 1897; 10d; near Slanesville B: Hampshire BUR: Pine Hill B/P: 1/92

4386 Wolford, Mrs. - married white female D: July 9, 1904; 65y B/P: 2/131

4387 Wolford, Nancy - widow white female D: Nov 24, 1905; 78y

17d B/P: 2/131

4388 Wolford, Nancy J. - white female D: Feb 26, 1903; 69y; Hampshire F: Shanholtzer B: 1834 DOI: husband C: Wolford, A. B/P: 1/80

4389 Wolford, Nellie - single white female D: May 19, 1908; 2y 6m B/P: 2/131

4390 Wolford, Nora - white female D: Apr 13, 1913; 16y 7m 13d B/P: 2/133

4391 Wolford, O.W. - white male D: May 10, 1896; 1y; Hampshire F: Wolford, Jos. M: Wolford, Mary M. B: May 1895 DOI: father B/P: 1/63

4392 Wolford, Oscar - single white male D: Apr 23, 1911; 19y 3m 16d B/P: 2/132

4393 Wolford, Phoebe J. - married white female D: Dec 12, 1898; 65y 9m 24d; Augusta BUR: Mt. Zion B/P: 1/104

4394 Wolford, Rosa - married white female D: Jan 22, 1907; 17y 9m 6d B/P: 2/131

4395 Wolford, Sam'l - single white male D: Mar 2, 1900; 80y; Pine Hill B: WV BUR: Pine Hill B/P: 1/105

4396 Wolford, Tilly - single white female D: Aug 5, 1921; 60y 2m; Hampshire F: Wolford, Daniel M: Wolford, Jane B: Virginia I: Saville, Hattie B/P: 1/132 N: housekeeper

4397 Wolford, Virginia M. - married white female D: Feb 2, 1894; 20y 8m 17d; Sherman District B: Hampshire BUR: Mt. Zion Church B/P: 1/83

4398 Wolford, Willie - single white male D: Oct 29, 1918; 21y 6d; Hampshire B/P: 1/127 N: farmer

4399 Wolford, Wm. - white male D: Oct 2, 1906; 84y 2m 11d B/P: 2/131

4400 Wood, George - single white male D: Oct 18, 1918; 10y; Hampshire B/P: 1/127 N: pupil at Deaf & Blind School

4401 Woodson, Chas, L. - white male D: Aug 8, 1891; 13y 1m 19d; Hampshire F: Woodson, T.L. M: Woodson, Mary B: Hampshire DOI: father B/P: 1/55

4402 Wotring, Florence V. - married white female D: Nov 24,

1922; 60y; Hampshire F: Hook, Isaac P. B: Hampshire I: Lupton, Geo. B/P: 1/135

4403 Wriggles, Gertrude - white female D: Nov 8, 1911; 15y 2m 6d B/P: 2/132

4404 Wright, Arlie Lee - single white female D: May 20, 1922; 13y 7m 1d F: Wright, Albert M: Wright, H. B: Hampshire DOI: father B/P: 1/135

4405 Wright, David H. - white male D: Sept 1881; 13y; Hampshire F: Wright, David M: Wright, Eliza B: Hampshire DOI: father B/P: 1/29

4406 Wright, David H. - married white male D: Jan 5, 1900; 80y; Augusta BUR: Augusta B/P: 1/110

4407 Wright, Gracie - single white female D: Aug 20, 1911; 19y 3m 1d B/P: 2/132

4408 Wright, Gracie - white female D: Aug 20, 1912; 19y 3m 1d B/P: 2/132

4409 Wright, Hannah C. - married white female D: May 7, 1920; 52y 16d; Hampshire F: Wolford, Ben B: Hampshire B/P: 1/129 N: housewife

4410 Wright, Robert M. - single white male D: June 30, 1898; B/P: 1/97

4411 Wright, Sarah Belle - married white female D: Nov 16, 1921; 56y 4m 26d; Hampshire F: Sandy, Ervin M: Sandy, Elizabeth B: Hampshire I: Wright, L. B/P: 1/132

4412 Wynkoop, W.A. - married white male D: Nov 29, 1917; 49y 2m 16d B/P: 2/133 N: physician

4413 Yost, Elza - white female D: Sept 12, 1876; 70y; Hampshire F: Trouton, I: Hott, Mrs. John DOI: sister C: Yost, Henry B/P: 1/21

4414 Yost, James P. - white male D: Mar 22, 1881; 61y; Hampshire B: Hampshire I: Yost, Wm K. DOI: son B/P: 1/29

4415 Yost, John A. - white male D: Dec 23, 1914; 68y B/P: 2/148

4416 Yost, Mary - widow white female D: Sept 15, 1914; 63y 7m 9d B/P: 2/148

4417 Yost, Mary A. - white female D: Feb 19, 1903; 21y; Sir John's Run F: Allen, T.E. M: Allen, Mary B: 1882 DOI: father B/P: 1/80

4418 Yost, Robert - white male D: May 22, 1880; 33y; Hampshire F: Yost, Henry M: Yost, Elizabeth B: Hampshire I: Saville, Mrs. DOI: mother in law C: Yost, Rachel C. B/P: 1/28

4419 Yost, Sallie - white female D: June 2, 1913; 65y B/P: 2/148

4420 Youst, Julia A. - white female D: May 28, 1888; 61y; Hampshire B: Hampshire I: Edwards, F.F. DOI: son in law B/P: 1/46

4421 Zeilor, Joshua - white male D: Mar 2, 1905; 65y B/P: 2/150

4422 Zepp, Irene B. - white female D: Feb 14, 1891; 31y; Hampshire F: Ginn, Chas M: Ginn, Mary B: Virginia DOI: husband C: Zepp, E.H. B/P: 1/55

4423 Ziler, J.R. - white male D: Aug 15, 1889; 9m; Hampshire F: Ziler, Vick B: Hampshire I: Ziler, J.R. DOI: grandfather B/P: 1/52

4424 Ziler, Peter W. - white male D: July 20, 1874; 2y 4m 5d; Hampshire F: Ziler, Jno R. M: Ziler, Elizabeth B. B: Hampshire DOI: father B/P: 1/13

4425 Ziler, Peter W. - widower white male D: Nov 8, 1899; 79y 7m; Rio B: Frederick Co., VA BUR: Salem Church Fred. Co. B/P: 1/109 N: Nationality: German

4426 Zimmerman, Mrs. - married white female D: Sept 10, 1896; 32y; near Levels X Roads B: WV BUR: Little Capon B/P: 1/92

4427 Zimmerman, Robt - white male D: Oct 16, 1900; 1y; Hampshire F: Zimmerman, S. M: Zimmerman, Margaret B: June 15, 1900 DOI: mother B/P: 1/73

Index of Father - Mother - Informant

Index of Father - Mother - Informant

Index of Father - Mother - Informant

Index of Father - Mother - Informant

Index of Father - Mother - Informant

Index of Father - Mother - Informant

Index of Father - Mother - Informant

Index of Father - Mother - Informant

Index of Father - Mother - Informant

www.ingramcontent.com/pod-product-compliance
Lightning Source LLC
Chambersburg PA
CBHW060142280326
41932CB00012B/1606